FROM THE LABORATORY
TO THE CLASSROOM

Over recent years the field of science of learning has grown dramatically. Unfortunately, despite claims that this work will have a major impact on education, very little research makes it into teacher practice. Although the reasons for this are varied, a primary concern is the lack of a proper translation framework.

From the Laboratory to the Classroom aims to consolidate information from many different research disciplines and correlate learning principles with known classroom practices in order to establish explanatory foundations for successful strategies that can be implemented in the classroom. It combines theoretical research with the diverse and dynamic classroom environment to deliver original, effective, and specific teaching and learning strategies and address questions concerning what possible mechanisms are at play as people learn. Divided into five sections, chapters cover:

- A framework for organizing and translating science of learning research
- Motivation and attention as foundations for student learning
- Memory and metamemory considerations in the instruction of human beings
- Science of learning and digital learning environments
- Educational approaches for students experiencing learning difficulties and developmental characteristics of gifted children
- Brain, behavior, and classroom practice
- Forging research/practice relationships via laboratory schools

This fascinating text gathers an international team of expert scientists, teachers, and administrators to present a coherent framework for the vital translation of laboratory research for educational practice. Applying the science of learning framework to a number of different educational domains, it will be an essential guide for any student or researcher in education, educational psychology, neuropsychology, educational technology, and the emergent field of neuroeducation.

Jared Cooney Horvath is a postdoctoral researcher at the Science of Learning Research Centre, University of Melbourne, a fellow at St. Vincent's Hospital, Melbourne, and co-founder of the Science of Learning Group—a team dedicated to bringing the latest in educationally relevant research to educators and students at all levels.

Jason M. Lodge is a psychological scientist and Senior Lecturer in the Australian Research Council funded Science of Learning Research Centre and the Melbourne Centre for the Study of Higher Education, University of Melbourne. His research focuses on the application of the learning sciences to higher education and the ways in which technology is influencing learning.

John Hattie is Professor and Director of the Melbourne Education Research Institute at the University of Melbourne, and Honorary Professor at the University of Auckland, New Zealand. He is the author of *Visible Learning for Literacy* by Corwin and *Visible Learning*, *Visible Learning for Teachers*, *Visible Learning and the Science of How We Learn*, *Visible Learning into Action*, and the *International Guide to Student Achievement*, all published by Routledge.

FROM THE LABORATORY TO THE CLASSROOM

Translating Science of Learning for Teachers

Edited by Jared Cooney Horvath,
Jason M. Lodge, and John Hattie

Routledge
Taylor & Francis Group

LONDON AND NEW YORK

First published 2017
by Routledge
2 Park Square, Milton Park, Abingdon, Oxon OX14 4RN

and by Routledge
711 Third Avenue, New York, NY 10017

Routledge is an imprint of the Taylor & Francis Group, an informa business

British Library Cataloguing in Publication Data
A catalogue record for this book is available from the British Library

Library of Congress Cataloging-in-Publication Data
Names: Horvath, Jared Cooney, editor. | Lodge, Jason M., editor. |
Hattie, John, editor.
Title: From the laboratory to the classroom : translating science of learning
for teachers / edited by Jared Cooney Horvath, Jason M. Lodge and John
Hattie.
Description: Abingdon, Oxon ; New York, NY : Routledge is an imprint
of the Taylor & Francis Group, an Informa Business, [2016]
Identifiers: LCCN 2016002126| ISBN 9781138649637 (hardback) |
ISBN 9781138649644 (pbk.) | ISBN 9781315625737 (ebook)
Subjects: LCSH: Learning--Research. | Learning, Psychology of--
Research. | Teaching--Research.
Classification: LCC LB1060 .F786 2016 | DDC 370.15/23--dc23
LC record available at http://lccn.loc.gov/2016002126

ISBN: 978-1-138-64963-7 (hbk)
ISBN: 978-1-138-64964-4 (pbk)
ISBN: 978-1-315-62573-7 (ebk)

Typeset in Bembo
by Saxon Graphics Ltd, Derby

Printed and bound in Great Britain by
TJ International Ltd, Padstow, Cornwall

CONTENTS

LIST OF CONTRIBUTORS

George Aranda is a Research Fellow at Deakin University, where he conducts research into science education, science communication, and education technology. With a Ph.D. in cognitive neuroscience, he is interested in examining the relationship between neuroscience and education, and exploring how knowledge is constructed and represented within the brain.

Anne Bellert is a lecturer in education at Southern Cross University. Previously she worked as a teacher, school adviser, and researcher. Her areas of research interest include students experiencing learning difficulties, cognitive processes of learning, effective teaching in the middle-school years, literacy and numeracy interventions, and teaching literacy and numeracy across the curriculum. She has also followed with interest the more recent development of links between education and cognitive neuroscience.

Robert A. Bjork is Distinguished Research Professor in the Department of Psychology at the University of California, Los Angeles. His research focuses on human learning and memory, and on the implications of the science of learning for instruction and training. He has served as President or Chair of multiple scientific organizations, including the Association for Psychological Science, and he is the recipient of multiple awards and honors, including UCLA's Distinguished Teaching Award and the American Psychological Association's Distinguished Service to Psychological Science Award. He is a Fellow of the American Academy of Arts and Sciences.

Brian Butterworth is Emeritus Professor of Cognitive Neuropsychology at University College London, Adjunct Professor at National Cheng Chi University, Taiwan, Professorial Fellow at Melbourne University, Australia, and Research Consultant at Ospedale San Camillo Istituto di Ricovero e Cura a Carattere Scientifico in Venice, Italy. He taught at Cambridge University for 8 years, and has held visiting appointments at Massachusetts Institute of Technology and the Max Planck Institute at Nijmegen, The Netherlands. He is currently working on the neuroscience and genetics of mathematical abilities and disabilities. He was elected Fellow of the British Academy in 2002.

Sharon M. Carver has been the Director of the Carnegie Mellon University Children's School since 1993. She is also a Teaching Professor in the Psychology Department and the Associate Training Director for the university's Program in Interdisciplinary Education Research (PIER), which is funded by the Institute of Education Sciences (U.S. Department of Education). She is actively involved in the International Association of Laboratory Schools (IALS), the National Coalition for Campus Children's Centers (NCCCC), and the National Association for the Education of Young Children (NAEYC).

Courtney Clark is a Ph.D. candidate at the University of California, Los Angeles. Under the guidance of Robert and Elizabeth Bjork, she is exploring the often helpful role of making mistakes in subsequent learning. She received the UCLA Department of Psychology's Distinguished Teaching Assistant Award in 2015.

Donna Coch is a Professor in the Department of Education at Dartmouth College. She teaches courses on child development and learning that connect mind, brain, and education, and conducts event-related potential research investigating aspects of reading.

Elena Egorova is a teacher of social sciences in Lyceum #44 in Cheboksary, Russia, designated as TOP 200 school for gifted and talented education in the Russian Federation. She has 19 years of experience in gifted and talented education, and held the "Teacher of the Year" award from the Russian Federation in 2008 and 2015.

Howard Gardner teaches psychology at the Harvard Graduate School of Education. Since 1967 he has been associated with Project Zero, a major research center in education. Best known in educational circles for his theory of multiple intelligences, he has published widely on creativity, leadership, ethics, curriculum, and the arts. For 20 years he was a leader of the Good Work Project, now incorporated into the Good Project.

Lorraine Graham is Foundation Professor of Learning Intervention at the University of Melbourne. She has taught in primary school and tertiary settings for over 30 years. Her research interests are focused on inclusion, literacy strategies, basic academic skill interventions in numeracy and literacy, and, ultimately, the effective teaching of all students.

Deirdre Greer is Dean of the College of Education and Health Professions at Columbus State University. Her teaching and research interests focus on the study of neurological and psychological factors to improve teaching and learning.

Vicki Hinesley is a graduate student at the University of Texas at Arlington. She has an M.Ed. from the University of North Texas, and teaching endorsements in gifted and talented education, bilingual education, and English as a second language. She has taught students in K–5 for 40 years, working for the last 15 years as a Gifted Specialist in the Gifted and Talented Program in the Grapevine-Colleyville ISD in the Dallas-Fort Worth Metroplex.

Wayne Holmes received his Ph.D. in Education (Learning and Technology) from the University of Oxford. Currently he is a researcher in the UCL Knowledge Lab, UCL

Institute of Education, University College London, and he teaches at the Graduate School of Education, University of Bristol.

Paul Howard-Jones is a Professor of Neuroscience and Education at the University of Bristol. His particular area of interest is the application of our understanding of cognition and neuroscience to enhance child and adult learning. His research explores the benefits offered to education by emerging technologies, aided by a critical consideration of underlying cognitive processes.

Sean Kang is an Assistant Professor in the Department of Education at Dartmouth College. He directs Dartmouth's Cognition and Education Laboratory, which is focused on applying the cognitive science of human learning and memory to the improvement of instructional practice.

Diana Laurillard is Professor of Learning with Digital Technologies at the UCL Knowledge Lab, UCL Institute of Education, University College London, leading research projects on developing the Learning Designer suite of tools and online community for teachers and trainers, on adaptive software interventions for learners with low numeracy and dyscalculia, and on the use of massive open online courses (MOOCs) for continuing professional development. She has previously been Head of the e-Learning Strategy Unit at the Department for Education and Skills, Pro-Vice-Chancellor for learning technologies and teaching at the Open University, a member of the Visiting Committee on IT at Harvard University, and a member of the Royal Society Working Group on Educational Neuroscience.

Wendell McConnaha has worked as an educator for the past 48 years. He has served as an elementary, middle-school, and high-school teacher, counsellor, and administrator. Since 1985 he has worked as a laboratory school administrator in a number of locations, including the University of Chicago and the University of Pittsburgh. He has worked and lived in the U.S.A., Nigeria, Romania, Indonesia, Chile, the United Arab Emirates, the U.K., and China. He is currently based at Tsinghua University in Beijing, China. He holds a Ph.D. from Purdue University .

Evie Malaia is currently a EURIAS-awarded fellow at the Netherlands Institute for Advanced Studies. Her research interests include computational cognitive neuroscience and learning in atypical populations (e.g. deaf, gifted and talented, children on the autism spectrum). She holds a Ph.D. from Purdue University, and has received multiple national and international research and teaching awards.

Richard Messina is the principal of the Dr. Eric Jackman Institute of Child Study Laboratory School, a nursery to sixth grade elementary school that is part of the Ontario Institute for Studies in Education (OISE) at the University of Toronto. With a mandate to "explore what is possible", the Laboratory School exists to make a difference in the public domain by providing new insights into research, teacher education, and student learning. Richard Messina was a teacher and researcher at the Laboratory School and taught in the public school system. He is a lead teacher (elementary cohort) at the Klingenstein Summer Institute, Teachers College, Columbia University.

Elizabeth Morley recently retired from her position as Principal of the Dr. Eric Jackman Institute of Child Study Laboratory School, a nursery to sixth grade elementary school that is part of the Ontario Institute for Studies in Education (OISE) at the University of Toronto. She has also held the position of President of the International Association of Laboratory Schools (IALS) and is a Visiting Scholar at Kobe Shinwa Women's University in Japan.

Daniel Mucinskas is currently the Project Manager for the Good Project at the Harvard Graduate School of Education. He oversees the Good Project's digital presence and maintains relationships with partners and practitioners. He is a graduate of Boston University.

John F. Nestojko is an Instructor and Post-Doctoral Research Associate in the laboratory of Dr. Henry L. Roediger at Washington University in St. Louis. He received his B.A., M.A., and Ph.D. degrees from the University of California, Los Angeles. His dissertation research, conducted in collaboration with Dr. Elizabeth Bjork and Dr. Robert Bjork at UCLA, investigated retrieval-induced forgetting. His research interests include retrieval as a memory modifier, principles of psychology that enhance education and training, how expectations influence memory processes, false memory, collective memory, and individuals with superior memory.

Amelia Peterson is a Ph.D. student in Education at Harvard University, and a fellow in the Inequality and Social Policy program at the Kennedy School of Government. Working with Professor Howard Gardner, she has been a research assistant at Harvard's Project Zero and a teaching fellow for the course "Good Work in Education." She is an Associate at Innovation Unit and the Royal Society of Arts in the UK, and a researcher for the Global Education Leaders' Partnership.

Adam L. Putnam is an Assistant Professor at Carleton College. After obtaining his B.A. at Earlham College, he completed his Ph.D. at Washington University in St. Louis with Henry L. Roediger. In his research exploring human memory he often focuses on questions with real-world applications, such as how the principles of memory can be used to improve education, how false memories are formed, and how people remember political information.

Martina Rau is an Assistant Professor in the Department of Educational Psychology in the area of learning sciences at the University of Wisconsin–Madison, and is affiliated with the Department of Computer Sciences. The goal of her research is to help students to learn with visual representations. To this end, she investigates how best to enhance learning environments with educational technologies that adapt to the individual student's representational competencies in real time.

Henry L. Roediger III is the James S. McDonnell Distinguished University Professor at Washington University in St. Louis. His main research interests focus on the study of learning and memory using behavioral techniques. In addition to applying basic research on learning to education, he also studies retrieval processes in remembering, the relationship between confidence and accuracy in reports from memory, memory illusions and false memories, implicit memory processes, and collective memory. In 2008 he was awarded the Howard Crosby Warren Medal from the Society for Experimental Psychology, and in 2012 he received the William James Lifetime Achievement Award from the Association for Psychological Science.

Russell Tytler is the Chair in Science Education at Deakin University, Melbourne. He has held a range of teaching positions, including Lecturer in Physics in Australia and Africa, and 10 years as a science teacher and coordinator in a secondary school. He has a strong interest in innovation in science teaching and science teacher education, with a particular focus on supporting reasoning in science, and the generation of authentic settings and inquiry approaches in the teaching and learning of science.

Yingmin Wang is the Director of the International Education Office, Assistant Principal of the Tsinghua International School, and Assistant Principal of Tsinghua High School in Beijing, China.

Veronica Yan is currently a postdoctoral researcher at UCLA and at the University of Southern California. Her research focuses on what it takes to be an effective, self-regulated learner, bringing together research investigating the strategies that enhance learning and the motivational mindsets required to appreciate them. She holds training workshops for educational organizations, and is a recipient of both the UCLA Department of Psychology's Distinguished Teaching Assistant Award and the UCLA Dissertation Launchpad.

INTRODUCTION

There is growing excitement surrounding the implementation of scientific research within education, and with good reason. From the cognitive revolution of the 1950s through to the emerging "century of the brain", researchers across many fields have been making great strides in addressing the question of how human beings learn.

It is unfortunate that applying research findings from the laboratory to the classroom has not always been a straightforward pursuit. In fact, in the past, many of the attempts to achieve this have fallen flat. Although the reasons for this are many and varied, one primary driver concerns the nature of scientific research. Put simply, in order to obtain valid scientific results, researchers must control for and eliminate as many external variables as possible. This means that the study of learning in a laboratory involves the use of abstracted stimuli under as sterile conditions as possible (imagine a single student sitting in a sound-proof, dimly lit room with little extraneous noise or interference). Learning under real-world conditions is rarely similar to learning in laboratory settings. In one afternoon at a typical school or university, a student may be asked to study several different topics with dozens of peers within several dynamic environments that are heavily influenced by social and personal factors. They may also be using one of many available resources, devices, or technologies to aid their learning. This means that answers found within a "neat" laboratory are rarely directly applicable to "messy" classrooms.

It is for this reason that the *science of learning* (SoL) field has been created. The goals of this field are fourfold. The first goal is to consolidate information from many different disciplines (including, but not limited to, education, psychology, neuroscience, technology, and design) in order to derive a series of foundational learning principles. For instance, research from fields ranging from artificial intelligence to economics suggests that error making and correction are essential for successful learning in both formal and informal settings. Many of these principles are domain general—that is, they can be adapted and applied to a wide range of different learning environments and educational scenarios.

The second goal is to correlate learning principles with known classroom practices in order to establish explanatory foundations for successful strategies. For instance, educators have long known that purposeful feedback is essential for effective learning. Pooling this knowledge with the above-mentioned learning principle, we come to understand that feedback works both as a mechanism by which one is made aware of errors, and as a guide towards corrective steps. Although these correlations may not generate novel teaching practices, they do serve as a solid evidence base that enables current practices to be better understood and evaluated.

The third goal is to work closely with educators to develop original, effective, and specific teaching and learning strategies. As noted earlier, the classroom is a far more diverse and dynamic environment than the laboratory. Therefore many unique ideas born in the laboratory must be explicitly tested in and adapted to a range of learning environments. Returning to feedback, although laboratory researchers may aim to derive a universal, one-size-fits-all definition of effective feedback, classroom practice elucidates the importance of knowing the context, the phase of learning, the intended outcomes, and other variables in order to deliver successful feedback.

The fourth goal is to work backwards from the classroom to the laboratory in order to address questions about the possible causal mechanisms that are involved as people learn. In many respects this final goal is reductionist, as it involves "seeing" in the brain what we can "see" in the real world—a process rife with procedural and philosophical gaps. Despite this limitation, however, this goal may help to contextualize learning within the person and suggest novel ways of thinking about education.

It is perhaps worth noting here that the field of SoL is not the first to attempt this type of work. In the past, the fields of *mind, brain, and education* (MBE), *educational neuroscience* (EN), and *learning sciences* (LS) have attempted similar endeavors. The major differences between modern SoL and other fields concern breadth and scope. In terms of breadth, both MBE and EN tend to draw primarily from neuroscientific, psychological, and educational research, whereas LS tends to draw more deeply from classical cognitive sciences and philosophy. SoL tends to incorporate aspects of all of these fields, drawing from classical as well as emerging sciences, along with input from seemingly tangential sources (e.g. design, political science). In terms of scope, both MBE and EN primarily employ laboratory-based research methodologies with a strong focus on establishing how knowledge of the brain can benefit education, whereas LS primarily employs field-based research methodologies with a strong focus on iterative experimentation. Again, SoL tends to incorporate aspects of both of these fields, employing both laboratory- and field-based research, with a strong focus on elucidating and linking foundations of learning to teacher and student practice.

We hope that the four primary goals of SoL—determination of learning principles, correlation of learning principles with current practice, generation of novel practices, and elucidation of the biological processes of learning—suffuse this volume and not only serve as a source for validation and corroboration, but also inspire and empower the reader.

To that end, we have organized the book into five sections. The first section lays the foundation upon which later sections can be scaffolded and understood. In Chapter 1, we explore the *how* of SoL; more specifically, we take a look at the means by which research from many different fields can be brought together to generate meaningful and practical ideas and tools for educators. In Chapter 2, we explore the *why* of teaching, namely what it means to engage in good work, how we can manifest this in education, and how can we instil these notions within our students in order to prepare them to carry out excellent, engaging, and ethical work in the future.

The second section explores domain-general issues of learning. These ideas reflect basic mechanisms of human learning and may prove influential to all teachers, regardless of level or subject. In Chapter 3 we examine the integral relationship between motivation and attention, explore the neurological and psychological foundations of both, and look at how these two concepts are manifested and can be leveraged within the classroom. We then consider the importance of "challenge" in effective learning, and how to leverage this concept in both physical and digital learning environments. Chapters 4 and 5 closely examine the concepts behind and application of three teaching and learning techniques based on foundational principles of memory, namely retrieval, spaced, and interleaved practice. Finally, in Chapters 6 and 7 we explore the key concepts that need to be considered in the push towards emerging "educational technology", and we look at the best ways to leverage technologies to engender learning.

The third section narrows the focus to domain-specific issues of learning. Chapters 8 and 9 look at the use of multimodal presentations of concepts within the field of science. Chapter 8 takes a more philosophical approach, exploring the neuroscientific evidence for *why* utilizing varied presentational material could improve learning, whereas Chapter 9 takes a more applied approach, examining how best to support students as they develop competency in the interpretation and utilization of multimodal scientific displays. In Chapter 10 we shift to mathematics and take a look at dyscalculia, its manifestation in the brain, behavior, and learning, and track a process by which research from each of these fields has been synthesized to develop a practical classroom tool. Finally, in Chapter 11 we explore the dynamic and complex processes behind the unique human ability to read, and we examine the impact that this knowledge can have on the teaching and learning of reading skills.

The fourth section takes a closer look at specific student groups within which learning processes may manifest in different ways. In Chapter 12 we examine the characteristics of and ways in which to engage and challenge gifted populations. In Chapter 13 we explore issues of differentiation, direct instruction, and teaching for meta-cognition in populations who demonstrate learning difficulties.

The fifth section of this book casts a net into the future, exploring what we may expect from SoL in years to come, and how all schools and educators can contribute to this growth. In Chapter 14 we look at the relationship between neuroscience and education in a bid to better elucidate how these two fields interact and what we can meaningfully expect from this flourishing relationship. Finally, in Chapter 15, we close by outlining the concept of the laboratory school—a unique collaborative opportunity between practicing educators and researchers. Through exemplar schools that have successfully undertaken this type of collaboration, we explore the benefits of cross-discipline interaction and look at several highly applicable ideas that have emerged from such work to date.

A key feature of this book is its applicability to classroom teachers. As noted earlier, because laboratory-based research will never be able to account for the uniqueness and complexity of each classroom, it must necessarily refrain from making overly specific and formulated suggestions. However, laboratory work can generate a number of principles and processes that may either serve as an evidence-based foundation for current practices, or inspire educators to develop and test novel practices unique to their environment.

In order to make it easy to locate these "take-home" ideas, each chapter has a section called *From the Classroom to the Laboratory*. It is within these sections that the reader will find concrete ideas relevant to teaching and learning that have been developed by the authors of each chapter.

Acknowledgments: ARC-SRI: Science of Learning Research Centre (Project Number SR120300015).

SECTION 1

The How and Why of Science of Learning

1

A FRAMEWORK FOR ORGANIZING AND TRANSLATING SCIENCE OF LEARNING RESEARCH

Jared Cooney Horvath and Jason M. Lodge

MELBOURNE GRADUATE SCHOOL OF EDUCATION, UNIVERSITY OF MELBOURNE

Introduction

The term *science of learning* (SoL) encompasses a broad range of scientific disciplines, from basic neuroscience to cognitive psychology to computer science to social theory. Despite this wide array of interests, however, the goal of many SoL programs is the same, namely to determine and develop methods that teachers and students can use to improve the learning experience.

As with any multidisciplinary endeavor with the ultimate aim of "application", an important consideration concerns how the knowledge obtained from disparate research programs fits together to form a coherent and useful whole (Glasgow *et al.*, 2003). As can be inferred, trying to determine how data obtained at micro-scales link to data obtained at macro-scales is not a trivial task. Furthermore, it is far from clear whether these types of links are meaningful or in any way beneficial for the larger goals of classroom education (Bruer, 1997). For instance, what support is there to suggest that knowledge of calcium-driven potentiation at the neural synapse can influence a typical teacher trying to help a student to differentiate between the numerator and the denominator in a fraction?

In order to ensure that research findings are correctly applied and educators are presented with only the most solid ideas, a coherent and structured framework through which relevant information can be localized, interpreted, understood, and built is required. It is a long way from the neuron to the neighborhood (Shonkoff & Phillips, 2000); more specifically, there is a tremendous gap between biochemical processes which occur in isolated regions of the brain and the socio-cultural interactions that help students to become good, educated citizens. What is needed is a clear pathway from the former to the latter that takes into account the contexts in which teachers apply their practice. This pathway is what we hope to build here.

Different Types of Translation

The primary aim of many SoL programs is successful *translation*. In the applied sciences, translation typically refers to the process of interpreting information and/or ideas devised during "research" into a form that relevant consumers can understand and utilize. The most obvious example of this translation process at work is in healthcare. Clear mechanisms are in place to translate findings from the basic sciences of chemistry, biology, and physics into meaningful *processes* and *procedures* that can be readily implemented by medical practitioners (Sussman *et al.*, 2006). With regard to SoL, this translation process similarly means adapting outcomes elucidated in the laboratory into a form that practicing teachers and students can easily grasp and apply to their own practices (however, there is a large and important difference between *medical* and *educational* translation, which will be further explored later in this chapter).

Although it is often spoken of in singular terms, *translation* can be divided into at least three unique types.

The first type of translation is termed *prescriptive*. Prescriptive translation aims to specify activities and/or behaviors that teachers and students can undertake to best ensure specific learning outcomes—essentially addressing the question "*What* should I do?" For instance, the concept of *priming* (whereby the presentation of specific information or activities prior to a lesson serves to scaffold how later material is interpreted and understood) has been well elucidated in SoL research, and several specific, prescriptive strategies are emerging that can be incorporated into daily teaching and learning practices (Wilde *et al.*, 1992).

The second type of translation is termed *conceptual*. Conceptual translation enables teachers and students to understand educational phenomena through the lens of varied scientific theories—essentially addressing the question "*Why* does this work?" It is important to note that this type of translation does not offer advice on what unique practices individuals should undertake; it merely contextualizes and offers a theoretical explanation as to why the said practices are (or are not) effective. For instance, although some educators may be inspired by the *concept* of neural adaptation and use that framework to justify the success or failure of specific activities, this interpretation does not affect the content, structure, or outcome of the activity itself (Walsh & Anderson, 2012).

The third type of translation is termed *functional*. Functional translation enables direct alterations of physiology to expand or restrict the number and type of educationally relevant practices that an educator or learner can successfully undertake. Again it is important to note that this type of translation does not advise on what practices an educator or learner should undertake. For instance, if a learner were to suffer damage to the auditory cortices, leading to deafness, all future learning activities would then need to utilize visual or other sensory modalities. Here it is important to note that damage to the auditory cortices does not instruct the teacher or learner with regard to which non-auditory activities to undertake, how best to undertake them, or how to measure their impact.

As the distinction between *prescriptive* and *functional* translation may be somewhat unclear, it might be helpful to clarify it further using a specific example. Some students who suffer from disorders of attention, such as attention deficit disorder/attention deficit hyperactivity disorder (ADD/ADHD), use pharmaceuticals in order to alleviate their symptoms, which in turn can lead to improved educational performance (Loe & Feldman, 2007). At first glance the ingestion of drugs may appear to be prescriptive. However, a closer examination reveals that, although taking a pill may enable an individual to interact more effectively with learning activities, this does not *engender* learning itself. Pharmaceuticals do not inform an individual as to which activities to undertake, how to structure them, or how to measure them in order to learn language, math, or geography. Accordingly, pharmaceuticals represent functional translation rather than a prescriptive translation.

As can be inferred, the most widely demanded form of translation from SoL research is prescriptive (Pickering & Howard-Jones, 2007; Hook & Farah, 2013). Although conceptual and functional translation are no doubt important, they are already extant in some form within many classrooms around the world. With regard to conceptual translation, educators and learners at all levels utilize ideas from many different SoL fields, such as neuroscience (plasticity; Ansari, 2012), biology (evolutionary theory; Geary, 2008), and computer science (information coding; Pressley *et al.*, 1989), to explain why certain practices do or do not work, even though these concepts do not instruct the individual how to specifically structure, perform, or measure these practices. Similarly, with regard to functional translation, educators and students at all levels are utilizing interventions, such as drugs (e.g. Ritalin; McCabe *et al.*, 2005), energy drinks (e.g. Red Bull; Malinauskas *et al.*, 2007), and therapies (e.g. deep breathing; Birkel & Edgren, 2000), to directly modulate brain and body function in order to enhance educationally related behaviorial and/or cognitive performance, even though these interventions do not indicate which behaviors and/or cognitions need to be undertaken in order to engender learning.

In this chapter we shall be exclusively considering the issue of *prescriptive* translation.

Characteristics of Prescriptive Translation

Attempts at prescriptive translation cannot aim to provide precise formulae that guarantee all students will achieve the intended learning outcomes in a variety of contexts. If the nuances of the educational setting are not taken into account, it can be deceptively simple to conjure up highly specific teaching and learning approaches that seem valid based on research in the laboratory, but suffer from a lack of generalizability. Any translation approach that aims to provide prescriptions for teachers to implement in their classes must therefore be mindful of the context in which teachers find themselves, rather than use the rigor of laboratory research to give the illusion that there is a "one size fits all" solution to a pedagogical issue.

Unfortunately, the desire and pressure to generate highly specific prescriptive translation of SoL research has led many to prematurely champion ideas which ultimately prove useless in the classrooms. In fact, most concepts that tend to be referred to as educational or neuromyths (e.g. "individuals have unique and specific learning styles"; see Lodge *et al.*, 2016) represent ideas that originated in a laboratory and were rushed to prescriptive application without proper and effective translation.

Ideally, SoL prescriptive translation serves to provide evidence-based advice for teachers that enables them to make informed decisions about what will work for them and their students in the unique contexts in which they find themselves. For this reason, rather than being overly dictatorial, effective prescriptive translation will necessarily remain moot on the point of specific implementation within specific contexts. Rather, the final stages of applicability ("where the rubber meets the road", so to speak) and iteration will always remain fluid and require the input, ideas, and professional judgement of individual teachers within individual settings.

This all serves to highlight the importance of developing a robust translation framework by which laboratory results can be explored further and prescriptive classroom applicability established in a meaningful fashion. This type of framework would be important not only to researchers (as it can guide them in the move towards applicability), but also to educators (as it can clarify what teachers can meaningfully expect from the laboratory).

Levels of Organization, Emergence, and Incommensurability

In order to understand the framework developed, there are several scientific and philosophical concepts that must first be elucidated.

The first important concept is that of *levels of organization*. Within a living system (e.g. humans), the most common definitions of levels of organization are compositional (Oppenheim & Putnam, 1958; Wimsatt, 1994; Kim, 1999). More specifically, each "level" that constitutes a living system is composed of the material extant in the preceding levels. For instance, within biology, levels of organization typically progress as follows:

Cellular → Tissue → Organ → Organ Complex → Organism → Population.

In this instance, tissues are composed of cells, organs are composed of tissues, and so on. It is commonly held that as compositional levels increase (from cell to tissue to organ, etc.), so too does complexity (in this case, complexity is simply defined as any increase in the quantity of individual parts that interact to form a "whole"; for a review, see Lewin, 1999). For instance, a *tissue* is composed of many different collaborative *cells*, thereby making a tissue more "complex" than a single cell. Similarly, an *organ* is composed of several varied yet interacting *tissues*, which in turn are composed of many different collaborative *cells*, thereby making an organ more complex than an isolated tissue or single cell.

The next concept to undergird our framework is *emergence*. This is the process whereby novel and coherent structures, patterns, and/or properties arise at ascending levels that are neither exhibited within nor predicted by preceding levels (for a discussion of this topics, see Bedau & Humphreys, 2008). As a simple example, the eventual unified size, shape, and functional coherence of an entire ant colony cannot be explained or predicted by observing the behavior of an individual ant (Johnson, 2002).

In order to address increasing complexity and emergence at ascending levels of compositional complexity, a number of unique *scientific specialties* have been developed. Interestingly, as different specialties approach topics from different levels, each necessarily utilizes a unique set of questions, definitions, tools, and success criteria (Pavé, 2006). To explore this, let us consider measles as an example. At the cellular level, cytologists might map proteins at the viral–cell interface using crystallography to characterize the measles virus binding process (Tahara *et al.*, 2008). At the tissue level, histologists might explore viral infolding using an eyepiece micrometer to characterize the susceptibility of different lymphoid tissues to measles (White & Boyd, 1973). At the organ level, post-mortem gross pathologists might directly measure necrosis patterns to characterize measles development and progression within the lung (Kascbula *et al.*, 1983). At the population level, epidemiologists might map the prevalence of measles across a country using aggregated medical record data to characterize viral spread (Santoro *et al.*, 1984).

These examples highlight the final concept that supports our framework, namely *incommensurability*. It is clear that each of the above specialties represents a valid method of defining and exploring measles. However, it is equally clear that each specialty is unique and difficult to integrate with the others. This is one of the foundations of incommensurability (Feyerabend, 1962; Kuhn, 1962). This concept is perhaps best explained by three statements:

1. Different paradigms are built upon different assumptions about what constitutes a "valid" scientific question and solution.

2. The way in which individuals interpret data is influenced by the baseline assumptions of each paradigm.
3. As the methods and vocabulary utilized within different paradigms are unique, such paradigms cannot be meaningfully compared with each other.

Although incommensurability was developed to explore conceptual evolution within scientific fields, replacing the term "paradigm" with the term "level" reveals why work between different specialties is largely independent. As was noted above, researchers at each level must necessarily use a unique set of questions (assumptions), definitions (vocabulary), tools (methods), and success criteria (solutions). Therefore work within each level is incommensurable with work at other levels. However, it is important to note that incommensurability does negate conceptual translation. Most specialties are built upon the same larger environmental references (e.g. germ theory of disease) and examine the same topic (e.g. measles). Accordingly, it is possible to conceptually contrast research conducted at different levels in order to demonstrate that the findings are non-contradictory, even if those findings are not directly comparable.

These three key concepts can be combined together as follows. Levels of organization represent a stepwise increase in compositional complexity. This increase leads to emergent properties, not predictable by preceding levels, which require unique language, tools, data, and success criteria for their explication. Due to this utilization of different assumptions, vocabularies, methods, and solutions, unique levels of organization are incommensurable (Fodor, 1974, 1997; Rohrlich, 2004; Rosenberg, 1994; Wimsatt, 1994; Oberheim & Hoyningen-Hueve, 2009).

Prescriptive Translation between Incommensurable Levels of Organization

The utilization of incommensurable methodologies and explanations imposes a limitation on prescriptive translation between different levels, and the difficulty in applying laboratory research to the classroom is symptomatic of what happens when there is failure to abide by this limitation. More specifically, although it is possible to generate prescriptive translation between *adjacent* levels, this can only be achieved by accepting several unproven (and largely un-provable) assumptions (Atlan, 1993). Returning to the measles example, it is possible that knowledge of viral binding at the receptors of a single cell *may* be useful for someone trying to characterize cellular membrane fusion within a tissue (composed of thousands of cells). However, in order for the former to influence the latter, a number of assumptions must be made and accepted—for instance, that the extracellular environment created by millions of competition/cooperative cells will not dramatically change membrane receptor sensitivity, or that the behavior of isolated cells will not change when they are joined into a cellular matrix. It is conceivable that, at some point in the future, we will be able to measure the activity of millions of individual cells simultaneously without loss of fidelity. However, until that time, it is necessary to accept these assumptions in order to fill in the gaps between adjacent levels.

Clearly, then, prescriptive translation between *non-adjacent* levels becomes risky as the weight and number of assumptions increases. However, it is of far more importance that the *emergence* of specific properties at each level, unpredictable by preceding levels, ultimately makes non-adjacent prescriptive translation deficient (Atlan, 1993; Mazzocchi, 2008). For example, researchers interested in exploring the workings of a single isolated cell are unconcerned with and cannot define the properties that *emerge* when many cells join together to form a tissue (e.g. permeability, elasticity, contractibility). However, it is precisely these properties that may influence researchers who are interested in elucidating how different tissues work in tandem to form an organ. Similarly, the properties that are irrelevant to and unpredictable by researchers examining tissues that *emerge* at the level of the organ (e.g. function, chemical production, structure) are precisely those properties that may be of prescriptive use to researchers interested in exploring how different organs form an organ complex. Therefore prescriptive translation between *non-adjacent* levels is ultimately meaningless, as it fails to account for the integral properties that emerge at intermediate levels.

As this is a rather important point, it is perhaps worth considering a more specific example. It is possible to see how the process by which the measles virus binds to a single epithelial cell may be of practical value for elucidating how this virus spreads across larger epithelial tissues (*adjacent* levels). However, as we ascend to higher levels, the practical value of viral binding specifics becomes less clear. For instance, of what practical value are the specifics of epithelial cell binding to researchers interested in describing the presentation of measles across the skin (composed of many different cell and tissue types), across the nervous system, across the entire human body, or across a whole population of human bodies (*non-adjacent* levels)? Of practical value to researchers at each level are those properties which emerge at the immediately preceding level (Huneman, 2008), such that the researcher interested in the population-wide prevalence of measles may find some prescriptive use in the tools used by and conclusions drawn by a researcher describing the gross symptomology of measles within an individual. Again, viral binding may confer *conceptual* and/or *functional* translation to non-adjacent levels, but our only concern here is *prescriptive* translation.

Interestingly, it is in accounting for emergent properties at ascending levels that the method of prescriptively translating between non-adjacent levels is manifested, namely via stepwise prescriptive translation through all intermediate levels. More specifically, it is possible that *cell* research may prescriptively influence *tissue* research (so long as certain assumptions are accepted), and it is possible that *tissue* research may prescriptively influence *organ* research (again, so long as certain assumptions are accepted). Accordingly, although direct prescriptive translation between the cellular and organ levels will be inadequate (as properties that emerge at the tissue level will be unaccounted for), prescriptive translation can be undertaken between the cell/tissue and tissue/organ levels, thereby forming an inclusive and comprehensive path between levels.

Although this idea may seem simple and obvious, it is of paramount importance. When attempting prescriptive translation between *non-adjacent* levels of organization, one must always and completely traverse each intermediate level. This stepwise ascension is the only method whereby properties that emerge at each level can be accounted for and ideas from *non-adjacent* levels can form a tentative prescriptive relationship.

Prescriptive Translation in the Science of Learning

The primary research fields that constitute SoL are neuroscience, psychology, and education, although it is recognized here that other disciplines are also involved. If we organize these unique fields into a compositional schema, we arrive at five unique organizational levels (see Table 1.1).

TABLE 1.1 Levels of organization for science of learning.

Level	Domain	Questions	Tools	Data	Example success criteria
E	Education (practice)	Which combination of integrated cognitions/behaviors and environments leads to the comprehension, memorization, and effective application of educationally relevant skills/information in a social environment?	Curricula; pedagogical theories; assessment tools	Educationally relevant integrated cognitions/ behaviors at the group level	Improved individual and social employability, well-being, and economic prosperity
D	Cognitive / behavioral psychology	How do isolated cognitions/behaviors combine to form an integrated "set" (e.g. arithmetic ability)? How do these unique "sets" develop, manifest, and evolve over time within an individual?	Psychometrics; questionnaires; cognitive function measures	*Integrated* cognitions/ behaviors at the individual level	Elucidation of how an individual visually scans a scene to achieve a pre-established goal
C	Cognitive / behavioral neuroscience	How are isolated cognitions/behaviors (e.g. numerical recognition) reflected in brain activity?	Functional magnetic resonance imaging; scalp electroenceph-alography; transcranial magnetic stimulation	*Isolated* cognitions/ behaviors and functional neural networks	Localization of primary neural linguistic vs. non-linguistic auditory processing regions
B	Systems neuroscience	How do neurons combine to form nuclei and how are unique nuclei organized?	Implanted multi-electrode arrays; animal experimentation; cell culture	Neuronal nuclei	Input/output patterns from the six layers of the lateral geniculate nuclei in response to photostimuli
A	Cellular neuroscience	How do nerve cells function, communicate, and interact with unique chemical environments?	Patch clamps; confocal imaging; laser scanning microscopy	Individual neurons	Impact of calcium influx on resting action potential firing rate

Note: Additional levels concerning educational policy and management could be included above the educational level. In addition, several social levels could be included tangentially to the educational and preceding level. These were omitted for the sake of clarity.

Since their inception, the learning sciences have been rife with debate concerning the prescriptive translation of neuroscience to education, with many considering this endeavor difficult, if not impossible (Bruer, 1997; Varma *et al.*, 2008; Hruby, 2012; Byrnes & Vu, 2015). From this framework we can clearly see why this has been the case—neuroscience and education are *non-adjacent* levels and are compositionally separated by psychology (at the very minimum). This means that any attempt to prescriptively translate directly between any level of neuroscience and education necessarily ignores and cannot predict or account for important properties that emerge at the psychological level—and, as we have seen above, it is precisely these properties which will probably confer prescriptive utility at the educational level.

To better appreciate this, let us use the scientific elucidation of language as an example. The primary focus of many linguistic researchers at the cognitive/behavioral (c/b) neuroscience level is to map different language functions to specific brain areas. In order to do this, they must decompose language into its constituent parts (e.g. verb comprehension), construct an artificial task that isolates and targets an isolated part (e.g. read aloud 100 unrelated context-free verbs), and ask an individual to perform this task while measuring an indirect correlate of neural activity in an artificial, highly controlled environment (e.g. blood oxygen level patterns as measured while lying prone in a 70-cm borehole) (for a review, see Vigliocco *et al.*, 2011).

Moving to the next level, the primary focus of many linguistic researchers at the c/b psychology level is to determine how the constituent parts of language recombine to create a complete and meaningful "language." Although it is possible to see how the conclusions derived by linguistic c/b neuroscientists may prescriptively influence linguistic c/b psychologists, several unproven (and unprovable) assumptions must be accepted—for example, that brain areas active during an isolated task will behave similarly during amalgamated network activation, that isolated behavioral functions will not change dramatically when integrated into larger behavioral sets, and that activation patterns will not undergo important shifts in response to varied environmental influences (Chomsky, 1995).

If one were to ignore c/b psychology and try simply to prescriptively translate findings from c/b neuroscience into education, not only would the amount and severity of the assumptions increase, but also utility would disappear. As noted earlier, in order for linguistic c/b neuroscientists to undertake their research, they must decompose language, create an artificial task, and measure neural activity in an unnatural environment. This method necessarily eliminates all competing environmental factors and removes any integrated utility or meaning from language. However, these are the very factors that one must account for in order to consider and have an impact on language learning in the classroom (Gibbons, 2002). Interestingly, environmental influences and integrated linguistic utility or meaning are reconstituted at the c/b psychology level, thereby outlining a path for prescriptive utility.

How does knowledge of occipital neuronal activation patterns in response to the visual perception of the letter "T" prescriptively influence an educator who is attempting to teach 20 students how to read? Of more use to this educator would be the knowledge that successful reading requires the successful integration of visual letter identification with auditory phonemic discrimination in order to derive meaning—a larger behavioral set that emerges within the psychological level and which can be elucidated using c/b psychological methods (Chall, 1996). Similarly, of what prescriptive utility is the understanding that sensory neurons are activated during adjective generation to an educator who is trying to help a class learn how to speak French? Again, of more use to this educator is the understanding that novel language learning requires the successful integration of object recognition, identification, and conceptual mapping—a larger behavioral set that emerges within the psychological level and which can be elucidated using c/b psychological methods (Barsalou *et al.*, 2003).

Again, according to this framework, prescriptive translation requires a stepwise transition between adjacent levels of organization. Any attempt to "skip" or otherwise omit intermediate levels will ultimately lead to ineffective prescriptive translation, as it ignores key emergent properties.

Using the Framework to Resolve the "Brain Training" Debate

Over the last decade there has been an ongoing debate in the science of learning concerning the role and efficacy of "brain training" programs and games. A scientific consensus statement published by the Stanford Center on Longevity (2014) and signed by 65 researchers concluded that brain training conferred only narrow, short-lived effects and was ultimately ineffective. Interestingly, only a couple of months later a counter-scientific consensus statement was published (Cognitive Training Data, 2014). This statement, signed by 117 researchers, argued that there was irrefutable evidence that brain training confers measurable and meaningful effects. (It should be noted that each statement included a number of non–researcher signatories, including marketing and business developers, who were omitted from these calculations.)

Although this issue may seem intractable, application of the above framework in fact clarifies where the discrepancy lies. More specifically, if one divides up the signatories of each consensus statement into their corresponding "level" of research, an interesting and telling pattern emerges. With regard to the anti-brain-training statement, of the 65 signatories, 83% conduct research at either the c/b psychology or education levels, whereas only 17% conduct research at the c/b neuroscience level. Conversely, with regard to the pro-brain-training statement, of the 117 signatories, 75% conduct research at the c/b neuroscience level, whereas only 25% conduct research at the c/b psychology or education levels.

This suggests that brain training probably *does* work when the questions of interest (e.g. whether functional brain patterns change) and outcome measures (e.g. electroencephalography) are derived from the neurological levels. However, this also suggests that brain training *does not* work when the questions of interest (e.g. whether training confers far transfer) and outcome measures (e.g. performance on a secondary memory task) are derived from behavioral or educational levels. In other words, both sets of researchers are probably correct—they are merely arguing from different levels of the framework.

Of importance for our purposes is that this occurrence demonstrates well the path of prescriptive translation. When utilizing the language, methods, tools, and outcomes of c/b neuroscience, brain-training programs and games appear to be effective (in that they modulate network activity). However, we now see that any attempt at prescriptive translation of this information for use at the educational level would ultimately have failed, due to emergence and incommensurability. Rather, in order to make sense of these data, the first step was to prescriptively translate this information into the c/b psychology level. It was here where evidence revealed that changes in neural function engendered by brain training do not confer lasting or transferable changes in behavior, let alone educationally relevant behavior. In other words, unpredictable properties which emerged at the c/b psychology level (namely, larger behavioral patterns) and the adoption of a new set of language, methods, tools, and outcomes made the potential prescriptive utility of information gleaned at a preceding level obsolete—although *brain* change was extant, it did not scale up to meaningful *behavioral* change. However, had brain training showed an important effect at the c/b psychological level, prescriptive translation for education would not have been complete. Rather, research within the classroom would have been required to account for any unpredictable properties to emerge at the socio-cultural educational level (e.g. environmental influences).

What is likely to have arisen from research in the classroom is a reinforcement of the importance of the context in which students are learning. Brain training provides an example of a digital learning environment that can be used across multiple settings. The extensive history of research on the use of educational technologies, within which digital brain-training tools broadly fit, is that the medium is not as important as the pedagogy relating to the tool (Clark, 1994). For teachers, then, prescriptive translation must take into account the socio-cultural aspects of the learning setting, so that tools like those developed as part of the brain-training trend can be used effectively within the context, rather than in a context-free, inert manner. The inert nature of brain-training programs probably partly explains why they have largely failed to have any clear or predictable impact on learning in real-world settings over the long term.

The Difference between Medical and Educational Translation

In the past, several authors have drawn a parallel between medical and educational translation (Sousa, 2010; Atherton & Diket, 2005; Thomas, 2013; Hale, 2015). More specifically, there is a well-established system by which research from varied levels translates up to a set of procedures and/or processes that medical professionals can utilize. Several individuals have argued that this established medical model can serve as a model for proper and effective educational translation. Unfortunately, there is a large and important difference between these two fields that makes this comparison untenable.

In many respects, the primary outcome of medicine (morbidity and mortality) can be regarded as binary—patients are either ill or well, and either alive or dead. For this reason, within medicine, the ultimate goal remains unchanged across different levels of organization. Researchers tackling the problem of disease at different levels (cells, tissues, organs, etc.) all have the same final objective, namely to ensure survival of the individual (i.e. well/alive). This makes the stepwise advance of prescriptive translation relatively straightforward—any endeavor that combats disease at one level without having a negative impact on overall morbidity and mortality will be adopted and progressed.

For example, suppose that a cytologist developed a method to effectively kill viral infections within blood cells, but that in order for this method to work, all other cell types must also be killed. In a purely *scientific* context, this method would be considered a breakthrough, as it could be used to further the goals of biological science—for example, by elucidating the mechanisms whereby blood cells multiply, protect themselves, and/or interact with foreign viral bodies. However, in a *medical* context this method would be considered deficient, as it does not further the goal of survival of the individual (well/alive).

Unlike the binary medical outcome, educational outcomes are multidimensional and multifaceted in nature. Beyond the mere retention of information (which may rightly be considered to be binary), the ultimate goals of education encompass varying degrees of a number of universal skills (e.g. comprehension, synthesizing, innovation) and socially specific factors (e.g. ethics, citizenship, confidence). It is perhaps because of this complexity that attempts to adopt the medical model in education have been unsuccessful, and there has been no clear process for prescriptive translation in SoL to date.

It is worth noting that, when we used measles as an exemplar in the earlier sections of this chapter, we deliberately did not broach the subject of medical treatment. Our reason for this should now be clear. We confined our discussion to the scientific *characterization* of measles across different levels of organization, as this more closely resembles the process of prescriptive educational translation than does the medical treatment of measles.

Implications for Science of Learning Researchers

Arguably the most obvious ramification of incommensurable levels of organization for researchers in the science of learning is the outlining of a path by which prescriptive translation can be pursued. During the last few years, a tremendous amount of resources and time have been expended considering the direct applicability of neuroscience to education. However, as this framework demonstrates, attempted prescriptive translation between *non-adjacent* levels is simply not a meaningful endeavor, as it ignores emergence at intermediate levels. This applies not only in the science of learning, but also within every multidisciplinary applied scientific pursuit.

In addition, incommensurable levels of organization should help to alleviate the pressure experienced by some researchers to apply their findings to non-adjacent levels. In this context, the current excitement about the direct application of neuroscience in the classroom is particularly important to consider, as this practice leads to the development of overly simplified models and is the ultimate foundation of neuromyths. These models also generally fail to provide teachers with sufficient flexibility to allow them to make informed decisions about how best to apply the recommendations to their own classroom setting. Perhaps, with this framework, it will be easier to justify the specification of prescriptive translation between adjacent layers in a bid to establish more comprehensive ideas for the classroom (as is the aim of this book).

Finally, the elucidation of levels of organization may also prove beneficial to the organization of science of learning laboratories and journals. For instance, in order to guide prescriptive translation, larger mind/brain/education labs may consider organizing space so as to ensure that researchers at *adjacent* levels have more direct contact. Similarly, SoL-themed journals may opt to organize articles according to their organizational levels. This practice may help researchers and practitioners at all levels to quickly and easily locate relevant articles from their own and adjacent levels.

Conclusion

There is a great deal of excitement and expectation surrounding science of learning, as indeed there should be! The concept of improving the education and lives of future generations by the application of multidisciplinary empirical research is incredible. However, as with any nascent endeavor, it is of paramount importance to establish a foundational framework to ensure that development and translation occur in the strongest and most beneficial manner. We believe that the framework presented here represents the most inclusive and comprehensive way forward, and that it will ultimately lead to quicker, more comprehensive, and more successful prescriptive translation between the laboratory and the classroom.

From the Laboratory to the Classroom

Recently, several SoL researchers have put forward the argument that, in order for educators to improve their efficacy, they need to become more knowledgeable about neuroscience and the brain (Busso & Pollack, 2015; Dekker *et al.*, 2012; Devonshire and Dommett, 2010). The levels-of-organization framework helps to illuminate the mistake with argument. Just as a jeweler does not need to comprehend the molecular bonding patterns of silver atoms in order to craft an engagement ring, or a chef does not need to understand how flavors are transduced into electrical signals at the tongue in to order to prepare a wholesome meal, an educator does not need to comprehend how neurons or neural networks function in order to teach students effectively. Education is a *behavioral* activity that is undertaken within a socio-cultural context. The assumptions, vocabulary, methods, and solutions important to education depend upon and reside within properties that emerge above the level of neuroscience. Therefore the two fields are prescriptively separate. This does not mean that knowledge of neuroscience cannot inspire (*conceptual* translation) or assist (*functional* translation) certain educators—it simply means that intimate knowledge of the brain is not a necessity and will not directly confer successful educational practices (*prescriptive* translation).

In addition, educators are currently being inundated with programs designed to influence and nurture the brain. Using this new framework, the importance and veracity of these programs can be put into perspective. More specifically, "brain change" is not an outcome that we, as educators, can readily measure in the classroom. Rather, we are rightly confined to utilizing and measuring behavioral and social outcomes. Therefore the important point when being presented with novel programs is not whether they *scale down* to confer brain change, but whether they *scale up* to confer meaningful, educationally relevant behavioral change. In short, educators do not need to be concerned with "brain" claims, but rather they only need to be concerned with behavioral and educational claims and how to make the best possible decisions about what will work best in their practice context.

Acknowledgments

ARC-SRI: Science of Learning Research Centre (Project Number SR120300015).

References

Ansari, D. (2012). Culture and education: new frontiers in brain plasticity. *Trends in Cognitive Sciences*, 16(2), 93–95.

Atherton, M. & Diket, R. (2005). Applying the neurosciences to educational research: can cognitive neuroscience bridge the gap? Part I. In: *Annual Meeting of the American Educational Research Association*. Montreal, Canada.

Atlan, H. (1993). *Enlightenment to Enlightenment: Intercritique of Science and Myth*. New York: SUNY Press.

Barsalou, L. W., Simmons, W. K., Barbey, A. K., & Wilson, C. D. (2003). Grounding conceptual knowledge in modality-specific systems. *Trends in Cognitive Sciences*, 7(2), 84–91.

Bedau, M. A. & Humphreys, P. E. (2008). *Emergence: Contemporary Readings in Philosophy and Science*. Cambridge, MA: MIT Press.

Birkel, D. A. & Edgren, L. (2000). Hatha yoga: improved vital capacity of college students. *Alternative Therapies in Health and Medicine*, 6(6), 55–63.

Bruer, J. T. (1997). Education and the brain: a bridge too far. *Educational Researcher*, 26(8), 4–16.

Busso, D. S. & Pollack, C. (2015). No brain left behind: consequences of neuroscience discourse for education. *Learning, Media and Technology*, 40(2), 168–186.

Byrnes, J. P. & Vu, L. T. (2015). Educational neuroscience: definitional, methodological, and interpretive issues. *Wiley Interdisciplinary Reviews: Cognitive Science*, 6(3), 221–234.

Chall, J. S. (1996). *Stages of Reading Development*. Fort Worth, TX: Harcourt Brace.

Chomsky, N. (1995). Language and nature. *Mind*, 104, 1–61.

Clark, R. E. (1994). Media will never influence learning. *Educational Technology Research and Development*, 42(2), 21–29.

Cognitive Training Data (2014). Available online at www.cognitivetrainingdata.org (accessed 30 December 2015).

Dekker, S., Lee, N. C., Howard-Jones, P., & Jolles, J. (2012). Neuromyths in education: prevalence and predictors of misconceptions among teachers. *Frontiers in Psychology*, 3, 429.

Devonshire, I. M. & Dommett, E. J. (2010). Neuroscience: viable applications in education? *The Neuroscientist*, 16(4), 349–356.

Feyerabend, P. (1962). Explanation, reduction, and empiricism. In: H. Feigl & G. Maxwell (Eds) *Scientific Explanation, Space, and Time*. Minneapolis, MN: University of Minneapolis Press.

Fodor, J. A. (1974). Special sciences (or: the disunity of science as a working hypothesis). *Synthese*, 28(2), 97–115.

Fodor, J. (1997). Special sciences: still autonomous after all these years. *Nous*, 31 (Suppl.), 149–163.

Geary, D. C. (2008). An evolutionarily informed education science. *Educational Psychologist*, 43(4), 179–195.

Gibbons, P. (2002). *Scaffolding Language, Scaffolding Learning: Teaching Second Language Learners in the Mainstream Classroom*. Portsmouth, NH: Heinemann.

Glasgow, R. E., Lichtenstein, E., & Marcus, A. C. (2003). Why don't we see more translation of health promotion research to practice? Rethinking the efficacy-to-effectiveness transition. *American Journal of Public Health*, 93(8), 1261–1267.

Hale, J. (2015). *Creating Infrastructure for Bridging Educational Neuroscience and Classroom-Based Practice*. Available online at http://news.ntu.edu.sg/rc-cradle/Documents/James HALE.pdf (accessed 30 December 2015).

Hook, C. J. & Farah, M. J. (2013). Neuroscience for educators: what are they seeking, and what are they finding? *Neuroethics*, 6(2), 331–341.

Hruby, G. G. (2012). Three requirements for justifying an educational neuroscience. *British Journal of Educational Psychology*, 82(1), 1–23.

Huneman, P. (2008). Emergence and adaptation. *Minds and Machines*, 18(4), 493–520.

Johnson, S. (2002). *Emergence: The Connected Lives of Ants, Brains, Cities, and Software*. New York: Simon & Schuster.

Kascbula, R. O., Druker, J., & Kipps, A. (1983). Late morphologic consequences of measles: a lethal and debilitating lung disease among the poor. *Review of Infectious Diseases*, 5(3), 395–404.

Kim, J. (1999). Making sense of emergence. *Philosophical Studies*, 95(1), 3–36.

Kuhn, T. S. (1962). *The Structure of Scientific Revolutions*. Chicago: University of Chicago Press.

Lewin, R. (1999). *Complexity: Life at the Edge of Chaos*, Second Edition. Chicago: University of Chicago Press.

Lodge, J. M., Hansen, L., & Cottrell, D. (2016). Modality preference and learning style theories: rethinking the role of sensory modality in learning. *Learning: Research and Practice*, 2(1), 4–17.

Loe, I. M. & Feldman, H. M. (2007). Academic and educational outcomes of children with ADHD. *Journal of Pediatric Psychology*, 32(6), 643–654.

McCabe, S. E., Knight, J. R., Teter, C. J., & Wechsler, H. (2005). Non-medical use of prescription stimulants among US college students: prevalence and correlates from a national survey. *Addiction*, 100(1), 96–106.

Malinauskas, B. M., Aeby, V. G., Overton, R. F., Carpenter-Aeby, T., & Barber-Heidal, K. (2007). A survey of energy drink consumption patterns among college students. *Nutrition Journal*, 6(1), 35–41.

Mazzocchi, F. (2008). Complexity in biology. *EMBO Reports*, 9(1), 10–14.

Oberheim, E. & Hoyningen-Huene, P. (2009). The incommensurability of scientific theories. In: E. N. Zalta (Ed.) *The Stanford Encyclopedia of Philosophy.* Stanford, CA: Stanford University Press.

Oppenheim, P. & Putnam, H. (1958). Unity of science as a working hypothesis. *Minnesota Studies in the Philosophy of Science,* 2, 3–36.

Pavé, A. (2006). Biological and ecological systems hierarchical organisation. In: D. Pumain (Ed.) *Hierarchy in Natural and Social Sciences.* Dordrecht, The Netherlands: Springer. pp. 39–70.

Pickering, S. J. & Howard-Jones, P. (2007). Educators' views on the role of neuroscience in education: findings from a study of UK and international perspectives. *Mind, Brain, and Education,* 1(3), 109–113.

Pressley, M., Borkowski, J. G., & Schneider, W. (1989). Good information processing: what it is and how education can promote it. *International Journal of Educational Research,* 13(8), 857–867.

Rohrlich, F. (2004). Realism despite cognitive antireductionism. *International Studies in the Philosophy of Science,* 18(1), 73–88.

Rosenberg, A. (1994). *Instrumental Biology, or the Disunity of Science.* Chicago: University of Chicago Press.

Santoro, R., Ruggeri, F. M., Battaglia, M., Rapicetta, M., Grandolfo, M. E., Annesi, I., & Cortellessa, C. M. (1984). Measles epidemiology in Italy. *International Journal of Epidemiology,* 13(2), 201–209.

Shonkoff, J. P. & Phillips, D. A. (Eds) (2000). *From Neurons to Neighborhoods: The Science of Early Childhood Development.* Washington, DC: National Academy Press.

Sousa, D. A. (Ed.) (2010). *Mind, Brain, and Education: Neuroscience Implications for the Classroom.* Bloomington, IN: Solution Tree Press.

Stanford Center on Longevity (2014). *A Consensus on the Brain Training Industry from the Scientific Community.* Available online at http://longevity3.stanford.edu/blog/2014/10/15/the-consensus-on-the-brain-training-industry-from-the-scientific-community/ (accessed 30 December 2015).

Sussman, S., Valente, T. W., Rohrbach, L. A., Skara, S., & Pentz, M. A. (2006). Translation in the health professions: converting science into action. *Evaluation and the Health Professions,* 29(1), 7–32.

Tahara, M., Takeda, M., Shirogane, Y., Hashiguchi, T., Ohno, S., & Yanagi, Y. (2008). Measles virus infects both polarized epithelial and immune cells by using distinctive receptor-binding sites on its hemagglutinin. *Journal of Virology,* 82(9), 4630–4637.

Thomas, M. (2013). *How Could Neuroscience Influence Education? (And Vice Versa!).* LEARNUS Mediated Workshop. Available online at www.learnus.co.uk/mw1report.html (accessed 30 December 2015).

Varma, S., McCandliss, B. D., & Schwartz, D. L. (2008). Scientific and pragmatic challenges for bridging education and neuroscience. *Educational Researcher,* 37(3), 140–152.

Vigliocco, G., Vinson, D. P., Druks, J., Barber, H., & Cappa, S. F. (2011). Nouns and verbs in the brain: a review of behavioural, electrophysiological, neuropsychological and imaging studies. *Neuroscience and Biobehavioral Reviews,* 35(3), 407–426.

Walsh, M. M. & Anderson, J. R. (2012). Learning from experience: event-related potential correlates of reward processing, neural adaptation, and behavioral choice. *Neuroscience and Biobehavioral Reviews,* 36(8), 1870–1884.

White, R. G. & Boyd, J. F. (1973) The effect of measles on the thymus and other lymphoid tissues. *Clinical and Experimental Immunology,* 13(3), 343–357.

Wilde, L. D., Koegel, L. K., & Koegel, R. L. (1992). *Increasing Success in School Through Priming: A Training Manual.* Santa Barbara, CA: University of California.

Wimsatt, W. C. (1994). The ontology of complex systems: levels of organization, perspectives, and causal thickets. *Canadian Journal of Philosophy,* 24(Suppl. 1), 207–274.

2

TEACHING FOR GOOD WORK, TEACHING AS GOOD WORK

Amelia Peterson, Daniel Mucinskas, and Howard Gardner

HARVARD GRADUATE SCHOOL OF EDUCATION

Introduction

When we describe work as "good", we might mean this in a number of different ways. We might say someone has done a "good job" when they have done a specific piece of work well—a mechanic who has repaired a car in a skillful way, or a reporter who has quoted all interviewees accurately. Equally, we might talk about a philanthropist or a charity doing "good work", doing something socially valuable.

Elucidating "good work" in other sectors might be more nebulous. How do we define whether a doctor or lawyer has really done good work? We might know when they have done "bad work"—if they clearly have been ineffective, or done something unethical or illegal. In addition, we might utilize metrics to establish whether they are particularly effective—for example, how many patients they see per hour, or how many cases they win. However, what if these criteria were to conflict? How would we judge a doctor who compromises on working comprehensively with patients in order to see more patients per hour, or a lawyer who avoids difficult cases in order to increase his win percentage? How can we recognize good work when it lies in balancing competing criteria rather than excelling in any single one of them?

In what follows, we introduce a 20-year research project that has sought to uncover the criteria and conditions of "good work."[1] We apply findings from the project to the work of teaching and learning, suggesting what it looks like to prepare students to do good work, and what it looks like when teachers are able to do their best work. We offer some frameworks for education professionals who might be asking themselves how they can best fulfill their responsibility to prepare young people for the future of work.

Why Study "Good Work"?

As we began preparing this chapter, news broke of the sentencing of eight educators in Atlanta, Georgia, U.S.A., with imprisonment of up to seven years (Fausset & Blinder, 2015). These teachers were convicted for their part in a cheating scandal in which 178 individual teachers and administrators altered student answers on a state-mandated achievement test. In a detailed profile of the case published in *The New Yorker*, the culprits were depicted as dedicated professionals who had veered off course in their pursuit of what they thought was best for their students (Aviv, 2014). These educators viewed the state testing regime and the demand that students meet the same requirement for progress regardless of initial competency or context as inhumane and unrealistic. As Damany Lewis, one of the teachers fired for these cheating allegations, said of his students, "I'm not going to let the state slap them in the face and say they're failures."

The U.S. education field was torn in its response. Was this a case of individual rotten apples who had lost their moral compass, or was it a sign that the pressure on schools to demonstrate continuous improvement had gotten out of hand? Were these educators truly motivated by what they thought was best for students, or were they motivated more by job security and the monetary bonuses that came with high scores? More generally, what professional confusion or lack of principles could lead a group of educators to commit a wrongdoing worthy of prison time?

Individuals in all lines of work face ethical dilemmas. Often a dilemma pits the interests of customers or shareholders against wider societal demands. A communications company served with a government request for customer data must weigh where its responsibilities lie—to individual customers, or to the ruling government. Where work takes place in competitive industries, dilemmas can arise from uncertainty concerning what other professionals may do. For instance, a journalist might debate whether to delay publishing unverified information because of the risk of a competitor releasing the story first. Sometimes an individual might find that their personal interests are at odds with their professional responsibilities. For example, a junior scientist who discovers that a senior member of her laboratory is manipulating data must decide whether to declare misconduct, at the risk of losing her academic mentors and future job prospects. In some cases, dilemmas may be missed or ignored. For instance, a doctor may not realize that their own misgivings about handling mental illness are causing them to minimize the time they spend with certain patients.

Because most work involves such ethical dilemmas, governments have sought to develop ways to manage these decisions, thereby maximizing the likelihood that choices are to the benefit of society. Across many fields, from businesses to frontline services, and in most countries, this management occurs via government regulations. Some forms of work, however, involve decisions that are highly contextual and so are not easily regulated. By and large, we put faith in professionals to carry out such work. Professionals perform tasks that are complex and require expertise. Consequently, these workers are given considerable latitude to police themselves in professional communities, by creating and upholding their own standards. Professionals also control who enters their profession by requiring particular credentials before candidates are allowed to carry out work.

In recent decades, however, an increasingly complex set of external conditions and public expectations of higher standards of service (especially in the wake of scandals involving professionals who do not live up to expectations) has created new demands on professionals. Credentials may no longer be adequate to ensure the continued improvement and evolution of professional expertise. Accountability based on outcomes is seen as a more effective means to motivate evolution and improvement. Consequently, in many sectors, including teaching, professionals are increasingly under pressure to demonstrate their efficacy and efficiency according to measurable outputs of their work.

In education, the increased emphasis on measurable outcomes has shifted the focus of the work. Although many teachers and school leaders continue to have considerable freedom in shaping the day-to-day experiences of young people, their work increasingly takes place against the background of a narrow set of measures regarded by the public as an indication of professional competence. This focus has been associated with mixed consequences—most jurisdictions have seen some improvement on measured indices, but many have flatlined. There is also concern about the appropriateness and rigor of the measures.

Most importantly, the pressure on educators to "optimize" their classrooms, schools, and systems for the production of results may have unintended consequences. For instance, in the last round of the Programme for International Student Assessment (PISA), one country that is among the highest performers in all subject areas, South Korea, saw its students report the lowest levels of well-being (Organisation for Economic Co-operation and Development, 2013). This finding (along with other, more anecdotal reports of student anxiety) has led Korean system leaders to ask serious questions about educational goals. For example, what is the proper response when a drive for achievement is too successful and incurs unanticipated costs? The use of student assessment data to measure the quality of systems, schools, and teachers raises important questions about what quality actually means. For example, what does "good work" look like in education?

The Origins of the Good Work Project

These broad questions, which should be asked in one way or another of all professions, led to the founding of the Good Work Project (the Good Work Project at the Harvard Graduate School of Education has been absorbed into the larger Good Project there, which investigates various areas, including digital life, collaboration, quality, civics, and family life; further information can be found at www.thegoodproject.org). The seeds of the project were planted in 1994–95 by three psychologists—Mihaly Csikszentmihalyi, William Damon, and Howard Gardner. Along with shared moral commitments, each of these researchers had experienced their ideas being taken in unexpected—and sometimes unwelcome—directions when they became known to the public. Following the publication in 1983 of *Frames of Mind*, which set out the theory of *multiple intelligences*, Gardner saw this theory rapidly applied in unintended ways. Most disturbingly, he was notified of an educational program in Australia which sought to build positive identities for different ethnic groups by listing the intelligence(s) they displayed most strongly and the ones that they allegedly lacked. Although this intervention was well intentioned, Gardner was so shocked by the discriminatory overtones that he made a television appearance denouncing it. Similarly, Csikszentmihalyi's notion of "flow" was often misinterpreted as advocating the pursuit of meaningless tasks that "feel good", and Damon's recommendations for the establishment of "youth charters" were sometimes distorted by advocacy groups.

Due to these occurrences, each of these three scholars had reason to ponder how good intentions could go awry if certain aspects of society were not aligned. The Good Work Project started out as an inquiry into this dilemma. As researcher Jeanne Nakamura recollects, it asked "Can work that should be humane in fact be humane?" (Gardner, 2010, p. 108). This is a question facing educators; for all intents and purposes, education should be good work—it is an intrinsic public good. Why, then, do educators not always feel that it is good work? Why are up to 40% of teachers in the U.S.A., the U.K., and Australia leaving their profession during the first five years? What set of factors is making it hard to do consistent good work, and what is motivating those who stay?

Questions of this kind gave shape to the first phase of the Good Work Project. With the help of a team of researchers ultimately spread across five campuses in the U.S.A., the project leaders conducted interviews with over 1,200 individuals representing nine "domains." These included established professions (law, medicine, and journalism) and more amorphous pursuits (theater, genetics, philanthropy, and business). K–12 and tertiary education completed the list. In each domain, participants were identified by asking individuals to nominate colleagues whom they perceived to be (by their own definition) "good workers." Each of the interviews was semi-structured (sample questionnaires can be found in the appendices of Gardner *et al.*, 2001, and Fischman *et al.*, 2004). Participants were asked to reflect on whom and what they admired in their respective professions, and why. What represented the core of what was good in their field? What changes did they expect to occur in their profession? Were these changes desirable or not? All interviews were transcribed and coded by multiple coders in order to achieve statistical reliability with regard to the principal themes.

Major Findings and Frameworks

The most fundamental framework that has arisen from the Good Work Project is that good work in practice must fulfill three specific requirements, all of which begin (for ease of recall) with the letter E (see Figure 2.1):

1. *Excellence.* In a technical sense, this means carrying out one's work with expertise and adapting as needed to changes and/or difficulties.
2. *Ethics.* This involves behaving in a way that demonstrates a moral understanding and nuanced handling of ethical dilemmas as they arise in the workplace.
3. *Engagement.* This refers to deriving enjoyment, satisfaction, and/or meaningfulness from one's work.

Excellence, ethics, and engagement have become the yardstick that is used to determine whether or not good work is occurring in a particular situation. When considering any environment, professional individual, or set of conditions through the lens of good work, the *triple helix* (often dubbed "ENA") provides the key to coherent analysis.

In order for good work to occur, all three Es must be present at once. Only when a worker is simultaneously excellent, ethical, and engaged will good work truly be carried out to the highest degree. For educators, the three Es are epitomized by superior content knowledge and teaching ability (which results in effective learning by students), skilled handling of moral or ethical dilemmas with students, colleagues, administrators, and other stakeholders in the educational process, and a feeling of enduring connectedness with and concern for students, one's particular school or institution, and the educational enterprise as a whole. Educators who embody these characteristics are likely to carry out good work as individuals.

Although the three Es must, of necessity, function as a solid and integrated unit in order to achieve good work, it may be tempting at times to separate these components for the purposes of analyzing good work. In the largely open-market global economy of the twenty-first century, in which professions are most frequently judged by deliverables, it is frequently

Excellence Ethics **Engagement**

FIGURE 2.1 The components of good work, illustrated as a triple helix.

the case that work is discussed only with reference to one of the criteria, namely excellence. Excellence, as a synonym for success (often judged by monetary gains or some other metric), overshadows engagement as well as ethics in public consciousness. If a job is done in a timely fashion with positive results, we may label it "good work" without considering how those results were produced or how the workers involved in the process felt both at the time and over the long term.

A second discovery of prime importance from the Good Work Project is what "good work" researchers have termed *alignment*—that is, the state of harmony that occurs when the goals of the major stakeholders involved in a profession or organization are the same or are directed towards complementary ends. When the goals or motivations of various stakeholders are not in agreement, the profession or organization is said to be misaligned. Although misalignment can occasionally open up pathways to the development of innovative solutions to problems, a state of alignment generally makes it easier for parties to achieve good work, as conflicts are less likely to arise, intense ethical dilemmas are less likely to be faced, and workers are more likely to derive a sense of satisfaction from their work.

Applying the concept of alignment to an actual field, genetics was a domain that was highly aligned at the time of the main "good work" research at the end of the twentieth century. The professional workers, research funders, and biomedical companies all wanted essentially the same thing—to make discoveries that would promote healthier and longer lives. This goal was aligned with the vocation of a scientist and with broader societal goals. Individuals could do work that was simultaneously excellent, ethical, and engaging with ease. Since then, the domain has been through some changes. As the science has matured, it has uncovered the true complexity of epigenetics (forestalling some early hopes), witnessed increased contention about the moral limits of genetics research, and resulted in numerous examples of excessive claims, perhaps in the search for funds in an increasingly competitive environment.

Using the overarching three Es and the organizational theory of alignment as its fundamental background, the Good Work Diamond illustrates the factors that influence whether good work is achieved. These factors, which may encourage or prevent good work, can be grouped under four headings, each placed at one of the four corners of the Diamond (see Figure 2.2):

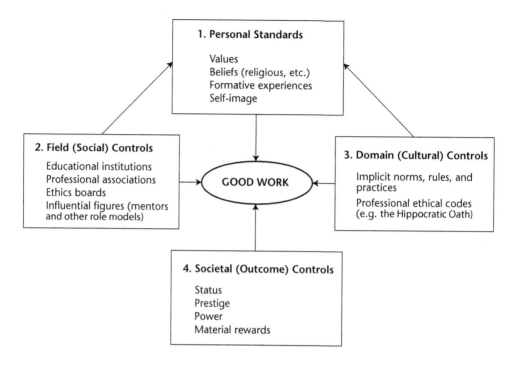

FIGURE 2.2 The Good Work Diamond, a visualization of the factors involved in good work outcomes.

1. *Personal standards*: the philosophies or moral values by which a person lives their life.
2. *Field or social controls*: the institutions or figures that train, employ, or support professionals in a certain domain.
3. *Domain or cultural controls*: the norms or codes that govern behavior in a profession over a considerable period of time.
4. *Societal or outcome controls*: the values, rewards, and sanctions that are at a premium in a society during a given time frame.

The Good Work Diamond is a convenient pictorial tool that prompts deep scrutinization of the many elements that have an impact on how work is carried out.

In 2001, the Good Work Project released its first extensive publication, *Good Work: When Excellence and Ethics Meet*, co-written by the three principal investigators, and thereafter introduced features including the three Es, alignment/misalignment, and the Good Work Diamond. For the first time, the findings uncovered and the frameworks created by the Project were released to the public.

However, the researchers did not feel that the Project was even close to completion; in fact, the many complex investigations had spurred several lines of questioning. Entering a new phase, the Good Work Project directed its attention to young people. Realizing that the dynamics of excellent, engaged, and ethical behavior in relation to work are often deeply ingrained from an early age, researchers interviewed scores of budding professionals about their conceptions of the personal and professional meanings of good work.

As reported in *Making Good: How Young People Cope with Moral Dilemmas at Work* (Fischman *et al.*, 2004), the findings of the study were alarming. Many of the young people who were interviewed recognized that good work and the three Es were intrinsically important, yet felt that they did not have the time or, as they saw it, the luxury of doing good work. This situation was particularly marked with regard to ethical behavior, as young professionals devoted the majority of their time and energy to satisfying surface-level primary responsibilities. Viewing (and to some extent dismissing) good work as a lofty ideal that was unattainable in their present circumstances, the interviewees spoke of their commitment to be excellent, engaged, and ethical at an undetermined future time.

Since *Making Good* was published, the situation with regard to good work among new and future professionals has become increasingly concerning in many countries. The prevailing attitudes of college students are one indicator of current dynamics (as many of these students will soon go on to enter graduate schools and the professional ranks). Studies of college enrollees in the U.S.A. show increased importance being attached to the "return on investment" of a university education, along with a simultaneous decreasing level of satisfaction with the educational experience, and a burgeoning emphasis on vocational training (Levine & Dean, 2012). Although the percentage of 18- to 24-year-olds enrolled in college is at the highest level on record in the U.S.A. (over 40%), indicating that higher education remains a desirable qualification (National Center for Education Statistics, undated), only 37% of the public believe that the main purpose of university is to foster personal and intellectual growth. By contrast, 47% believe that university should teach specific skills and knowledge related to the workplace (Pew Research Center, 2011). The Higher Education Research Institute of UCLA's annual survey of college freshmen reports that the most important factor for students who decide to pursue a degree is "to be able to get a better job," trumping "learning about topics of interest" (Higher Education Research Institute, 2014). Overall, student debt burden also continues to rise. The often desperate search for relevant post-graduation employment, along with strong financial and career pressures, mean that young professionals will undoubtedly feel that they are not able to practice good work in a vast number of cases This situation is compounded by a lack of ethics training or coursework, which is not generally a requirement of a high-school diploma or bachelor's degree in the U.S.A. Under these circumstances, many individuals also seek employment that is financially secure but not personally rewarding, thus limiting engagement.

According to the Good Work Diamond, this situation epitomizes misalignment. Good work is not likely to occur because the personal desire and need for a monetary return on a college education, as well as the societal mantra of monetary success, are in conflict with the field controls espoused by universities and professional societies (which seek to expand knowledge and profession-wide supports) and the domain controls of vocations (which encourage adherence to particular codes of conduct reinforcing particular behaviors).

In-depth awareness of the importance and complexity of good work and the three Es, which will ideally catalyze the achievement of good work, therefore eludes most young people embroiled in the current climate surrounding educational goals and outcomes. For this reason, teachers at all levels have a crucial role to play in bringing good work to the classroom and exposing students to ideas and materials that will cultivate a sense of what it means to do work that is excellent, ethical, and engaged, both within school and beyond.

Teaching for Good Work

We believe it is possible to educate students in such a way that they will be more likely to do good work. This involves helping students to experience, recognize, and ultimately seek out each of the three Es.

Excellence

It should not be hard to find a place for excellence in education today. Formal curricula and assessments enshrine certain standards. In many places these aspirational materials are becoming more demanding, as governments and parents respond to a sense of global competition in employment and higher education. From the perspective of the Good Work Project, these formal standards come from the "field" in the form of outcome controls. However, this source is only part of what might inform standards of excellence for each child and community.

Teachers and students may draw standards from the domain that they are studying. For instance, young people have an intuitive sense that excellence in sports is not the same as excellence in history or mathematics, and in some settings they have the opportunity to formalize this understanding by becoming involved in fleshing out standards. Assessment for learning practices, now used by many teachers around the world, involves students in establishing criteria for excellence (Wiliam, 2011, pp. 51–70). In this form of practice, teachers first use models to demonstrate to students what excellence looks like, and then work with the students to develop criteria for a good product. In this way, students work towards a concrete set of guidelines that they have helped to articulate, as opposed to an abstract mark or a rubric that they may not fully understand or endorse.

Teachers may still feel tension, however, when different players in the field (parents, government, students, local community members, and employers) have contrasting understandings and definitions of excellence. The government may give priority to curriculum coverage, employers may be calling for students to be given practice at working in groups or independently and more exposure to the adult world, and students may want the chance to develop their own areas of interest or skill.

Balancing these priorities is difficult. If students can be brought inside this process, however, it is good preparation for the challenge of doing good work. In life there will always be competing goals and standards, and competing opinions on what matters most or on what constitutes the essence of "excellence." When students are made aware of what excellence looks like in a given case, and why, they can build an understanding of how excellence relates to context. Ideally, through personal projects or a more open classroom model, students also have time to develop some of their own sense of what excellence means for them.

With current societal controls in particular, all of schooling might be taken up with exploring understandings of excellence. But what about the other Es, namely engagement and ethics? Researcher Katie Davis is concerned that sometimes those two Es get sidelined: "When I talk to educators about the 3Es they instantly understand it; of course we want students and professionals to be excellent, but you also want them to be ethical and engaged. Yet that's not always explicitly stated, or it's not often part of the review process or assessment process in schools" (personal communication, 26 February 2015).

Indeed, there is evidence that schooling often proceeds without engagement. How, then, might one prioritize student engagement in learning?

Engagement

A primary way in which the Good Work Project understands engagement is in relation to "flow"—that is, the psychological state in which one is completely immersed in a task (Csikszentmihalyi, 1990). Using a nationally representative sample and the experience sampling method, Csikszentmihalyi and colleagues have studied flow in schools in the U.S.A. They in fact found that flow was lowest inside classrooms, and that students spent up to 40% of their time within classrooms actively pondering non-academic matters (Shernoff *et al.*, 2003). As researcher Hans-Henrik Knoop points out, this is a problem shared by both students and workers: "poll after poll shows that many, indeed often majorities of workers find themselves disengaged in their work, just as pupils and students still often report their institutionalized learning to be boring" (personal communication, 22 February 2015).

In recognition of this situation, there have been notable efforts to place engagement front and center. For instance, the Canadian Education Association (2009) launched the project "What Did You Do In School Today?", which is a national inquiry into student engagement in learning. In Australia, "Learning Frontiers", an initiative spearheaded by the Australian Institute for Teaching and School Leadership (AITSL) (undated), has the explicit goal of developing new teaching practices aimed at increasing deep student engagement in learning. The highly influential OECD Program for International Student Assessment (PISA) investigates student engagement and motivation in its supplementary questionnaires, recognizing these as important contributors to academic learning (Organisation for Economic Co-operation and Development, 2013). Evidence that measures of school engagement are strong predictors of academic success and long-term employment outcomes makes these initiatives all the more important (Abbott-Chapman *et al.*, 2014; Upadyaya & Salmela-Aro, 2013). These findings imply that, far from being a mere embellishment, engagement and the attainment of excellence are intertwined in student learning, just as they are in professional (and all other kinds of) work.

But is engagement just about avoiding boredom and staying on task? What does it really mean for school to be "engaging"? David Shernoff, a colleague of Mihaly Csikszentmihalyi, has led the research on conditions for flow in schools (Shernoff *et al.*, 2014). One of the key findings of his studies is that students experience greater flow in settings where they are allowed a degree of choice over activities, and can remain with or move on from an activity when they are ready to do so. Enabling this more self-directed kind of work in a classroom often relies on different scheduling or timetable arrangements—for example, to allow teachers more time with the same group of students (Suttie, 2012).

The Canadian Education Association (CEA) describes three ways in which students might be engaged in school. An "academically engaged" student describes commitment to schoolwork, participation in lessons, and timely completion of assignments. A "socially engaged" student has a feeling of belonging at school, without necessarily being engaged by schoolwork. An "intellectually engaged" student displays serious emotional and cognitive investment in learning, building a personal learning identity beyond the simple completion of school tasks (Dunleavy & Milton, 2009; Munns & Martin, 2005).

The building of positive attitudes to learning is an important outcome of school at a time when the acquisition of a school certificate or diploma may no longer be a sufficient guarantee of a secure future (Dobbs *et al.*, 2012). Although high-school graduates continue to fare better than school dropouts, even students who perform well and attain higher qualifications may be among the many whose skills and knowledge are no longer at a premium in the job market (Carnevale *et al.*, 2014). In a volatile environment, the keys to resilience and success lie in being a confident and capable thinker and creator, and nothing is more important for this than the capacity to continue learning (Gardner, 2009). So what sets students on that path?

A key contributor to long-term engagement is a sense of purpose. In western contexts, psychologists have found that a sense of purpose is a key contributor to positive work and life outcomes for young people (Damon *et al.*, 2003; Steger & Dik, 2009). William Damon has synthesized his ongoing work with the Stanford Center on Adolescence into a variety of ways that teachers can help young people to develop purpose—an area of passion that extends beyond self-interest (Damon, 2008). Teachers can actively promote the development of purpose by creating opportunities for students to connect with schoolwork in individual ways. Out-of-school experiences or exposure to a wide range of adults are also important for igniting new interests. In fact, simply engaging in conversations with students about things that are personally meaningful to them can be hugely influential in this domain. Damon found that many of the American children in his studies were cynical about the possibility of purpose and meaning. Unless students hear from and get to know adults who have meaningful working lives, they will not be inclined to believe that they might find this for themselves, either in their schoolwork or in their future endeavors (Redding *et al.*, 2016).

As was indicated earlier in this chapter, engagement is a hugely complex concept, and the precise relationship between short- and long-term engagement, and its beneficial outcomes, remains unclear. Nevertheless, the notion of engagement reflected by the Good Work Project seems to have significant resonance for schools and students. It is not only about motivation and well-being in the experience of flow, but also about being engaged in the long term by the purpose and values of one's work. Interestingly, in order to find and appreciate this kind of purpose, engagement relies on a deeper understanding of ethics (Damon, 2008).

Ethics

What is the responsibility of schools to develop ethics? As several of our interviewees reflected, "ethics belongs everywhere." However, in schools, if it is not on the schedule it can be hard to see where it fits in. Most teachers would agree that promoting ethical behavior is part of the work of teaching, and indeed wording to this effect is written into the goals of many local and national curricula. Yet several factors are making ethical focus and development more challenging. Globalization, environmental disruption, and new technologies are just three major drivers of change that affect how people see their futures in the context of local and global conditions. Moreover, in many countries, young people are likely to be part of online communities, interacting with people from different cultural and social settings. In these settings, there are few models of how to behave in an ethical manner (James & Jenkins, 2014).

One of the key challenges is that ethics cannot take the form of a simple set of rules. The Good Work Project's studies of young people found that few of them have a clear sense of what qualifies as an ethical dilemma, let alone a straightforward compass to guide them in ethical decision making. Ethical decisions are as common in schools as in working life, but students may not recognize how complex they are. In secondary and high schools, copying of work or plagiarism is worryingly frequent in a range of countries where grades are "high stakes", as epitomized by our opening example from Atlanta public schools. Some students even articulate a rationale—if everyone is doing it, it would be unfair to oneself to resist doing the same. Directly addressing these kinds of decisions in class discussion can help students to see other perspectives. Students *need* to have conversations in order to develop a sense of the value of personal integrity and credibility—qualities whose pay-off is in the long term and not at the forefront of adolescent minds (Redding *et al.*, 2016).

Another set of ethical concepts that can readily be developed in a school setting is the ethics of care. Students are faced with decisions about how to treat others on a daily basis—for example, whom to sit with, whom to talk to, whether to laugh, whether to speak out—but many of these may pass by unnoticed. Bullying is a major concern for many schools, but sometimes the reaction has been to regiment students to the point where they are stripped of the opportunity to show care for others. If a school context indicates that "academic outcomes" are all-important, then it is easy for students to justify ignoring the suffering of others—an attitude which may remain with them throughout their lives. Instead, where schools actively embrace the complexity of being a community, and have explicit conversations about principles and incidents when they occur, students discover that making decisions about how we treat others is every bit as challenging as academic learning.

Schools now find themselves taking on, as sites of ethical development, some of the former responsibilities of communities or churches. This state of affairs has not been lost on governments or school leaders. Many have aimed for the development of "grit", "resilience", or "character building" as the route to developing upstanding citizens while simultaneously boosting achievement and academic success (Tough, 2012).[2] However, such traits may be unrelated to ethical behavior. Recent studies of resilience found that resiliency scales record high scores both for high-achieving students and for young offenders (Deakin Crick *et al.*, 2015). Perseverance and tenacity are only beneficial when students have also developed the disposition to seek out meaningful work and take heed of the needs of others. Therefore "wit" alone is not enough to direct grit. The development of "good grit" requires conversation and time to develop students' ethical understanding and awareness of others (Strauss & Gardner, 2014).

The question of "good grit" brings us back to a focus on purpose. Research suggests that the most effective and engaging purposes are those that are also ethically minded. In a longitudinal study, Hill *et al.* (2010) reported that college students who have a sense of purpose that is primarily prosocial demonstrate greater work productivity and well-being in later life than those who have either no purpose or one that is primarily financial. Researcher Hans-Henrik Knoop describes this in terms of "framing the idea of excellence with ethics, not only at the personal level but also the social" (personal communication, 22 February 2015). Worldwide, it is recognized that education needs to be oriented towards the ethical needs of societies as well as towards their economic needs. Most recently, this view has been reflected in efforts to establish global metrics for universal education. The Learning Metrics Task Force, a UNESCO-led coalition exploring the potential for global learning metrics, recommends that education systems should track the extent to which schools are helping young people to develop into "Citizens of the World" (Learning Metrics Task Force, 2013). Whether these goals can be reflected in empirical measures is still hotly contested, and potential measures are still nascent.[3] Nevertheless, educators can feel confident that they have support in the battle to create space for ethics in intensely competitive learning environments.

Bringing the Three Es Together

In the triple helix image mentioned earlier we saw that, in good work, engagement, excellence, and ethics are integrally linked. This concordance should be manifest in a good school: students need to understand the purpose of their work to be involved in developing criteria for excellence; connecting to a purpose creates engagement; and the most engaging and critically needed purposes are those that align with ethical principles. What does it look like when these three Es are brought together in a learning environment?

The early years might seem too early to be thinking about "work", but not too early to start nurturing dispositions towards ethics, engagement, and excellence (Perkins *et al.*, 2000). Reggio Emilia practices, which originated in a small city in northern Italy, aim to support the emergence of a child's identity in a way that fosters the development of personal standards of ethics and excellence. In preschools or early primary grades, students spend their time in a carefully designed learning environment, learning to express themselves at their own pace. Particular emphasis is placed on children learning how to work together and to question each other thoughtfully and respectfully. Children practice articulating the reasons for their actions and taking account of the perspectives of others (Krechevsky *et al.*, 2013; Project Zero, 2005).

As students develop, they need different types of activities to induct them into the language and skills of different academic disciplines (Ritchhart *et al.*, 2011). This altered focus, however, need not require abandonment of the large goals of engagement, ethics, and excellence. The practices of *expeditionary learning* (EL) schools, found across the U.S.A. and increasingly elsewhere, illustrate how the three Es can be united in elementary and secondary education. Students in EL schools learn to create "beautiful work" through practices of peer critique and redrafting. They come to appreciate that different types of work have different standards of excellence, and also that in any domain repeated reflective efforts can lead to excellence (Berger *et al.*, 2014). Teachers design projects that have real-world meaning and, potentially, an ethical purpose. For example, fourth graders test local water conditions to see if they are within safe ranges for local animal life. Sixth graders conduct interviews with homeless people and create a storybook to share with their school and community in order to foster care and inclusion. The challenging and purposeful nature of this kind of work makes it key to experiencing engagement and cultivating an ethical sense (Berger, 2003).

In adolescence, students can have even more opportunities to connect with purposes and meaning outside the classroom. Big Picture Learning (www.bigpicture.org) schools, found in the U.S.A., Australia, The Netherlands, and Israel, embrace the philosophy of "one child at a time" (Levine *et al.*, 2001). These high schools focus on personalization and helping students to learn through "real work", in the form of extensive internships and personal projects (Washor & Mojkowski, 2013). Their model helps students to develop their own goals for their future work and lives within the standards of a community (Littky & Grabelle, 2004). During internships, students work alongside adult mentors in an apprenticeship model. Studies of adolescent learning indicate the promise of apprenticeship-style learning, particularly in high school (Halpern, 2009). Jeanne Nakamura and colleagues have conducted numerous studies of mentoring and apprenticeship inspired by the "good work" framework. They show how informal talk and modeling are important carriers of values and standards between teachers and students (Nakamura *et al.*, 2009). Thus, in their learning, students are developing an appreciation of the standards of both ethics and excellence in the given domain (indeed, value systems of powerful mentors are often passed on from one generation to the next). In the classroom, Big Picture Learning teachers take on the role of "advisers", working with small groups of students throughout their time at the school, with an explicit remit to support their personal and social development.

In each of these examples, schools have been able to make structural changes. This alteration in the rhythm of the day provides teachers with collaborative time to plan long-term activities and to work with a group of students over the long term to build relationships (education in Reggio Emilia has foregrounded this endeavor). Even without such changes, however, an orientation towards the three Es can make a big difference. Educators are increasingly familiar with the calls to foster the "growth mindset" that enables long-term learning (Dweck, 2006). Focusing on ethics, engagement, and excellence as facets of the student experience can help to foster this mindset. When students think about the process and outcomes of their work in terms of the three Es, they see that there is more than one way to achieve excellence, and more to life and work than a simplistic notion of achievement. Simple comparisons recede, to be replaced by fuller notions of what it means to grow and be "better." Where competitive pressures can often lead students astray, it is more important than ever that students have access to a richer framework of values by which to orient themselves.

Teaching as Good Work

What can educators do to develop their own ability to do good work? To carry out their roles with precision and conviction, educators need a strong sense of the foundations and purposes of their work. "Good work" researchers have found that educators often do not get enough opportunity to develop these foundations. In the early 2000s, Jeanne Nakamura and her team carried out an extensive study of universities, asking them to consider their institutional mission, and found that educators were desperate for the opportunity to grapple with larger questions in their profession: "It's really striking how surprised people are, and how appreciative they are [to have the opportunity to speak with us on these topics]. They're committed to the mission [of their institution], but they don't get much chance to think about it" (personal communication, 23 January 2015). In too many of the universities visited by Nakamura and colleagues, a mission had been developed with little input from the professionals currently in the organization.

In K-12 education, the development of a mission statement or explicit goals can become a more public and engaging process. Delta School District in British Columbia, Canada, championed the creation of a new district vision through a multi-stage graphic visioning process. Each school worked with a graphic artist to develop its mission; thereafter, volunteers from the schools and parent communities came together to view a gallery of all the visions and develop a "unified" piece. The graphic of this final vision is now displayed in all schools as well as in every room of the district office, and is used to guide and connect all aspects of work at the schools. Other districts in British Columbia have now been through a similar process.

A clear sense of mission is particularly important when a field is in flux, as education is in many ways today. William Damon suggests that education may now be in a similar position to that of journalism 10 years ago—a field that is being disrupted by the effects of new technologies and globalization, with stark disagreement as to how this disruption should be responded to, managed, or embraced. Hans-Henrik Knoop reflects that while "teaching is small-scale" and "journalism big-scale", we increasingly see "examples of how educators scale up", via the likes of massive open online courses (MOOCs), or whole platforms, such as Khan Academy. Likewise, the teacher-leaders who are sharing their practices via online communities and in-person presentations represent an exciting new phase of the profession, filled with promise but also with pitfalls.

What can we recommend for those who feel that today's climate is too uncertain for fixed principles such as missions and professional ethics? Researcher Seana Moran thinks that, in uncertain situations, the consideration of ethics is more important than ever, but only if we nuance our understanding of what the word means: "ethics tends to be used in the sense of rules, not in the sense of responsibility. By that I actually mean 'response-ability'—response to a situation and how it might unfold. ... I am afraid of people that only see ethics as rules, because rules are too easy to subvert" (Seana Moran, personal communication, 3 February 2015).

The notion of "response-ability" was coined by researcher Susan Verducci in her attempt to describe the characteristics that singled out good workers (Verducci, 2007). Of those interviewed for the Good Work Project, some of the most memorable subjects demonstrated that they knew how to respond to the needs of others and maintain integrity in dynamic situations. Developing the ability to work with the notion of ethics involves developing an ethical sense as "a practice and a habit." Verducci has reported that when she works with education students on their ethical development, it is "a characterological thing—developing their character as a [future] teacher, as opposed to responding to a set of questions every month" (Susan Verducci, personal communication, 18 February 2015). Using initial reflection exercises to cultivate ethical thinking, Verducci then slowly allows the exercises to fall away as the ethical habits that they fostered gradually become part of everyday conversation and action.

Over time, we have found that the central mechanism necessary to cultivate a "good work" sensibility is reflection. Although it may seem a rather basic technique, simply allowing people the opportunity to ponder the meaning of good work is a valuable exercise. Reflection is just as indispensable to young students as it is to seasoned professionals, particularly when ethical dilemmas are in question (Light, 2015). During the research carried out by the Good Work Project, the resounding message from interview participants was that the interview process itself was not only enjoyable, but also provided important and much needed time to think about the meaning of work and how ethically gray situations have been handled in the past. In the workshops and sessions that the Good Work Project has held since, attendees have echoed these sentiments. The value of having a specific time and space for contemplating and discussing the meaning of good work should therefore not be underestimated; people benefit from a multifaceted approach to looking at good work, which is too often reduced to a single static dimension.

Reflection on one's work is a naturally ongoing process (which means that time must be devoted to it over the long term) that can occur either individually or in groups. In some cases, independent reflection is vital to arriving at an enhanced understanding of the points surrounding good work. For example, by performing an activity from the GoodWork Toolkit (see *From the Laboratory to the Classroom* section below), one can ponder the factors that motivate one's own work. By engaging with a hypothetical ethical dilemma about professionals in the workplace, one can review the pressures and responsibilities facing the actors in the narrative and, by extension, apply that insight to one's own life.

However, solitary reflection by itself is not enough. The Good Work Project encourages *shared* reflection and conversation in groups. Personal interaction is the key to in-depth and complex comprehension of the meaning(s) of good work, particularly when it comes to more difficult concepts or ethically "gray" situations in which the "right" course of action is not entirely clear. In group-level discussions, contributors are exposed to multiple perspectives from peers, resulting in more thorough meditation on the implications of good work. For this reason, the Good Work Project has developed materials that are interactive in nature and which encourage people to delve together into the concepts underlying good work.

Can this kind of reflection possibly be fitted into the daily work of teaching? One example illustrates how educators might make space for it. "Spirals of Inquiry" is a process developed through the work of school researchers and practitioners in New Zealand and British Columbia, and now used across parts of Australia, England, and the U.S.A. In Spirals of Inquiry, teachers are encouraged to assume responsibility for what happens in their classrooms and to work together with students to find ways to improve the educational experience. This collaborative reflection considers all aspects of students' lives, and firmly takes into account local performance standards with a focus on formative assessment. Weekly meetings between teachers provide the opportunity to maintain a focus on what matters most. Monthly network meetings and an annual symposium allow teachers from different schools to come together, build their professional knowledge, and renew their moral purpose. Linda Kaser and Judy Halbert, the creators of Spirals of Inquiry, have regularly drawn on the notion of good work as defined by the Good Work Project (Kaser & Halbert, 2009; Halbert & Kaser, 2012). In their writing about schools involved in Spirals of Inquiry, and about the networks that link those schools together, they use the concept of good work to describe what they are looking to promote and share through this program.

As Verducci has pointed out, group discussion and personal reflection on "good work" themes act as a form of "inoculation." In other words, when students or professionals at any level are introduced to good work as practitioners or via a lesson, workshop, or book, the ideas will, with any luck, plant a seed in their mind that they will then carry with them and discuss with others. In turn, individuals will come to their own understanding of good work and their own practices that align with the values of good work.

In fact, evidence indicates that contact with "good work" topics may have a long-term effect on both the professional and personal life of an individual. In 2014, a study of former students on the Harvard Graduate School of Education course, "Good Work in Education: When Excellence, Ethics, and Engagement Meet", surveyed graduates spanning a period of a decade. Respondents were asked to answer a series of questions about their memories of the course content and the influence of the ideas on their career and private life. Coding the responses for content areas revealed that 79% of the former students at least mentioned, and many of them illustrated anecdotally, the fact that the course had had an effect on their behavior both within and outside their workplace (Mucinskas & Nichols, 2014). For example, one graduate reported that the course helped to transform her view of education from a simple occupation into a true professional domain. Five individuals who had become teachers explicitly discussed how they communicated "good work" ideas to their students in their own teaching. Additional respondents reported a feeling of preparedness for tricky ethical quandaries, and a strengthened moral and ethical compass in general. Although a selection bias almost certainly meant that the former students who answered the survey disproportionately represented those who were influenced by the course content, the study shows the lasting effect of good work on people who are up to 10 years distant from short-term formal instruction in the area. Similar courses or initiatives are being or have been taught at institutions such as Amherst College, Bloomsburg University of Pennsylvania, Claremont Graduate University, Clark University, Colby College, Colorado State University, San Jose State University, the University of Maine, Farmington, and Aarhus University in Denmark (Mucinskas & Gardner, 2013).

Building a Community for Good Work

At the start of this chapter, we described scenarios where the pursuit of success might conflict with moral principles. The Good Work Project recognizes a tension between the goals of excellence and ethics unless the two are understood in relationship to each other. Seana Moran, in her course on ethics inspired by the Good Work Project, describes how students can come to recognize the qualities of this relationship. Initially, her students become "quite flustered" when they discuss situations in which success and ethics may diverge: "They don't like it at all. They want those two to be the same. … So then we have a conversation about what it means when something is excellent but not ethical, and vice versa" (Seana Moran, personal communication, 3 February 2015).

This is a conversation that all educators might have as we consider at what point the pursuit of measurable outcomes might begin to come at the cost of other important goals. It is clear that the education metrics that currently have the highest profile, although fundamentally important, cannot be our only guiding star in developing young people. In fact, educators of all types (particularly those responsible for training or mentoring professional realms, such as law, medicine, or journalism) have an obligation to help students to cultivate their ethical compasses to prepare them for the realities of the working world.

The ultimate goals of the Good Work Project, then, are that excellence, ethics, and engagement will become habitual practices, and that good work itself will be achieved on a larger scale. In stimulating good work, educators have a pivotal role to play—by setting students on the path to good work early and encouraging the three Es in school, they convey that these ideas are important for life in general, and are therefore worth the struggle. The components of the good work triple helix should not only exist in the classroom, but will also ideally become an underlying disposition that shapes thoughts and actions. In her teaching, Moran strives to connect ethical thinking to action by helping her students to recognize when they have an opportunity to do good. She calls the initial surprise of that recognition the "collywobbles"—the feeling that something important is going on to which an individual can contribute. Teaching to develop an ethical sense, in a way that is age appropriate, is crucial to overcome the prevailing attitude among young people that good work can be deferred until an undetermined point in the future when they can "afford" to act in an excellent, ethical, and engaged way. This behavior has to start now (Gardner, 2007).

Overall, the promotion of complex goods such as ethical development works best when it can be done in concert with others. Individuals need to be able to draw on social resources in order to have the strength to create time and space for these goods in their work, whether in the form of a mentor, a team, an organizational mission, or a set of professional standards. The examples in this chapter illustrate how, by working together, groups of educators can hold themselves accountable to more holistic visions of teaching and learning.

From the Laboratory to the Classroom

The Good Work Project offers a plethora of items for educators. The intentionally flexible Good Work "Toolkits" are curricula that aim to convey particular ideas from the Good Work Project. They are designed on the basis of research into how individuals at various life stages deal with complex questions and problems (Kuhn, 1999; Lipman, 2003), and how teaching can enhance those approaches (Grotzer & Perkins, 2000; Ritchhart & Perkins, 2005). The toolkits can serve a dual purpose in educational settings. Firstly, teachers can use toolkits with students in the classroom in order to facilitate discussions about issues such as the three Es, values, and responsibilities. Secondly, teachers can use the toolkits among themselves as part of their professional development efforts as workers, mentors, and citizens of their school communities. Our toolkits have been used by teachers in this way at an array of schools. In addition, the Good Work Project's website (www.thegoodproject.org) provides further information about other good-work-related courses and initiatives. Here we shall outline the most relevant available materials, all of which are accessible digitally for free.

1. *The GoodWork Toolkit.* Created in 2004, this toolkit is a curriculum and guidebook of narratives and associated activities intended to walk readers through ethical situations that they may encounter at school or in the workplace. Initially developed to expose secondary students to good work ideas and reflection, each of the narratives is a short story of a moral dilemma faced by a particular individual, inspired by the professional interviews carried out during the Good Work Project's research phase. This toolkit is intentionally adaptable to a multitude of settings, and has been used in a variety of environments. Educators can employ the toolkit as instructional material for students, and may also benefit from exploring it themselves in seminars so as to better understand their own relationship to situations in the workplace. Further information, sample materials, and the full free guidebook can be accessed via the Good Project website (at www.thegoodproject.org/toolkits-curricula/the-goodwork-toolkit/).
2. *The Elementary Good Work Toolkit.* Developed by elementary school teacher Amy Hoffman, the Elementary Good Work Toolkit is a set of curricular materials based on the original GoodWork Toolkit, but adapted for a younger audience. Using simpler language and emphasizing introductory concepts such as a basic knowledge of the three Es and their meanings, students who used the toolkit in Hoffman's class demonstrated that they retained the ideas presented and applied them to other areas of learning. Further information and the latest downloadable version of this toolkit can be accessed via the Good Project website (at www.thegoodproject.org/toolkits-curricula/the-elementary-good-work-toolkit/).
3. *The Good Collaboration Toolkit.* Launched in 2015, the Good Collaboration Toolkit was developed from a study of collaboration originating directly from the Good Work Project, mainly focused on collaboration between educational institutions and consortia. The study provided insight into how to forge collaborations at all levels and in various sectors. The toolkit is organized around eight specific elements that all effective collaborations should satisfy, and can facilitate good work at an organizational or group level in any setting. Narrative cases, group and individual activities, and specific guiding questions are all included in the text. The electronic materials can be accessed via the Good Project website (at www.thegoodproject.org/collaborationtoolkit/).

4. *Good work course materials and syllabuses.* Courses that incorporate "good work" themes have been taught at many K-12 schools and at institutions of higher education. Samples of these course materials and syllabuses can be accessed via the Good Project website (at www.thegoodproject.org/courses/good-work-course-materials/).
5. *Implementation information.* Partners of the Good Work Project, many of which have utilized "good work" ideas in educational settings, can be accessed via the Good Project website (at www.thegoodproject.org/good-project-friends/). Descriptions of various educational efforts to incorporate good work in the classroom and beyond are available on the Good Project's blog (at www.thegoodproject.org/good-blog/).

NOTES

1 This chapter draws on our experience of writing and teaching about the Good Work Project, and on interviews with "good work" researchers past and present, namely Kendall Cotton Bronk, Mihaly Csikszentmihalyi, William Damon, Katie Davis, Hans Henrik Knoop, Seana Moran, Jeanne Nakamura, and Susan Verducci. We draw also on the lines of inquiry that grew from the original project, as well as outside research that has complemented or amplified its findings. We are grateful to the funders who have supported the Good Work Project over the years. The Endeavor Foundation has been a steadfast supporter, and the authors owe an incalculable debt to President Julie Kidd, Program Officer Susan Kassouf, and Ashley Kidd.
2 In 2014–15, the British Government adopted a new strategy to "develop a set of character traits, attributes and behaviours that underpin success" (www.gov.uk/government/news/character-education-apply-for-2015-grant-funding). Leading charter schools focus on character as a route to "success" (www.kipp.org/our-approach/character).
3 Surveys of citizenship among students already exist, as do ethical assessments for adults (for example, https://lectica.org/visitors/about_lectatests.php). For students, the Education Testing Service in the U.S.A. has been involved in developing the "Mission Skills Assessment" for use by schools that wish to demonstrate how they develop aspects of students such as ethics, creativity, teamwork, resilience, and curiosity (http://indexgroups.org/msa/).

References

Abbott-Chapman, J., Martin, K., Ollington, N., Venn, A., Dwyer, T., & Gall, S. (2014). The longitudinal association of childhood school engagement with adult educational and occupational achievement: findings from an Australian national study. *British Educational Research Journal*, 40(1), 102–120.

Australian Institute for Teaching and School Leadership (AITSL) (undated). *Learning Frontiers*. Available online at www.aitsl.edu.au/learning-frontiers

Aviv, R. (2014). Wrong answer. *The New Yorker*. Available online at www.newyorker.com/magazine/2014/07/21/wrong-answer

Berger, R. (2003). *An Ethic of Excellence: Building a Culture of Craftsmanship with Students*. Portsmouth, NH: Heinemann Educational Books.

Berger, R., Rugen, L., Woodfin, L., & Expeditionary Learning (2014). *Leaders of Their Own Learning: Transforming Schools Through Student-Engaged Assessment* (Pap/DVD edition). Indianapolis, IN: Jossey-Bass.

Canadian Education Association (2009). *What Did You Do In School Today?* Available online at www.cea-ace.ca/programs-initiatives/wdydist

Carnevale, A. P., Cheah, B., & Strohl, J. (2014). *Hard Times: College Majors, Unemployment and Earnings*. Center on Education and the Workforce, Georgetown Public Policy Institute. Available online at https://cew.georgetown.edu/wp-content/uploads/2014/11/Unemployment.Final_.update1.pdf

Csikszentmihalyi, M. (1990). *Flow: The Psychology of Optimal Experience.* New York: Harper & Row.

Damon, W. (2008). *The Path to Purpose: How Young People Find Their Calling in Life.* New York: Free Press.

Damon, W., Menon, J., & Cotton Bronk, K. (2003). The development of purpose during adolescence. *Applied Developmental Science,* 7(3), 119–128.

Deakin Crick, R., Huang, S., Ahmed Shafi, A., & Goldspink, C. (2015). Developing resilient agency in learning: the internal structure of learning power. *British Journal of Educational Studies,* 63(2), 121–160.

Dobbs, R., Madgavkar, A., Barton, D., Labaye, E., Manyika, J., Roxburgh, C., Lund, S., & Madhav, S. (2012). *The World at Work: Jobs, Pay, and Skills for 3.5 Billion People.* McKinsey Global Institute. Available online at www.mckinsey.com/insights/employment_and_growth/the_world_at_work

Dunleavy, J. & Milton, P. (2009). *What Did You Do in School Today? Exploring the Concept of Student Engagement and its Implications for Teaching and Learning in Canada.* Canadian Education Association. Available online at www.cea-ace.ca/sites/cea-ace.ca/files/cea-2009-wdydist-concept.pdf

Dweck, C. (2006). *Mindset: The New Psychology of Success.* New York: Random House.

Fausset, R. & Blinder, A. (2015). Atlanta school workers sentenced in test score cheating case. *The New York Times,* 14 April. Available online at www.nytimes.com/2015/04/15/us/atlanta-school-workers-sentenced-in-test-score-cheating-case.html?_r=1

Fischman, W., Solomon, B., Schutte, D., & Gardner, H. (2004). *Making Good: How Young People Cope with Moral Dilemmas at Work.* Cambridge, MA: Harvard University Press.

Gardner, H. (Ed.) (2007). *Responsibility at Work.* San Francisco, CA: Jossey-Bass.

Gardner, H. (2009). *Five Minds for the Future.* Boston, MA: Harvard Business School Press.

Gardner, H. (Ed.) (2010). *Good Work: Theory and Practice.* The Good Work Project. Available online at www.thegoodproject.org/pdf/GoodWork-Theory_and_Practice-with_covers.pdf

Gardner, H., Csikszentmihalyi, M., & Damon, W. (2001). *Good Work: When Excellence and Ethics Meet.* New York: Basic Books.

Grotzer, T. A. & Perkins, D. N. (2000). Teaching intelligence: a performance conception. In: R. A. Sternberg (Ed.), *Handbook of Intelligence* (pp. 492–515). New York: Cambridge University Press.

Halbert, J. & Kaser, L. (2012). *Inquiring Learning Environments: New Mindsets Required.* East Melbourne, Victoria: Centre for Strategic Education.

Halpern, R. (2009). *The Means to Grow Up: Reinventing Apprenticeship as a Developmental Support in Adolescence.* New York: Routledge.

Higher Education Research Institute (2014). *The American Freshman: National Norms.* Available online at http://heri.ucla.edu/monographs/TheAmericanFreshman2014.pdf

Hill, P. L., Burrow, A. L., Brandenberger, J. W., Lapsley, D. K., & Quaranto, J. C. (2010). Collegiate purpose orientations and well-being in early and middle adulthood. *Journal of Applied Developmental Psychology,* 31(2), 173–179.

James, C. & Jenkins, H. (2014). *Disconnected: Youth, New Media, and the Ethics Gap.* Cambridge, MA: MIT Press.

Kaser, L. & Halbert, J. (2009). *Leadership Mindsets: Innovation and Learning in the Transformation of Schools.* New York: Routledge.

Krechevsky, M., Mardell, B., Rivard, M., & Wilson, D. (2013). *The Visible Learners: Promoting Reggio-Inspired Approaches in All Schools.* San Francisco, CA: Jossey-Bass.

Kuhn, D. (1999). A developmental model of critical thinking. *Educational Researcher,* 28(2), 16–46.

Learning Metrics Task Force (LMTF) (2013). *Towards Universal Learning: Recommendations from the Learning Metrics Task Force.* Washington, DC: Center for Universal Education at Brookings. Available online at www.uis.unesco.org/Education/Documents/lmtf-summary-rpt-en.pdf

Levine, A. & Dean, D. (2012). *Generation on a Tightrope: A Portrait of Today's College Student.* Hoboken, NJ: Jossey-Bass.

Levine, E., Peters, T., & Sizer, T. (2001). *One Kid at a Time: Big Lessons from a Small School.* New York: Teachers College Press.

Light, R. (2015). How to live wisely. *New York Times*, 31 July. Available online at www.nytimes. com/2015/08/02/education/edlife/how-to-live-wisely.html

Lipman, M. (2003). *Thinking in Education*, 2nd edition. New York: Cambridge University Press.

Littky, D. & Grabelle, S. (2004). *The Big Picture: Education Is Everyone's Business*. Alexandria, VA: Association for Supervision and Curriculum Development.

Mucinskas, D. & Gardner, H. (2013). Educating for good work: from research to practice. *British Journal of Educational Studies,* 61(4), 453–470.

Mucinskas, D. & Nichols, V. (2014). *The Impact of a Course on Good Work: Alumni Reflect on Their Experiences.* Cambridge, MA: The Good Project.

Munns, G. & Martin, A. (2005). *It's All About MeE: A Motivation and Engagement Framework.* Australian Association for Research in Education, International Education Research Conference, 2005.

Nakamura, J., Shernoff, D. J., & Hooker, C. H. (2009). *Good Mentoring: Fostering Excellent Practice in Higher Education.* San Francisco, CA: John Wiley & Sons.

National Center for Education Statistics (undated). *Fast Facts.* Available online at http://nces.ed.gov/ fastfacts/display.asp?id=98

Organisation for Economic Co-operation and Development (OECD) (2013). *PISA 2012 Results: Ready to Learn: Students' Engagement, Drive and Self-Beliefs (Volume III).* Paris: OECD.

Perkins, D., Tishman, S., Ritchhart, R., Donis, K., & Andrade, A. (2000). Intelligence in the wild: a dispositional view of intellectual traits. *Educational Psychology Review*, 12(3), 269–293.

Pew Research Center (2011). *Is College Worth It?* Available online at www.pewsocialtrends. org/2011/05/15/is-college-worth-it/

Project Zero (2005). *Making Learning Visible: Children as Individual and Group Learners.* Reggio Emilia: Reggio Children Publications.

Redding, A., James, C., & Gardner, H. (2016). Nurturing ethical collaboration. *Independent School Magazine*, 75(2), 58–64.

Ritchhart, R. & Perkins, D. N. (2005). Learning to think: the challenges of teaching for thinking. In: K. Holyoak (Ed.), *Cambridge Handbook of Thinking and Reasoning* (pp. 775–802). New York: Cambridge University Press.

Ritchhart, R., Church, M., & Morrison, K. (2011). *Making Thinking Visible: How to Promote Engagement, Understanding, and Independence for All Learners.* San Francisco, CA: John Wiley & Sons.

Shernoff, D. J., Csikszentmihalyi, M., Shneider, B., & Shernoff, E. S. (2003). Student engagement in high school classrooms from the perspective of flow theory. *School Psychology Quarterly*, 18(2), 158–176.

Shernoff, D. J, Abdi, B. A., Anderson, B., & Csikszentmihalyi, M. (2014). Flow in schools revisited: cultivating engaged learners and optimal learning environments. In: M. J. Furlong, R. Gilman, & E. S. Huebner (Eds), *Handbook of Positive Psychology in Schools*, 2nd edition (pp. 211–226). New York: Routledge.

Steger, M. F. & Dik, B. J. (2009). Work as meaning: individual and organizational benefits of engaging in meaningful work. In: N. Garcea, S. Harrington, & P. A. Linley (Eds), *Oxford Handbook of Positive Psychology and Work* (pp. 131–142). Oxford: Oxford University Press.

Strauss, V. & Gardner, H. (2014). Howard Gardner, creator of 'multiple intelligences' theory, launches new project on 'good' education. *The Washington Post.* Available online at www.washingtonpost. com/blogs/answer-sheet/wp/2014/10/01/
howard-gardner-creator-of-multiple-intelligences-theory-launches-new-project-on-good-education/

Suttie, J. (2012). *Eight Tips for Fostering Flow in the Classroom. Greater Good: The Science of a Meaningful Life.* Available online at http://greatergood.berkeley.edu/article/item/eight_tips_for_fostering_flow_in_the_classroom

Tough, P. (2012). *How Children Succeed: Grit, Curiosity, and the Hidden Power of Character.* New York: Houghton Mifflin Harcourt.

Upadyaya, K. & Salmela-Aro, K. (2013). Development of school engagement in association with academic success and well-being in varying social contexts: a review of empirical research. *European Psychologist*, 18(2), 136–147.

Verducci, S. (2007). The ability to respond. In: H. Gardner (Ed.), *Responsibility at Work: How Leading Professionals Act (or Don't Act) Responsibly* (pp. 43–63). San Francisco, CA: Jossey-Bass.

Washor, E. & Mojkowski, C. (2013). *Leaving to Learn: How Out-of-School Learning Increases Student Engagement and Reduces Dropout Rates*. Portsmouth, NH: Heinemann.

Wiliam, D. (2011). *Embedded Formative Assessment*. Bloomington, IN: Solution Tree Press.

Domain-General Issues and Classroom Strategies

3

MOTIVATION AND ATTENTION AS FOUNDATIONS FOR STUDENT LEARNING

Deirdre C. Greer

COLUMBUS STATE UNIVERSITY

Introduction

Motivation and attention are critical to learning, yet learning how to activate these constructs in the classroom is not typically part of teacher preparation programs. It is often assumed that students come to school ready to learn and participate, and while this may be true for some students, it is not typical. Teachers who understand the differences in students' readiness to participate in school often make efforts to develop engaging lessons that will interest their students, or they may introduce management plans that can have a negative effect on learning. Understanding the psychological constructs and neurological processes behind motivation and attention and how to utilize this knowledge in the classroom will increase the teacher's ability to engage all students in learning. The two constructs of motivation and attention are inextricably connected. Motivation drives attention, and therefore the more motivated we are, the more likely we are to pay attention (Ormrod, 2009). There are a number of practices related to school that can affect children's level of motivation and attention, such as rewards and punishment, verbal praise and feedback, social interaction, teacher and student expectations, and autonomy and control.

This chapter will discuss key components of social cognitive theory and self-determination theory along with some neurological processes that support motivation and attention. It will also consider effective classroom applications and practices, based on these theories and processes, to help educators to support the development of intrinsic motivation for learning, which can lead to increased student attention and achievement.

Extrinsic and Intrinsic Motivation

Motivation is the drive that influences us to do things. This drive can come from within (*intrinsic motivation*), or it can come from something external (*extrinsic motivation*). Students may be intrinsically motivated by their engagement in a classroom activity that is in some way rewarding to them. The activity may be fun, challenging, interesting, or provide some other internal satisfaction that drives the students' engagement in the activity. In contrast, many classrooms are set up to utilize an external reward system, such as a token economy, that many people perceive as motivation.

Extrinsic Motivation

Every day in classrooms, students' learning and behavior are managed through a variety of techniques, many of which fall into the category of "reward systems." This means that, essentially, children are being bribed to learn and behave. The bribes may be candy, toys, praise, special privileges, or other incentives that are often considered to be motivating to children. Regardless of the incentive that is used, what students actually learn from these kinds of systems is that there is a specific set of behaviors they are expected to perform at school, and if they exhibit these behaviors, they will receive a reward.

Commonly expected student behaviors include following school and classroom rules, giving correct answers to questions, and performing activities correctly. To some, this may sound like exactly what we want students to learn. However, the result is that students begin to understand learning as simply acquiring a set of facts or following a set of procedures for the purpose of obtaining a reward, and they fail to comprehend the broader goal of connecting learning to their lives. For example, a child may say to her parents, "If I make an 'A' on my spelling test, I get to go to the popcorn party!" This exclamation is very telling in terms of the child's underlying interpretation of the purpose of achieving an "A" in the spelling test. The message is about learning to spell words not in order to communicate effectively with others, but in order to be able to spell the words on test day so as to obtain the promised reward. This example clearly involves extrinsic motivation. In situations like this, students are motivated by the reward rather than by the activity itself.

Extrinsic motivation in the classroom, which is based on the desire to obtain something unrelated to the learning, often leads to superficial learning that is not retained on a long-term basis (Deci et al., 1991). Evidence of this fact is found when students spell words perfectly in a spelling test, but are unable to spell those same words correctly in their written work. This scenario is representative of what researchers have found to be a negative effect of external rewards on students' intrinsic motivation (Lepper et al., 1973). That is, extrinsic motivation works, but only so long as the external reward is available. True motivation involves thoughts, beliefs, and emotions, which is in direct contrast to responding to external rewards (Schunk & Usher, 2012).

Over the last few decades, research has been conducted to determine the effects of external rewards on intrinsic motivation (Deci, 1971; Deci et al., 1999, 2001; Deci and Ryan, 1985; Ledford et al., 2013; Morgan, 1984; Murayama et al., 2010). In many of these studies, external rewards have been shown to decrease intrinsic motivation. Providing an external reward for something that is already intrinsically motivating to an individual actually reduces the level of intrinsic motivation for doing that activity (Deci, 1971). Moreover, learning that occurs as a result of extrinsic motivation is often not sustained (Shindler, 2009), as in the example of the student who was motivated to learn how to spell words in order to obtain the reward of attending a popcorn party, because the effort put into the learning is often the minimum required to obtain the reward (Lei, 2010).

Intrinsic Motivation

So what *should* teachers do to motivate students? From birth, children are intrinsically motivated (Einon, 1999). According to Alphie Kohn, "children do not need to be motivated. From the beginning they are hungry to make sense of their world" (Kohn, 1993, p. 198). This premise is evident in the curious explorations of very young children eagerly trying to figure out how things work. The actions of parents and teachers can promote the development of intrinsic or extrinsic motivation. When children learn to expect external rewards, their intrinsic motivation decreases (Lepper *et al.*, 1973). Indeed, children are naturally driven to explore and learn about their world; it is the actions of the adults in their lives that can extinguish the natural intrinsic motivation.

While it is clear that children naturally possess intrinsic motivation, it is important to understand that *appropriate* extrinsic motivation is also beneficial. What is critical is to understand the difference between motivation that is self-directed and that which is influenced by external sources, such as family, school, culture, or economics. To address these aspects of motivation, we look to self-determination theory.

Self-determination, as defined in the *American Heritage Dictionary of the English Language* (www.thefreedictionary.com/self-determination), is the basic human quality of being able to make choices and decisions in order to meet personal needs. Self-determination theory is concerned with the innate motivation that drives people to make choices and decisions in order to grow and develop (Vansteenkiste *et al.*, 2006). Deci and Ryan (2012, p. 88) have identified two important assumptions of self-determination theory: first, that individuals are actively seeking growth and fulfillment, and secondly, that they have a "developmental tendency toward integration and organization of psychic material." That is, people have a drive to take in information from the outside world and integrate it with their personal knowledge and beliefs. These assumptions parallel the work of Jean Piaget, who stated that "the principal motive power of intellectual activity [is] the need to incorporate things into the subject's schemata" (Piaget, 1952, p. 46). People automatically take in information from the environment and incorporate it into what they already know. To use Piaget's terminology, we assimilate information by fitting it into our existing schemata, or we accommodate by changing our existing schemata to fit new information. These biological processes are a form of self-motivation at the subconscious level, and are present at birth. As we grow and develop, we continue to make choices and decisions that satisfy our innate needs, and it is these needs that drive us to do the things we do. This is intrinsic motivation.

Intrinsic motivation is a natural expression of human activity, and a predecessor to what Deci and Ryan (2012) call *autonomous motivation*, which can involve extrinsic motivation that is internalized. When the idea of autonomous motivation is considered, environmental information that is assimilated can be understood as a form of extrinsic motivation that becomes deeply internalized. Together, intrinsic motivation and internalized extrinsic motivation, two *self-directed* types of motivation, make up autonomous motivation. Autonomous motivation is based on individual identification of what is important and relevant to the individual, regardless of whether it is intrinsic or extrinsic (Deci & Ryan, 2012). The critical factor is whether someone else is using the extrinsic reward as a means of controlling the behavior of the individual, or the satisfaction gained from the reward emanates from within the individual.

It is important to understand that autonomous motivation is not purely intrinsic motivation, as it incorporates those extrinsic motivators from the environment that an individual assimilates for him- or herself. As it is typically understood, intrinsic motivation is then considered to be any motivation that comes from the exertion of autonomy (autonomous motivation), whereas extrinsic motivation is considered to be, that which is imposed with a feeling of control external to the individual (Deci & Ryan, 2012). LeDoux (2002) explains that intrinsic motivation also includes those incentives that satisfy our basic needs, such as food and water. The inclusion of this idea as part of the discussion may blur the distinction between intrinsic and extrinsic motivation in situations where students come to school hungry and respond strongly to a teacher's offer of food or candy as a reward. However, it must be understood that, in these instances, the students' motivation to satisfy their hunger is separate from the motivation to learn, and if the teacher's intention is to use the food or candy as a means of controlling the students' learning or behavior, the development of autonomous motivation is not being supported. According to self-determination theory, when motivation is more autonomous, the quality of student engagement, performance, and level of well-being are higher (Deci & Ryan, 2001).

In order for children to engage in autonomous motivation, three basic psychological needs must be met, namely a competence with tasks, a connection with others, and a sense of autonomy in goals and behavior (Deci & Ryan, 2001). These basic needs are addressed in social cognitive theory. For example, a teacher's consideration of task difficulty, as addressed through social cognitive theory, can lead to children's authentic success. That is, the students' success at tasks is based on their own construction of understanding, as opposed to being led through the task from the teacher's understanding. Only authentic success will result in students feeling more competent (Schunk & Usher, 2012). Therefore teachers must learn effective methods for supporting students' autonomous motivation. Some of these methods include verbal praise, social interaction, and goal setting.

Verbal Praise

Verbal praise is often used to encourage and motivate students. However, teachers may overly praise students or, in an attempt to spare a student's feelings, provide artificial praise when none is warranted. Deci (1971) reported that positive verbal reinforcement, when it is deserved, may increase intrinsic motivation. This finding is further supported by the work of Dweck (2006), who emphasizes that verbal praise should be directed toward children's *effort* rather than toward their intelligence. Dweck has identified two mindsets, namely a fixed mindset and a growth mindset, both of which develop from the way in which children are praised from a young age.

The fixed mindset, which is the traditional view, recognizes intelligence as a fixed characteristic that is innate, whereas the growth mindset acknowledges the dynamic nature of intelligence, with individual effort as the impetus for growth. According to Dweck (2006), when students are praised for their intelligence (e.g. "You are so smart!"), their motivation decreases, and any learning is temporary because their success at a task is attributed to a quality that exists within them, rather than the effort they expend in order to succeed. Furthermore, children who develop a fixed mindset see their performance as a reflection of their character, which leads to the feeling that success is equivalent to being "smart", and failure is the equivalent to being "dumb." Over time, students' performance is harmed, resulting in an aversion to difficult tasks and tasks that cannot be accomplished immediately (Dweck, 2006), because they associate academic struggle with lack of intelligence. In fact, students should be praised for their efforts regardless of whether those efforts are successful or not. Students need to learn to view errors and misunderstandings as opportunities to learn, and teachers who have a growth mindset understand and practice the kind of verbal praise that promotes this outlook.

Over time, as children develop a sense of self, they naturally begin to compare themselves with their peers. For students who have a fixed mindset, such social comparisons can result in decreased motivation in the classroom (Schunk & Usher, 2012), as they do not believe they have the power to increase their intelligence. In order to alleviate some of the negative effects of such social comparisons, teachers must be cautious in their use of verbal praise, and focus on praise for students' efforts rather than their intelligence. In other words, rather than responding to students' correct answers with "You're so smart", a teacher might say "You really worked hard to figure that out." Teachers are responsible for establishing the tone of the classroom, and modeling appropriate interactions in this way can be a valuable influence on the relationships between students.

Social Interaction

It is clear that interactions with others can have a significant effect on motivation (Bandura, 1989). The social interaction that occurs in schools can provide an opportunity for students to experience academic learning by interacting in the broader milieu of a community. In other words, school serves as a realistic context in which learning can be made applicable to the lives of the students. When students are able to immediately put their learning to use in authentic situations, they are motivated and will persevere with tasks. The social environment of the classroom also affects motivation (Bransford *et al.*, 2000). Students must be able to feel competent among their peers.

Social cognitive theory acknowledges that much of human behavior and learning is influenced by interactions in a social environment (Bandura, 1986). Beginning from birth and continuing throughout our lives, we learn appropriate and useful behaviors as well as the consequences of our behaviors through interaction with others and the environment. Bandura's social cognitive theory identifies behavioral, personal, and environmental influences that interact in a reciprocal manner. This means that children's thoughts, feelings, perceptions, and other cognitive actions (personal cognitions) influence their behavior and their environment, while at the same time the environment influences their personal cognitions and behaviors, which in turn influence the environment. Together, these interactions between behavior, environment, and personal cognitions direct children's behavior and help them to develop a sense of control over their own actions (Schunk & Usher, 2012).

According to social cognitive theory, there are several social factors that can motivate children to strive to accomplish tasks and achieve learning goals, beginning at a young age (Schunk & Usher, 2012), namely vicarious processes, symbolic processes, and/or self-regulatory processes. When students see others successfully doing something they would like to be able to do, they are vicariously motivated to do that same thing. Vicarious learning is most effective when students see themselves in some way "like" the person whom they are observing. This idea supports the use of heterogeneous grouping strategies in classrooms, so that children see their peers thinking through tasks and trying various strategies, and in turn they feel motivated to try those strategies themselves. Symbolic processes, like language and thought, also allow students to make sense of what they see others doing and to plan their own future actions. It is a teacher's knowledge of symbolic processes that supports interactive strategies such as thinking aloud and having students share their problem-solving solutions with the class. When students have opportunities to see and hear how others, specifically their peers, have completed a task, they may later attempt those same strategies themselves. Finally, self-regulatory processes, such as setting goals and identifying appropriate strategies for accomplishing a task, help students to persist in their efforts to complete tasks. Teachers can and should support the development of self-regulatory processes in the classroom.

Self-Regulation

Self-regulation is the ability to control one's actions and impulses, and it involves monitoring one's behavior, thoughts, and emotions in a given situation (Posner *et al.*, 2014). There is a distinct connection between self-regulation and attention (Posner *et al.*, 2014; Ruff and Rothbart, 1996), in that both are processed in the frontal lobe of the brain as part of a set of mental constructs known as executive functions. Executive functions include working memory, goal setting, planning, and carrying out plans effectively (Reeve & Lee, 2012). Part of this process includes the ability to inhibit behaviors that are not consistent with a goal or the plan for achieving that goal (Cuevas *et al.*, 2014). The connection between self-regulation and attention supports the observation that many students who have difficulty focusing their attention also struggle with organizing for learning, setting and completing goals, and performing tasks that involve memory (e.g. remembering basic math facts). Fortunately, teachers can incorporate strategies in the classroom that will help students to develop self-regulation.

The development of self-regulation is supported by autonomy, positive involvement, and structure, and begins with the mother's earliest attempts to pacify her crying infant as a precursor to the child's own ability to control emotion. Strong development of self-regulation begins at around the age of 3 years (Posner & Rothbart, 2007). It is an important component of motivation, because it allows students to set goals, plan strategies, and monitor the effectiveness of those strategies as they work towards accomplishing their goals (Zimmerman, 2008).

Helping students to develop strategies for becoming independent learners is a significant part of a teacher's role. Therefore teachers must be aware of and able to promote the development of autonomy, positive interaction, and structure, which support the development of self-regulation (Posner & Rothbart, 2007). In order to learn independently and function autonomously, students need to be aware of their thought processes as they learn. This awareness, which is known as metacognition, can be modeled by teachers to guide students' development of autonomy. Goal setting is a significant component of self-regulation. Students need to be able to determine how they will approach a task, set goals for their own learning, and monitor their progress towards meeting those goals.

Goal Setting

The use of explicit goals in the classroom can increase students' motivation and attention by helping them to identify important concepts. Teachers most often have multiple goals for each lesson that they teach, but do those goals resonate with their students? Social cognitive theory recognizes the identification of goals and the self-monitoring of progress towards those goals as important aspects of developing self-efficacy and maintaining motivation (Schunk & Usher, 2012). Students need to see their efforts result in the accomplishment of their goals in order to develop and strengthen self-efficacy. Other factors with regard to goal setting must also be considered in order to develop and strengthen self-efficacy and maintain motivation. For instance, goal difficulty is directly related to the amount of effort that must be expended in order to accomplish a particular goal. Goals that are overly difficult will require more effort than some children are able, or willing, to sustain. Conversely, goals that are perceived as too easy may result in students delaying their attempts to work towards them (Schunk & Usher, 2012). Therefore teachers must understand the individual needs of their students in order to assist them in setting goals at a level that supports motivation to accomplish those goals.

It is also important for teachers to understand the difference between learning goals and performance goals. Learning goals are aimed at improving skills or developing competence, and are typically associated with the growth mindset, which acknowledges intelligence as a malleable construct that is capable of being changed through effort. Performance goals are focused on completing a task (Dweck & Leggett, 1988; Schunk & Usher, 2012), and are typically aligned with the fixed mindset, which views intelligence as an innate characteristic that is possessed at various levels by different people, and which is unlikely to change very much over time (Dweck & Leggett, 1988). When learning goals are presented, students must attend to how the goal relates to what they know and what strategies they have for achieving the goal. A performance goal, on the other hand, focuses the students' attention on successful completion of a task with little regard for what is to be learned through engagement in the task (Dweck & Leggett, 1988, Schunk & Usher, 2012). Often a focus on performance goals results in a competitive atmosphere in which children believe those who finish the task first are the smartest. Social comparisons in this kind of environment can result in decreased self-efficacy and motivation (Schunk & Usher, 2012), which is the opposite effect to the one that the teacher wants to achieve.

For younger children, it is the teacher who must set reasonable learning goals based on the students' prior knowledge and developmental levels. In conjunction with setting appropriate goals, the teacher should clearly communicate the learning goals to the students in a way that they can understand. By carefully and strategically setting and communicating appropriate learning goals, teachers provide a model for young students to learn to set goals for themselves. As students become ready to do this, the teacher should provide support and encouragement for personal goal setting.

Self-efficacy is an important concept in social cognitive theory, and it is integral to learning. Self-efficacy is the belief that a person has about their ability to achieve a goal, and it is a necessary factor in motivation (Schunk & Usher, 2012). Students with low self-efficacy do not believe that they are capable of achieving a goal, and therefore they are not motivated to attempt tasks. Likewise, they may not persevere in academic tasks to achieve learning goals (Schunk & Usher, 2012).

Mastery experiences, in which students are able to be successful, are an important contributor to self-efficacy, and are closely linked to learning goals. According to Schunk and Pajares (2009), mastery experiences are the best predictor of self-efficacy, regardless of the content area and age of the individual. Children who have had successful experiences in school develop the belief that they are capable of doing well at school, which leads to increased self-efficacy. Conversely, children who have experienced many failures at school will have low self-efficacy with regard to academic work. However, it has been shown that if children have had many successes, occasional failures are not detrimental to their self-efficacy (Schunk & Usher, 2012).

Children who have had many experiences involving failure in school are likely to have developed a weak sense of self-efficacy. These children have developed low expectations from the outcomes of their efforts in school, and teachers should work to increase the self-efficacy of these students. Often the repeated failures are due to a mismatch between the teacher's goals for the student and the student's current capability in a particular subject area. Conversely, students who have had many successes in school develop an expectation of success, which is characterized by strong self-efficacy and perseverance (Schunk & Usher, 2012). Clearly, it is imperative that teachers understand how to support the development of self-efficacy in their students, which begins with success in school tasks. A student's self-efficacy can be an indicator of their level of perseverance (Schunk & Usher, 2012). Therefore supporting children's development of self-efficacy can simultaneously support increasing perseverance. However, there is more to the development of self-efficacy than just ensuring students' success with tasks.

There are a number of factors that can influence a child's perception of their performance on a task, such as the difficulty of the task, the effort the child expends in completing the task, the amount of assistance the child receives while completing the task, and the child's preconceived ideas about their competence to complete the task. It is the child's *perception* of their performance on a task, rather than their actual performance, that makes a difference in the development of self-efficacy (Schunk & Usher, 2012). For example, if a student requires a significant amount of assistance from the teacher to complete a task successfully, his cognitive interpretation of that experience will not lead to an increase in self-efficacy. In fact, if the teacher leads a student through a task step by step, the student will be aware, upon completion of the task, that he does not understand the task, and he may in fact be even more confused, which will lead to decreased self-efficacy.

In addition, with such a clear relationship between past experiences and the development of self-efficacy, there is also a strong physical link between the development of self-efficacy and memory—specifically episodic memory, which represents past personal experiences linked to particular times and places (Blakemore & Frith, 2008). During a learning task, the chemical dopamine is released into the brain when the student experiences a positive event, such as success. The release of dopamine in different areas of the brain improves working memory and opens the learner to a more creative and connected learning experience characterized by increased attention and positive social behavior (Ashby *et al.*, 1999). Thus positive experiences in school are critical to ensure that this physical process of dopamine release into the brain occurs.

Autonomy

Social cognitive theory contributes significantly to our understanding of the role of motivation in learning, by identifying social, cognitive, and behavioral influences on motivation, but there are also other considerations for teachers. Although children are intrinsically motivated at birth, they come to school with varying levels of autonomous motivation, based on their interactions with others that have either supported or suppressed this autonomous motivation (Deci & Ryan, 2012). For this reason, it is important for teachers to consider the level of intensity of students' intrinsic motivation in order to meet their individual needs.

School is the place where many children begin to form relationships with others, which leads to a sense of connection outside their family. Deci and Ryan (2001) identified this sense of connection as an important psychological need for the development of autonomous motivation. Allowing students to work together as they learn and develop competence is therefore critical to promoting motivation. Students are more likely to engage in autonomous behaviors in collusion with peers than with the teacher, who is most often seen as an authority figure (Deci & Ryan, 2012). Students are often more focused on producing or doing what the teacher wants than on what makes sense based on their own understanding. This is particularly true when teachers employ a behaviorist approach that utilizes external rewards in an attempt to control students' behavior and learning. It is incumbent upon teachers to understand motivation and how the use of rewards can undermine autonomous motivation. Students' sense of autonomy in their goals and behavior cannot develop under a system that is controlled by external rewards (Deci & Ryan, 2012).

Curiosity and Interest

Shiner (1998) linked curiosity and interest to mastery motivation in that an individual who is driven to accomplish a challenging task has a disposition characterized by curiosity and interest. According to Silvia (2012), curiosity and motivation can be viewed in three different ways. First, curiosity as a motivator can be seen as not just a simple desire to know something, but also a way to reduce discomfort due to a void in knowledge. This view identifies the motivation to know something out of curiosity as a desire to rid oneself of the feeling of not knowing. Second, curiosity can be regarded as intrinsic motivation—that is, one is simply motivated to find out more about an interesting topic. Third, there is the idea that variations in curiosity are inherent in individuals. Clearly, it is critical for teachers to consider this final aspect as they seek to provoke curiosity in students. Children are naturally curious and use their curiosity to explore their world. Teachers should be diligent in encouraging that curiosity (Willingham, 2014). Often curiosity arises as a result of an activity in which students develop an interest (Hidi & Renninger, 2006). As teachers strive to make learning interesting, students are more likely to become curious and motivated to learn more.

John Dewey was an early proponent of making school relevant to the interests of children (Dewey, 1913). He believed that interest ensures attention, and that the more effort a child expends due to interest, the more cohesive that child's activity will be. There are a number of child-centered theories that support and expand on Dewey's ideas about the use of children's natural interest to promote learning (Bruner, 1996; Edwards *et al.*, 1998; Piaget, 1973; Vygotsky, 1980). There is also evidence to support the view that children's interest in activities will lead to better engagement (Subramaniam, 2009) and decrease behavior problems (Kern & Clemens, 2007). In order for children to sustain interest, they need to be able to relate to the tasks in which they are engaged (Renninger & Lipstein, 2006).

Interest has been defined by Renninger and Su (2012, p. 167) as "a cognitive and motivational variable that both develops and can be supported to develop." Hidi and Renninger (2006) have identified four phases of interest development: (1) triggered situational interest; (2) maintained situational interest; (3) emerging individual interest; and (4) well-developed individual interest. The initial phase of interest can lead to the later phases when support is available through interaction with other individuals, such as a teacher. Students need to see how their learning is meaningful to their lives, which can be accomplished through support from teachers, peers, parents, or others. Again, a strong sense of self-efficacy and perseverance is helpful in developing interest.

Rothbart and Derryberry (1981) propose that curiosity and interest are inherently linked and arise as part of children's temperament, or innate differences in the way that children react to changes in stimuli and self-regulate their emotions, motor activity, and attention. As a part of personality, temperament plays a significant role in children's approach to various situations. That is, children differ in their willingness to approach or avoid situations or tasks. Clearly, when children are interested in a particular task, they are more likely to be curious about the subject of the task and will enjoy deeper engagement. It is this state of deep engagement that leads to what Csikszentmihalyi (1990) calls "flow", in which the learner becomes absorbed in a task to the point that the sense of time is lost, creating an impression that little time has passed during an activity when in fact much time has passed. Engaging students in authentic tasks can pique their interest and curiosity and result in this kind of deep engagement.

An authentic task is one that carries inherent meaning for students. Often teachers present tasks to students with the expectation that they will understand how the learning that comes from the task will be important for them at some time in the future. For example, teachers frequently present money-related tasks in the context of children's need to be able to manage money when they are adults. Although this reasoning makes sense to the teacher as an adult, young children are not able to think that far into the future to see a need for this skill. Rather, authentic tasks are immediately applicable to the children's current situations in a meaningful way, and will compel the children to immediately experience a need to learn in order to participate.

Alternatively, it is sometimes helpful to engage children in scenarios that operate within a real context, although they may not be authentic. For example, a teacher could stage a situation in which children are engaged in learning the economics concept of supply and demand by planning and making goods or providing services for peers to purchase with play money, developing advertisements for their products and services, and determining whether they experienced a profit or a loss. The level of engagement in an activity like this is such that children will maintain interest and develop lasting knowledge of the content.

Attention

From the foregoing account it seems that the route to increased attention is through better motivation. Attention is a process in which the brain focuses on particular inputs to accommodate for the fact that its resources are limited (Garrett, 2015). Attention is a vital component of learning, and with an understanding of some basic concepts of attention, teachers can develop lessons that maximize student attention. Attention consists of three basic functions, namely alerting, orienting, and executive attention (Johnson & Proctor, 2004). These functions begin to develop in infancy and are fully developed at the age of around 13 years (Posner *et al.*, 2014).

Alerting is a state of readiness to attend to some form of sensory input. It is the earliest function of attention to develop, and is necessary for the other functions. Teachers employ a variety of strategies to attract students' attention, such as playing music or using a clapping pattern. The next state of attention is orienting, which involves focusing attention on one input from among all of the sensory input from the environment. This means that teachers must attract the students to an activity to the point where they are not distracted by other things that are going on around them. This is where interest supports attention. When students are interested in what they are doing, they will be much less likely to shift their attention to other things (Posner, 2012). Orienting to a single input serves to strengthen its signal, to allow the brain to process it further. Orienting can occur as an intentional or spontaneous act. For example, if a loud noise occurs, most people will spontaneously turn toward the sound. Orienting can also be the result of an internal or external stimulus. Internally, orienting can occur due to interest, lack of interest, a change in thinking, or other non-observed occurrences. For example, if a student is not interested in an activity, their attention may shift to more desired thoughts, or they may engage in behaviors that are undesirable to the teacher and that distract other students. Externally, the stimulus that prompts orienting comes from outside the learner, like when someone calls your name. These internal and external distractions may pull a student's attention away briefly or lead to disengagement. Students may become disengaged by distractions, particularly if their interest in the activity is low. Whenever there are shifts in attention, there is a simultaneous shift in the neural activity of the brain (Garrett, 2015), disrupting learning as well as attention. Finally, executive attention is the mechanism that allows us to ignore distracting stimuli in order to maintain attention on a task. It is also critical for many of the kinds of learning tasks that are required in school that involve recall of information (Posner & Rothbart, 2007).

It is clear that motivation and attention are linked and contribute significantly to positive learning experiences. Teachers must learn to promote the development of autonomous motivation, which in turn will support increased attention and result in more engaged learning. Key requirements for accomplishing this task include an environment that is structured so that students know what to expect, teachers who are willing to allow students to operate autonomously with opportunities to have choices and make decisions about their learning, and an atmosphere that encourages the involvement of all students. When all of these components are in place, teachers can then employ strategies to support students' development of self-efficacy, autonomy, and social interaction, which will lead to greater engagement (Deci & Ryan, 2012).

Conclusion

This chapter has presented some concepts of social cognitive theory with features of self-determination theory along with classroom practices that are supported by cognitive psychology and neuroscience. The adoption of teaching practices that are sensitive to the development of children's autonomy, self-efficacy, and social interaction can engender motivation for learning that garners students' attention, allowing them to maximize their learning, and providing a strong foundation for the lifelong learning that is necessary for today's students. Teachers are no longer tasked with passing existing knowledge to their students; from an early age, children are able to obtain information from the Internet. Rather, teachers are now challenged to assist students in developing critical thinking, problem solving, creating new knowledge, and applying knowledge in new ways. These challenges can be addressed by integrating the ideas and strategies suggested in this chapter with the standards identified by school districts.

From the Laboratory to the Classroom

Helping students to develop feelings of self-efficacy, autonomy, and social interaction should be a focus in every classroom, and this work must be done intentionally. Establishing a positive climate in the classroom sets the tone for high expectations for students with individualized goals for learning, so that students know what they are expected to learn and how they can use what they already know to increase their learning. Having specific goals helps students to see that their efforts have resulted in accomplishing something, which motivates them to continue to put in more effort. Helping students to set incremental goals can be beneficial. Dopamine is naturally released in the brain when we have rewarding experiences, so when incremental goals are used, dopamine is released more frequently. In essence, the brain becomes trained to expect the dopamine response to tasks that are rewarding, and the feeling of enjoyment we derive from that dopamine release motivates us to continue the activity (LeDoux, 2002). It is important to pay attention to the level of difficulty of the goals for students at various levels. Some students will not attempt a task if it is too difficult and they do not believe it is achievable. It may be necessary to establish individual goals or teach students to set goals for themselves in order to address individual differences.

Teaching students to set personal learning goals will aid their development of self-efficacy, which will affect learning and motivation by influencing their level of self-regulation. Consequently, students will improve in their use of effective strategies, engage in more effective self-monitoring to seek help as needed, and begin to set more challenging goals. Although all students are expected to demonstrate the knowledge and understanding reflected in standards, they should have some choices with regard to how they develop that knowledge and understanding. When students are given choices in their learning and allowed to approach learning tasks in a way that makes sense to them, they learn more and become more autonomous. Students at any grade level can be taught to set personal goals through modeling, instruction, and support from the teacher.

Goal setting and determining potential strategies based on students' prior knowledge should precede engagement in a learning task. Calling students' attention to your goals for the lesson or activity can serve as a model. After presenting the goal, use questioning to scaffold students' personal goal setting and provide support to help individual students identify their personal goals, remembering to ensure that all goals, including yours, are learning goals rather than performance goals. One way to emphasize learning goals is by simply using language that supports learning goals, such as telling children what they are going to *learn* today instead of what they are going to *do* today. You can also help students to break down a big goal into several smaller more attainable goals. This can be especially helpful for students who have attention deficit disorder/attention deficit hyperactivity disorder (ADD/ADHD).

Supporting students as they work to achieve learning goals should *not* include the use of teacher-supplied rewards, as this can have negative effects on the students' academic progress. When students are given rewards for performing tasks or achieving goals, they can grow dependent upon the rewards. They may also begin to choose less challenging tasks or set less challenging goals in order to ensure that they obtain the reward. When students learn that they will be rewarded for accomplishing a task, they will often seek the greatest reward for the least amount of effort. The most productive way to encourage students to strive higher is to focus on learning goals and provide the necessary support for them to reach those goals. Using incremental goals to develop intrinsic motivation, and helping students to set progressively higher goals that are comparable to their ability at an appropriately challenging level will support their development of self-efficacy.

Another way to increase students' self-efficacy is to allow them time to reflect on their experience after completing a lesson or task. They need to see that they have learned something if they are to strengthen their self-efficacy and be motivated to continue learning. Reflection is sometimes disregarded for the sake of saving time. However, offering some guiding questions to support students' focused reflection is beneficial, and will provide them with information about their progress, leading to their development of intrinsic motivation. Students who are able to write their reflection should do so, and those who struggle to write their responses should verbalize their feedback and, whenever possible, have someone write it down for them. The benefits of having students who know they are learning and who are motivated are worth the investment of a little time early in the school year to support them as they learn to set personal goals and reflect on their learning. Once students have developed these habits, they will then continue them automatically.

It is also beneficial for students to learn to self-evaluate. The use of rubrics can help students to learn to see their strengths and weaknesses for themselves. Self-evaluation can improve their ability to set reasonable personal goals and develop autonomy, which will lead to greater self-efficacy. Gradually they will begin to set more challenging goals for themselves. As mentioned previously, greater self-efficacy also leads to greater perseverance. Often students who are learning to self-evaluate will initially present inflated, or even perfect, ratings. This should be expected, as students think the assessment is about them rather than about their work. Taking time to review the rubric alongside the student's work and asking questions about the evidence they see will lead to more accurate self-evaluation. This is another one of those tasks that can be overlooked due to time constraints. After all, it may be necessary to sit down with almost every student and review their work. However, the benefits of doing this once or twice, and maybe a few more times for some students, will be well worth the time and effort. They will quickly learn to use their work as evidence to support their self-evaluation, and their learning and perseverance will increase as they strive to do better. A word of caution is needed with regard to implementing self-evaluation—make sure the students understand that they are evaluating their learning, not themselves. Use intentional language to talk about what the evidence shows about the students' learning. This takes practice and personal patience. Remember that supporting the development of autonomy and self-efficacy in this way will result in more autonomously motivated students.

Support for autonomy will result in children who are more interested in the activity of school, and it aids the development of self-efficacy, self-regulation, and perseverance. Helping students to become more autonomous involves providing only the level of support that is needed to prevent them from becoming frustrated. Giving too much assistance has a negative effect on students' self-efficacy and may even lead to learned helplessness if it continues for an extended period of time. Releasing some of the control of the class to the students can be difficult, so set goals to gradually release control to allow the students to act more autonomously.

Along with goal setting and student self-evaluation, providing feedback that informs students about how they can improve can lead to increased self-efficacy and perseverance. Students' persistence and effort can be developed by providing clear, positive feedback that helps them understand how to improve on previous work to meet the stated criteria. Students also need to know what they do well. Therefore it is important to provide some feedback that focuses on this, so that they will more readily accept feedback that focuses on what they need to do differently next time, with sufficient detail to help them understand how to do better in the future. For students who have multiple areas for improvement, selecting a single focus area for improvement helps the student to successfully understand this and make corrections, rather than being overwhelmed, which could be detrimental to their self-efficacy.

Teachers need to be able to recognize when a student's interest is waning, and know how to provide appropriate support to move students from situational interest in the moment to prolonged interest that becomes individual interest. Classroom tasks and activities should be developed with the students' interests in mind. This requires more than just presenting the task and expecting students to maintain a high level of interest. The most significant way to help students to sustain their interest in a task or activity is to support their learning and curiosity by giving them choices. When they have some degree of choice as to what they are learning, students will be more likely to experience sustained interest.

References

Ashby, F. G., Isen, A. M., & Turken, A. (1999). A neuropsychological theory of positive affect and its influence on cognition. *Psychological Review*, 106, 529–550.

Bandura, A. (1986). *Social Foundations of Thought and Action: A Social Cognitive Theory*. Englewood Cliffs, NJ: Prentice Hall.

Bandura, A. (1989). Social cognitive theory. In: R. Vista (Ed.), *Annals of Child Development. Volume 6. Six Theories of Child Development* (pp. 1–60). Greenwich, CT: JAI Press.

Blakemore, S. J. & Frith, U. (2008). Learning and remembering. In: *The Jossey-Bass Reader on the Brain and Learning* (pp. 109–119). San Francisco, CA: John Wiley & Sons.

Bransford, J. D., Brown, A. L., & Cocking. R. R. (Eds) (2000). *How People Learn: Brain, Mind, Experience, and School: Expanded Edition*. Washington, DC: National Academy Press.

Bruner, J. S. (1996). *The Culture of Education*. Cambridge, MA: Harvard University Press.

Csikszentmihalyi, M. (1990). *Flow: The Psychology of Optimal Experience*. New York: Harper & Row.

Cuevas, K., Deater-Deckard, K., Kim-Spoon, J., Wang, Z., Morasch, K. C., & Bell, M. A. (2014). A longitudinal intergenerational analysis of executive functions during early childhood. *British Journal of Developmental Psychology*, 32, 50–64.

Deci, E. L. (1971). Effects of externally mediated rewards on intrinsic motivation. *Journal of Personality and Social Psychology*, 18, 105–115.

Deci, E. L. & Ryan, R. M. (1985). *Intrinsic Motivation and Self-Determination in Human Behavior*. New York: Plenum.

Deci, E. L. & Ryan, R. M. (2001). The "what" and "why" of goal pursuits: human needs and the self-determination of behavior. *Psychological Inquiry*, 11, 227–268.

Deci, E. L. & Ryan, R. M. (2012). Motivation, personality, and development within embedded social contexts: an overview of self-determination theory. In: R. M. Ryan (Ed.), *The Oxford Handbook of Human Motivation* (pp. 85–107). New York: Oxford University Press.

Deci, E. L., Vallerand, R. J., Pelletier, L. G., & Ryan, R. M. (1991). Motivation and education: the self-determination perspective. *Educational Psychologist*, 26, 325–346.

Deci, E. L., Koestner, R., & Ryan, R. M. (1999). A meta-analytic review of experiments examining the effects of extrinsic rewards on intrinsic motivation. *Psychological Bulletin*, 125, 627–668.

Deci, E. L., Koestner, R., & Ryan, R. M. (2001). Extrinsic rewards and intrinsic motivation in education: reconsidered once again. *Review of Educational Research,* 71, 1–27.

Dewey, J. (1913). *Interest and Effort in Eeducation*. New York: Houghton Mifflin Company.

Dweck, C. S. (2006). *Mindset: The New Psychology of Success*. New York: Random House, Inc.

Dweck, C. S. & Leggett, E. L. (1988). A social–cognitive approach to motivation and personality. *Psychological Review*, 95, 256–273.

Edwards, C., Gandini, L., & Forman, G. (Eds) (1998). *The Hundred Languages of Children: The Reggio Emilia Approach—Advanced Reflections*. Greenwich, CN: Ablex Publishing Corporation.

Einon, D. (1999). *Early Learning*. New York: Checkmark Books.

Garrett, B. (2015). *Brain and Behavior: An Introduction to Biological Psychology*, 4th edition. Thousand Oaks, CA: Sage Publications, Inc.

Hidi, S. & Renninger, K. A. (2006). The four-phase model of interest development. *Educational Psychologist*, 41, 111–127.

Johnson, A. & Proctor, R. W. (2004). *Attention: Theory and Practice*. Thousand Oaks, CA: Sage Publications.

Kern, L. & Clemens, N. H. (2007). Antecedent strategies to promote appropriate classroom behavior. *Psychology in the Schools*, 44, 65–75.

Kohn, A. (1993). *Punished by Rewards: The Trouble with Gold Stars, Incentive Plans, A's, Praise, and Other Bribes*. New York: Houghton Mifflin Company.

Ledford Jr., G. E., Gerhart, B., & Fang, M. (2013). Negative effects of extrinsic rewards on intrinsic motivation: more smoke than fire. *WorldatWork Journal*, Second Quarter, 17–29.

LeDoux, J. (2002). *Synaptic Self: How Our Brains Become Who We Are*. New York: Penguin Books.

Lei, S. A. (2010). Intrinsic and extrinsic motivation: evaluating benefits and drawbacks from college instructors' perspectives. *Journal of Instructional Psychology*, 37, 153–160.

Lepper, M., Greene, D., & Nisbett, R. (1973). Undermining children's intrinsic interest with extrinsic rewards: a test of the "overjustification" hypothesis. *Journal of Personality and Social Psychology*, 28, 129–137.

Morgan, M. (1984). Reward-induced decrements and increments in intrinsic motivation. *Review of Educational Research*, 54, 5–30.

Murayama, K., Matsumoto, M., Izuma, K., & Matsumoto, K. (2010). Neural basis of the undermining effect of monetary reward on intrinsic motivation. *Proceedings of the National Academy of Sciences of the United States of America*, 107, 20911–20916.

Ormrod, J. E. (2009). *Essentials of Educational Psychology*. Upper Saddle River, NJ: Prentice Hall.

Piaget, J. (1952). *The Origins of Intelligence in Children*. New York: International Universities Press.

Piaget, J. (1973). *To Understand is to Invent: The Future of Education*. New York: Grossman Publishers.

Posner, M. I. (2012). *Attention in a Social World*. New York: Oxford University Press.

Posner, M. I. & Rothbart, M. K. (2007). *Educating the Human Brain*. Washington, DC: American Psychological Association.

Posner, M. I., Rothbart, M. K., & Rueda, M. R. (2014). Developing attention and self-regulation in childhood. In: A. C. Nobre & S. Kastner (Eds), *The Oxford Handbook of Attention* (pp. 541–569). New York: Oxford University Press.

Reeve, J. & Lee, W. (2012). Neuroscience and human motivation. In: R. M. Ryan (Ed.), *The Oxford Handbook of Human Motivation* (pp. 365–380). New York: Oxford University Press.

Renninger, K. A. & Lipstein, R. (2006). Developing interest for writing: what do students want and what do students need? *Eta Evolutiva*, 84, 65–83.

Renninger, K. A. & Su, S. (2012). Interest and development. In: R. M. Ryan (Ed.), *The Oxford Handbook of Human Motivation* (pp. 167–187). New York: Oxford University Press.

Rothbart, M. K. & Derryberry, D. (1981). Development of individual differences in temperament. *Advances in Developmental Psychology*, 1, 37–86.

Ruff, H. A. & Rothbart, M. K. (1996). *Attention in Early Development: Themes and Variations*. New York: Oxford University Press.

Schunk, D. H. & Pajares, F. (2009). Self-efficacy theory. In: K. R. Wentzel & A. Wigfield (Eds), *Handbook of Motivation at School* (pp. 35–53). New York: Routledge.

Schunk, D. H. & Usher, E. L. (2012). Social cognitive theory and motivation. In: R. M. Ryan (Ed.), *The Oxford Handbook of Human Motivation* (pp. 13–27). New York: Oxford University Press.

Shindler, J. (2009). *Transformative Classroom Management: Positive Strategies to Engage all Students and Promote a Psychology of Success*. San Francisco, CA: Jossey-Bass.

Shiner, R. L. (1998). How shall we speak of children's personalities in middle childhood? A preliminary taxonomy. *Psychological Bulletin*, 124, 308–332.

Silvia, P. J. (2012). Curiosity and motivation. In: R. M. Ryan (Ed.), *The Oxford Handbook of Human Motivation* (pp. 157–166). New York: Oxford University Press.

Subramaniam, P. R. (2009). Motivational effects of interest on student engagement and learning in physical education: a review. *International Journal of Physical Education*, 46, 11–19.

Vansteenkiste, M., Lens, W., & Deci, E. L. (2006). Intrinsic versus extrinsic goal contents in self-determination theory: another look at the quality of academic motivation. *Educational Psychologist*, 41, 19–31.

Vygotsky, L. S. (1980). *Mind in Society*. Cambridge, MA: Harvard University Press.

Willingham, D. (2014). Making students more curious. *Knowledge Quest*, 42, 32–35.

Zimmerman, B. J. (2008). Investigating self-regulation and motivation: historical background, methodological developments, and future prospects. *American Educational Research Journal*, 45, 166–183.

4

MEMORY AND METAMEMORY CONSIDERATIONS IN THE INSTRUCTION OF HUMAN BEINGS REVISITED

Implications for Optimizing Online Learning

Veronica X. Yan, Courtney M. Clark, and Robert A. Bjork

DEPARTMENT OF PSYCHOLOGY, UNIVERSITY OF CALIFORNIA, LOS ANGELES

Introduction

With increasingly advanced tools available for online teaching and learning, it is easy to get carried away with the possibilities for designing flashy, fun, and seemingly motivating learning modules, games, and experiences. Inserting videos, animations, sounds, pop-ups, mouse-hovers, and so on may appear to enrich the learning experience in ways that have never before been possible. Implicit (or even sometimes explicit) in many training programs are the assumptions that if the experience is made enjoyable and easy, learning will occur, and that conditions which support quick acquisition and high performance accuracy during training will lead to effective long-term learning. Decades of research, however, have demonstrated that learners and instructors alike (and, more recently, learning technology developers) do not always understand what strategies are most effective for long-term learning, nor do they appreciate that conditions which appear to support rapid acquisition often do not promote long-term retention. For recent reviews of this subject, the reader is referred to Bjork *et al.* (2013) and Soderstrom and Bjork (2015).

What are the Goals of Training?

The ultimate goal of training is to create learning that is both durable and flexible. By "durable", we mean learning that lasts beyond the training program or study session and across subsequent periods of disuse. By "flexible", we mean learning that can be drawn upon and recalled in different conditions (e.g. both in and out of the classroom), and transferred and applied to new, real-life situations. For example, when teaching students algebra, we hope that they will be able to retain this information well beyond the end of the course, and that when these concepts reappear in subsequent modules or courses, or in real-life situations, they will be able to recognize, recall, and apply what they have learned to solve novel problems (e.g. calculating the original price of a dress, given its price after a 30% markdown, or how many gallons of gas one can buy with $20, or converting between degrees Celsius and Fahrenheit). Durable and flexible learning does not always happen, however, despite both instructors' and students' best intentions. From one class to the next, students and teachers alike are often dismayed to find that much of what was learned in a previous class has been forgotten. For example, high accuracy on one set of quizzes or exams does not always reflect high retention of information beyond those tests.

In other words, the goal of training is not—or at least, should not be—simply for students to perform well on quizzes, midterms, and final exams. However, one critical obstacle to effective long-term training is that we (either as learners or instructors) do not often assess long-term retention. Rather, assessments typically occur either throughout study (e.g. via homework and midterm exams) or immediately at the end of training (e.g. final exams). Performance on these relatively immediate assessments is then subsequently interpreted as a measure of learning—for instance, receiving an "A" grade is seen as a sign of completed and successful learning.

As simple as this sounds, it is important not to forget about forgetting. We all understand that information that is easily retrieved at one point in time may be difficult to recall at some later time, and this fact is especially true for newly learned information. For example, we have all had the experience of being introduced to new people at a party, only to find ourselves embarrassed to have forgotten their names only minutes later. While the information is still fresh in our minds, however, it can be easy to forget that what is recallable now may not be recallable later.

In one striking demonstration of this failure to predict forgetting, participants were given a list of word pairs (some easier and some more difficult) and asked to predict the likelihood that they would be able to recall the second word when shown the first word on a later cued-recall test. The retention interval between end of study and final test was described to different groups of participants as being either 10 minutes, 1 week, or 1 year. Amazingly, participants' predictions of how many of the word pairs they would be able to recall after a 1-year interval (37%) were no lower than the predictions given for recall after a 10-minute interval (35%) or a 1-week interval (40%) (Koriat et al., 2004). Had the participants actually been tested after 1 year, it is likely that many of them would have forgotten ever studying the list. There is evidence, too, that learners, in addition to overestimating remembering (i.e. underestimating forgetting) are prone to underestimating learning—that is, they are prone to underestimating the power of additional study or practice (Kornell & Bjork, 2009).

If we forget about forgetting, we fail to accurately assess our learning methods. We assume that performance on an immediate test is a reliable index of long-term learning. However, the cognitive psychology literature is rife with examples (some of which will be described in this chapter) where the study strategies that support current performance and give the appearance of rapid acquisition can in fact lead to worse long-term retention and learning than other study strategies that appear to slow down initial acquisition. That is, a study strategy which makes it appear that you are learning quickly *now* may not support your ability to remember the information *later*.

Overview of the Chapter

Throughout this chapter, we shall cover some of the most robust techniques for enhancing long-term learning. These learning strategies are often collectively referred to as "desirable difficulties", a term coined by Bjork (1994). They are "difficulties" because they engage the learner in effortful and elaborative processes, which in turn lead to the "desirable" outcome—deeper, longer-lasting learning. However, for the very same reason that these strategies are effective, learners and educators alike judge them to be ineffective and inefficient. The engagement of effort often appears to slow down the acquisition of learning, and this effort is often misinterpreted as unsuccessful learning.

Throughout this chapter, we shall also discuss the underlying mechanisms that make each of these strategies effective. We emphasize the underlying mechanisms, not just because we, as researchers, are interested in theoretical underpinnings, but also because it is important from a practical standpoint. Users (instructors and students alike) should understand that it is not the specific manifestation of any particular strategy that leads to long-term learning, but rather it is the *processes* which are engaged by these strategies that enhance learning. Using a strategy that is superficially similar to a desirable difficulty without engaging the correct processes will not optimize learning. As Bjork and Bjork stated:

> we need to emphasize the importance of the word *desirable*. Many difficulties are undesirable during instruction and forever after. Desirable difficulties, versus the array of undesirable difficulties, are desirable because they trigger encoding and retrieval processes that support learning, comprehension, and remembering. If, however, the learner does not have the background knowledge or skills to respond to them successfully, they become undesirable difficulties.
>
> *(Bjork & Bjork, 2014, p. 62)*

Finally, although these learning principles are generally applicable to all learning (whether this learning involves a classroom, an online environment, or just the individual learner on their own), each section will also discuss more specifically the ways in which these principles may be engaged in online learning—a platform that is increasingly popular and integral to education.

Strategies for Long-Term Learning: Desirable Difficulties

Retrieval Practice

The Testing Effect

One of the most beneficial things learners can do for themselves is to stop studying and take a test. Although self-administered tests are usually used as summative assessments—that is, to check what one does or does not know, and to practice for the real test after all studying has been completed—tests themselves are potent learning tools. Instead of leaving tests until the very end of study, numerous experiments (spanning a range of learner ages, motivation levels, and content types) have demonstrated that instead of repeated restudying, learners are far better off testing themselves, both early and often (Roediger & Karpicke, 2006). It is important to highlight here that the recommendation is *not* to simply give students more summative tests (i.e. high-stakes assessments), but rather to ensure that students are encouraged to retrieve previously learned information from memory more frequently (i.e. low-stakes or no-stakes retrieval practice).

The act of retrieval itself is a very powerful "memory modifier" (Bjork, 1975), and testing oneself (again, without any requirement that these tests are graded or even seen by the teacher, so long as learners make honest efforts to answer the test questions) is an effective and easy way to engage retrieval processes. Whatever information is retrieved becomes strengthened. In the absence of feedback or additional study opportunities after taking a test, therefore, retrieval must be successful in order for the learner to experience a benefit of taking a test—tests should be neither too difficult (resulting in unsuccessful retrieval) nor too easy. With feedback, either by seeing the answers to each test question after making an honest effort to answer that question, or by re-studying the information, the benefits of testing become even more powerful, given that feedback allows learners to correct errors and maintain correct responses (Bangert-Drowns *et al.*, 1991; Hays *et al.*, 2010; Pashler *et al.*, 2005; but see also the section on the benefits of reducing feedback).

Does the type of test matter? One could argue that open-ended, short-answer, or essay test questions are more likely to engage deeper retrieval processes than multiple-choice tests, as multiple-choice tests may engage less productive retrieval processes, given that the correct answer is provided among the answer options. However, recent research (Little *et al.*, 2012) has demonstrated that multiple-choice tests do not have to be considered inferior pedagogical tools, provided that the multiple-choice test options are constructed carefully. If the alternative answers in multiple-choice questions are competitive enough (often referred to as "tricky" questions by students) to engage the learner in retrieval processes as they determine whether to reject each option (i.e. why a particular answer is correct or why other answers are incorrect), these multiple-choice tests can strengthen learning beyond merely what is directly tested by the question. This feature of multiple-choice tests has the potential to make them even more powerful learning tools than short-answer test questions under some circumstances (see also Chan *et al.*, 2006), especially when used as practice tests.

Pre-Testing and the Role of Errors

If retrieval strengthens what is recalled, then it may be disastrous if students retrieve the incorrect response. Marsh *et al.* (2007) suggest that once an incorrect response has been selected, the likelihood that the error will persist increases, although they also conclude that the positive benefits of testing outweigh this cost. More recently, Kornell *et al.* (2009) demonstrated that being tested before study (i.e. pre-testing) can potentiate subsequent learning, even when learners cannot answer any of the questions correctly, and that result has been replicated and extended by a number of researchers (e.g. Grimaldi & Karpicke, 2012; Hays *et al.*, 2013; Huelser & Metcalfe, 2012; Kapur & Bielaczyc, 2012; Knight *et al.*, 2012; Richland *et al.*, 2009; Vaughn & Rawson, 2012; Yan *et al.*, 2014). In many of these experiments, not only do learners take pre-tests, but also these pre-tests come at the cost of extended study, and errors on the pre-tests are almost guaranteed. Despite taking time out of their study to generate what was almost always an incorrect and potentially competing response—for example, there was a 97% error rate in the research by Kornell *et al.* (2009) and Yan *et al.* (2014)—taking a pre-test leads to better learning than simply studying the correct answers straight away.

These benefits extend beyond simply drawing learners' attention to the pre-tested answers when they are finally allowed to study. Rather, the benefit of attempting to answer questions before study—even when these attempts are unsuccessful—is generally thought to be a result of more elaborative encoding following semantic activation. In other words, the act of attempting to answer a question (e.g. "What is the tallest geyser in Yellowstone National Park?") encourages learners to draw upon their prior knowledge about a topic (e.g. "I know that *Old Faithful* is the most famous, and that *Castle Geyser* is the oldest"), and this activation enables them to better encode new information. Indeed, when pre-tests do not activate the appropriate semantic network, they do not benefit learning (Grimaldi & Karpicke, 2012; Huelser & Metcalfe, 2012).

Benefits beyond Memory

We have described how tests strengthen what is retrieved as well as potentiating new, subsequent learning, but these are not the only benefits of testing. Introducing frequent no-stakes or low-stakes testing to a study routine also improves metacognitive monitoring (i.e. accurately knowing what you do and do not know; Amlund *et al.*, 1986; Soderstrom & Bjork, 2014), reduces mind wandering during lectures (Szpunar *et al.*, 2013), and the experience of these frequent no-stakes or low-stakes tests reduces students' test anxiety about high-stakes tests (Agarwal *et al.*, 2014).

We shall explore the practical applications of retrieval practice at the end of this chapter.

Distributing Practice: Effects of Spacing and Interleaving

Spacing Repeated Study Opportunities

If you have an upcoming exam, do you choose to cram all of your studying into the night before the exam (massed schedule), or do you prepare for the exam by studying a little here and there in the weeks and days before it (spaced schedule)? Consider the student who chooses the former option by studying for six straight hours the night before the exam, versus the student who chooses the latter option by spreading out those six hours to one hour per day in the week leading up to the exam. Both students have studied for the same total number of hours—only the distribution of that study time differs. On an immediate test, these two students may actually perform similarly, and studies comparing the massed versus spaced schedules have even found that the massed schedule can sometimes lead to better performance on an immediate test than does a spaced schedule (e.g. Peterson *et al.*, 1963).

However, on a delayed test— for example, if the teacher surprises the students with a pop quiz a couple of weeks later, or if the information becomes important in a subsequent course—the pattern is reversed, and the student who studied using a spaced schedule is much more likely to have retained that information than the student who massed their study. This benefit of spaced, or distributed, learning over massed learning is known as the *spacing effect*, and is one of the most robust effects in the cognitive psychology literature (for reviews and calls to incorporate spacing into the classroom, see Bjork, 1979; Carpenter *et al.*, 2012; Cepeda *et al.*, 2006; Dempster, 1988; Rohrer & Pashler, 2010).

There are several reasons why distributed study is so effective for learning. Spacing out one's study across multiple sessions offers the opportunity for the information to be encoded with more variability (Estes, 1955; Glenberg, 1976), whether this variability involves seeing the information from different perspectives, or encoding the information in different places (Smith *et al.*, 1978).

One of the most influential theories as to why spacing repeated study opportunities confers benefits on long-term learning is based, counterintuitively, on the fact that spacing leads to forgetting, a theory that is referred to in the literature as both *study-phase retrieval* (e.g. Thios

& D'Agostino, 1976) and *reminding* (e.g. Benjamin & Ross, 2011; Hintzman, 2004). The basic idea is that spaced out restudy sessions engage retrieval processes as learners recall (or are reminded of) what they learned in previous study sessions. In other words, spacing benefits learning for somewhat the same reasons that testing benefits it. On the other hand, when restudy sessions occur immediately after the initial study session without any forgetting, very little retrieval effort is required, given that the to-be-learned information is still so fresh (i.e. easily accessible) in learners' minds. This theory does, however, suggest a limit to the benefits of spacing. If the study presentations are spaced out far enough in time for the second session not to remind learners of the first one, and therefore not to engage retrieval processes, spacing is no longer beneficial for learning.

Expanding Retrieval Practice

Retrieval modifies memory, and the greater the effort required to retrieve information—as long as retrieval is successful—the greater the learning gains. As information becomes better and better learned, it takes longer to reach the asymptote of forgetting, and therefore we should be able to wait longer and longer before the next restudy session. For example, when learning new vocabulary, one might choose to study the same list of words on days 1, 2, 10, 25, and 50. Although early studies showed benefits of expanding retrieval schedules versus uniformly spaced schedules (Landauer & Bjork, 1978; Tsai, 1927), under conditions in which the same number of retrievals are attempted across the same total period of time, the findings of more recent research have been more mixed, with uniform schedules producing better recall under some circumstances. Recent findings (Maddox *et al.*, 2011; Storm *et al.*, 2010) suggest that expanding retrieval practice is optimal when the to-be-remembered material is subject to rapid forgetting.

What is uncontroversial is that when retrieval is successful at a given interval, the next retrieval should be scheduled after a longer interval (Kornell & Bjork, 2008c), and there is potentially another very good reason to expand one's study. By creating longer and longer intervals between repetitions, learners also create more opportunities to introduce new, additional learning. In other words, expanding retrieval schedules not only benefit learning of repeated information by engaging retrieval processes optimally, but they also allow the learner to expand their repertoire of knowledge (Yan *et al.*, 2013).

Interleaving Exemplars of To-Be-Learned Categories, Concepts, and Procedures

Spacing out repetitions to enhance memory may work, but what about those cases where what is repeated is related, but not exactly the same? In particular, how do we learn categories and concepts from examples of those categories and concepts? In such cases, the task is not the memorization of individual facts, but rather seeing the relationships or similarities across the examples that define a given category or concept. It seems reasonable that the examples of a category or concept should be studied in a massed (or "blocked") way so that the relevant relationships are easier to see.

To use a concrete example, imagine that you have to teach your students to calculate four different types of mathematics problems relating to prisms (e.g. the number of edges, faces, corners, and angles). A typical strategy that is adopted by instructors and textbooks alike is to focus on one problem type at a time—first, teach students how to calculate the number of edges to a prism, given that the base has x sides, then allow them to practice calculating the number of edges, given prisms with different bases, and then repeat this process with each of the remaining problem types. In the cognitive psychology literature, this scheduling strategy is known as "blocking." In contrast, at the other end of the spectrum, one might "interleave" learning by teaching students all four types of problems, and then practice all four problem types intermixed randomly together (see Chapter 5). Figure 4.1 illustrates the prototypical design of an experiment that compares blocked and interleaved schedules of practice. Note that in the schedules that we are now referring to as interleaving, the examples of any given to-be-learned concept are inherently spaced.

From a purely intuitive standpoint, blocked practice would appear to be more effective for learning. It is arguably more organized to focus on one concept at a time, and by not introducing multiple concepts, to allow the learner to become immersed in learning each concept thoroughly. In fact, blocking is found everywhere in the real world—teachers typically teach in a blocked manner, textbooks are certainly organized in a blocked manner, and even high-performance athletes often train by massively repeating one specific skill. However, the evidence from research tells us that our intuitions are wrong. Taylor and Rohrer (2010) conducted the prism study described above with fifth graders. If they had simply examined students' performance on the practice questions during learning, then we would be led to believe that blocking (98% accuracy on practice questions) is more effective than interleaving (79% accuracy on practice questions). However, Taylor and Rohrer also gave the students a final test 1 day later, which revealed a very different pattern of learning. Those who practiced the problem types interleaved (77%) significantly outperformed those who practiced the problem types blocked (38%).

This benefit of interleaving is not restricted to math learning, but has also been demonstrated across motor skills—for example, hitting baseball pitches (Hall *et al.*, 1994), serving volleyballs (Bortoli *et al.*, 1992), playing piano melodies (Abushanab & Bishara, 2013), and acquiring perceptual skills, such as learning to recognize artists' painting styles (Kornell & Bjork, 2008a) or identifying different butterfly species (Birnbaum *et al.*, 2013). Interleaving practice versus blocking practice is yet another example of the learning–performance distinction, where performance during training appears to be worse with interleaved practice, but long-term

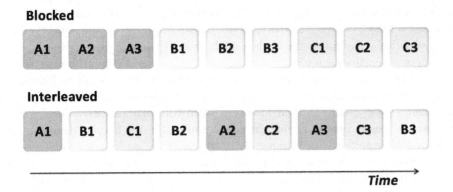

FIGURE 4.1 A comparison of blocked and interleaved schedules for the learning of three concepts. The letters A to C refer to the three concepts, and the numbers refer to different practice examples of each concept.

learning is better. Moreover, it is one of the most striking examples of learners failing to appreciate a desirable difficulty. In one study, despite classification test scores showing a very robust interleaving benefit (61% accuracy when study was interleaved, compared with 35% when study was blocked), the majority (78%) of participants indicated that they believed blocking was as good as or better than interleaving (Kornell & Bjork, 2008a).

Interleaving the study of exemplars from multiple to-be-learned concepts is effective for two reasons. First, interleaving inherently introduces spacing between successive examples from the same to-be-learned category, and therefore engages retrieval processes (Birnbaum *et al.*, 2013). Second, spacing category examples also allows learners to forget the less relevant features, which can facilitate the abstraction of categories (Vlach & Kalish, 2014; Vlach *et al.*, 2008). One of the biggest contributors to the interleaving benefit, however, appears to be that juxtaposing examples from different categories helps learners to see and encode the features that discriminate between those categories (Kang & Pashler, 2012; Kornell & Bjork, 2008a; Rohrer, 2012). For example, in the study by Taylor and Rohrer (2010), students who studied the different types of mathematics problems interleaved made fewer discrimination errors (i.e. applying the wrong formula).

We shall explore practical applications of distributing practice at the end of this chapter.

Varying Conditions of Practice

Interleaving the practice or study of different concepts or skills, versus blocking such study or practice by concept or skill, is one way of introducing variability. For instance, in an example mentioned earlier, students were better able to solve mathematics problems on a delayed test if they learned how to solve each type and then practiced all of the problems mixed up, as opposed to solving all the problems of one type before moving on to solve problems of another type (blocking). Solving problems in a mixed-up way, so to speak, incorporates spacing and also introduces variability of the type that requires more discriminative processing.

Another way to vary conditions of practice is to change the environment, or context, in which learning takes place. Students are often told to study in the same place each day, perhaps with the reasoning that the contextual cues associated with the place in question will become associated with studying, which will help them to get down to work and concentrate on the task at hand. However, research suggests that such advice may be misguided. Analogous to the way that walking into the kitchen might remind you that you need to buy milk, elements of the environment can become associated with material you are learning, and then act as cues later. When learners only have one opportunity to study, it may well be the case that studying and then taking a test in the same place is better than studying in one place and then taking a test in another location. However, when material is studied over several sessions and tested in a new context, varying the contexts of study—not keeping them constant— results in the best performance (Smith *et al.*, 1978). Practically speaking, it is rare for students to study something only once before taking a test, and their goal should be to form strong memories that they can retrieve anywhere. Therefore varying the conditions of learning, including where it takes place, should be incorporated as a study habit (for a review of environmental context effects, see Smith & Vela, 2001).

We shall explore practical applications of varying practice conditions at the end of this chapter.

Reducing or Delaying Feedback to the Learner

One feature of working with instructional technologies is that they offer the opportunity for immediate, individualized feedback. That is, computerized learning platforms can automatically score responses to specific questions and for individual students immediately, in a way that a teacher cannot. However, just because immediate feedback is an option this does not mean that we should adopt it. We may have the intuition that feedback should be provided as frequently or as soon as possible to avoid errors becoming ingrained (Guthrie, 1952; Skinner, 1958; Terrace, 1963), but the empirical evidence suggests that delaying (Kulhavy & Anderson, 1972) or even reducing the frequency of feedback (Schmidt & Bjork, 1992) can enhance long-term retention.

Delaying Feedback

Delaying feedback is more effective for long-term learning than providing immediate feedback—across a variety of learning materials, ranging from meaningless bigrams (Brackbill et al., 1962) to more complex, general factual knowledge (Butler et al., 2007; Sturges & Crawford, 1964), across a number of time scales, with feedback delayed by from just a few seconds (e.g. Boersma, 1966) to as long as a week (Mullet et al., 2014), and across a large age range, from children to adults (Metcalfe et al., 2009).

But does delaying feedback work in classroom settings? An early meta-analysis (Kulik & Kulik, 1988) suggested that the answer was no—that in real-life educational settings, immediate feedback was more effective for students' learning than was delayed feedback. However, subsequent research has not only shown that delaying feedback can have positive effects in the classroom, but underscores the importance of understanding the processes engaged by the learner. In most early delayed-feedback classroom studies, students were allowed to study the delayed feedback however they wanted. Given that students may be more interested in learning the answers immediately after the test, it is likely that some students do not read delayed feedback for some or all of the questions. Indeed, Mullet et al. (2014) showed that delayed feedback effects were more powerful in classroom settings when students were *required* to view feedback for each test problem (feedback was provided through an online homework system, which then tracked whether the feedback was viewed). It is therefore not enough simply to provide delayed feedback—measures need to be taken to ensure that the students actually process the feedback.

But is delaying feedback always beneficial? Whenever students engage in retrieval practice, they are likely to have a mixture of both correct and incorrect responses. Delaying feedback benefits correctly answered questions because it basically represents spaced learning of that information (Butler et al., 2007; Smith & Kimball, 2010). On the other hand, delaying feedback may not benefit learning when students generate incorrect responses on the test, and a handful of studies have shown that delaying feedback does not benefit error correction (Hays et al., 2013; Smith & Kimball, 2010). However, other studies have found the opposite— that delaying feedback can lead to better error correction and learning of the correct answers than providing immediate feedback (at least when using a multiple-choice testing format; Butler et al., 2007). Moreover, when participants are learning meaningful trivia questions, giving delayed feedback, even when all of the initial answers are incorrect, can be more effective than merely studying (and not trying to guess) in the first place (Kornell, 2014).

Reducing Feedback

Feedback does not have to be "all or nothing", and technology (e.g. online learning systems) now enables instructors to offer many different types of feedback. While immediate feedback can greatly help students to learn from incorrectly answered questions, there might not be any need to give feedback for correct answers (e.g. Kornell & Bjork, 2008b; Pashler *et al.*, 2005), and the time saved by not studying the feedback for those correct responses can be better used either to study less well-learned information for longer, or to engage in further retrieval practice to deepen learning (Karpicke & Smith, 2012). In other words, when considering when to give feedback, teachers should also consider how dropping unnecessary feedback can make learning more efficient.

Finally, other studies have looked at the effects of either scaffolding or reducing the amount of feedback given over time. For instance, giving scaffolding hints (e.g. revealing the correct answer one letter at a time) until the correct answer could be retrieved was found to be more effective for long-term learning than just receiving the correct answer (Finn & Metcalfe, 2010). In another investigation, the participants studied vocabulary translations in several rounds of retrieval practice (Finley *et al.*, 2011). Pairs in the accumulating cues (AC) condition were given more letters of the translation in each round, whereas pairs in the diminishing cues (DC) condition were given fewer letters in each round. Without feedback given for each round, DC pairs outperformed AC pairs. In this instance, we can think of the DC condition as representing another way to instantiate expanding retrieval practice, as retrieval is made easier initially and then harder as time goes on. In another experiment where feedback was provided for each round of retrieval practice, DC pairs were remembered only marginally better than AC pairs, suggesting that when feedback is provided, even initially very difficult and failed retrieval attempts can be quite productive (Finley *et al.*, 2011).

We shall explore practical applications of reducing or delaying feedback at the end of this chapter.

Undesirable Difficulties

"Desirable difficulties" may be regarded as an umbrella term that captures the range of different study strategies that enhance long-term memory by engaging the learner in effortful, elaborative processes. However, not all difficulties engage these elaborative processes; therefore not all difficulties are desirable. One mistake is to interpret the research as meaning that any type of introduced difficulty benefits learning. To use an absurd example, attempting to study while hanging upside down and nauseated would be difficult, but probably in no way beneficial for learning (except perhaps for being able to recall that same information again while hanging upside and nauseated).

To understand when difficulties are desirable, it is important to consider the processes that are being engaged by the learner. Dividing attention during retrieval practice, for example, is a manipulation that increases the difficulty of learning, but does not lead to any learning benefits (Gaspelin *et al.*, 2013). Whether helpful processes are engaged, however, is not simply a function of the specific manipulation, but can also be affected by the characteristics of the task (e.g. the processes that are already stimulated by the to-be-learned materials and therefore redundant, the processes that enhance deeper learning of that material, the processing required by the final test) and the characteristics of the individual learner (e.g. prior knowledge and/or ability level).

To illustrate the importance of the nature of the to-be-learned materials, McDaniel *et al.* (1986) compared two forms of active learning (word generation and sentence reordering) for the learning of either expository texts or fairy tales. Both learning activities are commonly considered to be better than passive reading. In the former, learners study a text passage in which many of the words are presented only as fragments (e.g. w_rd fr_gm_nts), and the learners must actively generate the full word from those fragments as they study. In the latter, learners study a text passage in which the sentences are out of order, and they must reorder the sentences so that the passage makes sense. However, the researchers found that these two types of activities were not necessarily always better than passive reading. Rather, word generation was a "desirable difficulty" for studying stories, and sentence reordering was a "desirable difficulty" for learning expository texts. However, word generation for the stories and sentence reordering for the expository texts were often not significantly better than passive reading.

The characteristics of the individual learner and what they bring to the learning experience are also important. If learners already experience difficulties with reading, then layering on the additional difficulty of having to generate words may be overwhelming and may impair learning instead of engaging deeper learning (McDaniel *et al.*, 2002). In another study (McNamara *et al.*, 1996), students were first asked to take a biology test to determine their prior knowledge before reading a biology textbook passage about heart disease. Some students read a less embellished and more difficult-to-read version, whereas other students read a more complete version that included more headings and subheadings and more transitions from one sentence to another. Unsurprisingly, learners with a low level of prior knowledge learned more from the more complete, easy-to-follow text. Surprisingly, however, learners with a higher level of prior knowledge benefited from reading the less embellished text—in other words, the lack of headings and transition sentences posed a desirable difficulty. Learners were apparently forced to draw upon their prior knowledge and actively fill in the gaps found in the text, and this active engagement promoted better learning. However, those with a low level of prior knowledge could not fill in the gaps and thus could not benefit from the difficulty of a minimally coherent text.

Finally, to really emphasize the importance of the underlying processes (rather than the specific manifestations of how learning is structured), studies have shown that combining different desirable difficulties does not always lead to a summative learning effect. For example, consider the case of trying to combine spacing and variation. We know that if some information is to be studied twice, it is better to space out those repetitions than to cram them in quick succession (i.e. the spacing effect) (Cepeda *et al.*, 2006). We also know that studying information in two different formats is better than studying it in the same format twice. However, one plus one does not always equal two. Appleton-Knapp *et al.* (2005) presented learners with advertisements for different products. For some of these products, learners were shown advertisements twice, either in rapid succession, spaced apart with only a short interval between the two presentations, or spaced apart with a longer interval between the two presentations. When the two presentations were identical, they found a classic spacing effect—the longer the interval between the two presentations, the better the final recall for those products. However, when the two presentations were varied, the variation did not give an extra boost of learning over that of spacing. Rather, variation boosted learning when the spacing interval was short, and impaired learning when the spacing interval was long. What was the reason for this? Consider the underlying process by which spacing enhances learning—spacing engages retrieval processes when the second presentation reminds learners of the first presentation. If the two presentations look too different and the second presentation does not therefore engage retrieval, spacing cannot benefit learning. Variation at longer spacing intervals can undermine the benefits of spacing.

Hence it is crucial that learners and instructors alike not only know the list of desirable difficulties to incorporate into learning, but also understand *why* these learning strategies are desirably difficult.

The Critical Distinction between Learning and Performance

In many of the examples discussed throughout this chapter, how well students perform during study or immediately after study differs from how well they have learned and are able to retain that information in the future. Re-reading may lead to greater initial access to information, but retrieving information leads to better long-term retention of what is retrieved. Although taking time out of one's study to take a pre-test on which there is very low accuracy may seem like a waste of time, the act of activating prior knowledge in fact potentiates subsequent study. Similarly, although taking a break to allow oneself to forget studied information feels counterproductive to immediately continuing study, distributing study leads to better long-term learning than does cramming study together. These examples (and many others) illustrate the critical distinction between performance (how easily accessible information is currently) and learning (how well that information has been encoded into existing knowledge and how easily and flexibly it can be retrieved in the future).

Without a deliberate awareness of and attention to the distinction between learning and performance, it is easy for both instructors and learners to fall prey to illusions of learning. Instructors often judge the effectiveness of their teaching methods by the current performance of their students, and students judge the effectiveness of their study methods by a sense of fluency with their assigned reading or with their score on a test taken after cramming. Restudying, cramming, and blocking can all lead to good performance that is merely fleeting. However, the methods (retrieval practice, spacing, and interleaving) that support durable and flexible learning—the ultimate goal—may not be apparent during acquisition (especially as they introduce "difficulties"), but only after a delay.

From the Laboratory to the Classroom

Retrieval Practice

One of the first verbal responses of most instructors and learners is some expression of dismay over the thought of adding more tests to a syllabus. These tests do not have to be exhaustive (especially if they are well-constructed multiple-choice tests—which, incidentally, are also easy to grade), nor do they even have to be graded by the course instructor (they can be low-stakes or even no-stakes tests). In fact, a survey of 1,400 middle- and high-school students who took no-stakes or low-stakes tests across a variety of subjects revealed that frequent retrieval practice (a "friendlier" term for tests) throughout the year alleviated test anxiety about unit tests and final exams (Agarwal *et al.*, 2014).

The online learning environment makes it very easy to incorporate retrieval practice into the learning experience. Quizzes can be easily inserted before learning (to potentiate study), as well as throughout and after study (to reduce mind wandering, alleviate test anxiety, and engage retrieval processes for deeper learning). Online systems also enable quizzes to be tailored to the evaluation of individual students' weaknesses, and for multiple-choice test questions to be scored automatically. The benefits of frequent testing are clear, though, and tests should be an integral part of the whole learning process, not just used as a summative assessment at the end.

Distributed Practice

Although distributed practice is often naturally incorporated into learning (e.g. when students restudy several weeks' worth of content when preparing for an exam), there are many ways in which it can, and should, be more deliberately incorporated into instruction. Distributing practice requires returning to previous content, and, given time constraints, is not always easy to incorporate into instruction. One simple way to distribute topics across time is to arrange lectures, homework, quizzes, and projects in a way that spaces and interleaves different topics, ensuring that students return to previously learned topics, rather than simply moving past them. Expanding retrieval may be incorporated by bringing back old topics less and less frequently as they become better learned, making way for practice of the more recently learned content. Interleaving—and its benefits—can be introduced by drawing explicit comparisons and contrasts between related topics and intermixing practice questions.

Another challenge is that spacing and interleaving simply feel confusing. Focusing on teaching one concept at a time (blocking), on the other hand, feels much more organized and easier to understand. Blocking is popular in classrooms and in textbooks, and is often an explicit feature of online learning platforms—educational content is divided into relatively short modules, learners watch videos and answer questions on a given topic, and provided that the learners achieve a certain score on the final test, they are considered to have mastered the information. Unfortunately, we know from research that blocking and massing support only the *illusion* of learning, not long-term retention and transfer. More recently, research into hybrid schedules that combine blocked and interleaved study has shown that these hybrid schedules are often just as effective as purely interleaved schedules, and better received by the learners (Yan, 2014). Hybrid schedules—briefly focusing some attention on one concept at a time, before intermixing and contrasting the many different concepts—may well be a natural fit for instruction. The initial blocked study provides the teacher with an organized way of introducing new concepts one at a time, and the subsequent interleaved study allows the learners to more deeply learn the full set of concepts.

One question that remains unanswered is whether unrelated concepts or topics (e.g. physics and English literature) should be interleaved. When concepts are related (e.g. two different molecular structures), studying them next to one another can draw attention to important features that make the concepts different from one another. With highly related but confusable topics, interleaving, by necessitating revisiting, may help learners to notice and resolve potential confusions. When concepts are unrelated, however, it is unclear whether putting them in contrast with one another is in any way helpful (Hausman & Kornell, 2014). For most practical applications, though, it is difficult to see how some degree of interleaving would harm learning. Interleaving incorporates spacing into repeated study episodes in a natural way, and when learning is spaced there is always the question of how to fill the lag between study sessions. To the dismay of students everywhere, filling a lag with more learning is probably more productive overall than filling that lag with other less academic online activities.

Varying Conditions of Practice

Students who are utilizing online tools for learning are likely to be using smartphones and other mobile technologies that allow for study in many varied locations (as opposed to heavy textbooks that lend themselves better to single-location study and storage). Online learning can therefore help to decontextualize learning. Research also suggests that it is important to incorporate retrieval practice (which is easy to do on online platforms) during study as a way to maximize the benefits of contextual variation (Smith & Handy, 2014).

Reducing or Delaying Feedback

How and when feedback is provided should be a carefully thought-out process. Feedback can be scaffolded to promote continued retrieval practice by the student, it can be withheld to promote spaced learning (this strategy may be especially appropriate when performance on a test is relatively good), or it can be provided immediately to promote error correction.

Conclusion

What links together the different learning strategies described in this chapter (retrieval practice, distributing learning, varying conditions of study and practice, and reducing or delaying feedback) is that they all make learning more active, engaging, and, in some respects, more *difficult*. This incorporation of difficulty in order to enhance learning flies in the face of a common intuition, namely that learning, when structured in the "right" way, should feel easy and fluent. More than simply introducing as many difficulties as possible, however, learners and instructors need to understand the processes that underlie durable and flexible learning. Thus the strategies outlined in this chapter should serve as general guidelines as to how these beneficial learning processes can be engaged. They also demonstrate the importance of being thoughtful in regulating one's own learning, because our intuitions can frequently steer us towards making precisely the wrong choice—which often involves selecting passive, ineffective strategies rather than more effective and efficient learning strategies. In short, as stated by Bjork and Linn (2002), one key to effective learning is to "be suspicious of the sense of ease and undeterred by the sense of difficulty."

References

Abushanab, B. & Bishara, A. J. (2013). Memory and metacognition for piano melodies: illusory advantages of fixed- over random-order practice. *Memory & Cognition*, 41(6), 928–937.

Agarwal, P. K., D'Antonio, L., Roediger, H. L., McDermott, K. B., & McDaniel, M. A. (2014). Classroom-based programs of retrieval practice reduce middle school and high school students' test anxiety. *Journal of Applied Research in Memory and Cognition*, 3(3), 131–139.

Amlund, J. T., Kardash, C. A. M., & Kulhavy, R. W. (1986). Repetitive reading and recall of expository text. *Reading Research Quarterly*, 21(1), 49–58.

Appleton-Knapp, S. L., Bjork, R. A., & Wickens, T. D. (2005). Examining the spacing effect in advertising: encoding variability, retrieval processes, and their interaction. *Journal of Consumer Research*, 32(2), 266–276.

Bangert-Drowns, R. L., Kulik, C. L. C., Kulik, J. A., & Morgan, M. (1991). The instructional effect of feedback in test-like events. *Review of Educational Research*, 61(2), 213–238.

Benjamin, A. S. & Ross, B. H. (2011). The causes and consequences of reminding. In: A. S. Benjamin (Ed.), *Successful Remembering and Successful Forgetting: A Festschrift in Honor of Robert A. Bjork* (pp. 71–88). New York: Psychology Press.

Birnbaum, M. S., Kornell, N., Bjork, E. L., & Bjork, R. A. (2013). Why interleaving enhances inductive learning: the roles of discrimination and retrieval. *Memory & Cognition*, 41(3), 392–402.

Bjork, R. A. (1975). Retrieval as a memory modifier. In: R. Solso (Ed.), *Information Processing and Cognition: The Loyola Symposium* (pp. 123–144). Hillsdale, NJ: Lawrence Erlbaum Associates.

Bjork, R. A. (1979). An information-processing analysis of college teaching. *Educational Psychologist*, 14, 15–23.

Bjork, R. A. (1994). Memory and metamemory considerations in the training of human beings. In: J. Metcalfe & A. Shimamura (Eds), *Metacognition: Knowing About Knowing* (pp. 185–205). Cambridge, MA: MIT Press.

Bjork, R. A. & Linn, M. C. (2002). *Introducing Desirable Difficulties for Educational Applications in Science (IDDEAS)*. Cognitive and Student Learning Program. Institute of Education Sciences (IES) grant proposal (grant award number R305H020113). Washington, DC: IES.

Bjork, E. L. & Bjork, R. A. (2014). Making things hard on yourself, but in a good way: creating desirable difficulties to enhance learning. In: M. A. Gernsbacher & J. Pomerantz (Eds), *Psychology and the Real World: Essays Illustrating Fundamental Contributions to Society*, 2nd edition (pp. 60–68). New York: Worth Publishers.

Bjork, R. A., Dunlosky, J., & Kornell, N. (2013). Self-regulated learning: beliefs, techniques, and illusions. *Annual Review of Psychology*, 64, 417–444.

Boersma, F. J. (1966). Effects of delay of information feedback and length of postfeedback interval on linear programed learning. *Journal of Educational Psychology*, 57(3), 140–145.

Bortoli, L., Robazza, C., Durigon, V., & Carra, C. (1992). Effects of contextual interference on learning technical sports skills. *Perceptual and Motor Skills*, 75(2), 555–562.

Brackbill, Y., Isaacs, R. B., & Smelkinson, N. (1962). Delay of reinforcement and the retention of unfamiliar, meaningless material. *Psychological Reports*, 11(2), 553–554.

Butler, A. C., Karpicke, J. D., & Roediger III, H. L. (2007). The effect of type and timing of feedback on learning from multiple-choice tests. *Journal of Experimental Psychology: Applied*, 13(4), 273–281.

Carpenter, S. K., Cepeda, N. J., Rohrer, D., Kang, S. H., & Pashler, H. (2012). Using spacing to enhance diverse forms of learning: review of recent research and implications for instruction. *Educational Psychology Review*, 24(3), 369–378.

Cepeda, N. J., Pashler, H., Vul, E., Wixted, J. T., & Rohrer, D. (2006). Distributed practice in verbal recall tasks: a review and quantitative synthesis. *Psychological Bulletin*, 132(3), 354–380.

Chan, J. C., McDermott, K. B., & Roediger III, H. L. (2006). Retrieval-induced facilitation: initially nontested material can benefit from prior testing of related material. *Journal of Experimental Psychology: General*, 135(4), 553–571.

Dempster, F. N. (1988). The spacing effect: a case study in the failure to apply the results of psychological research. *American Psychologist*, 43(8), 627–634.

Estes, W. K. (1955). Statistical theory of distributional phenomena in learning. *Psychological Review*, 62(5), 369–377.

Finley, J. R., Benjamin, A. S., Hays, M. J., Bjork, R. A., & Kornell, N. (2011). Benefits of accumulating versus diminishing cues in recall. *Journal of Memory and Language*, 64(4), 289–298.

Finn, B. & Metcalfe, J. (2010). Scaffolding feedback to maximize long-term error correction. *Memory & Cognition*, 38(7), 951–961.

Gaspelin, N., Ruthruff, E., & Pashler, H. (2013). Divided attention: an undesirable difficulty in memory retention. *Memory & Cognition*, 41(7), 978–988.

Glenberg, A. M. (1976). Monotonic and nonmonotonic lag effects in paired-associate and recognition memory paradigms. *Journal of Verbal Learning and Verbal Behavior*, 15(1), 1–16.

Grimaldi, P. J. & Karpicke, J. D. (2012). When and why do retrieval attempts enhance subsequent encoding? *Memory & Cognition*, 40(4), 505–513.

Guthrie, E. R. (1952). *The Psychology of Learning*. New York: Harper & Row.

Hall, K. G., Domingues, D. A., & Cavazos, R. (1994). Contextual interference effects with skilled baseball players. *Perceptual and Motor Skills*, 78(3), 835–841.

Hausman, H. & Kornell, N. (2014). Mixing topics while studying does not enhance learning. *Journal of Applied Research in Memory and Cognition*, 3(3), 153–160.

Hays, M. J., Kornell, N., & Bjork, R. A. (2010). Costs and benefits of feedback during learning. *Psychonomic Bulletin and Review*, 17(6), 797–801.

Hays, M. J., Kornell, N., & Bjork, R. A. (2013). When and why a failed test potentiates the effectiveness of subsequent study. *Journal of Experimental Psychology: Learning, Memory, and Cognition*, 39(1), 290–296.

Hintzman, D. L. (2004). Judgment of frequency vs. recognition confidence: repetition and recursive reminding. *Memory & Cognition*, 32, 336–350.

Huelser, B. J. & Metcalfe, J. (2012). Making related errors facilitates learning, but learners do not know it. *Memory & Cognition*, 40(4), 514–527.

Kang, S. H. & Pashler, H. (2012). Learning painting styles: spacing is advantageous when it promotes discriminative contrast. *Applied Cognitive Psychology*, 26(1), 97–103.

Kapur, M. & Bielaczyc, K. (2012). Designing for productive failure. *Journal of the Learning Sciences*, 21(1), 45–83.

Karpicke, J. D. & Smith, M. A. (2012). Separate mnemonic effects of retrieval practice and elaborative encoding. *Journal of Memory and Language*, 67(1), 17–29.

Knight, J. B., Ball, B. H., Brewer, G. A., DeWitt, M. R., & Marsh, R. L. (2012). Testing unsuccessfully: a specification of the underlying mechanisms supporting its influence on retention. *Journal of Memory and Language*, 66(4), 731–746.

Koriat, A., Bjork, R. A., Sheffer, L., & Bar, S. K. (2004). Predicting one's own forgetting: the role of experience-based and theory-based processes. *Journal of Experimental Psychology: General*, 133, 643–656.

Kornell, N. (2014). Attempting to answer a meaningful question enhances subsequent learning even when feedback is delayed. *Journal of Experimental Psychology: Learning, Memory, and Cognition*, 40(1), 106–114.

Kornell, N. & Bjork, R. A. (2008a). Learning concepts and categories: is spacing the "enemy of induction"? *Psychological Science*, 19(6), 585–592.

Kornell, N. & Bjork, R. A. (2008b). Optimising self-regulated study: the benefits—and costs—of dropping flashcards. *Memory*, 16(2), 125–136.

Kornell, N. & Bjork, R. A. (2008c). *Expanding Retrieval Practice in Theory and Practice*. Paper presented at the 49th Annual Meeting of the Psychonomic Society, Chicago, IL, 13–16 November 2008.

Kornell, N. & Bjork, R. A. (2009). A stability bias in human memory: overestimating remembering and underestimating learning. *Journal of Experimental Psychology: General*, 138(4), 449–468.

Kornell, N., Hays, M. J., & Bjork, R. A. (2009). Unsuccessful retrieval attempts enhance subsequent learning. *Journal of Experimental Psychology: Learning, Memory, and Cognition*, 35(4), 989–998.

Kulhavy, R. W. & Anderson, R. C. (1972). Delay-retention effect with multiple-choice tests. *Journal of Educational Psychology*, 63(5), 505–512.

Kulik, J. A. & Kulik, C. L. C. (1988). Timing of feedback and verbal learning. *Review of Educational Research*, 58(1), 79–97.

Landauer, T. K. & Bjork, R. A. (1978). Optimum rehearsal patterns and name learning. In: M. Gruneberg, P. E. Morris, & R. N. Sykes (Eds), *Practical Aspects of Memory* (pp. 625–632). London: Academic Press.

Little, J. L., Bjork, E. L., Bjork, R. A., & Angello, G. (2012). Multiple-choice tests exonerated, at least of some charges: fostering test-induced learning and avoiding test-induced forgetting. *Psychological Science*, 23(11), 1337–1344.

McDaniel, M. A., Einstein, G. O., Dunay, P. K., & Cobb, R. E. (1986). Encoding difficulty and memory: toward a unifying theory. *Journal of Memory and Language*, 25(6), 645–656.

McDaniel, M. A., Hines, R. J., & Guynn, M. J. (2002). When text difficulty benefits less-skilled readers. *Journal of Memory and Language*, 46(3), 544–561.

McNamara, D. S., Kintsch, E., Songer, N. B., & Kintsch, W. (1996). Are good texts always better? Interactions of text coherence, background knowledge, and levels of understanding in learning from text. *Cognition and Instruction*, 14(1), 1–43.

Maddox, G. B., Balota, D. A., Coane, J. H., & Duchek, J. M. (2011). The role of forgetting rate in producing a benefit of expanded over equal spaced retrieval in young and older adults. *Psychology and Aging*, 26(3), 661–670.

Marsh, E. J., Roediger, H. L., Bjork, R. A., & Bjork, E. L. (2007). The memorial consequences of multiple-choice testing. *Psychonomic Bulletin & Review*, 14(2), 194–199.

Metcalfe, J., Kornell, N., & Finn, B. (2009). Delayed versus immediate feedback in children's and adults' vocabulary learning. *Memory & Cognition*, 37(8), 1077–1087.

Mullet, H. G., Butler, A. C., Verdin, B., von Borries, R., & Marsh, E. J. (2014). Delaying feedback promotes transfer of knowledge despite student preferences to receive feedback immediately. *Journal of Applied Research in Memory and Cognition*, 3(3), 222–229.

Pashler, H., Cepeda, N. J., Wixted, J. T., & Rohrer, D. (2005). When does feedback facilitate learning of words? *Journal of Experimental Psychology: Learning, Memory, and Cognition*, 31(1), 3–8.

Peterson, L. R., Wampler, R., Kirkpatrick, M., & Saltzman, D. (1963). Effect of spacing presentations on retention of a paired associate over short intervals. *Journal of Experimental Psychology*, 66, 206–209.

Richland, L. E., Kornell, N., & Kao, L. S. (2009). The pretesting effect: do unsuccessful retrieval attempts enhance learning? *Journal of Experimental Psychology: Applied*, 15(3), 243–257.

Roediger, H. L. & Karpicke, J. D. (2006). Test-enhanced learning: taking memory tests improves long-term retention. *Psychological Science*, 17(3), 249–255.

Rohrer, D. (2012). Interleaving helps students distinguish among similar concepts. *Educational Psychology Review*, 24(3), 355–367.

Rohrer, D. & Pashler, H. (2010). Recent research on human learning challenges conventional instructional strategies. *Educational Researcher*, 39(5), 406–412.

Schmidt, R. A. & Bjork, R. A. (1992). New conceptualizations of practice: common principles in three paradigms suggest new concepts for training. *Psychological Science*, 3(4), 207–217.

Skinner, B. F. (1958). Teaching machines. *Science*, 128, 969–977.

Smith, S. M. & Vela, E. (2001). Environmental context-dependent memory: a review and meta-analysis. *Psychonomic Bulletin & Review*, 8(2), 203–220.

Smith, S. M. & Handy, J. D. (2014). Effects of varied and constant environmental contexts on acquisition and retention. *Journal of Experimental Psychology: Learning, Memory, and Cognition*, 40(6), 1582–1593.

Smith, S. M., Glenberg, A., & Bjork, R. A. (1978). Environmental context and human memory. *Memory & Cognition*, 6(4), 342–353.

Smith, T. A. & Kimball, D. R. (2010). Learning from feedback: spacing and the delay-retention effect. *Journal of Experimental Psychology: Learning, Memory, and Cognition*, 36(1), 80–95.

Soderstrom, N. C. & Bjork, R. A. (2014). Testing facilitates the regulation of subsequent study time. *Journal of Memory and Language*, 73, 99–115.

Soderstrom, N. C. & Bjork, R. A. (2015). Learning versus performance: an integrative review. *Perspectives on Psychological Science*, 10(2), 176–199.

Storm, B. C., Bjork, R. A., & Storm, J. C. (2010). Optimizing retrieval as a learning event: when and why expanding retrieval practice enhances long-term retention. *Memory & Cognition*, 38(2), 244–253.

Sturges, P. T. & Crawford, J. J. (1964). *The Relative Effectiveness of Immediate and Delayed Reinforcement on Learning Academic Material.* Washington, DC: ERIC, Institute of Education Sciences.

Szpunar, K. K., Khan, N. Y., & Schacter, D. L. (2013). Interpolated memory tests reduce mind wandering and improve learning of online lectures. *Proceedings of the National Academy of Sciences of the United States of America*, 110(16), 6313–6317.

Taylor, K. & Rohrer, D. (2010). The effects of interleaved practice. *Applied Cognitive Psychology*, 24(6), 837–848.

Terrace, H. S. (1963). Discrimination learning with and without "errors." *Journal of the Experimental Analysis of Behavior*, 6(1), 1–27.

Thios, S. J. & D'Agostino, P. R. (1976). Effects of repetition as a function of study-phase retrieval. *Journal of Verbal Learning and Verbal Behavior*, 15(5), 529–536.

Tsai, L. S. (1927). The relation of retention to the distribution of relearning. *Journal of Experimental Psychology*, 10(1), 30–39.

Vaughn, K. E. & Rawson, K. A. (2012). When is guessing incorrectly better than studying for enhancing memory? *Psychonomic Bulletin & Review*, 19(5), 899–905.

Vlach, H. A. & Kalish, C. W. (2014). Temporal dynamics of categorization: forgetting as the basis of abstraction and generalization. *Frontiers in Psychology*, 5, 1021.

Vlach, H. A., Sandhofer, C. M., & Kornell, N. (2008). The spacing effect in children's memory and category induction. *Cognition*, 109(1), 163–167.

Yan, V. (2014). *Learning Concepts and Categories from Examples: How Learners' Beliefs Match and Mismatch the Empirical Evidence.* Los Angeles, CA: University of California (UCLA). Available online at http://escholarship.org/uc/item/91q7z7z4

Yan, V. X., Garcia, M. A., Bjork, E. L., & Bjork, R. A. (2013). *Learning Better, Learning More: The Benefits of Expanding Retrieval Practice.* Poster presented at the 54th Annual Scientific Meeting of the Psychonomic Society, Toronto, Ontario.

Yan, V. X., Yu, Y., Garcia, M. A., & Bjork, R. A. (2014). Why does guessing incorrectly enhance, rather than impair, retention? *Memory & Cognition*, 42(8), 1373–1383.

5

THE BENEFITS OF INTERLEAVED PRACTICE FOR LEARNING

Sean H. K. Kang

DEPARTMENT OF EDUCATION, DARTMOUTH COLLEGE

Introduction

Practice is critical to successful learning. Teachers assign homework to give students additional experience with concepts taught in class, students know that they need to review their notes and other course material before an exam, and athletes put in many hours of training to improve and be at the top of their game. Indeed, a single exposure to a fact, concept, or activity will typically not yield effective and long-lasting knowledge or skill acquisition, no matter how attentive or well-intentioned a learner is. The importance of practice is supported by a wealth of anecdotal and scientific evidence (e.g. Ackerman, 2014; Ericsson *et al.*, 2007), and is probably intuitive to most people. What is less obvious, however, is *how* the practice should be organized or scheduled.

In particular, I am referring to situations in which the learner is presented with multiple examples pertaining to a certain topic or problem type (e.g. in mathematics), or when the learner has the opportunity to engage in repeated practice of a given activity (e.g. golf swing, tennis stroke). Does the sequencing of practice examples or activities within a study or training session affect learning, and, if so, are there ways to schedule or arrange practice so as to optimize this learning?

In this chapter, I shall offer an affirmative answer by reviewing research that has demonstrated that *interleaving* (or mixing together) different kinds of examples or activities during practice often produces superior learning to that achieved by *blocking* (or grouping together) the examples or activities by type, across a range of educationally relevant contexts. I shall also examine theoretical accounts of the interleaving advantage, compare how typical pedagogy lines up with the research findings, and discuss the practical implications for educators.[1]

Distributed Practice

Since this chapter deals with the sequencing of practice to optimize learning, it would be remiss of me not to mention the important finding that *distributed practice* enhances long-term learning to a greater extent than does *massed practice*. When the initial study and subsequent review/training opportunities are spaced out over time instead of occurring back to back, learning tends to be more durable (e.g. Cepeda *et al.*, 2006). This phenomenon, often referred to as the *spacing effect*, has been known by memory researchers for over a century. For instance, in the late nineteenth century, William James in his talks to teachers recommended distributed practice:

> You now see why 'cramming' must be so poor a mode of study. Cramming seeks to stamp things in by intense application immediately before the ordeal. But a thing thus learned can form but few associations. On the other hand, the same thing recurring on different days, in different contexts, read, recited on, referred to again and again, related to other things and reviewed, gets well-wrought into the mental structure. This is the reason why you should enforce on your pupils habits of continuous application.
>
> *(James, 1899/1914, p. 129)*

The benefit of spaced or distributed practice has been demonstrated repeatedly with a variety of study materials and learning tasks, and is widely regarded as one of the most robust learning and memory phenomena in the research literature (for a recent review, see Carpenter *et al.*, 2012; also see Chapters 4 and 6 of this volume). There is, however, another study sequencing effect that is related to and yet different from that of spaced practice, and it is the proper focus of this chapter.

Interleaving vs. Blocking

When a teacher sets homework assignments for students or when a sports coach designs practice drills for athletes, the teacher or coach has an important choice to make—either to have the student or athlete work on one kind of component skill many times in a row before moving on to the next skill, or to allow the various kinds of component skills to be mixed together throughout practice. These two alternatives in sequencing practice examples are referred to as *blocked* (e.g. $A_1A_2A_3B_1B_2B_3C_1C_2C_3$) and *interleaved* practice (e.g. $A_1B_1C_1B_2A_2C_2B_3C_3A_3$), respectively (it is, of course, possible to think of hybrid blocked–interleaved schedules, but for the sake of simplicity I shall focus primarily on the comparison between pure cases).

In the following sections, I shall review studies comparing the relative efficacy of interleaving vs. blocking practice. To foreshadow, research in three broad domains of learning—motor skill acquisition, category learning, and mathematics problem solving—has shown that interleaved practice often yields greater long-term gains. However, learners are typically unaware of the interleaving advantage, and commonly think that blocked practice is more effective for learning. Note that in all the studies described in this chapter the amount of practice or training did not differ between the interleaved and blocked conditions—that is, the number of practice trials or the items or examples presented during training were identical across conditions. The only difference was in how the practice trials or examples were sequenced.

Motor Skill Acquisition

Evidence

The domain of learning that has generated the most research on the sequencing effects of practice trials has been in the area of motor skill acquisition. Shea and Morgan (1979) were the first to demonstrate that interleaved practice led to better motor learning than blocked practice. In their experiment, participants practiced executing three different patterns of movement with their right arms in either an interleaved or blocked sequence of trials. During training, participants in the blocked practice condition exhibited better (i.e. quicker) performance than those in the interleaved condition. However, on a test administered either shortly after or 10 days after training, the participants who underwent interleaved practice displayed faster completion times when executing the movement patterns in which they had been trained. In addition, this group demonstrated faster performance when executing new, unpracticed movement patterns. In other words, interleaving the different kinds of practice trials led to superior retention (memory for the trained behavior) and transfer (the ability to generalize learning to novel contexts).

In a different study that examined the batting skills of collegiate baseball team members, players were given extra batting practice (on top of their usual training) twice a week for 6 weeks. In each practice session, players received 45 pitches (15 each of fastballs, curveballs, and change-ups) either blocked by type or randomly intermixed. On a batting test given after the extra practice sessions, players who had trained in the interleaved condition produced more solid hits than those who had trained in the blocked condition, regardless of whether the pitch type was blocked or random at test (Hall *et al.*, 1994). In a similar study, college students without previous experience of playing racquet sports learned three different badminton serves (short, long, and drive). Participants undertook three sessions of training per week for 3 weeks. In each session, participants performed 36 practice serves. One group practiced only one kind of serve during each training session (e.g. short serve in the first session, long serve in the second session, and drive serve in the third session), while another group practiced all three serves during each training session (i.e. 12 practice trials for each type of serve, randomly sequenced). A test was administered 1 day after the final training session, in which participants had to execute the three different serves. The group that received randomly interleaved training produced more accurate serves (the shuttlecock/birdie was more likely to attain the appropriate height and land within the target area) than the blocked practice group, both when the serves were made from the side of the court that the participants had practiced on (the right) and when the serves were made from the opposite, unpracticed side (the left). Again this demonstrates that interleaved practice led to superior retention and transfer of trained motor skills (Goode & Magill, 1986). Comparable results have been observed in other studies featuring novices learning golf (Porter *et al.*, 2007) and volleyball (Kalkhoran & Shariati, 2012).

In addition to sports, research has found advantages of interleaved practice for a number of other motor skills. For instance, Stambaugh (2011) trained beginning clarinet players (elementary school children) to play three brief series of notes. Over the course of a week, the children participated in three practice sessions, each consisting of 18 practice trials. One group practiced only one series during each session (i.e. they practiced the same series repeatedly 18 times), while a second group practiced all three series of notes during each session (i.e. six practice trials per series, all randomly interleaved). When retention was assessed 1 day after the final practice for each series, the children who underwent interleaved practice were able to play the series of notes more quickly than those who underwent blocked practice (see also Stambaugh, 2011). In a similar study, participants with previous formal training practiced playing a number of brief melodies on a piano with the goal of improving speed and maintaining accuracy. The melodies were practiced in pairs, with half of the pairs presented in a blocked fashion (repeated practice of one melody before moving on to the next melody) while the remaining pairs were randomly sequenced in an interleaved fashion. On a test administered 2 days after training, melodies that were practiced in the interleaved condition were played more quickly than those that were practiced in the blocked condition (Abushanab & Bishara, 2013).

Explanations

To help to explain the advantage of interleaved over blocked practice for motor skill learning, researchers often point to the role of *contextual interference* (Battig, 1979). The basic idea is that interleaved practice allows for a more variable training context than blocked practice, and that this variability introduces interference. Although increased interference typically slows the acquisition of a novel skill (e.g. Abushanab & Bishara, 2013), it is beneficial for long-term retention and transfer of learning. Although the exact reasons for this improvement remain uncertain, one hypothesis suggests that memory representations for the various motor sequences become more elaborate and distinctive following interleaved practice, because the learner needs to hold multiple motor sequences simultaneously in working memory during practice (thus allowing them to be compared) and use variable information-processing strategies depending on the specific task at hand (Shea & Zimny, 1983; Wright, 1991). Conversely, with blocked practice, the need to vary one's mental strategies is diminished, and comparisons among the tasks are precluded. Another prominent hypothesis is that during interleaved practice an action plan (or motor program) needs to be reconstructed anew for each trial, due to the interference (or forgetting) caused by intervening trials of varying types. In contrast, during blocked practice the same motor program can be applied on repeated trials. The continual reconstruction of action plans during interleaved practice, while effortful, facilitates future reconstruction and hence retention and transfer (Immink & Wright, 1998; Lee & Magill, 1985).

Metacognitive Considerations

Given that interleaved practice often feels more difficult and the associated performance improvements are usually more gradual (relative to blocked practice), might students perceive that they are not learning as well as they should? Put another way, given that blocked practice often fosters fluent processing, a sense of familiarity with the task, and relatively rapid improvements in performance, would students be misled into thinking that blocked practice leads to relatively greater gains in learning than interleaved practice? There is evidence to suggest that this might indeed be the case. In the above-mentioned study involving piano players, participants were asked during practice to judge how quickly they thought they would be able to play each melody on a test 2 days later. The participants predicted faster playing times for the melodies that were practiced in the blocked condition (despite actual test performance being faster in the interleaved practice condition). Moreover, when asked after the retention test about their preferences with regard to the two training conditions, the participants indicated that they would choose blocked over interleaved practice when learning melodies in the future (Abushanab & Bishara, 2013). In other words, the pianists were experiencing an illusion of competence, mistakenly believing that blocked practice was superior, when in fact the opposite was true (see also Simon & Bjork, 2001). The metacognitive aspects of training and instruction have important implications for educators, which will be discussed in a later section.

Category Learning

Evidence

In our everyday lives we encounter innumerable objects. Some of these objects we have encountered before and so they are known to us, some are novel examples of the kinds of things that we are familiar with, while others are entirely unknown to us. Our ability to recognize objects as belonging to particular categories allows us to generalize our knowledge about the categories to new instances (induction).

Although the bulk of research in this area has focused on how categories are learned and represented, recent work has explored how the sequencing of examples during training affects and can improve category learning (Richler & Palmeri, 2014). Intuitively, it would seem that interleaved practice would *harm* induction, since spacing out examples from a given concept or category might make it more difficult for the learner to notice the common features that define the concept or category (Kurtz & Hovland, 1956; Kornell & Bjork, 2008). Kornell and Bjork (2008) investigated this hypothesis using a task in which participants had to learn to identify the painting style of individual artists. During the training phase, participants viewed six paintings each by 12 artists. The paintings (accompanied by the name of the artist) were presented one at a time in one of two ways—either blocked according to artist (i.e. six paintings by a given artist were presented in a consecutive sequence) or interleaved (i.e. no two paintings by a given artist were presented consecutively). Shortly after training, the participants' inductive learning was assessed by presenting them with previously unseen paintings by the studied artists and asking them to identify the artist. Across two experiments, participants were better able to correctly classify the new paintings when they studied the artists' paintings in an interleaved rather than blocked fashion. These findings have since been replicated several times (e.g. Kornell et al., 2010), and with different category stimuli, such as types of birds and butterflies (Birnbaum et al., 2013; Wahlheim et al., 2011).

Beyond visual category learning, the interleaving advantage appears to generalize to a number of different category-based learning scenarios. For instance, across two experiments, Zulkiply et al. (2012) found that analyzing case studies of various mental disorders in an interleaved fashion yielded higher classification accuracy for new test cases than studying the cases in a blocked fashion (i.e. multiple case studies of the same disorder studied consecutively). Also, medical students learning to analyze electrocardiograms for various cardiac disorders (e.g. myocardial infarction, ischemia, pericarditis) exhibited higher diagnostic accuracy on a transfer test featuring novel examples if they undertook interleaved practice and were encouraged to contrast the features of different diagnostic categories, rather than if they undertook blocked practice (Hatala et al., 2003). Another study conducted with nursing students learning auscultation (using a stethoscope to listen to internal sounds of the body) found a benefit of interleaving for auditory category learning. The students in this study were presented with audio examples of various cardiac and respiratory sounds (e.g. mitral valve prolapse, wheeze) in either an interleaved or blocked manner during training, and were later tested using both old (retention) and new (transfer) examples. Test performance in the interleaved training group was demonstrably superior to that in the blocked training group, especially for the classification of new examples (Chen *et al.*, 2015).

Explanations

Although the findings of Kornell and Bjork (2008) were striking, they did not answer the question of whether the advantage of interleaving was due to the interleaving itself, or to increased temporal spacing between the presentation of paintings by the same artist. In a follow-up study that focused more directly on category induction, Kang and Pashler (2012) found that increasing temporal spacing between paintings while maintaining a presentation sequence that was blocked by artist produced test performances no better than those following typically blocked practice (both of which were worse than performance following interleaved practice). Moreover, presenting paintings by different artists *simultaneously* resulted in test performance as good as that with interleaved presentation, and better than that with blocked presentation. These results suggest that category learning was enhanced not because of increased temporal spacing per se, but rather because interleaving paintings by different artists facilitated discriminative contrast among the artists' styles. In other words, the juxtaposition of examples from different categories probably drew learners' attention to the relevant features that discriminate one category from another and/or promoted greater differentiation on the dimensions on which the categories varied, leading to better induction (e.g. Goldstone & Steyvers, 2001; Nosofsky, 1986). This supposition was supported by a study by Birnbaum *et al.* (2013), which examined the learning of bird and butterfly species. Interestingly, researchers in the latter study found that having more (rather than fewer) intervening items from different categories between successive presentations of a given category improved inductive learning. This suggests that the interleaving advantage in category learning and the temporal spacing effects need not be mutually exclusive (both could contribute to learning, depending on the particular conditions).

Metacognitive Considerations

There is ample evidence that learners perceive blocked presentation to be more effective for category learning than interleaved presentation. For instance, Kornell and Bjork (2008) found that the vast majority of participants, having experienced both interleaved and blocked presentations of different artists' paintings, judged that they had learned better in the blocked condition. What is perhaps especially remarkable is that the participants gave their judgments immediately after they had taken a test (with feedback provided!) in which classification accuracy was higher for the artists that had been interleaved (see also Zulkiply *et al.*, 2012; Zulkiply & Burt, 2013). Also, when undergraduate students were presented with a scenario based on the procedure of Kornell and Bjork and asked to predict whether interleaving or blocking would produce better learning, over 90% of them selected the blocked condition (McCabe, 2011). Finally, a study that gave learners control over the sequencing of study examples when learning to categorize types of birds found that the participants overwhelmingly chose blocked presentation (i.e. they preferred to study multiple examples of a particular bird family before switching to another bird family) (Tauber *et al.*, 2013). The preference for blocking may be driven by the subjective feeling of learning conferred by fluent processing when studying multiple examples of the same kind in a row. Another possibility is that learners simply hold the belief that blocked presentation is a superior method, perhaps due to its common use in instruction. The pedagogical implications of such inaccurate metacognitive monitoring and/or beliefs will be discussed later.

Problem Solving

Evidence

The final major area of learning in which interleaved practice has been explored is mathematics problem solving. Most of the relevant research on this topic has been undertaken by Doug Rohrer and colleagues, with experiments conducted both in the laboratory and in the classroom. In one laboratory experiment, college students were taught how to calculate the volume of four obscure solids (e.g. spheroid, wedge), after which they had two practice sessions separated by 1 week. During each session, the participants practiced solving four problems pertaining to each type of solid in either a blocked or an interleaved sequence, with corrective feedback provided immediately after each problem (the practice condition was consistent across both sessions for each participant). Performance during practice was higher in the blocked condition than in the interleaved condition. However, on a test containing new volume problems given 1 week after the second practice session, the interleaved group outperformed the blocked group by a wide margin of 63% vs. 20% (Rohrer & Taylor, 2007).

More recently, Rohrer and colleagues extended their research on interleaved practice into actual classrooms (Rohrer *et al.*, 2014, 2015). In their first classroom-based study, the mathematics homework assignments for seventh-grade students in a public middle school were manipulated across 9 weeks. Ten mathematics assignments were given out over that period (each consisting of 12 practice problems). For problem types assigned to blocked practice, all 12 problems in a single assignment would be of that type (and no other assignment would feature that problem type). For problem types assigned to interleaved practice, only the first four problems in the assignment would be of that type; the other eight problems in the assignment would pertain to previously covered topics or types, and the remaining eight practice problems pertaining to the current topic (of the first four problems) would be distributed across future assignments. In other words, the number of practice problems devoted to each type or topic was equal across the blocked and interleaved conditions (12 practice problems per topic), and the only difference was whether all 12 problems of a given type were completed in one assignment or whether they were spread out across multiple assignments (and therefore interleaved with other types of problems). The problem types or topics assigned to the blocked and interleaved practice conditions were counterbalanced among the students. On a test containing novel problems given 2 weeks after the final homework assignment, the students were substantially better at solving the types of problems that had been practiced in an interleaved manner than was the case for those that had undergone blocked practice (72% vs. 38%) (Rohrer *et al.*, 2014).

That study is notable because it was conducted in the context of a regular middle-school curriculum—that is, the mathematics teachers taught their lessons as they normally did, and apart from designing the homework assignments, the researchers had no control over the type or amount of mathematics-related activities that each student engaged in (inside or outside the classroom). Given the complexities of school-based interventions (e.g. Greene, 2015), the large effect of interleaved practice observed by Rohrer *et al.* (2014) is particularly impressive.

In the study by Rohrer *et al.* (2014), the scheduling of the mathematics problems over 9 weeks meant that problem types assigned to the interleaved condition (in which mathematics problems were spread out over multiple homework assignments) were practiced closer in time to the test than those assigned to the blocked condition (in which the problems appeared in a single homework assignment), raising the possibility that a difference in retention interval (the time between the last practice and the test) was responsible for the interleaving advantage. To overcome the retention interval problem, a follow-up study featured a review session of all the topics in class 5 days after the last homework assignment. A test consisting of new problems was administered either 1 day or 30 days after the review session, and the benefit of interleaved practice compared with blocked practice was still very apparent (performance after 1-day delay: 80% vs. 64%; performance after 30-day delay: 74% vs. 42%) (Rohrer *et al.*, 2015).

Explanations

Interleaving different kinds of mathematics problems naturally increases temporal spacing between successive presentations of problems of the same kind, and as discussed in the previous section on category learning, it is unclear whether the observed learning benefit is due to spacing or interleaving per se. In order to address this issue, Taylor and Rohrer (2010) asked elementary school children to learn to solve four types of mathematics problems (determining the number of faces, corners, edges, and angles that there are in a prism), with temporal spacing across the interleaved and blocked practice conditions kept constant. A filler task was inserted between practice items in the blocked condition, so that the amount of time between successive encounters with problems of the same type was equivalent to that of the interleaved condition. Performance during practice was higher in the blocked than in the interleaved condition. However, when asked to solve new prism problems 1 day after practice, students in the interleaved practice group performed considerably better than those who received blocked practice (77% vs. 38%). An analysis of the errors revealed that the interleaving advantage was mainly driven by students in the blocked condition using the formulae they had learned for problems that were not appropriate. In other words, they had difficulty discriminating between the different problem types and knowing when to use each learned formula.

Just as we saw in the case of category learning, interleaved practice seems to help learners to differentiate between the types of problems they are learning to solve. When learning mathematics, it is not sufficient to learn *how* to execute a strategy—one must also know *when* a particular strategy is appropriate (VanderStoep & Seifert, 1994). After all, there are problems that appear similar on the surface but which require different strategies (e.g. in statistics, independent versus repeated measures *t*-test). Moreover, with word problems there is often no explicit mention of the target mathematical concept or appropriate strategy, and it is left to the student to infer the type of problem that they are trying to solve (Rohrer, 2009). It is therefore not too surprising why blocked practice is less than ideal—the learner often already knows what strategy is required without even reading or analyzing the problem, and there is little need to figure out what kind of problem they are dealing with. In other words, the grouping together of problems of the same kind short-circuits learning to discriminate between the various problem types. As a result, less attention is paid to features of the problem that indicate what type of problem it is.

In the classroom study by Rohrer et al. (2014), the types of problems that the middle-school students were learning to solve were actually quite different (e.g. linear equations, determining the slope of lines, word problems involving proportions). When students' errors on the test were analyzed, there were very few instances in which students had used the wrong strategy, which was appropriate for a different kind of problem (and the rate of these discrimination errors did not differ between the interleaved and blocked practice conditions). This suggests that enhanced discrimination is not the only explanation for the interleaving advantage. Rohrer et al. propose that in addition to discrimination (i.e. learning to recognize the type of problem), association of a given problem type with an appropriate strategy is critical for successful problem solving. With blocked practice, the learner need only focus on executing a strategy (in repeated succession), without associating the problem with its strategy, whereas with interleaved practice, the switching between different problem types and strategies strengthens the association between a problem type and its strategy.

Is Blocked Practice Ever Helpful?

The research discussed in the preceding sections of this chapter clearly shows that interleaved practice is more effective than blocked practice across diverse forms of learning. However, to say that interleaving is *always* better, or that blocking is *never* useful, would be to oversimplify matters. After all, even in the above-mentioned studies by Rohrer et al. (2014, 2015), the homework assignments in the interleaved condition began with a mini-block of four mathematics problems on a given topic. Indeed, research in motor and category learning has revealed some boundary conditions with regard to the superiority of interleaved practice.

When one considers the theoretical explanation as to why interleaving enhances motor learning (i.e. increased contextual interference), one could perhaps anticipate that in certain situations the interference would be excessive and possibly overwhelm the learner, leading to either no benefit of interleaving (relative to blocked practice) or even a reduction in learning. One factor that has been shown to modulate the interleaving advantage is the complexity of the motor task. A meta-analysis of published studies found that the average effect size (the benefit of interleaved over blocked practice in terms of standard deviations) was larger in laboratory studies, which tend to feature simpler motor tasks, than in field studies, which tend to examine more complex, ecologically valid, sports-related motor skills (0.57 vs. 0.19) (Brady, 2004). With complex motor tasks, the level of expertise of the learner and the amount of practice also seem to matter. Although some of the studies mentioned in the earlier section on motor skill learning featured novices (e.g. learning badminton, volleyball), there are other studies that failed to find a benefit of interleaving for novices and young children (Magill & Hall, 1990). Also, a benefit of interleaved practice may emerge only after extensive practice (Shea et al., 1990). When dealing with beginners who are trying to learn a complex motor skill, a hybrid approach may be optimal—that is, starting with blocked practice and gradually transitioning to randomly interleaved practice (Porter & Magill, 2010).

For inductive learning of categories, the dominant explanation as to why interleaving is beneficial is that it facilitates discriminative contrast among the various categories (e.g. Kang & Pashler, 2012). If this is the case, interleaving should be advantageous for learning categories that are hard to tell apart (i.e. those which have high inter-category similarity), and indeed the research cited earlier which showed that interleaved presentation improved category learning generally featured categories that were highly similar (e.g. different kinds of birds or butterflies). However, when the members within each category share very few features in common (i.e. there is low intra-category similarity), there is evidence that learning of such categories is better with blocked than with interleaved presentation (Carvalho & Goldstone, 2014). Blocking the categories promotes the noticing of commonalities within each category (Kurtz & Hovland, 1956), which is especially useful when category members are of low similarity.

From the Laboratory to the Classroom

There is ample research evidence to support the benefit of interleaved practice for a variety of learning domains that are relevant both inside and outside the classroom. Of course, the complete picture regarding the relative utility of interleaved versus blocked practice is not as simple or straightforward as one would perhaps like (as the immediately preceding section has made clear). However, the existence of boundary conditions does not throw a spanner in the works when it comes to practical advice for educators. It just means that the recommendations must be nuanced and qualified at times. Let us first consider two major obstacles that stand in the way of teachers implementing interleaved practice.

There is evidence from the motor skill and category learning domains that learners, after having experienced both interleaved and blocked practice, tend to think that the latter is more effective, in direct contradiction to their actual learning demonstrated on a later test (e.g. Abushanab & Bishara, 2013; Kornell & Bjork, 2008; Zulkiply et al., 2012). The consecutive repetition of the same kinds of examples or motor actions one gets in blocked practice probably engenders a sense of relative fluency, which leads one to assume that great gains in learning have occurred. Another explanation for the discrepancy between subjective judgments and more objective measures of learning has to do with learners' beliefs or intuitions that blocking is more helpful than interleaving (e.g. McCabe, 2011). It should be noted that teachers are by no means immune from erroneous metacognitive beliefs. In a study conducted at a public university in Colorado, college instructors were just as likely as students to rate blocked presentation of paintings as being more effective than interleaved presentation for learning to recognize individual artists' styles (Morehead et al., 2016).

These erroneous metacognitive beliefs may pose a particular challenge to a teacher's intention to incorporate interleaved practice. During training or practice, interleaving sometimes yields poorer performance than blocking, giving the impression that the latter is more effective. Not only might the teacher question whether interleaved practice was the right strategy to adopt, but also the students might be unhappy about using this approach. A *New York Times* article on the study by Rohrer et al. (2014) stated that "The math students at Liberty Middle School were not happy. The seventh graders' homework was harder and more time-consuming at first, and many of the problems seemed stale" (Carey, 2013).

Later on in the article, though, the journalist mentions how the students eventually got used to the interleaving of different problem types in their homework assignments, and felt that it was easier to study for subsequent tests because all of the topics had recently been practiced. In other words, interleaved practice requires perseverance. The results may not be immediately apparent, but with some persistence the benefits to learning will become clear.

The second major barrier to the wider use of interleaving is convention. Traditional instructional practice typically favors a blocked approach. Inside the classroom, teaching materials and aids (textbooks, worksheets, etc.) are usually organized in a modular way, which promotes blocked practice. After presenting a new topic in class, it is common for teachers to give students practice with the topic via a homework assignment or worksheet. However, apart from that block of practice shortly after the introduction of a topic, there is usually no further practice until a review session prior to a major test. What this means for teachers who have decided to incorporate interleaved practice in their classrooms is that some planning is required. The classroom studies by Rohrer *et al.* (2014, 2015) described earlier demonstrate how a small tweak in homework assignments—switching from having the practice problems in a given assignment devoted to just a single topic to having a mix of problems pertaining to various topics appearing in each assignment—can produce impressive improvements in mathematics learning. Apart from rearranging the problems in the homework assignments and presenting the correct answers to the assignments in class (corrective feedback is important, because students tend to make more errors during interleaved practice), the mathematics classes were conducted in the same way as in the past. There was no increase in class time spent on mathematics instruction, no disruption to the regular teaching of mathematics topics, and the number of practice problems that students received for homework remained the same.

For optimal implementation of interleaved practice, a few practical issues need to be considered. First, of all the knowledge or skills that a student is expected to learn, which (sub) topics should one attempt to interleave during a given practice session? For instance, should topics from science, history, English, and mathematics be interleaved when a student is practicing using flashcards? In this instance, there is unlikely to be any benefit from interleaving of such disparate topics (Hausman & Kornell, 2014). Research findings suggest that interleaving helps students to notice the differences between categories or concepts (e.g. Birnbaum *et al.*, 2013; Kang & Pashler, 2012), which means that when the categories or concepts that have to be learned are, to some extent, similar or confusable, interleaving should be particularly useful. Within a given academic discipline (e.g. mathematics, physics), often the concepts that are being learned have some degree of similarity or overlap, and therefore the concepts within a discipline would be prime targets for interleaved practice. However, topics between disciplines (e.g. between history and chemistry) are probably too dissimilar to confer any benefit of cross-subject interleaving. This might be convenient, as any attempt at interleaving would probably remain within a single class or subject, which means that there would be no real need to coordinate multiple teachers across different subjects.

A second issue is the degree of interleaving during practice. Does practice have to be purely interleaved (i.e. with no blocking whatsoever) in order for a benefit to be obtained? There is evidence that blocked practice is helpful for novices, especially initially (e.g. Shea *et al.*, 1990). Also, grouping items of the same kind or topic together helps students to detect the commonalities across the items, which is useful when intra-category similarity is low (Carvalho & Goldstone, 2014). What this means is that taking interleaving to an extreme is probably not optimal in all situations. Teachers might consider providing a certain amount of blocked practice after introducing a new topic or concept, and perhaps feature practice items that appear to be quite different yet tap the same underlying concept. For instance, in mathematics, understanding of a given solution strategy or formula can be assessed or practiced in a variety of ways (e.g. problems containing diagrams, algebraic equations, word problems describing different scenarios), and it is important for students to figure out what these different forms share in common. Another potential advantage of blocked initial practice is that performance improvements tend to be more rapid, which might reduce learner anxiety and/or increase self-efficacy (e.g. Schunk, 1991). Of course, these performance gains are usually short term, and practicing the same kinds of items repeatedly could lull students into a state of complacency. Beyond blocked practice in the initial stages, therefore, the goal should be to transition to interleaved practice.

Current educational norms are heavily oriented towards blocked practice. Blocked practice feels effective, instructors are accustomed to it, and instructional materials generally facilitate it. However, there is a substantial body of evidence in favor of increasing the degree of interleaving during practice. Across a variety of learning domains, studies have found an advantage of interleaved over blocked practice. Some of these studies have examined the learning of ecologically valid material in educationally relevant contexts, increasing our confidence that the findings will apply to students in everyday classrooms. Whether you are an art history instructor teaching students to recognize the differences in style between various Impressionist painters (e.g. Manet vs. Monet), a biology instructor teaching students how to differentiate between various crocodilian species (e.g. alligators vs. crocodiles), or a mathematics instructor teaching students how to solve different calculus problems (e.g. integration by parts vs. substitution), you have a choice in terms of how you present examples in class and also how practice problems are sequenced in assignments. Although making a decision to increase the level of interleaving will require some effort and planning (because it is a departure from the default blocked practice), it need not entail a radical overhaul of one's teaching practices. Something as simple as shuffling the problems that appear in homework assignments—without significant changes to classroom instruction or the amount of homework—can produce great gains in learning (Rohrer et al., 2014, 2015). Also, with the increasing use of computers in instruction (e.g. computer-assisted tutoring tools), it is likely that introducing interleaved practice will become easier (for an example implemented in a college classroom, see Kirchoff et al., 2014). My hope is that educators reading this chapter will think of creative ways to ensure that their students are exposed to a variety of examples or problem types during practice, which more closely approximates the situation that they will face during a test (or in real life). Indeed, the benefits of interleaving are most apparent for learning that is inductive or that can be generalized to new situations or problems—precisely the kind of learning that is a primary goal of education!

NOTE

1   This work was supported by a faculty research grant from the Nelson A. Rockerfeller Center (Dartmouth College) and a Walter and Constance Burke Research Initiation Award. The author thanks Michael Blum for assisting with the literature review, and Amanda Bean for helpful comments on an earlier version of the manuscript.

References

Abushanab, B. & Bishara, A. J. (2013). Memory and metacognition for piano melodies: illusory advantages of fixed- over random-order practice. *Memory & Cognition, 41*, 928–937.

Ackerman, P. L. (2014). Nonsense, common sense, and science of expert performance: talent and individual differences. *Intelligence, 45*, 6–17.

Battig, W. F. (1979). The flexibility of human memory. In: L. S. Cermak & F. I. M. Craik (Eds), *Levels of Processing in Human Memory* (pp. 23–44). Hillsdale, NJ: Erlbaum.

Birnbaum, M. S., Kornell, N., Bjork, E. L., & Bjork, R. A. (2013). Why interleaving enhances inductive learning: the roles of discrimination and retrieval. *Memory & Cognition, 41*, 392–402.

Brady, F. (2004). Contextual interference: a meta-analytic study. *Perceptual and Motor Skills, 99*, 116–126.

Carey, B. (2013). Cognitive science meets pre-algebra. *The New York Times.* Available online at www.nytimes.com/2013/09/03/science/cognitive-science-meetspre-algebra.html

Carpenter, S. K., Cepeda, N. J., Rohrer, D., Kang, S. H. K., & Pashler, H. (2012). Using spacing to enhance diverse forms of learning: review of recent research and implications for instruction. *Educational Psychology Review, 24*, 369–378.

Carvalho, P. F. & Goldstone, R. L. (2014). Putting category learning in order: category structure and temporal arrangement affect the benefit of interleaved over blocked study. *Memory & Cognition, 42*, 481–495.

Cepeda, N. J., Pashler, H., Vul, E., Wixted, J. T., & Rohrer, D. (2006). Distributed practice in verbal recall tasks: a review and quantitative synthesis. *Psychological Bulletin, 132*, 354–380.

Chen, R., Grierson, L., & Norman, G. (2015). Manipulation of cognitive load variables and impact on auscultation test performance. *Advances in Health Sciences Education, 20*, 935–952.

Ericsson, K. A., Prietula, M. J., & Cokely, E. T. (2007). The making of an expert. *Harvard Business Review, 85*, 114–121.

Goldstone, R. L. & Steyvers, M. (2001). The sensitization and differentiation of dimensions during category learning. *Journal of Experimental Psychology: General, 130*, 116–139.

Goode, S. & Magill, R. A. (1986). Contextual interference effects in learning three badminton serves. *Research Quarterly for Exercise and Sport, 57*, 308–314.

Greene, J. A. (2015). Serious challenges require serious scholarship: integrating implementation science into the scholarly discourse. *Contemporary Educational Psychology, 40*, 112–120.

Hall, K. G., Domingues, D. A., & Cavazos, R. (1994). Contextual interference effects with skilled baseball players. *Perceptual and Motor Skills, 78*, 835–841.

Hatala, R. M., Brooks, L. R., & Norman, G. R. (2003). Practice makes perfect: the critical role of mixed practice in the acquisition of ECG interpretation skills. *Advances in Health Sciences Education, 8*, 17–26.

Hausman, H. & Kornell, N. (2014). Mixing topics while studying does not enhance learning. *Journal of Applied Research in Memory and Cognition, 3*, 153–160.

Immink, M. A. & Wright, D. L. (1998). Contextual interference: a response planning account. *The Quarterly Journal of Experimental Psychology, 51*, 735–754.

James, W. (1914). *Talks to Teachers on Psychology: And to Students on Some of Life's Ideals.* New York: Henry Holt.

Kalkhoran, A. F. & Shariati, A. (2012). The effects of contextual interference on learning volleyball motor skills. *Journal of Physical Education and Sport, 12*, 550–556.

Kang, S. H. K. & Pashler, H. (2012). Learning painting styles: spacing is advantageous when it promotes discriminative contrast. *Applied Cognitive Psychology, 26*, 97–103.

Kirchoff, B. K., Delaney, P. F., Horton, M., & Dellinger-Johnston, R. (2014). Optimizing learning of scientific category knowledge in the classroom: the case of plant identification. *CBE—Life Sciences Education, 13*, 425–436.

Kornell, N. & Bjork, R. A. (2008). Learning concepts and categories: is spacing the "enemy of induction"? *Psychological Science, 19*, 585–592.

Kornell, N., Castel, A. D., Eich, T. S., & Bjork, R. A. (2010). Spacing as the friend of both memory and induction in young and older adults. *Psychology and Aging*, 25, 498–503.

Kurtz, K. H. & Hovland, C. I. (1956). Concept learning with differing sequences of instances. *Journal of Experimental Psychology*, 51, 239–243.

Lee, T. D. & Magill, R. A. (1985). Can forgetting facilitate skill acquisition? In: D. Goodman, R. B. Wilberg, & I. M. Franks (Eds), *Differing Perspectives in Motor Learning, Memory, and Control* (pp. 3–22). Amsterdam: North-Holland Publishing Company.

McCabe, J. (2011). Metacognitive awareness of learning strategies in undergraduates. *Memory & Cognition*, 39, 462–476.

Magill, R. A. & Hall, K. G. (1990). A review of the contextual interference effect in motor skill acquisition. *Human Movement Science*, 9, 241–289.

Morehead, K., Rhodes, M. G., & DeLozier, S. (2016). Instructor and student knowledge of study strategies. *Memory*, 24, 257–271.

Nosofsky, R. M. (1986). Attention, similarity, and the identification-categorization relationship. *Journal of Experimental Psychology: General*, 115, 39–57.

Porter, J., Landin, D., Hebert, E., & Baum, B. (2007). The effects of three levels of contextual interference on performance outcomes and movement patterns in golf skills. *International Journal of Sports Science and Coaching*, 2, 243–255.

Porter, J. M. & Magill, R. A. (2010). Systematically increasing contextual interference is beneficial for learning sport skills. *Journal of Sports Sciences*, 28, 1277–1285.

Richler, J. J. & Palmeri, T. J. (2014). Visual category learning. *Wiley Interdisciplinary Reviews: Cognitive Science*, 5, 75–94.

Rohrer, D. (2009). The effects of spacing and mixing practice problems. *Journal for Research in Mathematics Education*, 40, 4–17.

Rohrer, D. & Taylor, K. (2007). The shuffling of mathematics practice problems improves learning. *Instructional Science*, 35, 481–498.

Rohrer, D., Dedrick, R. F., & Burgess, K. (2014). The benefit of interleaved mathematics practice is not limited to superficially similar kinds of problems. *Psychonomic Bulletin & Review*, 21, 1323–1330.

Rohrer, D., Dedrick, R. F., & Stershic, S. (2015). Interleaved practice improves mathematics learning. *Journal of Educational Psychology*, 107, 900–908.

Schunk, D. H. (1991). Self-efficacy and academic motivation. *Educational Psychologist*, 26, 207–231.

Shea, C. H., Kohl, R., & Indermill, C. (1990). Contextual interference: contributions of practice. *Acta Psychologica*, 73, 145–157.

Shea, J. B. & Morgan, R. L. (1979). Contextual interference effects on the acquisition, retention, and transfer of a motor skill. *Journal of Experimental Psychology: Human Learning and Memory*, 5, 179–187.

Shea, J. B. & Zimny, S. T. (1983). Context effects in memory and learning information. In: R. A. Magill (Ed.), *Memory and Control of Action* (pp. 345–366). Amsterdam: North-Holland Publishing Company.

Simon, D. A. & Bjork, R. A. (2001). Metacognition in motor learning. *Journal of Experimental Psychology: Learning, Memory, and Cognition*, 27, 907–912.

Stambaugh, L. A. (2011). When repetition isn't the best practice strategy: effects of blocked and random practice schedules. *Journal of Research in Music Education*, 58, 368–383.

Tauber, S. K., Dunlosky, J., Rawson, K. A., Wahlheim, C. N., & Jacoby, L. L. (2013). Self-regulated learning of a natural category: do people interleave or block exemplars during study? *Psychonomic Bulletin & Review*, 20, 356–363.

Taylor, K. & Rohrer, D. (2010). The effects of interleaving practice. *Applied Cognitive Psychology*, 24, 837–848.

VanderStoep, S. W. & Seifert, C. M. (1994). Learning "how" versus learning "when": improving transfer of problem-solving principles. *Journal of the Learning Sciences*, 3, 93–111.

Wahlheim, C. N., Dunlosky, J., & Jacoby, L. L. (2011). Spacing enhances the learning of natural concepts: an investigation of mechanisms, metacognition, and aging. *Memory & Cognition*, 39, 750–763.

Wright, D. L. (1991). The role of intertask and intratask processing in acquisition and retention of motor skills. *Journal of Motor Behavior*, 23, 139–145.

Zulkiply, N. & Burt, J. S. (2013). The exemplar interleaving effect in inductive learning: moderation by the difficulty of category discriminations. *Memory & Cognition*, 41, 16–27.

Zulkiply, N., McLean, J., Burt, J. S., & Bath, D. (2012). Spacing and induction: application to exemplars presented as auditory and visual text. *Learning and Instruction*, 22, 215–221.

6

IMPROVING STUDENT LEARNING

Two Strategies to Make It Stick

Adam L. Putnam, John F. Nestojko, and Henry L. Roediger III
WASHINGTON UNIVERSITY IN ST. LOUIS

Introduction

The aim of this book is to take research from the laboratory to the classroom. This is an important goal because, despite decades of research by cognitive psychologists, there is not a strong tradition of translational educational research, where findings are clarified in controlled laboratory settings and slowly introduced to real-world classrooms (Roediger, 2013). Several books written for non-specialists, such as *Make It Stick: The Science of Successful Learning* (Brown *et al.*, 2014) and *Why Don't Students Like School?* (Willingham, 2009), highlight some main points about educationally relevant research. Of course, we hope that books like the one you are holding will also help to spread the word about how findings from cognitive psychology can be used to improve education. In this chapter we take a close look at two strategies—retrieval practice and spaced learning—that most cognitive psychologists agree are some of the strongest candidates in terms of having a significant impact on education.

Students' Understanding of Learning

One question that needs to be posed at the outset is why learning is so hard. After all, humans are natural learners, and we learn from birth without necessarily trying hard to do so. Children do not have to *try* to understand and speak the language that surrounds them when they are growing up—it happens naturally. Why can't they learn to read or do arithmetic the same way? The answer to this question is complex, of course, but let us supplant it with a seemingly easier one. Because children *do* have to learn topics for which they are not naturally prepared (as they are with language), why don't they discover good learning strategies and stick with those? Why is education so hard for so many students?

Students display wide individual differences, of course, but even in excellent universities (and medical schools), students report that they do not know how to study effectively. In addition, when they think they are using good strategies, they may be wrong. Survey studies that have examined what students actually do when they study typically reveal that they choose to read and reread as their primary strategy (e.g. Karpicke *et al.*, 2009). They read the text and highlight or underline certain passages. They then reread the material (especially the critical highlighted parts) repeatedly to prepare for the test. As we shall see later in this chapter, rereading, despite its ubiquity as a study strategy, is not particularly effective. Much better strategies are possible (such as retrieval practice, discussed below). And even when students do reread material, they often do so under less than optimal conditions. That is, they often read materials over and over again with little time between rereadings. One main theme of this chapter is the spacing out of repeated rereadings to make them effective.

Repeated reading seems to have another drawback—it makes students overconfident about what they know (e.g. Roediger & Karpicke, 2006a). If you read something repeatedly, it will become quite familiar and you may be fooled into thinking you understand it when you do not. The familiarity or fluency of the material can be mistaken for knowledge and understanding. Unless the student can actively use the material—that is, they can call it up when necessary to answer questions or solve problems—the information is not useful. The first technique we shall discuss in this chapter, namely retrieval practice via testing, permits students to do this. Testing oneself also helps to correct overconfidence from rereading, because students can learn what they know and what they do not know by quizzing themselves.

The remainder of this chapter is devoted to discussion of the two topics introduced in this section—retrieval practice via quizzing, and spacing. These are certainly not the only topics important to education that have emerged from research in cognitive psychology, but they represent two central principles. Other important points are discussed elsewhere in this volume.

Retrieval Practice

One of the most effective learning tools available to teachers and students is retrieval practice. Also called the testing effect, retrieval practice refers to the idea that retrieving something from memory not only measures what someone has learned, but also changes the retrieved memory, making it easier to recall in the future. Psychologists have periodically studied this concept over the past 100 years (e.g. Abbot, 1909), but the last decade has seen a surge of interest, with researchers exploring both why retrieval practice can enhance memory (e.g. Carpenter, 2009; Karpicke *et al.*, 2014; Pyc & Rawson, 2009, 2010) and how it can be used to improve education (e.g. Karpicke & Blunt, 2011; Karpicke & Grimaldi, 2012; Roediger *et al.*, 2011a) (for reviews, see Roediger *et al.*, 2010; Roediger & Karpicke, 2006b).

Taking a test generally enhances later retention, because tests require some form of retrieval from memory. Even thinking about information and not saying it or writing it down improves retention (e.g. Putnam & Roediger, 2013; Smith *et al.*, 2013). Although the exact mechanisms involved remain unclear, retrieving a memory makes it easier to retrieve that memory again in the future. Critically for education, retrieving information during a test often leads to better future recall than rereading that same information, particularly if the final test occurs at some delay after the initial study session (Roediger & Karpicke, 2006a). The long-term benefits of testing make it a good candidate for use in education. However, testing sometimes does not help performance relative to restudying when a final test occurs shortly after studying, which may explain why students and teachers do not intuitively use testing as a learning strategy. That is, students learn that repeated studying (i.e. cramming) can get them through a test if the test occurs immediately after studying, but research shows that cramming leads to fast forgetting over time. Finally, testing does not just improve recall for factual information, but can also enhance the organization of information and the ability to transfer knowledge to new situations (for a description of ten benefits of testing, see Roediger *et al.*, 2011b).

As we shall show below, retrieval practice can be implemented in a variety of ways, both in the classroom and in students' own study routines. Testing also has indirect benefits for learning beyond directly enhancing retention of the tested information.

Types of Test

Students take many different kinds of tests and quizzes in the classroom, with a range of formats (including essay, short answer, and multiple choice) and levels of formality (including pop quizzes, weekly exams, mid-terms, and finals). The goal of most of these activities is to assess what students have learned from readings and lectures, but in some situations these assessments can also provide an opportunity for retrieval practice. Are some test formats (e.g. short answer or multiple choice) more effective than others at promoting learning?

On the one hand, McDermott *et al.* (2014) directly investigated the role of test format in a set of experiments that were conducted in real middle-school and high-school classrooms. In Experiment 4 the students took three short-answer or three multiple-choice quizzes about a particular topic covered in their history class. A research assistant administered the quizzes, so the teachers did not know what material was being covered in the quizzes. The day after the third quiz, the students took a unit exam consisting of a combination of multiple-choice and short-answer questions. Figure 6.1 shows that both multiple-choice and short-answer questions led to better performance on the unit exam compared with material that was not previously tested (other experiments in the study showed that the testing conditions consistently led to better performance on the unit exams than did restudying). Critically, the short-answer and multiple-choice test formats led to similar benefits in terms of performance on the unit exam. Furthermore, both quiz formats were equally effective regardless of whether the final test was short answer or multiple choice. Several other papers (e.g. Little *et al.*, 2012; Smith & Karpicke, 2014) have shown that multiple-choice and short-answer questions can lead to similarly large testing effects.

On the other hand, the two test formats are not equally effective under all conditions. Several studies have shown an advantage of short-answer questions over multiple-choice questions (Butler & Roediger, 2007; Kang *et al.*, 2007; McDaniel *et al.*, 2007). One explanation for this outcome is that short-answer questions, in which students are asked to generate the correct response, require more effortful retrieval than multiple-choice questions, in which students recognize and select the correct answer from among several alternatives. This is a prime example of what is known as a desirable difficulty in learning—some condition that is more difficult or effortful may seem to slow learning at first, but leads to memory benefits in the long term (Bjork, 1994; Karpicke & Roediger, 2007; Pyc & Rawson, 2009). Many researchers (e.g. Pyc & Rawson, 2009) have proposed that the difficulty involved in retrieval is the reason why testing is a powerful learning tool.

Retrieval effort is not the only factor that determines whether a question will lead to enhanced recall on a later test. Another factor is initial retrieval success. If students fail to answer a question on a practice quiz, they are unlikely to answer it correctly on a final test unless they get feedback or a chance to restudy. Not surprisingly, multiple-choice tests are

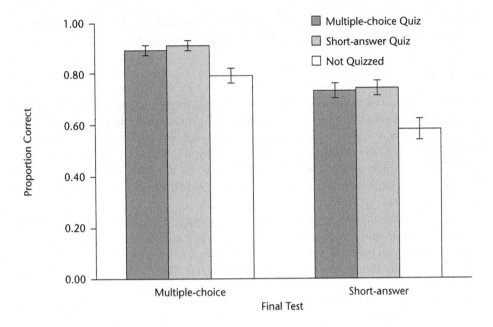

FIGURE 6.1 The results of Experiment 4 by McDermott *et al.* (2014). Both short-answer and multiple-choice quizzes led to enhanced performance on the final test (a unit exam) compared with a no-quiz control condition. The test format of the final test did not moderate the size of the testing effect.

Source: © 2013 American Psychological Association. Adapted with permission.

often easier than short-answer tests. Thus, in some experiments where performance on a short-answer practice quiz is low, multiple-choice questions can be more effective than short-answer questions (e.g. Kang *et al.*, 2007; Little *et al.*, 2012). Of course, one way to compensate for low initial test performance is to provide feedback after each question, which can lead to short-answer questions being more effective than multiple-choice questions (e.g. Kang *et al.*, 2007). We discuss feedback in more detail below.

One element that is important for multiple-choice questions is the construction of the questions themselves. Little *et al.* (2012) showed that properly constructed multiple-choice questions can enhance learning for both the correct and incorrect responses. Critically, the lures for the multiple-choice questions must be plausible and competitive; this requires students to retrieve information about why a particular response option is correct and why other response options are incorrect. In essence, a well-written multiple-choice question will require the test taker to retrieve information about all of the response options. Unfortunately, writing challenging multiple-choice questions is difficult, and many questions provided in test banks seem to have some implausible answers, which may not enhance future performance.

In summary, both multiple-choice and short-answer questions can be used to encourage retrieval-based learning, with much recent research suggesting that the two formats lead to similar testing effects. Both retrieval effort and retrieval success appear to be important in determining how effective a question is at engendering learning. Test questions should require some degree of retrieval effort, but if a question is too hard, performance feedback should be provided. On a related note, some research suggests that open-book tests (where students have access to their notes and other study materials) may be just as effective for promoting future learning as closed-book tests (Agarwal *et al.*, 2008).

Feedback

Although taking a test without feedback will enhance future recall, providing feedback (or providing students with the opportunity to restudy) almost always magnifies the size of a testing effect. Many aspects of feedback have been explored, such as how it affects later learning, what form the feedback should take (whether you simply say "right" or "wrong", or provide the correct answer), when feedback should be provided, and how taking a test allows people to learn more during their next study episode. We shall now consider each of these issues in turn.

As noted earlier, one important factor in finding a testing effect is initial test performance. If a student fails to answer a question correctly during the initial test, they are unlikely to answer that question correctly at a later date unless they are provided with feedback or given a chance to restudy (Butler & Roediger, 2008). Kang *et al.* (2007) had students read passages and then complete a short-answer or multiple-choice test before taking a final test later on. In one experiment they showed that when correct answer feedback was not provided, multiple-choice tests led to better final test performance than short-answer tests, because initial performance for the multiple-choice questions was better. When feedback was provided in a second experiment, however, that pattern was reversed, and short-answer tests led to better final recall than multiple-choice tests. Kang *et al.* attributed this reversal to the low initial test performance in the short-answer condition (compared with the multiple-choice condition) in the first experiment. Providing feedback (in the second experiment) allowed the students to correct any mistakes that they had made in the short-answer condition. Perhaps more interestingly, feedback can also help to strengthen correct responses, especially those made with low confidence on the initial test (Butler *et al.*, 2007, 2008).

Providing feedback is also important for multiple-choice tests, because when students take a multiple-choice test they are presented with a stem and several incorrect completions or answers along with one correct answer. The problem is that just reading (and definitely selecting) an incorrect lure can lead students to think that the response is correct, even if it is not. Roediger and Marsh (2005) showed that when students selected an erroneous response on a multiple-choice test and were later retested with a short-answer test, they often gave the incorrect response from the multiple-choice test, even though they were instructed to respond only if they were sure that their answer was correct. Furthermore, presenting additional lures on a multiple-choice test can decrease the size of a testing effect if performance is low (Butler *et al.*, 2006). Fortunately, providing feedback can ameliorate any negative effects of misleading lures, decreasing the likelihood that a wrongly endorsed lure will be reproduced on a later test (Butler & Roediger, 2008; see also Butler *et al.*, 2006; Marsh *et al.*, 2007).

Feedback can take many different shapes and forms (for a review, see Bangert-Drowns *et al.*, 1991). For example, verification feedback consists of telling the student whether their response was "right" or "wrong", whereas answer feedback provides the student with the correct answer after they have responded. Several studies have shown that, in general, simply telling students whether they are right or wrong leads to performance comparable to that observed when no feedback is provided (Fazio *et al.*, 2010; Pashler *et al.*, 2005; but for a discussion of how verification feedback can help with multiple-choice tests, see Marsh *et al.*,

2012). Thus, in general, feedback should at the very minimum involve providing students with the correct response.

Curiously, providing *more* information in a feedback message, such as explaining why an answer is correct, may or may not be helpful. Bangert-Drowns *et al.* (1991) conducted a meta-analysis and concluded that explanatory feedback did not provide any benefits over correct answer feedback. However, more recent research by Butler and colleagues has indicated that explanatory or elaborative feedback can be more effective than correct answer feedback *if* the final test includes inference or transfer questions (where students have to use knowledge in a new way). Butler *et al.* (2013) asked subjects to read a non-fiction text and then take a short-answer quiz in which they answered questions about the reading. After answering each question, students received either no feedback, correct answer feedback (where they were presented with the correct answer), or explanation feedback (where they received the correct answer along with more details about why that answer was correct). Two days later the students returned to take a final test in which half of the questions were repeated from the initial test and the other half required the students to make inferences based on knowledge that they had acquired from readings. The latter questions required students to extrapolate their knowledge. The results, shown in Figure 6.2, indicated that for the repeated questions the correct answer and explanation feedback conditions led to similar

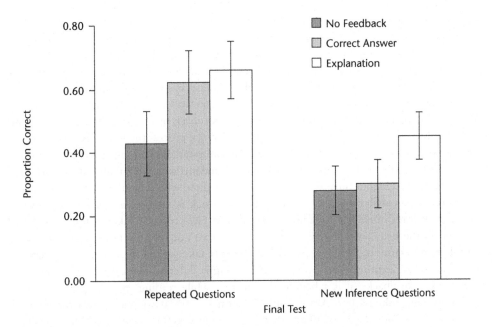

FIGURE 6.2 The results of Experiment 1 by Butler *et al.* (2013), Participants took an initial test with no feedback, correct-answer feedback, or explanation feedback. Performance on the final test (shown here) suggested that explanation feedback enhanced performance for inference questions compared with correct-answer feedback and the no-feedback condition. For the repeated questions, both correct-answer feedback and explanation feedback enhanced performance. Error bars are 95% confidence intervals estimated from Butler *et al.* (2013).

Source: © 2012 American Psychological Association. Adapted with permission.

recall on the final test, and that both led to better performance than the no feedback condition. In contrast, for the inference questions, only the explanatory feedback condition led to increased performance; recall on the final test was similar in the no feedback and correct answer conditions. Thus these results indicate that simple correct answer feedback is sufficient to improve performance when the final test questions are repeated from early tests, but that explanatory feedback can provide additional benefits to learning if the final test requires the making of new inferences.

When should feedback be provided? Early research on this question was murky (for a meta-analysis, see Kulik & Kulik, 1988). One view, grounded in behaviorist schools of thought, is that feedback should be provided as soon as possible after learning in order to reinforce correct responses and remediate incorrect ones. More recent research, however, has consistently shown that delaying feedback (by either a few seconds, minutes, or days) can be more effective than providing feedback immediately. For example, Mullet *et al.* (2014) conducted an experiment in a college engineering course in which students completed practice homework assignments throughout the semester. Sometimes students received feedback immediately after they had submitted their assignments, and sometimes they received feedback a week later. In two experiments, performance on the final course exam was better when students received delayed feedback than when they received immediate feedback. Mullet *et al.* suggested that the delayed feedback was more effective in promoting learning because it created a spacing effect. Another possible explanation was that the delay between the initial test and the presentation of feedback would allow the students to forget any incorrect responses, which would reduce interference with learning the correct response. Other research (Butler & Roediger, 2008; Metcalfe *et al.*, 2009) has provided further support for the view that delayed feedback is more effective than immediate feedback.

One caveat with regard to delayed feedback is that students must actually attend to the feedback in order to benefit from it. With delayed feedback there is the chance that students may simply look at their score on an assignment and not process the feedback related to any particular question. Mullet *et al.* (2014) required some students to look at feedback in order to receive credit for their assignments, and indeed students who were required to look at the feedback showed higher final test performance than those who were not required to do so.

Finally, one concept related to testing and feedback is test potentiation—the idea that people will learn more from reading a text if they have recently taken a test on material covered in the text, compared with people who have not recently taken such a test (e.g. Arnold & McDermott, 2013b; Izawa, 1966). That is, taking a test on material potentiates or increases future learning. Test-potentiated learning is different from the direct benefits of testing or of feedback—it is a benefit that accrues while reading something as a result of having recently taken a test. Arnold and McDermott (2013a) conducted an experiment in which students studied a set of 40 line drawings of objects before taking a final free recall test (writing down the names of the drawings). They were assigned to one of four conditions, with each group doing a different combination of practice tests and restudying before the final recall test. The experiment was a 2×2 between-subjects design: students took either no practice tests or three practice tests on the drawings, and they either restudied or did not restudy before the final test. All of the practice tests were free recall, and did not include feedback. The results (see Figure 6.3) showed a main effect of practice testing (more tests led to higher levels of recall on the final test), a main effect of restudying (restudying boosted recall on the final test), and, critically, a significant interaction. The interaction suggested that

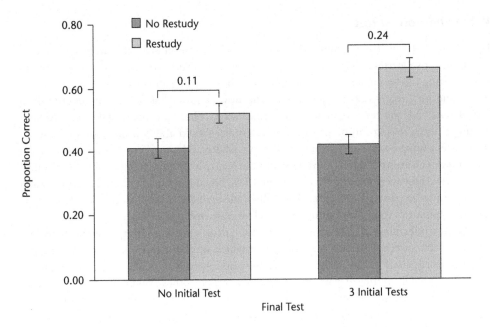

FIGURE 6.3 The results of Experiment 1 by Arnold and McDermott (2013a), showing the proportion recalled on the final test as a function of the number of previous tests and the restudy condition. Restudying after taking three tests led to a significantly better improvement than restudying after taking no initial tests. Error bars represent standard error of the means and are estimated from the original figure.

Source: © 2012 Psychonomic Society. Reprinted with permission.

students learned more from the restudy session after taking three practice tests than if they had not taken the practice tests. In other words, taking practice tests potentiated the students' ability to learn during the restudy phase.

Arnold and McDermott (2013a) suggested that test potentiation may occur because taking tests can lead to increased organization (Zaromb & Roediger, 2010), which helps people to learn more when they are restudying. However, taking a test can also have other positive effects on future studying. For example, Soderstrom and Bjork (2014) showed that students made better study decisions after taking a test, as they spent more time studying difficult word pairs compared with easy word pairs, and were more likely to study items that they had missed on the practice test. So testing helps to improve metacognition—students can learn what they know and what they don't know, and use that knowledge to guide their future studying.

To summarize, feedback is a valuable tool for use with retrieval-based learning. Feedback can help to correct mistakes and reinforce low-confidence accurate responses. At the very minimum, feedback should include the correct answer, but providing more detailed feedback can be helpful when the final test requires students to transfer knowledge. Finally, taking a test can help students to learn more from their next study session through test potentiation.

When and How to Test

By now we hope we have convinced you that tests (or retrieval practice) can be an effective way to improve learning. The next two sections in this chapter address some of the ways in which testing can be implemented, examining both the timing and dosage of tests (i.e. when to test and how many tests to administer), and how retrieval practice can be used both in formal tests and quizzes and in more informal ways. There are many different questions relating to how testing can be implemented, and we should also consider issues relating to differences among people (e.g. young children vs. adults) and topics (e.g. multiplication tables vs. history or chemistry). These considerations can lead to a dizzying number of combinations. Fortunately, however, research has revealed a few broad principles of test implementation that appear to be generally positive. We shall consider research that has documented several specific approaches to implementing tests in classroom environments.

The first principle is that more testing is better than less testing. Karpicke and Roediger (2008), for instance, reported an experiment in which students were asked to learn foreign-language word pairs. First the students learned the pairs relatively well. Then in some conditions students repeatedly retrieved pairs via testing, whereas in other conditions they repeatedly studied pairs. The results showed that after a 1-week delay, recall for the pairs that had been repeatedly retrieved was much better (80%) than recall for the pairs that had been repeatedly studied after being retrieved once (around 35%). Retrieving something on multiple occasions is much more effective than retrieving it once (see also Pyc & Rawson, 2009).

A second principle is that if an item or concept is going to be retrieved on multiple occasions, it is generally more effective if the retrieval practice is spaced apart in time, rather than being massed together (e.g. Pyc & Rawson, 2009). Massing tests will often lead to good performance on a test that occurs immediately after studying, but if there is a longer delay between studying and the final test, spacing practice tests apart will lead to better performance (another example of a desirable difficulty; Bjork, 1994). One extensively researched question concerns which schedules of spacing are most effective—that is, whether it is better for retrieval practice attempts to be spaced equally apart over time, or whether they should start immediately after study, and then occur less and less frequently over time (i.e. an expanding schedule). In general, most research suggests that expanding and equally spaced schedules are of similar effectiveness (Karpicke & Roediger, 2007; Logan & Balota, 2008; Kang et al., 2014). In summary, more tests are better than fewer tests, and when multiple tests are administered, those tests should be spaced apart in time.

Memory researchers have also documented specific approaches to using retrieval practice in the classroom. One effective strategy is called the PUREMEM technique (Lyle & Crawford, 2011). This approach involved students taking a short quiz (5 to 10 minutes) at the end of every class, which covered content from that day's lecture (rather than the readings). Questions were displayed on PowerPoint slides and students wrote their answers on a sheet of paper (a clicker system or handing out paper quizzes would probably be equally effective). The course instructor reviewed the quiz at the start of the next day's class, and this provided an additional opportunity to learn the material. Overall, the quizzes accounted for 8% of each student's grade in the course, so the students took them seriously, but without having any individual quiz count for too much of their grade. The final tests consisted of four non-cumulative exams throughout the semester. As the PUREMEM quizzes targeted the most important content from the courses, questions from the quizzes did appear on the exams, but never as an exact repetition. Students in the PUREMEM classes scored an average of 86% in the exams, whereas students in control classes scored an average of 78% in the exams. Clearly, the quizzes were beneficial, although it is unclear whether the effect is a direct function of retrieval practice, or an indirect one (perhaps students studied more before each class and paid more attention when they knew that they would be quizzed every day). Other research has shown that practice quizzes can be effective even if they occur only weekly (McDaniel *et al.*, 2007).

Taking daily quizzes has been shown to have other benefits in addition to enhancing final test performance. Lyle and Crawford (2011) had students take a survey at the end of the course. Students in the PUREMEM class reported that the quizzing technique helped them to learn in a variety of ways—it allowed them to practice questions, encouraged them to come to class, and motivated them to pay attention in class. Thus the use of daily quizzes may have helped the students to realize the mnemonic benefits of testing.

Quizzing does not have to happen at the end of class. Leeming (2002) reported success with the use of quizzes at the start of class, whereas another approach is to include quizzes throughout a lecture. Szpunar *et al.* (2013) conducted an experiment in which students were asked to watch a 21-minute online lecture video about statistics. One group of participants took three 2-minute quizzes that were equally spaced throughout the lecture, whereas a second group of subjects did unrelated math problems instead of taking the quizzes. Performance on the cumulative final was better in the testing group than in the control group. In addition, students in the testing group took more notes, reported less mind wandering, and reported experiencing less anxiety when going into the final exam. The findings of a subsequent study (Szpunar *et al.*, 2014) suggested that taking the interpolated quizzes led to better metacognitive monitoring—students were more accurate in their predictions of their future test performance after taking a test. Thus the inclusions of short quizzes during a lecture can improve later test performance, encourage students to pay attention in class, and improve metacognition. The optimum spacing of such quizzes still needs to be clarified. Schacter and Szpunar (2015) have provided a teacher-friendly review of many of these issues.

Finally, we shall end this section by encouraging the use of cumulative tests. Although students typically dislike cumulative exams, testing material from the entire semester provides an opportunity for spaced retrieval practice. Carpenter *et al.* (2012) have recommended that in addition to final exams being cumulative, unit tests should be cumulative throughout the semester. Not only does this provide spaced retrieval practice, but also students who know that they will be taking a cumulative exam will study material from the entire course before each test. Using such exams will make it more likely that students will remember course content beyond the current semester. The aim of education is (or should be) for long-term learning to occur, rather than just "getting through the test on Friday."

Formal and Informal Testing

Retrieval practice can work with any activity that requires students to retrieve information from memory. Although formal tests and quizzes in the classroom have provided one of the most straightforward ways to implement retrieval-based learning, retrieval practice can also be used in more informal ways. In both the PUREMEM approach described above (Lyle & Crawford, 2011) and the experiments conducted by Szpunar *et al.* (2014), the main goal of the quizzes is not to evaluate students, but rather to increase classroom engagement and encourage learning. Retrieval practice can also be effective when it is integrated into classroom assignments and discussion.

One recent study (Lindsey *et al.*, 2014) had eighth-grade Spanish students use a computerized review system during class time. The computer program cued students with an English word or phrase and asked them to recall the Spanish translation. Whether or not they were correct, students saw feedback. The students used this computerized flashcard system each week to study material from 10 different chapters over the semester. Some of the material was studied in a massed fashion (in which students only studied material from the current week), some of the material was studied in a generic spaced fashion (in which students studied a combination of material from the current and previous weeks), and finally some of the material was presented in a personalized spaced fashion (a computer algorithm selected specific items for students to study based on the item difficulty, the student's ability, and how often the student had seen the item before). In a cumulative final exam, the material that was studied with the personalized review led to the best performance (73%), followed by the generic spaced schedule (67%), and the worst performance (although not by much) was for the massed study condition (65%). As the authors noted, this finding is striking, in view of the fact that the manipulation only required 30 minutes of time per week (about 10% of the time for which students were engaged with the material overall), and students were free to spend as much time as they wished studying, paying attention in class, and doing additional reading. Despite the lack of a non-tested control condition, these results suggest that retrieval practice can be effective when used as a classroom activity, rather than a formal quiz.

Another simple way to use informal retrieval practice in the classroom is to ask students questions. Obviously most teachers present questions to their class every day, but with a little prior thought they can ask questions in a way that promotes retrieval practice for all of their students. Previous research suggests that people can derive benefit from retrieval practice even if they only *think* about the answer to a question—writing the answer down or saying it aloud is not necessary (Putnam & Roediger, 2013; Smith *et al.*, 2013). So how can a teacher ask questions in a way that encourages students to covertly answer them? One approach promoted by Pashler (personal communication, 24 September 2013) is called the "On the Hook" procedure. In this approach, each student in the class has their name written on a Popsicle stick, which is kept in a coffee can. The teacher asks the class a question and allows a few moments for everyone to think of an answer. Then, instead of calling on a student who has their hand raised, the teacher pulls a stick at random from the coffee can and asks that student to answer the question. Thus every student has a chance to covertly answer the question, and is motivated to do so because they know that they might be called upon to answer the question aloud in front of the class. Pashler reported that this technique is effective, and in at least one case it has been adopted by an entire school with huge success.

Retrieval Practice as a Study Strategy

Students can also use retrieval practice when they are studying. Unfortunately, survey studies suggest that students of many different ages report using and preferring relatively ineffective study strategies, such as highlighting or rereading, rather than using effective strategies such as retrieval practice and spaced study (Agarwal *et al.*, 2014; Hartwig & Dunlosky, 2012;

Karpicke *et al.*, 2009; Kornell & Bjork, 2007). Here we highlight some of the ways in which students can use retrieval practice in their own study routines.

First, students may already use retrieval practice with flash cards (Kornell & Bjork, 2008). When these are used correctly, students should look at the cue on one side of the card and attempt to recall the answer before looking at the other side of the card for feedback. In other words, they are practicing covert retrieval. One important idea to note here is that most students stop studying too soon—they remove a card from the stack once they have recalled it correctly once (Karpicke, 2009; see also Kornell & Bjork, 2007, 2008). As discussed throughout this chapter, students often have a poor understanding of their own learning. Therefore they should be encouraged to successfully retrieve information more than they think is necessary. Rawson and Dunlosky (2012) recommend recalling an item three times during initial learning, and then learning it again during three future study sessions.

Second, with some foresight students can turn other activities into opportunities for retrieval practice. For example, students are sometimes asked to create concept maps, where they use circles and lines to portray diagrammatically the relationships between different ideas (Novak, 1990). The creation of concept maps is often touted as an effective study strategy, and it does force students to think about the meaning of material and the relationships between concepts. However, Karpicke and Blunt (2011) showed that creation of concept maps was less effective than straightforward retrieval practice, where students are simply asked to recall everything they can remember from a chapter. Fortunately, a simple shift in procedure can turn concept mapping into a relatively effective study aid. Rather than creating a concept map while looking at a textbook, students should attempt to create concept maps from memory, and then consult the textbook after they have finished a first draft of the map. In this way, creating the concept map becomes a form of retrieval practice, and rereading the text after doing so may lead to test-potentiated learning. Blunt and Karpicke (2014) conducted an experiment in which they had students read a text and then recall information either by writing a paragraph about what they had learned (the standard approach to retrieval practice), or by creating a concept map from memory. No feedback was provided in either condition. The results showed that both conditions led to similar positive effects on a delayed test.

Finally, students can use various forms of retrieval practice to improve their recall of text materials. In one system, called the Read–Recite–Review strategy (or 3R strategy), students are asked first to read the chapter, then to take a few minutes to recall aloud everything they can remember, and then to re-skim the chapter to evaluate how well they did. This strategy enhances learning as assessed on both immediate and delayed free recall tests, compared with simply rereading or taking notes, and with some types of materials it can enhance performance on multiple-choice tests as well (McDaniel *et al.*, 2009). Given that rereading is a favorite study strategy of students (Karpicke *et al.*, 2009), the 3R strategy might be an important and useful technique for them to know.

In summary, students do not have to rely on their teachers to formally quiz or test them in order to derive benefits from retrieval practice, as they can also use such techniques in their own study sessions.

Indirect Benefits

So far the discussion has primarily focused on the direct memorial benefits of testing—retrieving something from memory aids learning. However, frequent testing or quizzing can have additional side effects. We have already considered a few examples, such as how interspersing quizzes throughout a lecture can enhance attention and reduce mind wandering (Szpunar *et al.*, 2014), or how cumulative exams can encourage students to study material from the entire semester before each test (Carpenter *et al.*, 2012). Roediger *et al.* (2011b) explored ten different benefits of testing (see Table 6.1). The first benefit was the direct benefit, and the other nine benefits were positive side effects that can occur after using frequent, low-stakes quizzes in the classroom, such as the fact that testing can help students to transfer knowledge to new situations. Here we highlight two of the benefits covered by Roediger *et al.* (2011b), and describe an additional indirect benefit.

One benefit, already noted earlier, is that testing improves metacognition and allows students to identify gaps in their own knowledge. As discussed in the introduction, students have a tendency to reread material rather than test themselves, both because rereading seems easier than quizzing oneself, and because rereading can lead to increased feelings of fluency, or knowing (Karpicke *et al.*, 2009). This can be dangerous, because students will often report being more confident about having learned something after repeatedly reading, even though such confidence is unwarranted (e.g. Roediger & Karpicke, 2006a). For this reason, practice tests are important—students will realize what they know and what they do not know, and will update their predictions of their performance appropriately. For example, Szpunar *et al.* (2014) showed that taking one quiz lowered students' expectations of their future performance to match their actual future performance, whereas taking three tests raised their performance on future tests to match their initially overly confident estimates. Other research has shown that, after taking a quiz, students spend more time studying material that they initially answered incorrectly (Son & Kornell, 2008), and also that they spend more time studying more difficult material (Soderstrom & Bjork, 2014). Although students tend not to use self-testing while studying, Kornell and Bjork (2007) reported a survey which suggested that when students did test themselves, 68% of the time it was in order to measure what they had learned (they did not seem to know about the direct benefit of retrieval practice). Thus using frequent tests and quizzes in the classroom can help students to identify what material they know and what they do not know, as well as help them to make more accurate predictions about the state of their own learning.

TABLE 6.1 The ten benefits of testing listed by Roediger *et al.* (2011b). Benefit 1 refers to the direct benefit of testing, whereas Benefits 2–10 refer to positive indirect benefits of testing.

Benefit 1	The testing effect: retrieval aids later retention.
Benefit 2	Testing identifies gaps in knowledge.
Benefit 3	Testing causes students to learn more from the next learning episode.
Benefit 4	Testing produces better organization of knowledge.
Benefit 5	Testing improves transfer of knowledge to new contexts.
Benefit 6	Testing can facilitate retrieval of information that was not tested.
Benefit 7	Testing improves metacognitive monitoring.
Benefit 8	Testing prevents interference from previous material when learning new material.
Benefit 9	Testing provides feedback to instructors.
Benefit 10	Frequent testing encourages students to study.

Source: Roediger *et al.* (2011b). Reprinted with permission.

A second important benefit of frequent classroom quizzing is that it encourages students to study more often. As you might know from your own experience and that of friends, most students report that they do the majority of their studying the night or day before an exam (Mawhinney *et al.*, 1971). Agarwal *et al.* (2014) surveyed middle-school and high-school students about their study habits in different classes. Critically, in some of the classes students were participating in experiments where retrieval practice was integrated within the course (e.g. McDermott *et al.*, 2014). The results of the survey showed that across all grade levels and topics, students studied for approximately 19 minutes per week outside of class when there was no test scheduled for that week, but they studied for 43 minutes per week outside of class when a test was scheduled. Thus, not surprisingly, integrating daily or weekly quizzes into a class can encourage students to study more often and more consistently throughout the semester.

One additional indirect benefit of testing which was not listed by Roediger *et al.* (2011b) is that frequent classroom testing can reduce test anxiety. Agarwal *et al.* (2014) had students complete a survey at the end of the year, in which they answered several questions about testing and taking clicker quizzes in class. All of the students were included in at least one classroom study that used retrieval practice (e.g. McDermott *et al.*, 2014). The most salient finding was that 72% of the 1,408 middle-school and high-school students reported that taking the practice tests made them less anxious about unit exams, whereas 22% said that they were equally anxious, and only 6% said that they were more anxious. Thus, in contrast to the assumption that quizzing students more often may increase test anxiety, these results suggested that frequent quizzing actually reduces test anxiety, either by giving students more practice in taking tests, or by helping them to learn the material better.

In summary, including frequent low-stakes quizzes can have a variety of benefits in the classroom. In addition to the direct memorial benefits of retrieval practice, frequent quizzes can enhance students' metacognition of their own learning, encourage them to study more, and decrease test anxiety.

Distributed Practice and Spacing

One lesson is typically insufficient to create learning that lasts over time. Therefore repetition is a necessity in education, and so the issue of *when* students should restudy is central to instruction. When students study material more than once (or when a teacher reviews material), the timing of the subsequent learning sessions is important. When a student reviews a critical section of a textbook, should it be soon after the first reading, or should she wait a week? When a teacher plans review sessions to prepare his students for the final exam, should the review of a topic be included at the end of the lesson for that topic, or should he spend time today reviewing material covered a month ago? A century of research (Ebbinghaus, 1885/1964) suggests that students should space their repetitions of learning over time, and that longer spacing gaps are more effective than shorter ones. Distributing practice over time enhances learning. Below we review research on distributed practice, focusing primarily on research conducted with educationally relevant materials, learners, settings, and time scales.

What is the Spacing Effect?

Repeated sessions of study spaced over time lead to more effective learning than repetitions that occur back to back. This finding is referred to as the spacing effect or the distributed practice effect (Cepeda *et al.*, 2006). The term lag, or spacing gap, refers to the amount of time (or sometimes the number of other episodes) that elapses between two episodes of learning a piece of information. Repetitions with a lag of zero constitute massed practice (back to back), whereas distributed (or spaced) practice includes any lag greater than zero. For example, a student learning vocabulary might choose to repeat a word-definition pair in massed fashion (e.g. "paucity–shortage", "paucity–shortage", "paucity–shortage"). Alternatively, he could use a spaced practice schedule, by studying this pair with other vocabulary pairs between repetitions (e.g. "paucity–shortage", "loggia–balcony", "sobriquet–nickname", "paucity–shortage"). This constitutes within-session spacing (e.g. Dempster, 1987). Another option would be to study the vocabulary pair(s) across many days (e.g. once a day on Monday, Wednesday, and Friday). This constitutes between-session spacing (Küpper-Tetzel, 2014). In this example, both types of spacing (within-session and between-session) would lead to better long-term learning than massed practice. Researchers sometimes distinguish the spacing effect, which suggests that distributed practice is more effective than massed practice, from the lag effect, which suggests that longer lags between repetitions promote more durable learning than shorter lags (Crowder, 1976). However, for the purposes of this review we shall use the terms "distributed practice" and "spacing" to describe all variations of these basic findings.

The simplest design for evaluating distributed learning is shown in Figure 6.4, and includes (1) initial learning, (2) relearning, (3) a lag between the two learning sessions, (4) a final test, and (5) a retention interval between relearning and the final test. Note that the overall amount of time spent studying is equated across conditions, so any differences in performance on the final test must be due to the *distribution of time* spent studying, rather than to the *amount of time* spent studying. The key manipulation in this type of experiment is that of the spacing gap (i.e. the lag between the two learning trials), but as we shall see later, the length of the final retention interval is also important.

As noted earlier, spacing can be manipulated within sessions or between sessions (Küpper-Tetzel, 2014). Within-session spacing occurs when the lag between items in a series is manipulated by inserting other items between repetitions. Thus, in the within-session paradigm, spacing occurs on timescales ranging from seconds to minutes. One specific method that induces within-session spacing is called interleaving (Rohrer, 2009), which consists of mixing up practice with related types of materials. Practice problems in mathemematics textbooks are often *not* interleaved—students typically practice a block of problems about one topic (e.g. calculating the volume of a spheroid), and then in another

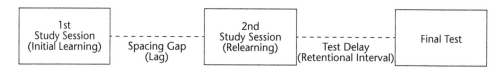

FIGURE 6.4 Design of a typical spacing experiment. Participants study information in two sessions that are separated by an interval ranging from zero (massed practice) up to years (but typically shorter than that). This interval is referred to here as the spacing gap (or lag). Participants are finally tested after what is referred to as a test delay (or retention interval). The spacing gap is typically manipulated, and the retention interval is manipulated in some (but not all) studies.

section practice a block of problems about a different topic (e.g. calculating the volume of a spherical cone). In an interleaved schedule, different kinds of problems would be mixed together (e.g. students might calculate the volume of a spheroid, then a half cone, then a wedge). Although blocked practice is common in education, it may be less effective than interleaving. Rohrer and Taylor (2007) demonstrated this by showing that interleaving practice problems led to better performance on a final mathematics test (63%) than blocked practice (20%), even when the test occurred after a 1-week delay. Despite the fact that students often report feeling that massed practice is more effective than interleaving, the benefits of interleaving have been shown in many domains (see Rohrer, 2009; see also Chapter 5 in this volume).

In contrast to within-session spacing, between-session spacing occurs when material is studied in one session and then covered again in a second session. The lag between the sessions is filled with something completely unrelated to the target material (e.g. taking a nap, working on a different class, or simply doing nothing), and can be as short as a few minutes between lists or as long as a few years (Bahrick *et al.*, 1993). Both within-session and between-session spacing can enhance learning compared with massed practice.

The Benefits of Distributed Practice

Although the advantage of distributed practice over massed practice has been demonstrated most commonly on retention tests involving college-aged students learning discrete verbal materials, many studies have extended the effect beyond these basic conditions. The spacing effect has been shown to occur in many different animal species and at nearly every stage of human development. It has also been demonstrated with a wide range of learning materials and across multiple measures of learning (for an in-depth review of the breadth of the spacing effect, see Gerbier and Toppino, 2015). Although researchers are still debating why exactly the spacing effect occurs (for reviews, see Delaney *et al.*, 2010; Hintzman, 1974), the robustness of the effect makes it a prime candidate for educational applications.

One notable boundary condition for the spacing effect is that massed study can sometimes be more effective than spacing when the final test occurs immediately after the last study session. Balota *et al.* (1989) reported an experiment in which subjects took a test either immediately after a second presentation of a paired associate or after a delay. With the immediate test, massing led to better recall than spacing, but with the delayed test, spacing led to better recall than massing. Although this finding is an important boundary condition of the spacing effect, in educational scenarios students are rarely tested immediately after study.

Spacing Makes It Stick

Having reviewed the basic research on the spacing effect, we shall now examine research that has used educationally relevant materials and studies conducted in real classrooms.

Translational Laboratory Research

Many investigators have recently begun exploring spacing effects with educationally realistic materials. Fortunately, the results generally corroborate basic research in showing advantages for distributed learning. There are many studies like this, but here we highlight two which show that spacing can enhance multiple forms of learning.

The first, by Gluckman *et al.* (2014), is a laboratory study of elementary school students that examined whether spaced practice would enhance both their memory and their ability to generalize science concepts to new domains. The experimenters presented first- and second-grade children with four lessons about food chains. Each lesson covered a different biome (grasslands, arctic, ocean, and swamp), but key concepts were repeated across lessons (e.g. the definition of a predator). The children either completed all four lessons in a single day (the massed condition) or received one lesson on each of four consecutive days (the spaced condition). One week after the last lesson, the students took a final test that assessed memory for facts (e.g. what a carnivore eats), simple generalization (e.g. larger animals typically eat smaller animals), and complex generalization (e.g. animals in a food chain are dependent on one another for food and survival). Critically, the memory questions corresponded directly to facts that the students learned in the lessons, whereas the generalizations (both simple and complex) were taught with one set of animals during the lessons, but tested with a new set of animals from a novel biome (e.g. desert). Figure 6.5 shows performance on the final test, and reveals that the spaced condition led to betterperformance on all three kinds of test than did the massed condition. Thus spacing enhanced both memory and transfer.

In another study using realistic materials, Kapler *et al.* (2015) examined the effects of spaced practice on memory and higher-order learning. They simulated a science class by having introductory psychology students watch a lecture about meteorology in a lecture hall. This design provided more external validity than is typically present in a laboratory, but allowed the researchers to control other variables, such as studying outside of class (the meteorology lecture was excluded from students' grades). After the initial lecture, students completed an online review module 1 day or 8 days later, and then took a final test in class 35 days after the review module. The online review session incorporated testing to capitalize on the benefits of retrieval practice. Critically, the review module and the final test contained both factual questions (in which students simply had to recall a fact) and higher-order questions (in which students had to apply a concept to a new problem). The 8-day spacing gap led to better final test performance than the 1-day spacing gap for both factual questions (54% vs. 47%) and higher-level questions (43% vs. 36%). Thus, in an experiment involving fairly realistic materials, delays, and tests, spacing led to an increase in performance of 7%, or the equivalent of half a letter grade.

Research in Instructional Settings

Spacing effects have also been shown to enhance memory and other forms of learning in real classrooms and in other training environments. For example, Sobel *et al.* (2011) had students in a fifth-grade classroom learn GRE vocabulary words and definitions (e.g. "gregarious: outgoing and social") in two learning sessions that were spaced by either 1 minute (massed condition) or 7 days (spaced condition). Five weeks after the second learning session, students were given the vocabulary words and asked to recall the definitions. Not surprisingly, recall was better after spaced practice (20.8%) than after massed practice (7.5%), demonstrating that middle-school students can benefit from distributed practice in their normal classroom environments (see also Carpenter *et al.*, 2009).

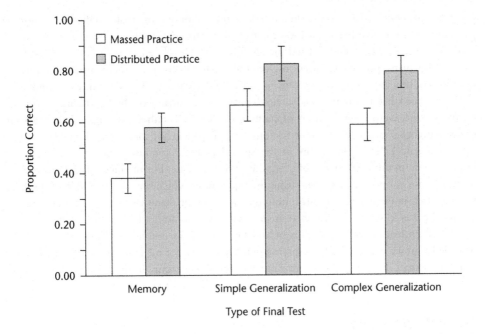

FIGURE 6.5 Performance on the final test in the study by Gluckman *et al.* (2014), expressed as proportion correct on three types of test (memory, simple generalization, and complex generalization), plotted as a function of practice condition (massed practice vs. distributed practice). In this experiment, early elementary school children were taught about food chains in four lessons that were either distributed across 4 days (distributed practice) or took place over the course of 1 day (massed practice). They were then tested 1 week after the last lesson. Distributed practice led to significantly better performance on all three test types. Error bars are standard error of the mean (calculated from Table 1 in the original report; Gluckman *et al.*, 2014, p. 270).

Source: © 2014 John Wiley & Sons Ltd. Adapted with permission.

Moving beyond basic learning, Bird (2011) manipulated the spacing of practice sessions in which students learned English syntax in a college-level second-language learning course for native Malay speakers. Students practiced identifying sentences with syntax errors (e.g. "I have seen that movie with my brother last week"), and were given feedback on their performance in practice sessions that occurred either 3 or 14 days apart. The final test, which was 7 or 60 days later, required students to read novel sentences that were not part of the learning phase and mark whether the sentence used correct syntax. Thus the test required the abstraction of syntactical rules rather than rote memory. When the retention interval was 7 days, the 3-day and 14-day conditions led to similar performance on the final test, but when the retention interval was 60 days, the 14-day condition led to enhanced performance compared with the 3-day condition. Bird's study demonstrated that spaced practice can promote transfer of learning to new material, and that this benefit persists over time.

Finally, researchers have also examined the benefits of distributed practice in training domains outside standard classrooms. Efficient training that leads to durable learning is highly valued in many fields, including medicine and police work, particularly because the skills required in such fields require advanced forms of learning. For example, the Enhanced

Cognitive Interview (ECI) is a police interviewing technique originally crafted by cognitive psychologists to standardize eyewitness interrogation procedures while reducing the influence of interviewer bias and other related pitfalls (Fisher & Geiselman, 1992). The ECI has been adopted by many police organizations, yet there have been some problems with regard to questions of how best to train new officers in the ECI approach. A recent study by Heidt *et al.* (2016) revealed that distributed practice holds promise for teaching the ECI. In their experiment, 60 participants were given 2 hours of training on the ECI, either in a single 2-hour session (massed practice) or in two 1-hour sessions with a spacing gap of 1 week between sessions (spaced practice). The participants in the spaced practice condition showed much greater improvement in multiple aspects of using the ECI technique. For instance, spaced practice led to greater use of open-ended (non-suggestive) questions, which is a core principle of the ECI. In short, the simple change of distributing practice—rather than massing—has the potential to change the way in which eyewitnesses are interviewed by police, which in turn could affect the quality of evidence used in the pursuit and prosecution of criminals. Moulton *et al.* (2006) provided a similar example of how spacing practice sessions for medical students enhanced their ability to learn a difficult and dangerous microsurgical technique. In short, distributed practice enhanced a training program for a complex motor skill that can save lives.

The Optimal Spacing Gap

So far, we have illustrated that spacing typically outperforms massing. But how long should the spacing gap be? Is 5 minutes enough or should learning sessions be spread out as far as possible? A complete answer undoubtedly depends on a variety of factors (e.g. what is being studied, who is studying, how learning will be assessed, etc.). One factor that does appear to be important is how long learning needs to be maintained, or the length of the retention interval between the last study session and the final test. As we noted earlier, one boundary condition of the spacing effect is when the retention interval is very short. Indeed, recent research suggests that an optimal spacing lag depends on the length of the retention interval, and that longer retention intervals require longer spacing gaps (although, as with any rule, there are exceptions).

In what is almost certainly the most comprehensive examination to date of the effects of spacing gaps as assessed after various retention intervals, Cepeda *et al.* (2008) recruited 1,350 people online for a long-term investigation of spacing effects (for a similar laboratory study, see Cepeda *et al.*, 2009). In this experiment, the participants studied a set of obscure but true trivia facts (e.g. "What European nation consumes the most spicy Mexican food?" Answer: "Norway"). The participants then reviewed the trivia facts after lag periods of 0, 1, 2, 4, 7, 11, 14, 21, or 105 days following the initial learning (different groups were given different lag periods). Finally, the participants were tested at retention intervals of 7, 35, 70, or 350 days after the review session. The results are somewhat complex, but two conclusions seem unequivocal. First, non-zero spacing gaps produced better learning than did massed practice—across retention intervals, the optimal gap improved recall performance over the massed condition by 64%. Second, and more relevant for the current discussion, there was a different optimal gap at each retention interval. For example, the optimal spacing gap at the 350-day retention interval was 21 days, whereas at the 7-day retention interval it was only 1 day. Thus the simple conclusion that longer spacing gaps between presentations are always better for performance is wrong. Instead, the optimal spacing gap depends on the length of the retention interval.

Critically, this pattern has also been shown with educationally relevant materials. Rawson and Kintsch (2005) had students read a 1,730-word text from a *Scientific American* article and then reread the text either immediately or after 1 week. The final test took place either 5 minutes after or 2 days after the second learning session, and consisted of both a free recall section and a series of short-answer questions that required the making of inferences and application. Figure 6.6 shows the students' performance on the short-answer questions. At the immediate test (5-minute retention interval) the massed practice condition led to similar performance to that produced by the spacing condition, but at the delayed test (2-day retention interval), spaced practice led to better performance than massed practice. The same pattern occurred in the free recall section of the test. Similar results were reported by Verkoeijen *et al.* (2008), who showed that when the retention interval between the second study session and the final test was 2 days, a spacing gap of 4 days led to better performance than either massed rereading or a spacing gap of 3.5 weeks. Taken together, these studies show first that massed rereading appears to be advantageous only when the test is administered immediately after studying, and second, that spacing gaps that are too long can sometimes be ineffective.

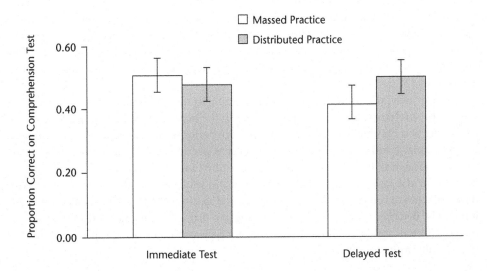

FIGURE 6.6 The results of Experiment 2 by Rawson and Kintsch (2005), showing performance as a proportion of correct scores on a comprehension test consisting of short-answer questions, plotted as a function of practice condition (massed practice vs. distributed practice) and test delay (immediate test vs. delayed test). In this experiment, the participants read a passage of text twice, with the readings separated by a lag of either zero or 1 week, and they were then tested either 5 minutes or 2 days after the second reading. Performance was not significantly different between the practice groups on the immediate test (although it slightly favored massed practice), but spaced practice produced higher comprehension scores on the delayed test. Error bars are standard error of the mean (K. Rawson, personal communication, 25 August 2015).

Source: © 2005 American Psychological Association. Adapted with permission.

Finally, the finding that retention interval influences the optimal spacing gap between presentations has also been demonstrated in a classroom field study (Küpper-Tetzel *et al.*, 2014). German sixth-grade students studied German–English vocabulary in an initial session, and they then studied the same vocabulary terms in a second session either immediately, 1 day later, or 10 days later. The final test took place 7 or 35 days after the second session. In line with the laboratory studies reviewed here, the optimal spacing lag at the short (7-day) retention interval was 1 day, whereas the 1- and 10-day spacing gaps were equally advantageous over the massed practice condition when the retention interval was longer (35 days).

There has now been enough research—in the laboratory and in the classroom—to allow some initial conclusions to be drawn about the relationship between spacing gaps and the retention interval. Clearly, students should avoid massed repetitions, as these appear to be of little or no benefit to long-term retention (in fact, they are sometimes no better than a single exposure to material; e.g. Callender & McDaniel, 2009; Rawson & Kintsch, 2005). Once spacing is introduced, though, a rough guideline is that longer retention intervals generally require longer spacing gaps. However, there is a limit—for any given retention interval, test performance is an inverted U-shaped function such that increasing the spacing gap first increases performance until an optimal lag, after which performance declines with increasing lag periods. Determining an optimal spacing gap for any given setting would require additional research, but the available data suggest that the optimal gap is often 5–40% of the retention interval, and that this ratio gets smaller as the retention interval gets longer. For example, Cepeda *et al.* (2009) found that when the retention interval was 1 week the optimal gap was 14% (1 day), whereas when the retention interval was 1 year the optimal gap was 6% (21 days).

Unfortunately, this makes planning for practical purposes more difficult. Teachers cannot simply plan a relearning session far in the future in the hope that the longest spacing gap will lead to the best possible performance. To optimize performance, the retention interval must be taken into consideration. One way to conceptualize this is that, after a very long delay, sufficient forgetting has occurred for rereading to be functionally equivalent to reading the material for the first time. However, educators and students should be able to work with these estimates to roughly determine what is a good spacing schedule. One final caveat is that it might be better to err on the side of a spacing gap that is too long rather than too short, as the cost (in terms of lowered test performance) of an overlong spacing gap is much smaller than the alternative (Rohrer, 2015).

How to Use Spacing

In summary, the timing of learning sessions can have powerful effects on retention even when the overall time on task is equated. The spacing of repetitions nearly always enhances long-term learning, and longer spacing gaps (but not too long!) typically lead to more durable learning. Empirical research suggests that these effects apply to numerous types of learning, in many environments, with many kinds of students. Here are a few recommendations for using distributed practice in the classroom.

First, instructors can add review sessions at the start of each lesson where they cover key concepts from previous lessons. In many cases, old content can be used to introduce new concepts, perhaps by comparing and contrasting related topics, or by pointing out connections between seemingly unrelated concepts. Class time is obviously limited, so these reviews should be brief and focus on the most important concepts from a lesson. A second strategy that serves a similar purpose without taking up class time is the setting of homework assignments that target both old and new material. In this way students can both practice new concepts and refresh their understanding of old concepts. Third, instructors should keep retention interval in mind when considering when to schedule review sessions. Longer retention intervals require longer spacing gaps (but be careful of overlong gaps). In schooling situations, we suspect that spacing gaps of weeks or months are ideal. Finally, one particularly effective strategy is to pair distributed practice with retrieval practice. As noted earlier, one good way to do this is to administer cumulative (or semi-cumulative) exams. For example, in a psychology research methods course (taught by the second author), each of the five exams conducted during the semester consisted of a mixture of old (20%) and new (80%) content. The final exam covered the entire course. With semi-cumulative exams students are given spaced exposure, get retrieval practice, and are motivated to study lessons from the entire course.

Conclusion

In summary, both retrieval practice and distributed practice are powerful learning tools that can enhance performance in a variety of situations. In reviewing the literature we have attempted to summarize basic research, research with educationally relevant materials, and research conducted in real classrooms. Fortunately, the basic principles discovered in the laboratory appear to translate readily to the classroom. In an effort to continue the translational research cycle, we shall close with a few practical applications of retrieval practice and spacing. In addition to being effective strategies, these suggestions are easy to implement, and require little or no extra equipment or resources.

From the Laboratory to the Classroom

Retrieval Practice

- One of the easiest ways to integrate retrieval practice into a study routine is by using flashcards. Flashcards can be used to remember vocabulary words, definitions, and more. To use flashcards correctly, it is important to attempt to retrieve the answer before turning the card over. In addition, spacing effect research (e.g. Kornell, 2009) suggests that using one larger stack of flashcards is more effective than using several smaller stacks.
- Teach students to use the Read–Recite–Review method (McDaniel *et al.*, 2009) when reading textbooks and other written materials. Briefly, students should read a chapter and then spend a few minutes recalling aloud everything they can remember from the passage (they could also write down their responses). The students should then review the chapter to see what they missed and what they remembered.
- Low-stakes in-class quizzes are an effective way to boost grades in a course (Lyle & Crawford, 2011). Quizzes can be given at the beginning or end of class, and can be administered with a clicker system or using pencil and paper. The quizzes should not represent a large proportion of a student's grade, but should be worth a few points so that

students take them seriously. Daily quizzes can directly improve memory for the tested material, and will encourage students to keep up with the reading and to ask questions in class. Reviewing the quizzes at the start of the next class session builds in a spaced presentation of the material.

- Instructors can use the "on the hook" method to encourage covert retrieval practice in their classrooms. Each student's name is written on a Popsicle stick and put in a coffee can. When the teacher asks a question she poses it to the whole class, waits a few seconds, and then draws a name from the coffee can and asks that student to answer the question. This structure means that most students will covertly retrieve an answer so that they can respond if called upon to do so.
- Finally, instructors can take advantage of technology to integrate short quizzes into material presented online. Short quizzes inserted in a lecture video posted online can reduce mind wandering and reduce the amount of anxiety that students feel about a final exam (Szpunar et al., 2013). Alternatively, instructors could post short online quizzes (perhaps via a course management system such as Blackboard or Moodle) that tests material from both readings and class lectures.

Distributed (Spaced) Practice

- Instructors can provide brief reviews of previously covered content at the start of each new lecture. Although it may be somewhat useful to briefly remind students of the most recent material (e.g. reviewing Monday's content on Tuesday), the biggest pay-offs will come from delaying in-lecture review by a week or more, when long-term retention is the instructional goal.
- Instructors can create homework assignments that require review of previously covered content. Ideally, old and new topics should be mixed together.
- When creating a distributed practice schedule, instructors should consider how long they want students to retain the information. As a rough rule, longer spacing intervals increase the duration of retention. However, spacing intervals can be too long. As quick (but somewhat rough) guidelines, here are some suggested spacing intervals for a few retention intervals:
  - One-day spacing is good for 1 week of retention.
  - One-week spacing is good for 2 months of retention.
  - One-month spacing is good for 1 year of retention.
- Many of the methods we suggest for retrieval practice can (and should) be implemented on a distributed schedule. For example, low-stakes quizzes at the start of a lesson can act as a form of spaced retrieval of important topics from previous lessons. Cumulative exams also provide spaced retrieval practice.

References

Abbott, E. E. (1909). On the analysis of the factors of recall in the learning process. *Psychological Monographs*, 11, 159–177.

Agarwal, P. K., Karpicke, J. D., Kang, S. H. K., Roediger, H. L., & McDermott, K. B. (2008). Examining the testing effect with open- and closed-book tests. *Applied Cognitive Psychology*, 22, 861–876.

Agarwal, P. K., D'Antonio, L., Roediger, H. L., McDermott, K. B., & McDaniel, M. A. (2014). Classroom-based programs of retrieval practice reduce middle school and high school students' test anxiety. *Journal of Applied Research in Memory and Cognition*, 3, 131–139.

Arnold, K. M. & McDermott, K. B. (2013a). Free recall enhances subsequent learning. *Psychonomic Bulletin & Review*, 20, 507–513.

Arnold, K. M. & McDermott, K. B. (2013b). Test-potentiated learning: distinguishing between direct and indirect effects of tests. *Journal of Experimental Psychology: Learning, Memory, and Cognition*, 39, 940–945.

Bahrick, H. P., Bahrick, L. E., Bahrick, A. S., & Bahrick, P. E. (1993). Maintenance of foreign language vocabulary and the spacing effect. *Psychological Science*, 4, 316–321.

Balota, D. A., Duchek, J. M., & Paullin, R. (1989). Age-related differences in the impact of spacing, lag, and retention interval. *Psychology and Aging*, 4, 3–9.

Bangert-Drowns, R. L., Kulik, C. C., Kulik, J. A., & Morgan, M. T. (1991). The instructional effect of feedback in test-like events. *Review of Educational Research*, 61, 213–238.

Bird, S. (2011). Effects of distributed practice on the acquisition of second language English syntax. *Applied Psycholinguistics*, 32, 435–452.

Bjork, R. A. (1994). Memory and metamemory considerations in the training of human beings. In: J. Metcalfe & A. P. Shimamura (Eds), *Metacognition: Knowing About Knowing* (pp. 185–205). Cambridge, MA: MIT Press.

Blunt, J. R. & Karpicke, J. D. (2014). Learning with retrieval-based concept mapping. *Journal of Educational Psychology*, 106, 849–858.

Brown, P.C., Roediger, H. L., & McDaniel, M. A. (2014). *Make It Stick: The Science of Successful Learning*. Cambridge, MA: Harvard University Press.

Butler, A. C. & Roediger, H. L. (2007). Testing improves long-term retention in a simulated classroom setting. *European Journal of Cognitive Psychology*, 19, 514–527.

Butler, A. C. & Roediger, H. L. (2008). Feedback enhances the positive effects and reduces the negative effects of multiple-choice testing. *Memory & Cognition*, 36, 604–616.

Butler, A. C., Marsh, E. J., Goode, M. K., & Roediger, H. L. (2006). When additional multiple-choice lures aid versus hinder later memory. *Applied Cognitive Psychology*, 20, 941–956.

Butler, A. C., Karpicke, J. D., & Roediger, H. L. (2007). The effect of type and timing of feedback on learning from multiple-choice tests. *Journal of Experimental Psychology: Applied*, 13, 273–281.

Butler, A. C., Karpicke, J. D., & Roediger, H. L. (2008). Correcting a metacognitive error: feedback increases retention of low-confidence correct responses. *Journal of Experimental Psychology: Learning, Memory, and Cognition*, 34, 918–928.

Butler, A. C., Godbole, N., & Marsh, E. J. (2013). Explanation feedback is better than correct answer feedback for promoting transfer of learning. *Journal of Educational Psychology*, 105, 290–298.

Callender, A. A. & McDaniel, M. A. (2009). The limited benefits of rereading educational texts. *Contemporary Educational Psychology*, 34, 30–41.

Carpenter, S. K. (2009). Cue strength as a moderator of the testing effect: the benefits of elaborative retrieval. *Journal of Experimental Psychology: Learning, Memory, and Cognition*, 35, 1563–1569.

Carpenter, S. K., Pashler, H., & Cepeda, N. J. (2009). Using tests to enhance 8th grade students' retention of U.S. history facts. *Applied Cognitive Psychology*, 23, 760–771.

Carpenter, S. K., Cepeda, N. J., Rohrer, D., Kang, S. H. K., & Pashler, H. (2012). Using spacing to enhance diverse forms of learning: review of recent research and implications for instruction. *Educational Psychology Review*, 24, 369–378.

Cepeda, N. J., Pashler, H., Vul, E., Wixted, J. T., & Rohrer, D. (2006). Distributed practice in verbal recall tasks: a review and quantitative synthesis. *Psychological Bulletin*, 132, 354–380.

Cepeda, N. J., Vul, E., Rohrer, D., Wixted, J. T., & Pashler, H. (2008). Spacing effects in learning: a temporal ridgeline of optimal retention. *Psychological Science*, 19, 1095–1102.

Cepeda, N. J., Coburn, N., Rohrer, D., Wixted, J. T., Mozer, M. C., & Pashler, H. (2009). Optimizing distributed practice: theoretical analysis and practical implications. *Experimental Psychology*, 56, 236–246.

Crowder, R. G. (1976). *Principles of Learning and Memory*. Hillsdale, NJ: Lawrence Erlbaum Associates.

Delaney, P. F., Verkoeijen, P. P. J. L., & Spirgel, A. (2010). Spacing and testing effects: a deeply critical, lengthy, and at times discursive review of the literature. In: B. Ross (Ed.), *The Psychology of Learning and Motivation, Volume 53* (pp. 63–148). Burlington, VT: Academic Press.

Dempster, F. N. (1987). Effects of variable encoding and spaced presentations on vocabulary learning. *Journal of Educational Psychology, 79*, 162–170.

Ebbinghaus, H. (1885/1964). *Memory: A Contribution to Experimental Psychology* (translated by H. A. Ruger & G. E. Bussenius, 1913). New York: Dover.

Fazio, L. K., Huelser, B. J., Johnson, A., & Marsh, E. J. (2010). Receiving right/wrong feedback: consequences for learning. *Memory, 18*, 335–350.

Fisher, R. P. & Geiselman, R. E. (1992). *Memory Enhancing Techniques for Investigative Interviewing: The Cognitive Interview*. Springfield, IL: Charles C. Thomas.

Gerbier, E. & Toppino, T. C. (2015). The effect of distributed practice: neuroscience, cognition, and education. *Trends in Neuroscience and Education, 4*, 49–59.

Gluckman, M., Vlach, H. A., & Sandhofer, C. M. (2014). Spacing simultaneously promotes multiple forms of learning in children's science curriculum. *Applied Cognitive Psychology, 28*, 266–273.

Hartwig, M. K. & Dunlosky, J. (2012). Study strategies of college students: are self-testing and scheduling related to achievement? *Psychonomic Bulletin & Review, 19*, 126–134.

Heidt, C. T., Arbuthnott, K. D., & Price, H. L. (2016). The effects of distributed learning on enhanced cognitive interview training. *Psychiatry, Psychology and Law, 23*, 47–61.

Hintzman, D. L. (1974). Theoretical implications of the spacing effect. In: R. L. Solso (Ed.), *Theories in Cognitive Psychology: The Loyola Symposium* (pp. 77–97). Potomac, MD: Lawrence Erlbaum Associates.

Izawa, C. (1966). Reinforcement-test sequences in paired-associate learning. *Psychological Reports, 18*, 879–919.

Kang, S. H. K., McDermott, K. B., & Roediger, H. L. (2007). Test format and corrective feedback modify the effect of testing on long-term retention. *European Journal of Cognitive Psychology, 19*, 528–558.

Kang, S. H. K., Lindsey, R. V., Mozer, M. C., & Pashler, H. (2014). Retrieval practice over the long term: should spacing be expanding or equal-interval? *Psychonomic Bulletin & Review, 21*, 1544–1550.

Kapler, I. V., Weston, T., & Wiseheart, M. (2015). Spacing in a simulated undergraduate classroom: long-term benefits for factual and higher-level learning. *Learning and Instruction, 36*, 38–45.

Karpicke, J. D. (2009). Metacognitive control and strategy selection: deciding to practice retrieval during learning. *Journal of Experimental Psychology: General, 138*, 469–486.

Karpicke, J. D. & Roediger, H. L. (2007). Expanding retrieval practice promotes short-term retention, but equally spaced retrieval enhances long-term retention. *Journal of Experimental Psychology: Learning, Memory, and Cognition, 33*, 704–719.

Karpicke, J. D. & Roediger, H. L. (2008). The critical importance of retrieval for learning. *Science, 319*, 966–968.

Karpicke, J. D. & Blunt, J. R. (2011). Retrieval practice produces more learning than elaborative studying with concept mapping. *Science, 331*, 772–775.

Karpicke, J. D. & Grimaldi, P. J. (2012). Retrieval-based learning: a perspective for enhancing meaningful learning. *Educational Psychology Review, 24*, 401–418.

Karpicke, J. D., Butler, A. C., & Roediger, H. L. (2009). Metacognitive strategies in student learning: do students practise retrieval when they study on their own? *Memory, 17*, 471–479.

Karpicke, J. D., Lehman, M., & Aue, W. R. (2014). Retrieval-based learning: an episodic context account. In: B. H. Ross (Ed.) *The Psychology of Learning and Motivation. Volume 61* (pp. 237–284). San Diego, CA: Elsevier Academic Press.

Kornell, N. (2009). Optimising learning using flashcards: spacing is more effective than cramming. *Applied Cognitive Psychology, 23*, 1297–1317.

Kornell, N. & Bjork, R. A. (2007). The promise and perils of self-regulated study. *Psychonomic Bulletin & Review*, 14, 219–224.

Kornell, N. & Bjork, R. A. (2008). Optimising self-regulated study: the benefits—and costs—of dropping flashcards. *Memory*, 16, 125–136.

Kulik, J. A. & Kulik, C. C. (1988). Timing of feedback and verbal learning. *Review of Educational Research*, 58, 79–97.

Küpper-Tetzel, C. E. (2014). Understanding the distributed practice effect: strong effects on weak theoretical grounds. *Zeitschrift für Psychologie*, 222, 71–81.

Küpper-Tetzel, C. E., Erdfelder, E., & Dickhäuser, O. (2014). The lag effect in secondary school classrooms: enhancing students' memory for vocabulary. *Instructional Science*, 42, 373–388.

Leeming, F. C. (2002). The exam-a-day procedure improves performance in psychology classes. *Teaching of Psychology*, 29, 210–212.

Lindsey, R. V., Shroyer, J. D., Pashler, H., & Mozer, M. C. (2014). Improving students' long-term knowledge retention through personalized review. *Psychological Science*, 25, 639–647.

Little, J. L., Bjork, E. L., Bjork, R. A., & Angello, G. (2012). Multiple-choice tests exonerated, at least of some charges: fostering test-induced learning and avoiding test-induced forgetting. *Psychological Science*, 23, 1337–1344.

Logan, J. M. & Balota, D. A. (2008). Expanded vs. equal interval spaced retrieval practice: exploring different schedules of spacing and retention interval in younger and older adults. *Aging, Neuropsychology, and Cognition*, 15, 257–280.

Lyle, K. B. & Crawford, N. A. (2011). Retrieving essential material at the end of lectures improves performance on statistics exams. *Teaching of Psychology*, 38, 94–97.

McDaniel, M. A., Anderson, J. L., Derbish, M. H., & Morrisette, N. (2007). Testing the testing effect in the classroom. *European Journal of Cognitive Psychology*, 19, 494–513.

McDaniel, M. A., Howard, D. C., & Einstein, G. O. (2009). The read-recite-review study strategy: effective and portable. *Psychological Science*, 20, 516–522.

McDermott, K. B., Agarwal, P. K., D'Antonio, L., Roediger, H. L., & McDaniel, M. A. (2014). Both multiple-choice and short-answer quizzes enhance later exam performance in middle and high school classes. *Journal of Experimental Psychology: Applied*, 20, 3–21.

Marsh, E. J., Roediger, H. L., Bjork, R. A., & Bjork, E. L. (2007). The memorial consequences of multiple-choice testing. *Psychonomic Bulletin & Review*, 14, 194–199.

Marsh, E. J., Lozito, J. P., Umanath, S., Bjork, E. L., & Bjork, R. A. (2012). Using verification feedback to correct errors made on a multiple-choice test. *Memory*, 20, 645–653.

Mawhinney, V. T., Bostow, D. E., Laws, D. R., Blumenfeld, G. J., & Hopkins, B. L. (1971). A comparison of students' studying behavior produced by daily, weekly, and three-week testing schedules. *Journal of Applied Behavior Analysis*, 4, 257–264.

Metcalfe, J., Kornell, N., & Finn, B. (2009). Delayed versus immediate feedback in children's and adults' vocabulary learning. *Memory & Cognition*, 37, 1077–1087.

Moulton, C.-A. E., Dubrowski, A., MacRae, H., Graham, B., Grober, E., & Reznick, R. (2006). Teaching surgical skills: what kind of practice makes perfect? A randomized, controlled trial. *Annals of Surgery*, 244, 400–409.

Mullet, H. G., Butler, A. C., Verdin, B., von Borries, R., & Marsh, E. J. (2014). Delaying feedback promotes transfer of knowledge despite student preferences to receive feedback immediately. *Journal of Applied Research in Memory and Cognition*, 3, 222–229.

Novak, J. D. (1990). Concept mapping: a useful tool for science education. *Journal of Research in Science Teaching*, 27, 937–949.

Pashler, H., Cepeda, N. J., Wixted, J. T., & Rohrer, D. (2005). When does feedback facilitate learning of words? *Journal of Experimental Psychology: Learning, Memory, and Cognition*, 31, 3–8.

Putnam, A. L. & Roediger, H. L. (2013). Does response mode affect amount recalled or the magnitude of the testing effect? *Memory & Cognition*, 41, 36–48.

Pyc, M. A. & Rawson, K. A. (2009). Testing the retrieval effort hypothesis: does greater difficulty correctly recalling information lead to higher levels of memory? *Journal of Memory and Language*, 60, 437–447.

Pyc, M. A. & Rawson, K. A. (2010). Why testing improves memory: mediator effectiveness hypothesis. *Science*, 330, 335.

Rawson, K. A. & Kintsch, W. (2005). Rereading effects depend on time of test. *Journal of Educational Psychology*, 97, 70–80.

Rawson, K. A. & Dunlosky, J. (2012). When is practice testing most effective for improving the durability and efficiency of student learning? *Educational Psychology Review*, 24, 419–435.

Roediger, H. L. (2013). Applying cognitive psychology to education: translational educational science. *Psychological Science in the Public Interest*, 14, 1–3.

Roediger, H. L. & Marsh, E. J. (2005). The positive and negative consequences of multiple-choice testing. *Journal of Experimental Psychology: Learning, Memory, and Cognition*, 31, 1155–1159.

Roediger, H. L. & Karpicke, J. D. (2006a). Test-enhanced learning. *Psychological Science*, 17, 249–255.

Roediger, H. L. & Karpicke, J. D. (2006b). The power of testing memory: basic research and implications for educational practice. *Perspectives on Psychological Science*, 1, 181–210.

Roediger, H. L., Agarwal, P. K., Kang, S. H. K., & Marsh, E. J. (2010). Benefits of testing memory: best practices and boundary conditions. In: G. M. Davies & D. B. Wright (Eds), *Current Issues in Applied Memory Research* (pp. 13–49). Brighton, UK: Psychology Press.

Roediger, H. L., Agarwal, P. K., McDaniel, M. A., & McDermott, K. B. (2011a). Test-enhanced learning in the classroom: long-term improvements from quizzing. *Journal of Experimental Psychology: Applied*, 17, 382–395.

Roediger, H. L., Putnam, A. L., & Smith, M. (2011b). Ten benefits of testing and their applications to educational practice. In: J. Mestre & B. H. Ross (Eds), *Psychology of Learning and Motivation: Advances in Research and Theory. Volume 55* (pp. 1–36). Oxford: Elsevier.

Rohrer, D. (2009). The effects of spacing and mixing practice problems. *Journal for Research in Mathematics Education*, 40, 4–17.

Rohrer, D. (2015). Student instruction should be distributed over long time periods. *Educational Psychology Review*, 27, 635–643.

Rohrer, D. & Taylor, K. (2007). The shuffling of mathematics problems improves learning. *Instructional Science*, 35, 481–498.

Schacter, D. L. & Szpunar, K. K. (2015). Enhancing attention and memory during video-recorded lectures. *Scholarship of Teaching and Learning in Psychology*, 1, 60–71.

Smith, M. A. & Karpicke, J. D. (2014). Retrieval practice with short-answer, multiple-choice, and hybrid tests. *Memory*, 22, 784–802.

Smith, M. A., Roediger, H. L., & Karpicke, J. D. (2013). Covert retrieval practice benefits retention as much as overt retrieval practice. *Journal of Experimental Psychology: Learning, Memory, and Cognition*, 39, 1712–1725.

Sobel, H. S., Cepeda, N. J., & Kapler, I. V. (2011). Spacing effects in real-world classroom vocabulary learning. *Applied Cognitive Psychology*, 25, 763–767.

Soderstrom, N. C. & Bjork, R. A. (2014). Testing facilitates the regulation of subsequent study time. *Journal of Memory and Language*, 73, 99–115.

Son, L. K. & Kornell, N. (2008). Research on the allocation of study time: key studies from 1890 to the present (and beyond). In: J. Dunlosky & R. A. Bjork (Eds), *A Handbook of Memory and Metamemory* (pp. 333–351). Hillsdale, NJ: Psychology Press.

Szpunar, K. K., Khan, N. Y., & Schacter, D. L. (2013). Interpolated memory tests reduce mind wandering and improve learning of online lectures. *Proceedings of the National Academy of Sciences of the United States of America*, 110, 6313–6317.

Szpunar, K. K., Jing, H. G., & Schacter, D. L. (2014). Overcoming overconfidence in learning from video-recorded lectures: implications of interpolated testing for online education. *Journal of Applied Research in Memory and Cognition*, 3, 161–164.

Verkoeijen, P. P. J. L., Rikers, R. M. J. P., & Özsoy, B. (2008). Distributed rereading can hurt the spacing effect in text memory. *Applied Cognitive Psychology*, 22, 685–695.

Willingham, D. B. (2009). *Why Don't Students Like School?* San Francisco, CA: Jossey-Bass.

Zaromb, F. M. & Roediger, H. L. (2010). The testing effect in free recall is associated with enhanced organizational processes. *Memory & Cognition*, 38, 995–1008.

7

SCIENCE OF LEARNING AND DIGITAL LEARNING ENVIRONMENTS

Jason M. Lodge and Jared Cooney Horvath

MELBOURNE GRADUATE SCHOOL OF EDUCATION, UNIVERSITY OF MELBOURNE

Introduction

Of all the areas where it is possible for the science of learning to have an impact on educational practice, it is arguably in the use of technologies where research from the laboratory can have the greatest influence. The introduction of new technologies raises profound (but also mundane) questions about education in the future. Learning that occurs in digital environments also offers opportunities for personalization and adaptive learning design that cannot always be achieved in face-to-face educational settings. Moreover, educational technologies provide opportunities to capture aspects of learning that are not easy to evaluate in complex, often chaotic classrooms.

In this chapter we shall provide an overview of some of the main research traditions underpinning the understanding of learning in digital environments with an eye to the future. Although this work has been translated to real-life educational settings to some degree to date, there is substantial potential for further research to have an impact on future education. We shall conclude with guidance to teachers on how best to conceptualize and use educational technologies in their practice.

The Trouble with Technology

The exponential growth in power and affordability of technologies has changed numerous aspects of modern life. Although there is some conjecture about the extent of the impact that these developments have had on education (e.g. Selwyn, 2013), what is undisputed is that information can now be more easily and efficiently accessed than ever before in history. Information is no longer limited to particular sources or locations—it is now possible to access information about almost any topic at any time from anywhere so long as you have a device and some means of accessing the Internet. The development of smaller, more mobile, more powerful devices means that it is common for many people throughout the world to have this persistent access to information.

As educational practices are notoriously difficult to change, these fundamental transformations of the relationship between students and information have yet to be integrated into most educational environments. One of the most obvious examples of this is in higher education, where the traditional lecture is still dominant on many campuses, although it is more suited to an era when information was scarce and difficult to obtain (Friesen, 2011). This slow rate of change is occurring despite pressure being placed on universities by numerous innovations and global competition. Not only are mobile devices changing the way that students interact with knowledge on campus, but also the development of massive open online courses (MOOCs) and other innovations (e.g. social media) are changing the way in which students interact with content, faculty, and each other. Higher education provides, perhaps, a particularly striking example of a collision between traditional teaching practices and new technologies. However, the same forces are evident at all levels of education (Ertmer *et al.*, 2015).

Although the use of new, networked technologies undoubtedly has the potential to provide access to knowledge and educational opportunities, some caution is required until these innovations reach their full potential. Educational technologies are particularly prone to hyperbole and myth (see De Bruyckere *et al.*, 2015). Technology and its potential for use in society (broadly) and in education (specifically) are evolving at a pace that far outstrips the capacity of researchers to determine what impact (if any) new devices or innovations have on learning. The situation is worsened by the overly optimistic and closed attitude adopted by many researchers in the educational technology community (Selwyn, 2011). In fact, many practitioners and policy makers are surprised to learn that educational technologies appear to have a negligible effect on the enhancement of student learning (Hattie, 2009). Reeves and Reeves (2015) in particular have been vocal in lamenting the inability of rigorous research into these technologies to find statistically significant differences across and between media platforms. Clark has further argued that the different media used in education are "mere vehicles that deliver instruction but do not influence student achievement any more than the truck that delivers our groceries causes changes in our nutrition" (Clark, 1983, p. 445).

These critiques of research on educational technology (and particularly of rigorous, controlled studies on the use of these technologies) have some merit. That is not to say that these views are held unanimously (Butler *et al.*, 2014; Lodge, 2016). What these diverse views do suggest, however, is that there is still work to be done to determine whether and how technologies have an impact on student learning.

The lack of research evidence demonstrating clear benefits of particular technologies is problematic for teachers and policy makers who need such evidence in order to make sound choices about what tools and innovations to adopt in practice. The void left by the lag between the introduction of technologies and the provision of evidence with regard to how they can be best utilized is often filled with hype and rhetoric (De Bruyckere *et al.*, 2015). In some cases, these misconceptions are used in order to sell devices or software; in other cases, these myths can be unequivocally detrimental to student learning.

There are many examples of hype outpacing solid evidence in relation to educational technologies and innovations. Perhaps the most (in)famous recent example is that of massive open online courses (MOOCs). These were developed as a way of democratizing higher education through the provision of free access to some of the world's leading professors from the highest-ranking universities. MOOCs created so much hype that the *New York Times* declared 2012 "The Year of the MOOC" (Pappano, 2012). As the hype around MOOCs grew, there were commentators claiming that MOOCs would be responsible for completely changing the way in which higher education is delivered globally, and would herald the emergence of a new model for the design and delivery of university education (Daniel, 2012). Subsequently it has become evident that MOOCs will not force a fundamental change in the global higher education sector. Although MOOCs have raised some questions about the role of the Internet in modern higher education (e.g. Porter, 2015) and the ways in which credentials are conceptualized and recognized (e.g. Lewis & Lodge, 2016), they have not had the impact that was predicted. Instead, the MOOC phenomenon has highlighted a lack of appreciation of several decades of published research into the subject of online and distance learning (Bates, 2014).

Other examples of hype surrounding new educational technologies include the interest focused on tablet computers (e.g. El-Gayar *et al.*, 2011), brain training (e.g. Rabipour & Raz, 2012) and the now almost ubiquitous learning management systems (e.g. Weaver *et al.*, 2008). In each of these instances, the hype cycle followed a similar pattern, as illustrated by the widely cited Gartner Hype Cycle (Gartner Inc., 2015), with an initial period of excitement about the introduction of a new technology being followed by a period of disillusionment when the reality failed to live up to the inflated expectations of the new innovation. Eventually, however, technologies and innovations find their niche in the educational landscape. The over-hyping of new innovations is particularly problematic. Technology is often seen as a panacea, and is promoted as such by marketers, who could cynically be accused of attempting to profit from the hype and lack of immediate evidence about new technologies (see also Selwyn, 2012).

While technology companies attempt to gain a foothold in the education market, there is simultaneously increasing pressure at all levels of education for institutions and schools to cut costs. Many Western countries are spending less per capita on education in relation to GDP than they have in the past (Organisation for Economic Co-operation and Development, 2015; Yang & McCall, 2014). This creates pressure both on schools and on individual teachers to do more with less. The outcome of these pressures is that simplified technological solutions begin to look appealing as a way of cutting costs and ostensibly providing a superior learning experience for students. However, the evidence for this is far from definitive, and without sufficient support from rigorous research studies into these new technologies, there is the possibility that new technologies could potentially *increase* costs through implementation and upgrade requirements, while at the same time being detrimental to student learning. The implementation of educational technologies in practice is therefore mired in complex economic and political circumstances that affect the potential for research to have an impact on practice.

Technology, the Internet, and Rotting Brains

The hype surrounding various technologies is a problem not only in relation to educational economics and politics, but also more broadly in relation to learning. The use of technology in learning is often seen as deleterious to the basic thinking skills that have proved to be necessary throughout history. Many authors (e.g. Brabazon, 2002; Carr, 2008; Daniel & Willingham, 2012) have argued that the use of educational technologies and the Internet is resulting in students underperforming in education. This argument is consistent with claims that the Internet is leading to a general decrease in intelligence in the population. Furthermore, authors such as Susan Greenfield (e.g. Greenfield, 2014) claim that technology is leading to wholesale detrimental changes in the brain. Thus there are numerous examples of researchers and other commentators claiming that the Internet and associated technologies are causing harmful effects on student learning and on society more broadly. However, the evidence in support of these arguments is equivocal at best, and non-existent at worst (Loh & Kanai, 2015).

The mixture of technologies and neuroscience is particularly prone to the development and perpetuation of myths and misconceptions that have led to these sorts of negative views about technology and learning. Both are areas that have a certain intuitive appeal. In each area, discoveries are often seen as groundbreaking and at the cutting edge of science and innovation. The inclusion of a neuroimage (e.g. McCabe & Castel, 2008) or the mention of a new technological or educational innovation (e.g. Ritchie *et al.*, 2012) have both been shown to make readers more susceptible to believing the claims that are made in the publication. Beneath the hype, there is a need for discoveries that combine these two fields to be treated with considerable caution. The brain is an extremely complex organism. Similarly, new and emerging technologies (e.g. learning analytics, machine learning, artificial intelligence) are highly complicated and sophisticated, and designed for implementation in complex educational settings. Attempts to simplify the developments in either field for blanket use in education are fraught with problems, particularly when the two areas are combined—for example, when evidence from neuroscience is used to support the efficacy of particular innovations or technologies. This suggests that research which aims to determine how best to use neuroscience to inform the effective implementation of innovations in education is difficult, complex, and will require substantial investments of time and resources. There will be no simple answers or quick fixes. Translation from the laboratory to the classroom is perhaps more complex here than in other areas of education, while simultaneously there is increased pressure to provide useful guidance to teachers and policy makers as technologies rapidly evolve.

Theory and Evidence of Learning in Digital Environments

The steady stream of hype surrounding the introduction of new technologies suggests that there is a dearth of evidence about how best to use educational technologies in practice. However, this is not the case. There is an extensive history of research that has been conducted both in laboratory and in educational settings in relation to educational technologies. These activities have tended to sit within one of three distinct paradigms or research traditions, and although there are other ways and means of evaluating the use of educational technologies (Phillips *et al.*, 2012), these are the dominant approaches. Each has a different level of focus and has contributed in different ways to the overall understanding of the use of educational technology.

The first area of focus is on the technologies themselves. This research tradition has focused closely on the technical aspects of educational technology development. Often this work is carried out by computer scientists in collaboration with educational practitioners. Perhaps the most prototypical area of research within this tradition is that associated with the development of intelligent tutoring systems. Stretching back to the pioneering work of Alan Newell (e.g. Newell, 1990), there has been a long-standing focus on the development and implementation of technologies that can interact with and adapt to students' learning needs in real time. One example of these systems is AutoTutor (Nye *et al.*, 2014), which has been developed and used in classroom settings in numerous studies (e.g. Craig *et al.*, 2004; Graesser *et al.*, 2005). Of greater importance to the development of a more sophisticated understanding of how educational technologies can be most effectively used in practice, these systems have also been used extensively to create computational models of the student learning process (Koedinger *et al.*, 2015). For example, AutoTutor has been used in experimental studies examining the effect of emotion on student learning (Craig *et al.*, 2004). It is a requirement for the evolution of intelligent tutoring systems that these systems have built into them a sophisticated algorithmic model for predicting the processes by which students are learning. The tradition that is the study of educational technologies from the technical viewpoint has therefore been useful both in aiding the development of the actual technologies, and in better understanding aspects such as confusion that are an important part of the student learning process. We shall return to the research in this area later in the chapter, when we discuss the current state of the field.

Another research paradigm that has had an impact on educational technology is research that adopts an approach akin to that commonly used in experimental psychology. This tradition tends to look at aspects of learning in digital environments in a controlled laboratory setting. This research is often conducted by experimental psychologists, cognitive neuroscientists, and/or learning scientists, and is often done in collaboration with educational practitioners and/or educational technologists. The advantage of these studies is that they are able to isolate various processes and features of technologies and enable an inference to be made about a cause-and-effect relationship between technologies, features of these technologies, and learning. For example, Mueller and Oppenheimer (2014) conducted an experimental examination comparing handwritten note taking with note taking on a notebook computer (the handwritten notes were more effective for studying in this experiment). This tradition aligns with the established subdiscipline of the learning sciences (as discussed in the Introduction to this volume). Although there are advantages to using these studies for determining cause-and-effect relationships, laboratory studies such as those conducted in this paradigm have also been criticized for being difficult to generalize to practice (e.g. Reeves & Reeves, 2015). As is the case with many of the areas of educational practice discussed in this volume, the distance from the experimental laboratory to the classroom is great. In the case of educational technologies, this distance has the potential to provide further fertile ground for the development of myths and misconceptions about the efficacy of technologies in practice, as highlighted above.

At the opposite end of the spectrum to highly controlled, rigorous laboratory research are studies that are conducted in real educational settings. These studies can involve the use of particular devices or applications in physical classrooms or online. These types of studies may be based on paradigms such as action research (Zuber-Skerritt, 1992) or design-based research (Van den Akker *et al.*, 2006), and are often carried out primarily by teachers and/or applied educational researchers. The aim of these studies is to evaluate particular technologies or features of those technologies in specific educational settings. For example, Venema and Lodge (2013) investigated the use of a USB tablet and "digital ink" in a live lecture setting to determine whether the use of this tool led to enhanced learning compared with the use of a whiteboard or other similar tools (this tool did appear to help student learning in this case). Although these types of studies are primarily useful for obtaining a qualitative evaluation of a tool or innovation in teaching practice, they are highly context specific. The proliferation of studies of this type that cannot be generalized broadly across educational settings has recently led the editors of the *British Journal of Educational Technology* (a top-ranked educational technology journal) to seek beyond small-sample, highly contextualized studies, and instead call for more systematic and generalizable research on the use of educational technologies (Latchem, 2014).

Research investigating the use of educational technologies thus spans a number of different paradigms, as does the study of education more broadly. Whether the focus is on the technologies, on cause-and-effect relationships, or on situated practice, there are advantages and disadvantages to each approach. One source of tension in recent times has been the balance between rigor and relevance in the research on educational innovations (Lodge & Bosanquet, 2014; Ross *et al.*, 2010). Reeves (2006) suggests that one remedy for this tension is research that is conducted within the tradition of educational design research. Such research is based on iterative cycles of design and evaluation, building on approaches commonly used in instructional and educational design. Goodyear (2015) further suggests that educational design research and design thinking are critical for "actionable knowledge" that can be utilized in educational practice, particularly practice involving innovation and technology. It would seem, then, that educational design research and design thinking are crucial to bridging the gap between the laboratory and the classroom, and between rigor and relevance (as has been discussed elsewhere in this volume).

Multimedia Learning Theory

Of the theories and approaches that have developed from the dominant paradigms in educational innovation, it is perhaps the work of Richard E. Mayer and his colleagues (e.g. Mayer, 2014b) that has been most influential. Mayer's multimedia learning theory (Mayer, 2009) is the most prominent example of laboratory research on educational technology that has been effectively translated and applied to practice. Multimedia learning theory is an information-processing theory which implies that learning occurs via the active process of filtering, organizing, and integrating information. In summary, multimedia information enters the brain via different sensory channels, each of which has limited capacity and integrative capabilities (Mayer, 2009). From this foundation, it is possible to carefully consider how information that is being presented via these multiple channels affects the learning process.

Multimedia learning theory has been used as the underpinning theoretical framework for the conceptualization of much research examining the role of technologies in learning (e.g. Horvath, 2014). Several handbooks have in fact been developed on the basis of this work (Clark & Mayer, 2011; Mayer, 2005, 2009, 2014b). The success of multimedia learning theory in this context has predominantly been due to the rigor that Mayer and his colleagues have applied to the research that informed the development of the theory. It has also proved to be robust to further elaboration, particularly by Moreno (2006), who made important contributions to multimedia learning theory by incorporating aspects of motivation and emotion (Mayer, 2014a). Again, the findings of rigorous laboratory studies were used as evidence to support these enhancements of the theory.

One reason why multimedia learning theory has been particularly influential in the use of educational technologies in practice is that it has generated solid, easy-to-follow guidelines for practitioners that can be easily adapted according to environmental and contextual pressures. These guidelines are commonly referred to as "multimedia principles." For example, the redundancy principle states that learning is impaired when identical (rather than non-conflicting supportive) information is presented to two sensory channels simultaneously—for example, task instructions simultaneously being presented verbally (auditory) and textually (visual) (Mayer & Fiorella, 2014). (We shall explore this principle further later in this chapter.) Thus the real genius of the work of Mayer and his colleagues is not just that they have been able to draw on rigorous research from the laboratory to develop a robust theory about how students learn with technologies, but also that they have been able to distil this work into a set of principles that provide clear, evidence-based guidance to teachers on the use of technology in their own practice (Mayer, 2014b). This process of translating from laboratory research to basic principles that can be picked up and used by teachers is common to the emerging work in design for learning and design thinking (mentioned earlier in this chapter).

Cutting-Edge Research on Learning in Digital Environments

Multimedia learning theory provides a solid basis for the understanding of learning in digital environments. Although it has been particularly useful in guiding the development of educational technologies and providing principles for teachers to apply to their practice, research on the use of these technologies in the future will continue and will need to increase. One example of the constantly dynamic nature of work in this area is the emergence of the discipline of learning analytics. This new area of research has grown out of the powerful new techniques that are available for collecting data about and from students in various digital environments and then integrating these data for deep analysis about their learning (Koedinger et al., 2015). The early focus of this work was to determine which students were most at risk of falling behind and potentially withdrawing from their university studies (e.g. Macfadyen & Dawson, 2010), but the field has rapidly evolved and is now focusing on more nuanced and sophisticated aspects of the student learning experience (e.g. de Barba et al., 2016). This rapid rise in the use of these data collection, integration, and analysis processes suggests that there is going to be a continuing need to better understand and conceptualize how learning occurs as both the technologies and the methods for analyzing student learning continue to evolve (Lodge & Lewis, 2012).

Perhaps the area that best exemplifies the cutting edge of research in educational technologies in the early twenty-first century is the work on intelligent and adaptive tutoring systems. The sophisticated modeling that has now been made more powerful through the use of learning analytics has allowed the ongoing development of these systems. There are now many examples of the kinds of adaptive systems that were first envisaged by Alan Newell and his colleagues at Carnegie Mellon University (Newell, 1990). The critical factor underpinning this development is the expansion of data integration and analysis approaches. Coupled with more powerful computing and an increase in networked devices, this has led to the development of more adaptive systems (Nye, 2014). For example, the adaptive learning platform Smart Sparrow can provide a personalized student learning experience that is responsive to the student's progress through a lesson in a digital environment (Marcus et al., 2011). The combination of better data collection, integration, and analysis together with more powerful, connected devices is thus steadily increasing the scope for personalized learning.

Another growing area of research falls within the broad umbrella term "affective computing" (Picard, 2000). Researchers in this field are particularly interested in the emotional aspects of human–computer relationships. This includes both the ways in which humans respond to machines, and the ways in which machines are able to detect and respond to human emotions of interest. Within this broad field there is a substantial focus on the use of these sorts of technologies to provide emotionally responsive systems for student learning (D'Mello & Graesser, 2015). For example, a system that is attuned to student confusion could be programmed in such a way as to detect confusion and provide a targeted intervention to ensure that the episode of confusion leads to a productive learning outcome (Lehman *et al.*, 2012).

Learning analytics, intelligent and adaptive tutoring systems, and affective computing are all examples of the research that is being conducted at the forefront of educational technologies. In each of these cases the research has a particular focus. For learning analytics, the research has often (but not always) been conducted in real-life settings drawing on large data sets. Research on intelligent tutoring systems and affective computing has been often conducted in the laboratory, where the complex, messy reality of the classroom can be controlled. Interestingly, there are examples where these trends have been reversed. Learning analytics have been used to look at learning during specific tasks in the laboratory (e.g. Lodge & Kennedy, 2015), and intelligent tutoring systems have similarly been deployed in school systems broadly (e.g. Koedinger *et al.*, 1997). It is when these reversals occur that the power of some of these new innovations and research approaches becomes evident. This will become even more apparent as these fields intermingle and merge. In the more mature field of health informatics, this collaborative cross-disciplinary process has already been established (Coiera, 2015). There has similarly been a call for synthesis and integration from neuroscience, laboratory-based experimental work, and large data sets in psychology for the purpose of better understanding personality and other psychological factors. This subfield has come to be referred to as psycho-informatics (Yarkoni, 2012). It is reasonable to expect that a more systematic, data-driven means of working from the laboratory to the classroom in education may emerge. There has indeed already been some work towards the development of educational informatics (see Ford, 2008), and this may herald a more systematic future for the investigation of learning with technology.

Future Challenges and Possibilities

Developments in intelligent tutoring systems, artificial intelligence, machine learning, and personalized education have the potential to radically transform formal and informal education in the near future. Computers and networked digital learning environments are becoming exponentially more powerful and less costly. There is no possible way to forecast what impact these advances in technology will have on education in the long term. Particularly in the case of artificial intelligence, the consequences of the creation of these possibly super-intelligent systems are nearly impossible to predict (Bostram, 2014). Learning analytics, adaptive learning, and affective computing suggest ways in which the technology will progress. In the meantime, however, there is ongoing research that suggests possibilities for the incremental evolution of our understanding of learning in digital environments. In other words, we shall continue to learn more about the human side of the human–computer interaction, too.

One particular area that appears to have great potential is the ongoing research into the experience of insight (Bowden *et al.*, 2005). Otherwise known as a "eureka" or "ah-ha!" moment, insight is commonly experienced when students have crossed a threshold and developed a new, more sophisticated understanding of an issue or concept (Topolinski & Reber, 2010). Although these experiences are relatively common, they have been hard to research because it is difficult both to predict when they will occur and, once they do occur, to replicate them. Replication of a phenomenon is vital for neuroimaging and experimental studies to separate the regular activity occurring in the brain and mind from the process of interest (in this case, the process leading to insight). Similar projects are under way looking at how error, feedback, and confidence contribute to the understanding of learning across the span from the laboratory to the classroom.

As we continue to learn more about how the brain and mind work, and as technologies become more sophisticated, phenomena such as "ah-ha!" moments and error correction will become more viable as areas of investigation. Synthesizing this research with the ongoing work in data science, computer science, and design for learning has the potential to create powerful new approaches for supporting student learning. In contrast to the more reactionary evaluation of new technologies that has occurred as these have become available in the past, there are now real opportunities for research to be at the forefront in the development of these innovations from their inception. For example, it is not difficult to see that a fuller understanding of the process of developing insight could be used to create a computational model of insight in the brain. This model could then be used to develop an adaptive intelligent system that can respond to students and give them exactly the individualized support and feedback that they need in real time. This system would thus help students to gain the insight necessary to develop a more sophisticated appreciation of a concept. In this way, what we learn about these processes in the brain can have a direct impact on how students are learning in a real-life educational setting, albeit a virtual setting in this example.

From the Laboratory to the Classroom

Technology and the introduction of new educational innovations provide unique challenges for teachers. As we have discussed in this chapter, there is an illusion that technologies can provide a panacea for student learning that rarely plays out in practice. The reality is that technologies introduce substantial complexity to what is an already complex and difficult task, which is preparing students for an unknowable and increasingly unpredictable future. There is a tendency for researchers and practitioners to adopt either a strong techno-positivist or an overly skeptical position with regard to technologies in education. This is thus an area that tends to cause polarization, with strong views for and against the use of technologies in education settings. Such polarization unfortunately hinders the provision of clear guidance to teachers.

Ultimately it remains the case that teachers are often (if not always) best placed to make informed decisions about what works for them and for their students in their own classroom setting. The lag in evidence relating to the efficacy of new innovations in education certainly warrants some level of skepticism until such time as better evidence becomes available. For teachers, this means drawing on what has been shown to be effective over the longer term. In other words, technology should not be privileged over pedagogy. There are very good reasons why educational practices are taught to pre-service teachers in the way that they are—because they have been shown to be effective. When new technologies and innovations are introduced, the same cannot be said of them until the necessary research has been conducted to determine whether the same standard can be applied to these new innovations. Until such time as that occurs, teachers are best placed to make professional judgements about what happens in their classroom.

If an educator decides that an established or novel technology suits the learning goals, there are several foundational principles grounded in the cognitive theory of multimedia learning to consider. As noted earlier, the first of these is the redundancy principle, which states that learning is impaired when identical information is presented to two sensory channels simultaneously (Clark & Mayer, 2011). In terms of learning design, this suggests that one should avoid including text-based information when identical material is being covered by either visual or auditory means. For instance, when utilizing a video or animation to illustrate a learning concept, do not also include text illustrating the same concept. In this instance, the video or animation and text will compete for limited attentional resources, thereby impairing comprehension and memory for each of them (Kalyuga *et al.*, 2004; Sorden, 2005; Soon Fook & Aldalalah, 2010).

A second principle to consider is the coherence principle, which states that learning is improved when extraneous material is reduced or excluded from multimedia material (Clark & Mayer, 2011). Extraneous information typically is typically presented in three forms. The first is extraneous audio—when unnecessary music, sound effects, or auditory cues are utilized (typically in a bid to attract attention), overall comprehension and memory for the learning material have been shown to be decreased (Moreno & Mayer, 2000). The second form is extraneous graphics—although images outlining key concepts are useful, the inclusion of secondary, irrelevant images (typically included to sustain attention) has been demonstrated to reduce learning (Mayer *et al.*, 2008). The third form is extraneous text—the utilization of large, dense blocks of text (typically included to allow for deeper understanding) actually impairs comprehension as compared with the utilization of short, simple keywords and phrases (Butcher, 2006).

A final principle to consider is the segmentation principle, which states that breaking down larger processes or concepts into their component parts and presenting each of these in turn improves comprehension and memory (Clark & Mayer, 2011). For instance, when teaching students how a diesel engine works, utilizing a video or animation that self-pauses at each major step along the process ensures that each student has ample time to link novel information with previously acquired knowledge (Mayer *et al.*, 2002, 2003). Although this principle is intuitively applicable to physical processes (e.g. tying a knot, cooking a meal), it is equally applicable to more "conceptual" material (e.g. the development of a democracy, the composition of a sentence).

These principles provide a starting point for teachers to consider the utility of technologies and different forms of media in their practice. The science of learning will continue to provide foundational knowledge about the learning process that will inform the development of new innovations in education. The increasing impact of machine learning, learning analytics, data science, and design will lead to incremental improvements in technologies that already exist, and to the development of new technologies specifically designed on the basis of what we are coming to know about the brain and mind. In the meantime, it behoves teachers to continue to draw on established, evidence-based teaching and learning practice. Despite the exciting developments that are occurring in neuroscience, data science, computer science, and educational technology, innovation in education will be via an evolution, not a revolution.

References

Bates, T. (2014). MOOCs: getting to know you better. *Distance Education*, 35, 145–148.

Bostrom, N. (2014). *Superintelligence: Paths, Dangers, Strategies*. Oxford, UK: Oxford University Press.

Bowden, E. M., Jung-Beeman, M., Fleck, J., & Kounios, J. (2005). New approaches to demystifying insight. *Trends in Cognitive Sciences*, 9, 322–328.

Brabazon, T. (2002). *Digital Hemlock: Internet Education and the Poisoning of Teaching*. Sydney: UNSW Press.

Butcher, K. R. (2006). Learning from text with diagrams: promoting mental model development and inference generation. *Journal of Educational Psychology*, 98, 182–197.

Butler, A. C., Marsh, E. J., Slavinsky, J. P., & Baraniuk, R. G. (2014). Integrating cognitive science and technology improves learning in a STEM classroom. *Educational Psychology Review*, 26, 331–340.

Carr, N. (2008). Is Google making us stupid? *The Atlantic*, July/August issue. Available online at www.theatlantic.com/magazine/archive/2008/07/is-google-making-us-stupid/306868/ (accessed 10 October 2015).

Clark, R. C. & Mayer, R. E. (2011). *E-Learning and the Science of Instruction: Proven Guidelines for Consumers and Designers of Multimedia Learning*, 3rd edition. San Francisco, CA: John Wiley & Sons.

Clark, R. E. (1983). Reconsidering research on learning from media. *Review of Educational Research*, 53, 445–459.

Coiera, E. (2015). *Guide to Health Informatics*. Boca Raton, FL: CRC Press.

Craig, S., Graesser, A., Sullins, J., & Gholson, B. (2004). Affect and learning: an exploratory look into the role of affect in learning with AutoTutor. *Journal of Educational Media*, 29, 241–250.

Daniel, D. B. & Willingham, D. T. (2012). Electronic textbooks: why the rush? *Science*, 335, 1570–1571.

Daniel, J. (2012). Making sense of MOOCs: musings in a maze of myth, paradox and possibility. *Journal of Interactive Media in Education*, 2012(3), Art-18.

de Barba, P., Kennedy, G., & Ainley, M. (2016). The role of students' motivation and participation in predicting performance in a MOOC. *Journal of Computer Assisted Learning*, DOI: 10.1111/jcal.12130

De Bruyckere, P., Kirschner, P. A., & Hulshof, C. (2015). *Urban Myths about Learning and Education*. New York: Academic Press.

D'Mello, S. K. & Graesser, A. C. (2015). Feeling, thinking, and computing with affect-aware learning technologies. In: R. A. Calvo, S. K. D'Mello, J. Gratch, & A. Kappas (Eds), *The Oxford Handbook of Affective Computing* (pp. 419–434). New York: Oxford University Press.

El-Gayar, O., Moran, M., & Hawkes, M. (2011). Students' acceptance of tablet PCs and implications for educational institutions. *Journal of Educational Technology & Society*, 14, 58–70.

Ertmer, P. A., Ottenbreit-Leftwich, A. T., & Tondeur, J. (2015). Teachers' beliefs and uses of technology to support 21st-century teaching and learning. In: H. Fives & M. G. Gill (Eds), *International Handbook of Research on Teachers' Beliefs*. New York: Routledge.

Ford, N. (2008). Educational informatics. *Annual Review of Information Science and Technology*, 42, 497–544.

Friesen, N. (2011). The lecture as a transmedial pedagogical form: a historical analysis. *Educational Researcher*, 40, 95–102.

Gartner Inc. (2015). *Research Methodologies: Gartner Hype Cycle*. Stamford, CT: Gartner Inc. Available online at www.gartner.com/technology/research/methodologies/hype-cycle.jsp (accessed 10 October 2015).

Goodyear, P. (2015). Teaching as design. *HERDSA Review of Higher Education*, 2, 27–50.

Graesser, A., Chipman, P., Haynes, B., & Olney, A. (2005). AutoTutor: an intelligent tutoring system with mixed-initiative dialogue. *IEEE Transactions on Education*, 48, 612–618.

Greenfield, S. (2014). *Mind Change: How Digital Technologies Are Leaving Their Mark On Our Brains*. London, UK: Random House.

Hattie, J. A. C. (2009). *Visible Learning: A Synthesis of Over 800 Meta-Analyses Related to Achievement*. New York: Routledge.

Horvath, J. C. (2014). The neuroscience of PowerPoint™. *Mind, Brain, and Education,* 8, 137–143.

Kalyuga, S., Chandler, P., & Sweller, J. (2004). When redundant on-screen text in multimedia technical instruction can interfere with learning. *Human Factors,* 46, 567–581.

Koedinger, K. R., Anderson, J. R., Hadley, W. H., & Mark, M. A. (1997). Intelligent tutoring goes to school in the big city. *International Journal of Artificial Intelligence in Education,* 8, 30–43.

Koedinger, K. R., D'Mello, S., McLaughlin, E. A., Pardos, Z. A., & Rosé, C. P. (2015). Data mining and education. *Wiley Interdisciplinary Reviews: Cognitive Science,* 6, 333–353.

Latchem, C. (2014). *BJET* Editorial: Opening up the educational technology research agenda. *British Journal of Educational Technology,* 45, 3–11.

Lehman, B., D'Mello, S., & Graesser, A. (2012). Interventions to regulate confusion during learning. In: *Intelligent Tutoring Systems: 11th International Conference, ITS 2012, Chania, Crete, Greece, June 14–18, 2012. Proceedings* (pp. 576–578). Berlin: Springer.

Lewis, M. J. & Lodge, J. M. (2016). Keep calm and credential on: linking learning, life and work practices in a complex world. In: D. Ifenthaler, N. Bellin-Mularski, & D.-K. Mah (Eds), *Foundation of Digital Badges and Micro-Credentials: Demonstrating and Recognizing Knowledge and Competencies.* Berlin: Springer.

Lodge, J. M. (2016). Do the learning sciences have a place in higher education research? *Higher Education Research & Development,* 35(3), 634–637. DOI: 10.1080/07294360.2015.1094204

Lodge, J. M. & Lewis, M. J. (2012). Pigeon pecks and mouse clicks: putting the learning back into learning analytics. In: M. Brown, M. Hartnett, & T. Stewart (Eds), *Future Challenges, Sustainable Futures. Proceedings of the Annual ascilite Conference, Wellington, New Zealand, 25–28 November 2012.* Tugun, Queensland: Australasian Society for Computers in Learning in Tertiary Education (ascilite).

Lodge, J. M. & Bosanquet, A. (2014). Evaluating quality learning in higher education: re-examining the evidence. *Quality in Higher Education,* 20, 3–23.

Lodge, J. M. & Kennedy, G. E. (2015). Prior knowledge, confidence and understanding in interactive tutorials and simulations. In: T. Reiners, B. R. von Konsky, D. Gibson, V. Chang, L. Irving, & K. Clarke (Eds), *Globally Connected, Digitally Enabled. Proceedings of the Annual ascilite Conference, Perth, Western Australia, 29 November – 2 December 2015* (pp. 190–200). Tugun, Queensland: Australasian Society for Computers in Learning in Tertiary Education (ascilite).

Loh, K. K. & Kanai, R. (2015). How has the Internet reshaped human cognition? *The Neuroscientist.* DOI: 1073858415595005

McCabe, D. P. & Castel, A. D. (2008). Seeing is believing: the effect of brain images on judgments of scientific reasoning. *Cognition,* 107, 343–352.

Macfadyen, L. P. & Dawson, S. (2010). Mining LMS data to develop an "early warning system" for educators: a proof of concept. *Computers & Education,* 54, 588–599.

Marcus, N., Ben-Naim, D., & Bain, M. (2011). Instructional support for teachers and guided feedback for students in an adaptive e-learning environment. In: *Eighth International Conference on Information Technology: New Generations (ITNG), 11–13 April 2011, Las Vegas, NV* (pp. 626–631). New York: Institute of Electrical and Electronics Engineers (IEEE).

Mayer, R. E. (2005) *Cambridge Handbook of Multimedia Learning.* New York: Cambridge University Press.

Mayer, R. E. (2009). *Multimedia Learning.* New York: Cambridge University Press.

Mayer, R. E. (2014a). Incorporating motivation into multimedia learning. *Learning and Instruction,* 29, 171–173.

Mayer, R. E. (2014b). *Cambridge Handbook of Multimedia Learning,* 2nd edition. New York: Cambridge University Press.

Mayer, R. E. & Fiorella, L. (2014). Principles for reducing extraneous processing in multimedia learning: coherence, signaling, redundancy, spatial contiguity, and temporal contiguity principles. In: R. E. Mayer (Ed.), *The Cambridge Handbook of Multimedia Learning,* 2nd edition (pp. 279–315). New York: Cambridge University Press.

Mayer, R. E., Mathias, A., & Wetzell, K. (2002). Pictorial aids for learning by doing in a multimedia geology simulation game. *Journal of Educational Psychology,* 94, 171–185.

Mayer, R. E., Dow, G., & Mayer, S. (2003). Multimedia learning in an interactive self-explaining environment: what works in the design of agent-based microworlds? *Journal of Educational Psychology*, 95, 806–812.

Mayer, R. E., Griffith, E., Jurkowitz, I. T., & Rothman, D. (2008). Increased interestingness of extraneous details in a multimedia science presentation leads to decreased learning. *Journal of Experimental Psychology: Applied*, 14, 329–339.

Moreno, R. (2006). Does the modality principle hold for different media? A test of the method-affects-learning hypothesis. *Journal of Computer Assisted Learning*, 22, 149–158.

Moreno, R. & Mayer, R. E. (2000). A coherence effect in multimedia learning: the case for minimizing irrelevant sounds in the design of multimedia instructional messages. *Journal of Educational Psychology*, 92, 117–125.

Mueller, P. A. & Oppenheimer, D. M. (2014). The pen is mightier than the keyboard: advantages of longhand over laptop note taking. *Psychological Science*, 25, 1159–1168.

Newell, A. (1990). *Unified Theories of Cognition*. Cambridge, MA: Cambridge University Press.

Nye, B. D. (2014). Intelligent tutoring systems by and for the developing world: a review of trends and approaches for educational technology in a global context. *International Journal of Artificial Intelligence in Education*, 25, 177–203.

Nye, B. D., Graesser, A. C., & Hu, X. (2014). AutoTutor and family: a review of 17 years of natural language tutoring. *International Journal of Artificial Intelligence in Education*, 24, 427–469.

Organisation for Economic Co-operation and Development (OECD) (2015). *Education at a Glance 2015: OECD Indicators*. Paris, France: OECD Publishing.

Pappano, L. (2012). The year of the MOOC. *The New York Times*. Available online at www.nytimes.com/2012/11/04/education/edlife/massive-open-online-   courses-are-multiplying-at-a-rapid-pace.html?pagewanted=1 (accessed 10 October 2015).

Phillips, R., McNaught, C., & Kennedy, G. (2012). *Evaluating e-Learning: Guiding Research and Practice*. New York: Routledge.

Picard, R. W. (2000). *Affective Computing*. Cambridge, MA: MIT Press.

Porter, S. (2015). *To MOOC or Not to MOOC: How Can Online Learning Help to Build the Future of Higher Education?* Waltham, MA: Chandos Publishing.

Rabipour, S. & Raz, A. (2012). Training the brain: fact and fad in cognitive and behavioral remediation. *Brain and Cognition*, 79, 159–179.

Reeves, T. C. (2006). Design research from a technology perspective. In: J. V. Akker, K. Gravemeijer, S. McKenney, & N. Nieveen (Eds), *Educational Design Research* (pp. 52–66). London, UK: Routledge.

Reeves, T. C. & Reeves, P. M. (2015). Reorienting educational technology research from things to problems. *Learning: Research and Practice*, 1, 91–93.

Ritchie, S. J., Chudler, E. H., & Della Sala, S. (2012). Don't try this at school: the attraction of 'alternative' educational techniques. In: S. Della Sala & M. Anderson (Eds), *Neuroscience in Education: The Good, the Bad, and the Ugly* (pp. 244–264). Oxford, UK: Oxford University Press.

Ross, S. M., Morrison, G. R., & Lowther, D. L. (2010). Educational technology research past and present: balancing rigor and relevance to impact school learning. *Contemporary Educational Technology*, 1, 17–35.

Selwyn, N. (2011). Editorial: in praise of pessimism—the need for negativity in educational technology. *British Journal of Educational Technology*, 42, 713–718.

Selwyn, N. (2012). Ten suggestions for improving academic research in education and technology. *Learning, Media and Technology*, 37, 213–219.

Selwyn, N. (2013). *Distrusting Educational Technology: Critical Questions for Changing Times*. New York: Routledge.

Soon Fook, F. & Aldalalah, O. (2010). Effects of computer-based instructional designs among internals-externals: a cognitive load perspective. *European Journal of Social Science*, 14, 164–182.

Sorden S. D. (2005). A cognitive approach to instructional design for multimedia learning. *Information Science Journal*, 8, 263–279.

Topolinski, S. & Reber, R. (2010). Gaining insight into the "Aha" experience. *Current Directions in Psychological Science*, 19, 402–405.

Van den Akker, J., Gravemeijer, K., McKenney, S., & Nieveen, N. (2006). Introducing educational design research. In: J. Van den Akker, K. Gravemeijer, S. McKenney, & N. Nieveen (Eds), *Educational Design Research* (pp. 3–7). New York: Routledge.

Venema, S. & Lodge, J. M. (2013). Capturing dynamic presentation: using technology to enhance the chalk and the talk. *Australasian Journal of Educational Technology*, 29, 20–31.

Weaver, D., Spratt, C., & Nair, C. S. (2008). Academic and student use of a learning management system: implications for quality. *Australasian Journal of Educational Technology*, 24, 30–41.

Yang, L. & McCall, B. (2014). World education finance policies and higher education access: a statistical analysis of World Development Indicators for 86 countries. *International Journal of Educational Development*, 35, 25–36.

Yarkoni, T. (2012). Psychoinformatics: new horizons at the interface of the psychological and computing sciences. *Current Directions in Psychological Science*, 21, 391–397.

Zuber-Skerritt, O. (1992). *Action Research in Higher Education: Examples and Reflections*. London, UK: Kogan Page.

SECTION 3

Domain-Specific Issues and Classroom Strategies

8

ALIGNING NEUROSCIENCE FINDINGS WITH SOCIO-CULTURAL PERSPECTIVES ON LEARNING IN SCIENCE

George Aranda and Russell Tytler

DEAKIN UNIVERSITY

Introduction

There has been increasing recognition, both in writing about science learning in schools and in the way that knowledge is produced in science, of the material basis of learning and knowledge creation (Pickering, 1995). Thirty years ago, Latour (1986) argued that the emergence of scientific thought depended on the development of effective representational tools or inscriptions, such as tables, graphs, figures, and models, which could be combined, quantified, graphed, written, and reproduced. Digital, material, and symbolic representations are seen as crucial tools for reasoning in science, rather than simply as records of resolved ideas and theories (Gooding, 2006).

These ideas provide new insights into and explanations of the nature of learning in science classrooms. Increasingly, there is recognition of the multi-modal nature of student learning in science (Lemke, 1990, 2004). There is a substantial science education literature based within socio-cultural perspectives that argues first that learning occurs through mediation processes involving these multi-modal representational tools (Vygotsky, 1981), and second, that learning to use these tools can be seen as a process of enculturation into the discursive practices of science (Lave & Wenger, 1991) that are shaped around a set of discipline-specific and generic literacies used in science to build and validate knowledge (Moje, 2007). Ainsworth (2006, 2008) has explored how the use of multi-model representations relates to their form and function. The recognition and coordination of multiple representations are key to visualization and problem solving in science (Gilbert, 2005; Kozma & Russell, 1997, 2005). Learning in science is thus not simply the memorization of abstracted concepts and the processes by which these apply to the world, but rather it involves the recognition and command of representational practices (Tytler & Prain, 2010; Tytler *et al.*, 2013). These practices involve the use of visual, spatial, symbolic, textual, and embodied representational tools. In this chapter we shall explore the evidence as to how these might involve, at the neurophysical level, brain structures specific to visual, auditory, spatial, and motor perceptions.

Further studies have argued that representations play a defining rather than supporting role in learning and problem solving (Klein, 2001; Tytler *et al.*, 2009; Zhang, 1997), consistent with pragmatist beliefs (see Peirce's collected papers in Hartshorne *et al.*, 1997; Wittgenstein, 1972) that we can only talk about conceptual understanding in terms of the effective and practical application of the multi-modal representational practices that underpin it. Again this implies that rather than the traditional focus on building expertise around formal, verbal definitions of concepts, classroom teaching and learning processes need to be built around the representational resources that underpin scientific concepts and practices (Moje, 2007). An inquiry process in which students generate and negotiate representations as a key aspect of learning has been explored by a number of researchers (Hubber *et al.*, 2010; Lehrer & Schauble, 2006; Manz, 2012; Waldrip *et al.*, 2010), who argue that representations can be used as tools for many different forms of reasoning (Cox, 1999; Ford & Forman, 2006)—for example, for initial, speculative thinking, to record observations, to show a sequence or process in time (Ainsworth *et al.*, 2011), to sort information, or to predict outcomes. We have argued that representations in different modes have different affordances by virtue of offering productive constraints on student perceptions and understanding (Prain & Tytler, 2012, 2013). Each visual, spatial, symbolic, or embodied representation acts to channel thinking. The essence of conceptual understanding lies in the capacity to coordinate across these different modes in solving problems and developing explanations.

These ideas provide fresh perspectives on the fundamental nature of learning, reasoning, and knowing in science. In generating and using representations, scientists reason not only through formal logic but also through informal processes such as visual and spatial pattern recognition and metaphoric association (Klein, 2006). Gooding (2004, 2006) has shown how visual images have been key to the creative advancement of scientific theory, and argues that the central role of visualization relates to "our ability to recognize regularities as visual or auditory patterns ... [and] our ability to integrate different kinds of sensory information into a single representation—not just consider one variable at a time. These abilities underlie the use of patterns and the construction of phenomenal and explanatory models" (Gooding, 2006, p. 41). Gooding's link between science knowledge-building practices and human cognitive capability mirrors our concern in this chapter to link learning in science with neuroscience findings about brain structure and function. We argue that reasoning and conceptual learning must fundamentally involve multiple brain structures and processes dedicated to auditory, visual, spatial, and linguistic processing, even where traditional accounts might predict that only abstracted logical manipulation is involved.

These insights suggest that the process of learning in science classrooms, like knowledge building in science, is much richer than generalized accounts suggest, involving not only formal reasoning but also perceptual reasoning across multiple modes. We have taken these ideas, together with advocacy of inquiry teaching and learning approaches in which students are accorded agency in exploring phenomena and producing and evaluating ideas, to develop a "representation construction" inquiry approach to science teaching and learning. The key principles underpinning the approach are first that students engage with real phenomena to construct, with guidance, representations in multiple modes, and second, that learning and knowing are judged in terms of the ability to create and coordinate multi-modal representations to solve problems.

In this chapter we shall take a number of core ideas within these socio-cultural, multi-modal perspectives on learning and knowing, and explore the educational neuroscience literature for evidence that might support or challenge this. In this process we see neuroscience findings as suggestive and confirmatory rather than as providing an explicit causal explanation. They can also suggest refined ways of thinking about these socio-cultural constructs. The core ideas that we take from these socio-cultural theoretical perspectives are as follows:

1. Perceiving, learning, and knowing are fundamentally distributed across multiple, multi-modal representations.
2. Abstraction is underpinned by multi-modal representations that link to perceptual experience.
3. Active construction leads to deeper learning.

We shall now consider each of these in turn and explore the relevant neuroscience findings. Each point is not strictly distinct, and in fact the neuroscience studies overlap in their implications. However, the three ideas provide a structure around which we have been able to explore the neuroscience literature.

Perceiving, Learning, and Knowing are Fundamentally Distributed Across Multiple, Multi-Modal Representations

As described in the Introduction to this chapter, from the perspective of socio-cultural pragmatist views of learning, conceptual learning involves the recognition and coordination of representations across multiple modes. Learning in science relies on students being able to recognize, construct, and interpret diagrams with both visual and spatial elements, and embodied representations (Lemke, 2004). A major implication of this is that teachers need to incorporate into their lessons experiences and representations in multiple perceptual modes, and to support students in coordinating these. Thus learning about evaporation might involve experiments with water, role plays of particles changing from liquid to gas state, drawings of water molecules in different states, and writing about evaporative processes.

Natural language is also one of the key representational tools that mediate understanding of a concept in science, and language often works through metaphoric association. We would thus expect that learning will generally involve activation of multiple areas of the brain that relate to different perceptual modes. We therefore look for neuroscience studies that show such multi-region activation, as validation that learning is inherently distributed across multiple representational modes. There is a common misconception that learning of a particular idea will occur in a particular region of the brain, and that recollection is like accessing a file on a computer. In fact many parts of the brain are coordinated with perception and learning that occur in the brain, and while consciousness feels as though it has a unity to it, the process of perceiving something to be learned relies on the coordination of different regions of the brain.

Neuroanatomy of Music

A complex task such as learning music requires the coordination of many regions of the brain, each responsible for processing different qualities that exist within the music itself. According to Koelsch's neurocognitive model of music perception (Koelsch, 2011), to perceive (and therefore learn about) music requires the coordination of different brain regions responsible for processing aspects of music.

Research by Koelsch (2011) has shown that the perception and learning of music require the coordination of many different brain regions, which themselves are not unique to music perception. Table 8.1 shows the multiple brain regions that correspond to different aspects of appreciation of musical quality.

There is general recognition of the multi-modal, multi-conceptual nature of learning music:

> listening to and producing music involves a tantalizing mix of practically every human cognitive function. Even a seemingly simple activity, such as humming a familiar tune, necessitates complex auditory pattern-processing mechanisms, attention, memory storage and retrieval, motor programming, sensory-motor integration, and so forth.
>
> *(Zatorre, 2005)*

Music education, like science, involves the development of a specialized language, and again these constructs draw on multiple perceptual modes. Although the above-mentioned aspects can develop naturally, they can also be influenced by learning, and it is the aim of music education to "make processing a conscious experience and develop the student's understanding and vocabulary to express musical concepts" (Collins, 2013, p. 223).

Thus, as with science, a crucial skill is the coordination of multiple perceptual modes. The perception and learning of music require the coordination of many different brain regions, which themselves are not unique to music perception. For example, the process of language learning relies on similar neural and cognitive structures to those involved in music perception, requiring a different coordination of somewhat similar neural structures: "the human brain, particularly at an early age, does not treat language and music as strictly separate domains, but rather treats language as a special case of music" (Koelsch, 2011, p. 16).

The ways in which multiple senses and modes of perception relate to learning and knowing are a function of the way that the brain encodes incoming information.

TABLE 8.1 Broad stages of Koelsch's model for music perception (Koelsch, 2011).

Musical quality	Perception and manifestations of processed music	Brain regions
Feature extraction	Perceiving the timing, timbre, and localization of sound	Auditory brainstem, thalamus, primary auditory cortex
Gestalt formation, auditory sensory memory, analysis of intervals, structure building, structural re-analysis and repair	Allow grouping and conceptualizing of music according to remembered patterns	Auditory cortices, the inferior and ventral frontal regions of the brain
Vitalization and premotor actions	Allow for embodied manifestations of music, such as toe tapping or a euphoric feeling coming from the music	Autonomic nervous system, frontal and parietal cortices

Encoding Involves Multiple Regions of the Brain

As stimuli are perceived, the information must be stored within the brain. This is a process known as encoding, in which the stimuli (visual, auditory, bodily, etc.) are converted into a form that the brain can store and retrieve at a later time. This encoding causes changes in the brain, such as the creation or modification of synapses and proteins. Information is stored in the brain via a mechanism known as long-term potentiation, which increases the strength of connections between two neurons that fire in succession. This process is thought to occur in a subcortical region of the brain known as the hippocampus, damage to which can lead to an inability to form new memories (Lynch, 2004; Scoville & Milner, 1957).

Other regions of the brain can be implicated depending on the type of encoding involved. For example, the amygdala, a subcortical structure near the hippocampus, can be activated during encoding of visual information (Lynch, 2004; Belova *et al.*, 2006).

Music is a good example of this learning, with many regions of the brain participating in many different aspects of the task. While the physical perception of music may occur as a consistent whole, the underlying processing of the brain suggests that multiple regions of the brain are responding to the underlying spatial structure of music.

It is clear from these neuroscience findings that learning in a domain can involve the recruitment of multiple, often surprising sensory perceptual modes that are considered to be fundamental to the conceptual challenge with which the person is engaging. This is consistent with the socio-cultural insight that learning (in science as elsewhere) is fundamentally multi-modal, and involves the recognition and coordination of a variety of representations that are perceptually based.

Thus our contention that in science teaching and learning it is important to expose students to representations in multiple perceptual modes is consistent with the evidence from music, and the argument that effective learning involves coordinating across multiple modes is consistent with Koelsch's advocacy that this coordinating should be made a conscious experience.

Remembering Multi-Modally as a Key Element of Knowing

A core characteristic of expert problem solvers in chemistry is the ability to recall and coordinate representations in response to contextual problems (Kozma & Russell, 2005). Logically, this involves processes of re-creation, re-constitution, and representational re-description. Second-generation cognitive science (Klein, 2006) emphasizes the importance of associative reasoning and perception, rather than having an exclusive focus on formal reasoning based on logical semantic structures that relate abstracted concepts. This shifts us towards an understanding that conceptual learning and knowing involve coordination of multiple perceptual elements. Furthermore, the role of representational re-creation and re-description raises the issue of memory as a perceptual process.

Findings from neuroscience indicate that learnt memories are not held as coherent unitary events, but are reconstructed from their constituent parts and modified each time they are recalled. Given that any demonstration of understanding in solving contextual problems in science will inevitably involve recall of concepts, laws, and episodes of application of ideas in context, findings concerning memory have relevance for demonstrating conceptual understanding. In fact, neuroscience research has demonstrated that the process of remembering involves not simply recall, but rather the active reconstruction of the events that have been laid down in our memories. Although it appears that we have a complete memory when we remember something that has happened, the reconstruction of a memory can be influenced by events or biases that occur at the time of recollection.

We argue from this that, in order to support student learning, teachers need to provide multiple perceptual experiences relating to a concept, to help students to form rich and multi-modal perceptions and associations that they can use in problem solving and explanation. It is not enough to imagine the task of understanding as committing to memory verbal and formal relationships such as laws and theories. Problem solving involves re-creation and re-description at a perceptual level.

Memory as a Constructive Process

Similar to encoding, recollection is influenced by biases at the moment of remembering. Studies of eyewitness testimony demonstrate that even though we may be quite confident about the accuracy of our memories, this may not truly represent what actually took place (discrepancies in the memory performance differ between laboratory and real-world studies) (Lacy & Stark, 2013). The misinformation effect has been widely studied, and demonstrates that certain cues can subtly alter the memory of an event.

For example, cues—such as the wording of a question after participants have viewed footage of a car collision—can influence memory. For instance, the questions "How fast were the cars going when they smashed into each other?" and "How fast were the cars going when they hit each other?" led participants to estimate the speed of the cars to be 20% faster when responding to the former question compared with their responses to the latter. In addition, participants are more likely to report a false memory of seeing broken glass at the site of the crash when the word "smash" is used (Loftus, 1979). Memory distortions can also occur as a result of positive or negative feedback to testimony (making the witness more or less confident about their memory of the event), or as a result of the passage of time or repeated recounting of events (Lacy & Stark, 2013).

Similarly, when introducing students to new concepts or representations, there must be a negotiation between previously learned concepts or representations so that students do not come away from the learning interaction with incorrect associations between similar concepts. Moving between representations allows students to add to or broaden their understanding of a particular concept.

What Happens in the Brain?

The process of retrieving an event or information from the past is known as recall. Proposed by Tulving (1972), recall consists of two types of memory, namely episodic memory, which involves the recollection of information about an autobiographical event in time and space (e.g. your tenth birthday), and semantic memory, which involves words, abstract concepts, and rules (Tulving, 1972).

The two types of memory are related, with semantic memory being derived from accumulated episodic memories. For example, our semantic concept of "ball" will be derived from all the previous experiences we have had with a ball, including visual, auditory, and tactile experiences. Similarly, future experiences we have of a ball will influence the semantic concept that we currently have. As time passes, it may be difficult to recall the episodes during which we experienced particular events, but the semantic concept remains.

Although each of the sensory modalities are required to successfully recall a memory, none of them hold all the information about the memory itself. Rather it is the coordination between primary and secondary sensory regions, typically by the prefrontal cortex and the hippocampus, that allows for the reconstruction of a memory that can be rich in sensory detail.

Thus neuroscience research into memory provides considerable support for the view that our memories—both semantic and episodic—are reconstructed each time they are recalled. This supports the argument that memories and associated conceptual understandings should not be regarded as unitary, but rather are fundamentally distributed across a range of different perceptual elements. It appears that our thinking and reasoning are distributed across a variety of multi-modal representations (visual, spatial, and motor) and coordination centres as we call on our knowledge to solve problems.

Thus, in classrooms, teachers need to provide students with a rich network of semantic and episodic multi-modal experiences, which can be drawn upon when interpreting, explaining, and problem solving in new situations. Learning and remembering are inherently associative and strengthened through practice, so teachers also need to provide students with multiple opportunities to explore and utilize associative links in solving problems.

Abstraction is Underpinned by Multi-Modal Representations that Link to Perceptual Experience

Teachers of science need to build students' capacity to move between multiple representations at different levels of abstraction in problem solving and inquiry situations. This will involve presenting tasks in which students are challenged to interpret scientific ideas through multiple and multi-modal perceptual experiences and representations.

The capacity to abstract is a key characteristic of expert representational practices. Concepts that are expressed in verbal form (e.g. definitions of the ideal gas model, evolutionary understandings of adaptation, or the mole) are powerful abstractions that constitute the discursive currency of experts in a field. A study by Hay *et al.* (2013) of undergraduate, graduate, and expert drawings of neuronal synapses found that experts tended to represent these in terms of abstracted functions, whereas undergraduate students tended to reproduce structures from textbooks. Thus abstraction is often concerned with purposes, processes, and underpinning principles, separated from surface descriptions of structures and functions.

The predominant approach to these conceptual abstractions used in science textbooks is to offer verbal descriptions and definitions, and introduce a range of visual and other representations as illustrative material to support the concept. Abstracted concepts then become the subjects of laws and theories that are separated from the everyday representations and experimental data through which they are instantiated. However, Latour (1999) described the process of representational re-description that underlies the scientific knowledge-building process. He followed scientists studying soils associated with changes in Amazonian rainforest boundaries to show how they transformed soil analysis data from ordered sample arrays of soils located geographically, to tables of soil constituent measurements, to graphs that could be transported back to France, to papers that could be circulated and debated. These circulating representations are typical of the way that scientific data are transformed into abstracted communications. An understanding of the abstractions generated by this process involves the recognition of the representational chains connecting high-level constructs and findings to the base data. Recognition of the successive chains that link theory to evidential data is a key aspect of understanding the nature of science and the status of the claims that are made.

Thus we argue that problem solving with abstracted concepts in science and other subjects must involve a recognition of the relationship between the higher-level abstractions that are concepts, and the networks of representations that support these abstractions and link them to their evidential bases. We argue that abstractions are ineffective for problem solving without coordination of the representational chains that give them meaning. We look for evidence from the neuroscience literature of ways in which abstracted concepts and perceptual elements are linked, and how this linking might operate to support problem solving.

The human brain is continually coordinating activity in different parts of the brain as it abstracts multi-modal representations of concepts. For example, a study by Fernandino *et al.* (2015) examined which sensory and motor regions of the brain were involved in neural representations of concepts. In this study, the participants looked at words on a screen and were asked the question "Does the item refer to something that can be experienced with the senses?" The changes in the participants' brain activity were measured using an fMRI scanner.

They were shown around 900 words, one at a time, and asked to press a button for "Yes" or "No" in response to the question. In a previous study, the words themselves had been demonstrated to load on five attributes closely tied to sensory–motor experiences, namely colour, shape, sound, visual motion, and physical manipulation. The last attribute referred to the extent to which the object affords physical manipulation. These attributes were examined as the brain networks that underpin their functions had been well established in the neuroscience literature. The words were a mixture of concrete and abstract words that ranged from objects that were or were not manipulable, to animals, emotions, professions, time spans, and events. One example is "tomato", which loaded highly on attributes such as colour and shape, but moderately on manipulation; another example is "apology", which loaded moderately on sound and manipulation.

The results of this study indicated that the word concepts activated regions of the brain that were involved with multi-modal integration of the senses. The functional purpose of these brain regions could be differentiated into two functions. The first was concerned with how we interact with an object, such as its visual and haptic shape, and motor representations about object-directed body interactions. The second was concerned with the temporal–spatial perception of the object, typically for those objects that we do not manipulate (e.g. people, events). The authors considered that this might be "a basic ontological distinction between static objects and dynamic events" (Fernandino *et al.*, 2015, p. 11).

The authors proposed a top–down model in which the concept of a word activates multi-modal integration networks of the brain, and that information is then passed on to other networks involved with higher- and then lower-order processing of sensory information. The degree to which each brain network contributes to the neural representation of the concept will vary depending on the concept, but the study clearly demonstrates that concepts are embodied in neural representations.

Another example of abstraction can be observed in children who are seen to be gifted. Studies indicate that children who are gifted use more parts of their brain for a given task with greater regional activity than non-gifted children (Desco *et al.*, 2011), but also that they demonstrate greater coordination between planning and executive frontal regions of the brain (Zhang *et al.*, 2006; Lee *et al.*, 2006; O'Boyle *et al.*, 2008) and sensory–motor regions, consistent with the findings of Fernandino *et al.* (2015) described above.

We speculate that one of the reasons why gifted children are able to abstract better than non-gifted children is that they are able to efficiently coordinate information between different regions of the brain. This may be consistent with models of giftedness and the notion of metacognition (Nelson & Narens, 1990, 1994; see also Chapter 12).

If we assume that abstract logical thinking is associated with problem-solving activity, this would indicate that higher levels of function involve the coordination of multiple sensory processes, and that abstract reasoning does not proceed separately from these. This supports our proposition that abstraction cannot be thought of as distinct from the multi-modal perceptual underpinnings through which abstraction is rendered meaningful. Teachers need to support students to develop flexibility in problem solving through experience of coordinating representations in different perceptual modes and levels of abstraction, rather than focusing on formal abstracted thinking.

Active Construction Leads to Deeper Learning

In this section we shall look to neuroscience findings to support the contention that setting students tasks in which they actively construct and discuss representations leads to deeper learning. This is a basic premise of inquiry learning.

As described in the Introduction to this chapter, there is general acknowledgment that learning science involves being able to recognize and coordinate representations across multiple modes. Some researchers have focused on the implications of this for explicit teaching of key canonical modal representations, such as the form and function of graphs, or diagrams such as molecular models or food webs, or symbolic representations of chemical reactions. However, there is a strand of research that investigates the effectiveness for learning of students constructing, negotiating, and coordinating representations in authentic contexts (Lehrer & Schauble, 2006; Tytler *et al.*, 2013). These approaches are consistent with inquiry approaches to science more generally, which have a substantial literature claiming that conceptual and procedural learning are both enhanced by this process. A number of meta-analyses have been conducted of studies comparing inquiry with more directed approaches, yielding somewhat inconclusive results but generally concluding that there is a learning advantage when students actively inquire and discuss the evidence for scientific ideas (Furtak *et al.*, 2012). Chi (2009) characterized three levels of student activity that describe differences from teacher-centred approaches in which students are cast in the role of passive recipients of knowledge. First, active activities involve students "actively doing something" in response to input. Second, constructing activities are those in which students produce outputs that go beyond the presented information. Third, interactive activities include dialogue in which ideas are discussed, challenged, argued for, and defended. Chi argues that there is a progressive learning advantage as one moves from passive activities through to interactive activities.

For evidence of student involvement in constructing representations and ideas that go beyond what is given, we look to the neuroscience literature concerning student construction that goes beyond reproduction.

An example of how construction leads to deeper learning can be observed in letter learning in children. The process of learning letters requires a complex understanding of the visual aspects of the letters, their sounds, how they sit within the context of words, and how they are written. When we perceive letters as adults, we activate neural networks for both the letter perception and motor regions responsible for writing, particularly in the left hemisphere of the brain (Flowers *et al.*, 2004; Menon & Desmond, 2001).

The Evidence from Children Learning about Letters

Children who are learning about letters activate similar parts of the brain, and the question has arisen as to how adult-like brain activity when recognizing letters emerges from child-like brain activity. Various strategies have been used in the teaching of letters, but it is unclear which teaching strategy might lead to an explanation of how this adult-like brain activity during letter recognition might occur.

To investigate this question, James (2010) trained pre-literate students using a variety of teaching methods, including story readings, where the letters and words were pointed out by the experimenter, and writing practice, where the children wrote the words from a story and received feedback on their accuracy. In the control condition, the letters from the story were identified by the children and they were given feedback. Children were tested both before and after training using an fMRI design, where they viewed letters, shapes, and pseudoletters (i.e. characters that have the qualities of a letter, but which are not real letters), but were not required to give a response. The results indicated that those children who had written the letters down showed significantly greater increases in brain activity compared with those children who had only viewed the letters. An important finding from this study was that the regions of the brain responsible for visual processing demonstrated increases in activity specifically to sensorimotor training. While it may be argued that this increase could have been due to greater attention when writing the letters, behavioral data did not show any significant differences between the conditions. They did demonstrate that there were potential learning gains when one combined sensory and motor processes: "perceptual learning is most efficient when observers are allowed to explore the environment through the combination of sensory and motor systems" (James, 2010, p. 286).

But were these learning gains specific to writing, or could comparable sensorimotor processes lead to similar outcomes?

James and Engelhardt (2012) examined the question of sensorimotor processes and how they contributed to letter learning. The study participants were pre-literate children who undertook a range of sensorimotor training activities, including printing letters, typing letters, or tracing letters and shapes. It was hypothesized that allowing students to write their own letters enhances their understanding of letters, by the creation of varied examples, all of which fit into the category of the letter that they are attempting to write. However, if any sort of sensorimotor activity involved with letters was able to enhance learning outcomes, there should be no difference in brain response or learning.

Participants underwent training in each condition, with stimuli that were presented only once in each type of training. This allowed an examination of stimuli unique to each training type to be compared in the fMRI study design. The results of the study indicated that printing letters produces greater increases in brain activity than typing letters in the inferior frontal gyrus, the anterior cingulate, and the fusiform gyrus; printing recruits greater brain activity than tracing in the posterior parietal cortex and the fusiform gyrus, and tracing recruits more brain activity than typing letters in the inferior frontal gyrus.

These four regions of the brain are important for reading in literate adults (Shaywitz & Shaywitz, 2008), while the inferior frontal gyrus and the posterior parietal cortex are involved with writing (Lobrano et al., 2004; Menon & Desmond, 2001).

The results suggest that although different sensorimotor practice can benefit letter learning, the greatest recruitment of important regions occurs for conditions where children are allowed to make their own mistakes, while carefully monitoring their own progress.

Embodied Cognition

Closer to science learning, Kontra et al. (2015) studied the role of embodied cognition in the learning of angular momentum in higher education physics classes. They compared students who had been briefly exposed to the physical experience of angular momentum, by holding a spinning wheel and axle, to those who only witnessed their classmates' exposure to the experience. Using fMRI, the brain activity of the two groups was examined when they took a quiz in which they viewed a computer-generated model of the same physical experience and were asked to decide which way the wheel would move due to angular momentum generated by the speed of the spinning wheel. Those who had been exposed to the physical experience demonstrated greater activity in the dorsal premotor cortex, the primary motor/somatosensory cortex, the superior parietal lobe, the supplementary motor area, and the cerebellum. These are the parts of the brain responsible for action planning, action production, and sensitivity to previous action experience, of which the primary motor/somatosensory cortex and the supplementary motor area were significantly correlated with quiz performance scores. These results suggest that students who had been exposed to the physical experience of angular momentum were better able to activate those parts of the brain involved with the original experience, which allowed them to more successfully answer the quiz question.

This finding can be interpreted using the model of Fernandino et al. (2015) which links high-level conceptual abstraction with a hierarchical perceptual network that includes sensorimotor perceptions as well as visual and auditory components. Understanding of angular momentum inevitably involves multiple perceptual experiences and representations.

These neuroscience findings concerning the implications of active construction for learning broadly support the contention that active engagement in constructing, such as drawing letters rather than tracing or typing, or being able to represent objects, provides support for learning beyond that conferred by practice that does not challenge individual construction. Moreover, the handwriting example showed that the particular affordance of free-form writing over tracing was the demand it created to monitor error, and the opportunity for correction. This is an example of the affordances offered by representation construction, through the productive constraint offered by the particular mode—in this case a motor mode. The example also demonstrates the close relationship between motor perception and conceptual understanding. The paper by Kontra et al. (2015) showed the advantage of active physical construction in learning physical science concepts, identifying sensorimotor brain regions as being more highly activated than in a non-constructive control group, leading to enhanced reasoning. This illustrates the importance of embodied representational work in developing deeper understanding of science concepts.

Thus we have identified substantial neuroscience findings that support the fundamental inquiry teaching and learning proposition that a powerful learning advantage is provided by having students actively explore and construct representations in close association with the introduction of the abstracted ideas and representations of science.

Conclusion

In this chapter we have presented three claims based on multi-modal pragmatist perspectives on teaching and learning in science, based within a socio-cultural tradition of research on student learning in science. For each of the claims (that perceiving, learning, and knowing are fundamentally distributed across representations involving multiple sensory modes, that abstraction is underpinned by representations that link to perceptual experience, and that active construction leads to deeper-level and more robust learning), we have sought neuroscience findings that speak to these claims, and in each case we have found research results that are compatible with them. In addition, in each case we have drawn out the messages from these results for teacher classroom practices.

From this exploration of the neuroscience literature we have also gained insights into the mechanisms by which reasoning in science across multiple perceptual modes enhances learning. For instance, the active construction of letters helps students to recognize letters by offering the opportunity to adjust motor processes and learn through mistakes—an assertion consistent with our notion of affordances of representation as productive constraint. We see also how the assertion that knowledge production through representational re-description across modes, including visuo-spatial and motor perceptions, is a fundamental aspect of learning language and music. Thus it becomes clear that learning and knowing are fundamentally distributed activities involving multiple senses and coordination processes. We conclude that the laying down of rich conceptual networks is dependent on multi-modal experiences in problem solving and representational work that reflects the creative nature of knowledge production in science. Planning for effective learning of abstract concepts is hindered by prevailing views that these are unitary, platonic ideals somehow separated from the multiple multi-modal representational practices that instantiate them. We would argue, with Gooding (2006), that the multi-modal representational reasoning processes by which scientific knowledge is built reflect the way that the human brain is wired. We would further argue that the essence of this wiring is that perceptual processes are distributed across differentiated brain structures, and that knowledge building fundamentally involves a process of coordination and reconstruction of perceptual events. Further still, we argue that learning in science needs to proceed in ways that reflect these reasoning processes, and that active construction of representations and interactions that enable negotiation and refinement of these should be a core aspect of effective classroom approaches to learning.

From this exploration we have also gained insight into the relationship between the findings of neuroscience research and the complex realities of classroom practice. In previous writing (Tytler, 2013), we have pointed out the seemingly intransigent translational difficulties in aligning socio-cultural with neuroscience research insights, relating to the different learning paradigms, problems of complexity and scale, epistemological and/or methodological incompatibilities, and incommensurate theoretical underpinnings that exist in the two areas. In this chapter we have not claimed direct causal connections between what happens at the individual brain level and what happens in classroom situations based on complex language exchanges and human interactions. We have not attempted to work directly from neuroscience findings to make pronouncements on how classroom teaching and learning practice should proceed. Rather we have taken insights into reasoning and learning from a coherent theoretical framing of knowledge production processes in science and in science classrooms, and looked for parallel findings in the neuroscience literature that could make sense of these at the biological level. The links are not direct, since the neuroscience findings do not address science learning explicitly, nor do they speak to language and representation. Nevertheless, they establish the complex perceptual processes that underpin conceptual learning, which are also recognized by recent thinking in cognitive science (Klein, 2006) and by pragmatist semiotic perspectives.

Clarke and Hollingsworth (2013) argue that a challenge for any research project seeking to connect socio-cultural research with neuroscience is how to interweave the complementary accounts provided by each analytical approach. We suggest that, in the same way that the unit of analysis in socio-cultural research and in neuroscience research is different, so the nature of the explanations provided will be fundamentally different. It is not different explanations of the same phenomenon that are being offered, but explanations of related phenomena that are different in scale, in complexity, and in the relative prominence given to the individual as cognizing agent or as participant member of a social group. We anticipate drawing on the findings of one discipline to explicate, elaborate, and explain learning as it is conceived in the other discipline.

This is the nature of what we have done—to draw on the neuroscience literature to elaborate and explain insights generated from socio-cultural perspectives on individual and collaborative learning in science.

The search for relevant neuroscience research to support socio-cultural insights into learning in science exposed a dearth of studies that spoke directly to science learning and classroom teaching, but unearthed a range of types of study relevant to these findings on the multi-modal multi-sensory nature of conceptual learning in science. There is a need for further research in neuroscience that investigates more explicitly the ways in which embodied, visual, and spatial perceptions are involved in different aspects of conceptual learning in science or other disciplines, the role of active engagement and interaction in establishing robust understandings, and the implications of this for classroom practice. It is our belief that such research has the capacity to provide new insights into the nature of abstraction in learning, and to challenge current platonic orthodoxies concerning the nature of conceptual knowledge. Such a program could potentially offer a new perspective on learning as the capacity for active problem solving using representation across multiple modes, involving multiple sensory inputs. It could also help to establish more robust, evidence-based recommendations as to how science classroom teaching should be framed.

References

Ainsworth, S. (2006). DeFT: a conceptual framework for considering learning with multiple representations. *Learning and Instruction*, 16(3), 183–198.

Ainsworth, S. (2008). The educational value of multiple representations when learning complex scientific concepts. In: J. K. Gilbert, M. Reiner, & M. Nakhlel (Eds), *Visualization: Theory and Practice in Science Education* (pp. 191–208). New York: Springer.

Ainsworth, S., Prain, V., & Tytler, R. (2011). Drawing to learn in science. *Science*, 333, 1096–1097.

Belova, M. A., Morrison, S. E., Paton, J. J., & Salzman, C. D. (2006). The primate amygdala represents the positive and negative value of visual stimuli during learning. *Nature*, 439, 865–870.

Chi, M. (2009). Active-constructive-interactive: a conceptual framework for differentiating learning activities. *Topics in Cognitive Science*, 1(1), 73–105.

Clarke, D. & Hollingsworth, H. (2013). Challenges and opportunities for neuroscience: how to explain the connection between socio-cultural practices and cognition? In: *Proceedings of the Australian Council for Educational Research (ACER) Annual Conference: How the Brain Learns* (pp. 103–110). Camberwell, Melbourne: ACER.

Collins, A. (2013). Neuroscience meets music education: exploring the implications of neural processing models on music education practice. *International Journal of Music Education*, 31(2), 217–231.

Cox, R. (1999). Representation construction, externalised cognition and individual differences. *Learning and Instruction*, 9(4), 343–363.

Desco, M., Navas-Sanchez, F. J., Sanchez-González, J., Reig, S., Robles, O., Franco, C., Guzmán-De-Villoria, J. A., García-Barreno, P., & Arango, C. (2011). Mathematically gifted adolescents use more extensive and more bilateral areas of the fronto-parietal network than controls during executive functioning and fluid reasoning tasks. *NeuroImage*, 57(1), 281–292.

Fernandino, L., Binder, J. R., Desai, R. H., Pendl, S. L., Humphries, C. J., Gross, W. L., Conant, L. L., & Seidenberg, M. S. (2015). Concept representation reflects multimodal abstraction: a framework for embodied semantics. *Cerebral Cortex*. DOI: 10.1093/cercor/bhv020

Flowers, D. L., Jones, K., Noble, K., VanMeter, J., Zeffiro, T. A., Wood, F. B., & Eden, G. F. (2004). Attention to single letters activates left extrastriate cortex. *NeuroImage*, 21(3), 829–839.

Ford, M. & Forman, E. A. (2006). Refining disciplinary learning in classroom contexts. *Review of Research in Education*, 30, 1–33.

Furtak, E., Seidel, T., Iverson, H., & Briggs, D. (2012). Experimental and quasi-experimental studies of inquiry-based science teaching: a meta-analysis. *Review of Educational Research*, 82(3), 300–329.

Gilbert, J. K. (Ed.) (2005). *Visualization in Science Education*. New York: Springer.

Gooding, D. (2004). Visualization, inference and explanation in the sciences. In: G. Malcolm (Ed.), *Studies in Multidisciplinarity. Volume 2. Multidisciplinary Approaches to Visual Representations and Interpretations* (pp. 1–25). Amsterdam, The Netherlands: Elsevier.

Gooding, D. (2006). From phenomenology to field theory: Faraday's visual reasoning. *Perspectives on Science*, 14(1), 40–65.

Hartshorne, C., Weiss, P., & Burks, A. W. (Eds) (1997). *Collected Papers of Charles Sanders Peirce*. Cambridge, MA: Harvard University Press.

Hay, D. B., Williams, D., Stahl, D., & Wingate, R. J. (2013). Using drawings of the brain cell to exhibit expertise in neuroscience: exploring the boundaries of experimental culture. *Science Studies and Science Education*, 97(3), 468–491.

Hubber, P, Tytler, R., & Haslam, F. (2010). Teaching and learning about force with a representational focus: pedagogy and teacher change. *Research in Science Education*, 40(1), 5–28.

James, K. H. (2010). Sensori-motor experience leads to changes in visual processing in the developing brain. *Developmental Science*, 13(2), 279–288.

James, K. H. & Engelhardt, L. (2012). The effects of handwriting experience on functional brain development in pre-literate children. *Trends in Neuroscience and Education*, 1(1), 32–42.

Klein, U. (2001). Introduction. In: U. Klein (Ed.). *Tools and Modes of Representation in the Laboratory Sciences*. Boston, MA: Kluwer Academic Publishers.

Klein, P. (2006). The challenges of scientific literacy: from the viewpoint of second-generation cognitive science. *International Journal of Science Education*, 28(2-3), 143–178.

Koelsch, S. (2011). Toward a neural basis of music perception – a review and updated model. *Frontiers in Psychology*, 2, 110.

Kontra, C., Lyons, D. J., Fischer, S. M., & Beilock, S. L. (2015). Physical experience enhances science learning. *Psychological Science*, 26(6), 737–749.

Kozma, R. & Russell, J. (1997). Multimedia and understanding: expert and novice responses to different representations of chemical phenomena. *Journal of Research in Science Teaching*, 34(9), 949–968.

Kozma, R. & Russell, J. (2005). Students becoming chemists: developing representational competence. In: J. Gilbert (Ed.), *Visualization in Science Education* (pp. 121–145). Dordrecht, The Netherlands: Springer.

Lacy, J. W. & Stark, C. E. L. (2013). The neuroscience of memory: implications for the courtroom. *Nature Reviews: Neuroscience*, 14, 649–658.

Latour, B. (1986). Visualization and cognition: drawing things together. *Knowledge and Society*, 6, 1–40.

Latour, B. (1999). *Pandora's Hope: Essays on the Reality of Science Studies*. Cambridge, MA: Harvard University Press.

Lave, J. & Wenger, E. (1991). *Situated Learning: Legitimate Peripheral Participation*. Cambridge, UK: Cambridge University Press.

Lee, K. H., Choi Y. Y., Gray, J. R., Cho, S. H., Chae, J., Lee, S., & Kim, K. (2006). Neural correlates of superior intelligence: stronger recruitment of posterior parietal cortex. *NeuroImage*, 29(2), 578–586.

Lehrer, R. & Schauble, L. (2006). Cultivating model-based reasoning in science education. In: K. Sawyer (Ed.), *Cambridge Handbook of the Learning Sciences* (pp. 371–388). New York: Cambridge University Press.

Lemke, J. L. (1990). *Talking Science: Language, Learning, and Values*. Westport, CT: Ablex Publishing.

Lemke, J. (2004). The literacies of science. In: E. W. Saul (Ed.), *Crossing Borders in Literacy and Science Instruction: Perspectives on Theory and Practice* (pp. 33–47). Newark, DE: International Reading Association/National Science Teachers Association.

Lobrano, V., Roux, F. E., & Démonet, J. F. (2004). Writing-specific sites in frontal areas: a cortical stimulation study. *Journal of Neurosurgery*, 101(5), 787–798.

Loftus, E. F. (1979) *Eyewitness Testimony*. Cambridge, MA: Harvard University Press.

Lynch, M. A. (2004). Long-term potentiation and memory. *Physiological Reviews*, 84(1), 87–136.

Manz, E. (2012). *Engaging Students in the Epistemic Functions of Scientific Argumentation*. Paper presented at the Annual Conference of the American Educational Research Association, Vancouver, 13–17 April 2012.

Menon, V. & Desmond, J. E. (2001). Left superior parietal cortex involvement in writing: integrating fMRI with lesion evidence. *Brain Research: Cognitive Brain Research*, 12(2), 337–340.

Moje, E. (2007). Developing socially just subject-matter instruction: a review of the literature on disciplinary literacy learning. *Review of Research in Education*, 31(1), 1–44.

Nelson, T. O. & Narens, L. (1990). Metamemory: a theoretical framework and new findings. In: G. H. Bower (Ed.), *The Psychology of Learning and Motivation* (pp. 1–45). New York: Academic Press.

Nelson, T. O. & Narens, L. (1994). Why investigate metacognition? In: J. Metcalfe & A. P. Shimamura (Eds), *Metacognition: Knowing About Knowing* (pp. 1–25). Cambridge, MA: MIT Press.

O'Boyle, M. W. (2008). Mathematically gifted children: developmental brain characteristics and their prognosis for well-being. *Roeper Review*, 30(3), 181–186.

Pickering, A. (1995). *The Mangle of Practice: Time, Agency, and Science*. Chicago, IL: University of Chicago Press.

Prain, V. & Tytler, R. (2012). Learning through constructing representations in science: a framework of representational construction affordances. *International Journal of Science Education*, 34(17), 2751–2773.

Prain, V. & Tytler, R. (2013). Learning through the affordances of representation construction. In: R. Tytler, V. Prain, P. Hubber, & B. Waldrip (Eds), *Constructing Representations to Learn in Science* (pp. 67–82). Rotterdam, The Netherlands: Sense Publishers.

Scoville, R. M. & Milner, B. (1957) Loss of recent memory after bilateral hippocampal lesions. *Journal of Neurology, Neurosurgery, and Psychiatry*, 20(1), 11–21.

Shaywitz, S. E. & Shaywitz, B. A. (2008). Paying attention to reading: the neurobiology of reading and dyslexia. *Development and Psychopathology*, 20(4), 1329–1349.

Tulving, E. (1972). Episodic and semantic memory. In: E. Tulving & W. Donaldson (Eds), *Organization of Memory* (pp. 38–403). New York: Academic Press.

Tytler, R. (2013). *Aligning Socio-Cultural, Classroom Perspectives on Learning with Neuroscience Perspectives and Findings*. Paper presented at the symposium "Contemporary Approaches to Research in Mathematics, Science, Health and Environmental Education", 23–29 November 2013, Deakin University, Melbourne.

Tytler, R. & Prain, V. (2010). A framework for re-thinking learning in science from recent cognitive science perspectives. *International Journal of Science Education,* 32(15), 2055–2078.

Tytler, R., Haslam, F., Prain, V., & Hubber, P. (2009). An explicit representational focus for teaching and learning about animals in the environment. *Teaching Science,* 55(4), 21–27.

Tytler, R., Prain, V., Hubber, P., & Waldrip, B. (Eds) (2013). *Constructing Representations to Learn in Science*. Rotterdam, The Netherlands: Sense Publishers.

Vygotsky, L. (1981). *Thought and Language* (revised and edited by A. Kozulin). Cambridge, MA: MIT Press.

Waldrip, B., Prain, V., & Carolan, J. (2010). Using multi-modal representations to improve learning in junior secondary science. *Research in Science Education,* 40(1), 65–80.

Wittgenstein, L. (1972). *Philosophical Investigations,* 2nd edition (translated by G. E. M. Anscombe, and edited by G. E. M. Anscombe & R. Rhees). Oxford: Basil Blackwell.

Zatorre, R. (2005). Music, the food of neuroscience? *Nature,* 434, 312–315.

Zhang, J. (1997). The nature of external representations in problem solving. *Cognitive Science,* 21(2), 179–217.

Zhang, Q., Shi, J., Luo, Y., Zhao, D., & Yang, J. (2006). Intelligence and information processing during a visual search task in children: an event-related potential study. *NeuroReport,* 17(7), 747–752.

9

SUPPORTING STUDENTS' LEARNING WITH MULTIPLE VISUAL REPRESENTATIONS

Martina A. Rau

DEPARTMENT OF EDUCATIONAL PSYCHOLOGY, UNIVERSITY OF WISCONSIN–MADISON

Introduction

Visual representations are ubiquitous in science, technology, engineering, and mathematics (STEM) domains. Many learning materials include a variety of visual representation (Arcavi, 2003; Cook *et al.*, 2007; Kozma & Russell, 2005b; Nathan *et al.*, 2011; van der Meij & de Jong, 2006; Van Someren *et al.*, 1998).

Visual representations have two important roles in instruction. First, they play a cognitive role. Visual representations can make domain-relevant concepts accessible to students (Arcavi, 2003; Cook *et al.*, 2007; Kordaki, 2010; Lewalter, 2003), and different visual representations often emphasize complementary conceptual aspects (Ainsworth, 2006; Bodner & Domin, 2000; Cheng & Gilbert, 2009; Cokelez & Dumon, 2005; Won *et al.*, 2014). From this perspective, the goal of using multiple visual representations in instruction is to help students to integrate multiple conceptual aspects of the to-be-learned content into a coherent mental model (Ainsworth, 2008; Schnotz, 2005; Seufert, 2003). Second, visual representations have a socio-cultural role. Representations are tools that members of a scientific or professional community use to think, to solve problems, and to communicate—in other words, visual representations are an integral part of discourse within the discipline (Airey & Linder, 2009; Kozma *et al.*, 2000; Schönborn & Anderson, 2006). To become legitimate members of STEM professions, students have to learn how to communicate using visual representations, and how to use visual representations as tools for problem solving (Cobb, 1995; Kozma & Russell, 2005b; Vygotsky, 1978; Wertsch & Kazak, 2011). From this perspective, the goal in using multiple visual representations in instruction is to enculturate students into STEM practices.

In this chapter I shall begin by describing research documenting the importance of representational competencies for STEM learning. I shall then present the theoretical framework that I will use as an organizing device for the remainder of the chapter. The focus of this chapter is on presenting research-based principles that can help instructors to develop effective types of support that help their students to acquire representational competencies, with the ultimate goal of enhancing their learning of domain knowledge.

Importance of Representational Competencies for STEM Learning

Visual representations play a crucial role in STEM because many key concepts are inherently visuo-spatial (Gilbert, 2005, 2008; Uttal & O'Doherty, 2008). For example, astronomers have to visualize the solar system, and chemists have to visualize the movements of atoms and electrons. To make these concepts accessible to students, STEM instruction relies heavily on representations (Kozma & Russell, 2005b; Stieff, 2007). For example, chemistry instruction typically uses a variety of visual representations (Bodner & Domin, 2000; Coll & Treagust, 2003a, 2003b) both because many key phenomena cannot be observed with the naked eye (Davidowitz & Chittleborough, 2009) and because many concepts are highly abstract (Justi & Gilbert, 2002). Representations can visualize these invisible phenomena and abstract concepts (Coll & Treagust, 2003a, 2003b; Kozma & Russell, 2005a). For example, Lewis structures are commonly used to show which atoms form which types of bonds in molecules, but ball-and-stick models are typically used to illustrate the geometrical arrangement of atoms in the molecule. Another example from a mathematics domain is fractions instruction. Different visual representations emphasize different conceptual aspects of fractions (Charalambous & Pitta-Pantazi, 2007; Post et al., 1982). For example, circle diagrams show fractions as parts of a whole (Cramer, 2001), number lines show fractions as measures of length (Siegler et al., 2011), and sets show fractions as ratios (Lamon, 1999). Helping students to integrate these different conceptual interpretations of fractions into a coherent understanding of fractions as proportions is considered to be key to their success in mathematics (Siegler et al., 2012).

These two examples illustrate the fact that students' success in STEM depends on their ability to make sense of abstract concepts depicted by visual representations (Ainsworth, 2008; Gilbert, 2004, 2008). Yet learning with visual representations is challenging, because students often fail to correctly interpret the representations and to integrate information across different representations (Ainsworth, 2006; de Jong et al., 2013). Indeed, students' failure to acquire such critical representational competencies jeopardizes their learning in STEM domains (Airey & Linder, 2009; Dori & Barak, 2001; Moss, 2005; Schönborn & Anderson, 2006; Taber, 2001; Talanquer, 2013). Unfortunately, students' lack of representational competencies often goes unnoticed by instructors, who tend to assume that students know how to interpret visual representations and how to navigate the multiplicity of visual representations that are available (Airey & Linder, 2009; Jong et al., 2005; Schönborn & Anderson, 2006). Therefore it is not surprising that much research has investigated how best to help students to acquire representational competencies. Indeed, there is an immense literature documenting the finding that interventions designed to help students to acquire representational competencies improve their learning of the domain knowledge (e.g. Ainsworth & van Labeke, 2002; Bodemer & Faust, 2006; Plötzner et al., 2008; Seufert, 2003; van der Meij & de Jong, 2006, 2011).

Theoretical Framework

To organize the presentation of research-based principles for the design of instructional support for representational competencies in the remainder of this chapter, I shall make use of a theoretical framework that is inspired by cognitive science research, research on instructional design, research on domain expertise, and research on discipline-based practices (Rau, in press). This framework proposes a taxonomy of representational competencies that play a role in students' learning with multiple visual representations (for an overview, see Table 9.1). First, students need to acquire *visual understanding*—that is, the ability to conceptually make sense of each individual visual representation by mapping the visual features of the given representation to information that is relevant to understanding the target domain knowledge (Ainsworth, 2006; Schnotz, 2005; Schnotz & Bannert, 2003). Cognitive theories of learning refer to the process by which students learn to map visual features to domain-relevant concepts as sense-making processes. Sense-making processes are verbally mediated explanation-based processes by means of which students reason about principles (Chi *et al.*, 1989; Gentner, 1983; Koedinger *et al.*, 2012). When students engage in verbally mediated sense-making processes they acquire principled conceptual knowledge about which visual features of the visual representation map onto analogous referents of the domain knowledge.

Second, students need to acquire *visual fluency* with each individual visual representation— that is, the ability to quickly and with minimal mental effort "see" what a visual representation shows (Airey & Linder, 2009; Kellman & Massey, 2013). The fact that experts perceive information differently from novice students has been well researched (e.g. Chi *et al.*, 1981; Gegenfurtner *et al.*, 2011). This research demonstrates that domain experts "see at a glance" what a given representation shows without any perceived mental effort. Visual fluency is an important aspect of expertise because it frees "cognitive head room" to engage in higher-order conceptual thinking about domain-relevant concepts (Gibson, 2000; Goldstone & Barsalou, 1998; Kellman & Massey, 2013; Richman *et al.*, 1996). According to socio-cultural theories of learning, visual fluency allows members of a professional or scientific community to communicate and to infer shared meaning about processes and phenomena (Airey & Linder, 2009; Wertsch & Kazak, 2011). Cognitive theories of learning suggest that visual fluency is the result of non-verbal inductive learning processes (Koedinger *et al.*, 2012; Richman *et al.*, 1996). Inductive processes are learning processes that students engage in when they learn to discriminate, classify, categorize, and become more accurate in doing so (Koedinger *et al.*, 2012), which—as theories on perceptual learning propose—is what characterizes perceptual expertise (Goldstone, 1997). Perceptual learning processes are considered to be non-verbal because they do not rely on explicit reasoning (Kellman & Garrigan, 2009; Kellman & Massey, 2013). They are implicit because they occur unintentionally and unconsciously (Shanks, 2005), through experience with numerous cases (Airey & Linder, 2009; Gibson, 1969; Kellman & Massey, 2013; Richman *et al.*, 1996).

Third, students need to acquire *connectional understanding*—that is, the ability to conceptually make sense of connections between multiple visual representations. Connectional understanding is important because it allows students to integrate the information shown by multiple visual representations into a coherent mental model of the domain knowledge (Ainsworth, 2006; Schnotz, 2005; Schnotz & Bannert, 2003). To do so, students map visual features of different representations that show corresponding concepts (Gentner, 1983). Understanding connections between multiple visual representations requires explicit, verbally mediated reasoning about how conceptually relevant visual features map onto one another (Chi *et al.*, 1989; Gentner, 1983; Koedinger *et al.*, 2012). When students map corresponding visual features, they reason conceptually about similarities between visual representations (e.g. two representations depict the same information or the same concept), and learn about differences between visual representations (e.g. two representations provide complementary information or depict different concepts about the domain knowledge) (Ainsworth, 2006).

TABLE 9.1 Overview of processes involved in learning with multiple visual representations and resulting competencies.

Scope	Representational learning processes	Representational competencies
Individual visual representations	Verbally mediated, conceptual learning processes	Visual understanding
	Non-verbal, perceptual learning processes	Visual fluency
Multiple visual representations	Verbally mediated, conceptual learning processes	Connectional understanding
	Non-verbal, perceptual learning processes	Connectional fluency

Fourth, students need to acquire *connectional fluency*—that is, the ability to "just see" whether different visual representations show the same information, to combine information from different visual representations without considerable mental effort, and to quickly translate between different visual representations (Airey & Linder, 2009; Chase & Simon, 1973; Kellman & Garrigan, 2009; Kellman & Massey, 2013). As with visual fluency, perceptual fluency in making connections frees "cognitive head room" to engage in higher-order conceptual thinking about domain-relevant concepts (Gibson, 2000; Kellman & Massey, 2013; Richman *et al.*, 1996). Furthermore, it allows students to spontaneously infer information that is not explicitly shown in the given representation, because seeing one representation automatically invokes a different visual representation (Airey & Linder, 2009). The ability to fluently translate between different visual representations is an important aspect of domain expertise, and is common to practices in scientific and professional communities (Cobb, 1995; Kozma *et al.*, 2000). Similar to visual fluency, the processes by which students learn to fluently translate between representations based on visual features are based on inductive learning processes that are non-verbal and implicit (Koedinger *et al.*, 2012). Connectional fluency results from experience with numerous cases (Airey & Linder, 2009; Kellman & Massey, 2013).

Table 9.1 provides an overview of this taxonomy of representational competencies and of the learning processes that students need to engage in to acquire them. The remainder of this chapter is organized by this taxonomy. I shall discuss research that provides principles for the design of instructional support for each of these representational competencies.

Instructional Support for Representational Competencies

Research has investigated how best to support students in acquiring the different types of representational competencies introduced in the previous section of this chapter. Here I shall summarize the principles of the design of instructional support for each of these competencies, while considering examples of empirical studies that provide evidence for these principles. I shall also suggest tangible recommendations for instructional practices that emerge from this research.

Support for Visual Understanding

Students acquire visual understanding by engaging in conceptual, verbally mediated sense-making processes involved in relating the visual features of the representations to the concepts that they depict. In doing so, students learn principles that describe how the given visual representation depicts information. To help students to relate a novel visual representation to concepts, they can relate the novel representation to another representation that they have already mastered. Because students can be assumed to have mastery over interpreting text or spoken narration, previous research has investigated how best to support students in relating a visual representation to text-based representations (i.e. symbolic representations, expository texts, spoken narration). Two important principles emerge from this research. First, prompting students to self-explain how the visual representation corresponds to text (Ainsworth & Loizou, 2003; Butcher & Aleven, 2007; Butcher, 2006; Seufert, 2003; Seufert & Brünken, 2006) or to symbolic representations has been shown to be effective (Berthold & Renkl, 2009; Berthold et al., 2008; Rau et al., 2015a). To this end, students may be asked to self-explain what concept a specific visual feature depicts (e.g. the number of shaded sections in a circle diagram depicts the numerator of a fraction; Rau et al., 2015a), in order to explain how the visual representation illustrates domain-specific principles (e.g. the angles in a triangle add up to 180 degrees; Butcher & Aleven, 2007), or to fill in information from a visual representation in a text-based version of the same information (e.g. translating the visual representation of a specific problem scenario into a word problem that describes the same scenario; Berthold et al., 2008). Self-explanation prompts have been shown to be particularly effective if they help students to focus on "why" questions, because this may elicit self-explanations of principled knowledge (Berthold & Renkl, 2009). Furthermore, self-explanation prompts are more effective if they ask students to self-explain specific connections than if they are open-ended (Berthold et al., 2008; van der Meij & de Jong, 2011).

A second principle regarding the support of visual understanding is that students should actively establish the relations between the visual representation and the familiar representation (e.g. text or symbols) themselves. Research shows that students should actively create connections between representations, rather than passively observing correspondences (Bodemer & Faust, 2006; Bodemer et al., 2004, 2005; Gutwill et al., 1999). For example, asking students to relate keywords that describe concepts in a text to the corresponding parts of a visual representation is more effective than providing these correspondences for students (Bodemer & Faust, 2006).

Figure 9.1 shows an example from an intervention for fractions learning in which students are prompted to self-explain how a circle representation depicts fractions. This example is taken from the Fractions Tutor—a computer-based tutoring system for fractions learning that focuses on supporting students' representational competencies (Rau et al., 2013a, 2015a). In providing their explanation, students are prompted to reflect on how the visual representation illustrates fractions principles (e.g. the more sections into which a circle is partitioned, the smaller the sections become, which explains the inverse relationship between the size of the denominator and the magnitude of the fraction). Furthermore, students have to become active themselves in establishing these connections because they fill in the gaps in the self-explanation prompts themselves.

For instructors, it is important to ensure that their students have the ability to make sense of how a given visual representation depicts information about the to-be-learned content. Instructors often take it for granted that their students know what a visual representation shows (Airey & Linder, 2009; Jong et al., 2005; Schönborn & Anderson, 2006; Uttal & O'Doherty, 2008). Yet there is extensive evidence that students often struggle to understand

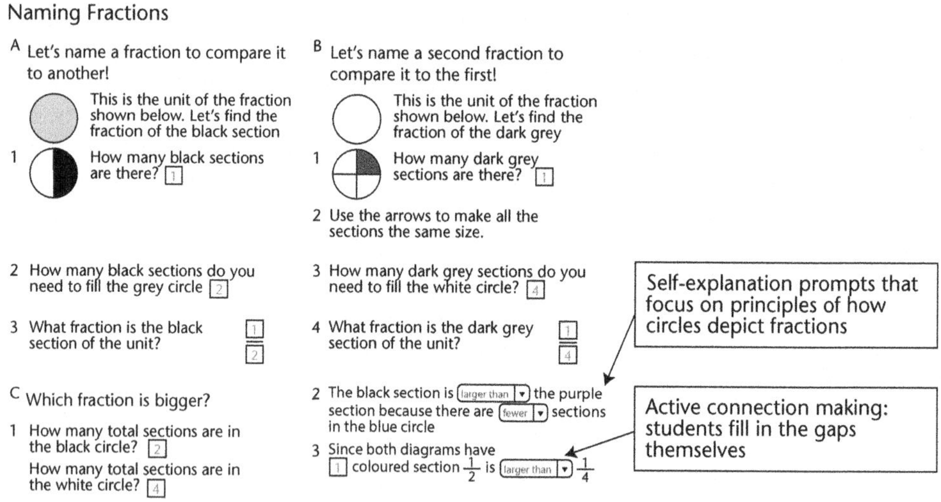

Naming Fractions

FIGURE 9.1 Example problem from the Fractions Tutor in which students are prompted to self-explain how circle representations depict the principle of the inverse relationship between the size of the denominator and the magnitude of the fraction when the numerators of two fractions are the same.

individual visual representations (for more extensive overviews, see Ainsworth, 2006, 2008; Uttal & O'Doherty, 2008). Instructors should ask students to explain what is being depicted by specific visual features of a visual representation (e.g. the number of shaded sections in a circle diagram that denotes a fraction, or the blue spheres in a ball-and-stick model of a chemical molecule). Students need to learn which visual features of the given representation convey conceptually relevant information (e.g. the proportion of the area in the circle diagram conveys the magnitude of the fraction) and which visual features are incidental (e.g. the blue color in a ball-and-stick model of ammonia does not mean that nitrogen atoms are blue, but follows the CPK color coding convention). To do so, they may be given a familiar representation, such as symbols or text—but they might also be given a different visual representation that they have already mastered. Students should be encouraged to actively establish these relationships themselves, and to refer to principles that can help them to understand a variety of examples with the same visual representation (e.g. the red color in a ball-and-stick model of water does not mean that oxygen atoms are red). If a familiar representation is not available—for instance, if the student is encountering an entirely new topic—the instructor may provide principled explanations of how to interpret the novel visual representation, and then ask students to actively make sense of new examples of the visual representation by themselves.

Support for Visual Fluency

Students acquire visual fluency by engaging in perceptual, non-verbal inductive learning processes. Two principles are important to adhere to when designing instructional materials that foster visual fluency. First, we can help students to engage in perceptual learning processes by exposing them to numerous examples of the visual representation while varying incidental features of the visual representation and keeping conceptually relevant features constant (Massey *et al.*, 2011). For example, if students should learn that the coloring of a circle diagram that shows a fraction is irrelevant but the proportion that the shaded part covers is conceptually relevant, the student should encounter a variety of circle diagrams that use different colors in problems where attending to the proportion that is shaded (regardless of its color) leads to the correct solution. This principle emerges from research on the so-called interference effect (de Croock *et al.*, 1998; Shea & Morgan, 1979), which suggests that interleaving aspects of a learning task that vary irrelevant features improves students' abstract understanding of the relevant features of the learning task. This attuning to the relevant features of the learning task does not require verbal processes, but can happen via implicit forms of learning (Koedinger *et al.*, 2012).

A second principle proposes that students should frequently switch between different problems for which the given visual representation is used (Rau *et al.*, 2013b). This principle also emerges from the contextual interference effect. If students encounter the visual representation across a variety of problem types for which the given representation provides useful information, they are likely to reactivate their knowledge about which visual features are conceptually relevant frequently. This process of repeated reactivation increases the likelihood that they will be able to recall this knowledge more easily later on, without having to invest mental effort in doing so (de Croock *et al.*, 1998; Lee & Magill, 1983, 1985; Sweller, 1990). For example, students may learn better if they use a coordinate system to solve an algebra problem that focuses on slope followed by an algebra problem that focuses on intercepts, rather than solving multiple slope problems one after another.

A third principle that draws on the contextual interference effect suggests that students should frequently switch between different visual representations (Rau *et al.*, 2014). Switching between different visual representations also requires that students reactivate their knowledge about the visual features of each individual representation, thereby increasing the likelihood that they will be able to quickly access that knowledge later on. For example, students may learn better if they solve a problem with a coordinate system followed by another problem that uses a bar chart than if they use coordinate systems to solve several problems in a row. Figure 9.2 shows an example of a sequence that interleaves different visual representations of fractions (circle, rectangle, number line) across consecutive problems. This sequence was demonstrated to be more effective in supporting students' learning of fractions knowledge in an experiment that contrasted interleaved and blocked sequences (Rau *et al.*, 2014).

In summary, in order to help students to acquire visual fluency, instructors should expose them to a variety of examples that vary irrelevant visual features while keeping

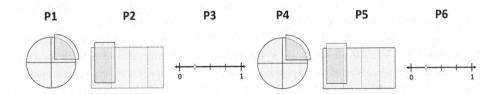

FIGURE 9.2 An example of a sequence in which different visual representations of fractions are presented in an interleaved fashion across a sequence of problems (P1–P6).

conceptually relevant visual features constant. For this type of instruction, students do not need to engage in verbally mediated explanations, but rather they should be asked to solve problems based on visual features by relying on their perceptual intuitions (Kellman *et al.*, 2009; Massey *et al.*, 2011).

Support for Connectional Understanding

Students acquire connectional understanding by engaging in conceptual, verbally mediated sense-making processes involved in relating visual features of one representation to visual features of another representation because they show corresponding conceptual aspects of the domain knowledge. The processes that students engage in when making sense of connections between multiple visual representations are somewhat similar to the processes they engage in when making connections between a visual representation and a text-based representation (see *Support for Visual Understanding* section), because in both cases the students engage in mapping of conceptually relevant features. However, the nature of these mappings is different, because connection making between multiple visual representations involves mapping visual features, whereas connection making between a visual representation and a text-based representation involves mapping a visual feature to a textual or symbolic feature. According to structure mapping theory (Gentner & Markman, 1997), making mappings between representations that share many features that are conceptually relevant should be easier than making connections between representations that share fewer features. When students make connections between multiple visual representations, the visual representations may share visual features that are conceptually relevant, but they may also share surface-level features (i.e. shared visual features that are *not* conceptually relevant, but incidental), which may lead the students to make incorrect connections. Therefore a student's ability to make connections between multiple visual representations may build, at least to some extent, on their visual understanding—the student needs to conceptually understand how a given visual representation denotes information, and has to be able to distinguish conceptually relevant visual features from surface-level features. Indeed, Ainsworth (2006) proposes that the ability to make connections between representations depends on prior visual understanding. Therefore students should have acquired at least a moderate level of visual understanding before they receive instructional support for connectional understanding.

Empirical research has yielded a number of principles that can guide the design of interventions that support students in conceptually making sense of connections between multiple visual representations. First, *explicitly comparing* multiple visual representations is effective in enhancing conceptual sense making of connections. Instructional support for conceptual sense making typically asks students to compare different representations by mapping visual features that show analogous information or different, complementary information about the concepts that the representations depict (Bodemer & Faust, 2006; Seufert, 2003; Seufert & Brünken, 2006; van der Meij & de Jong, 2006; Van Labeke & Ainsworth, 2002; Vreman-de Olde & De Jong, 2007). Instruction should provide step-by-step guidance to make sense of corresponding elements shown in the different representations (Bodemer & Faust, 2006; Gutwill *et al.*, 1999; Özgün-Koca, 2008). Furthermore, instruction should focus not only on similarities between representations (i.e. ways in which both visual representations show the same information) but also on differences between representations (i.e. ways in which one visual representation shows information that the other visual representation does not show). For example, an experiment on chemistry learning showed that students who received step-by-step guidance to reflect on the similarities and differences between multiple visual representations showed higher learning outcomes on a domain knowledge test than students who were not asked to do so (Rau & Wu, 2015).

Second, *prompting students to self-explain* is effective in enhancing sense-making processes (Berthold & Renkl, 2009; Berthold *et al.*, 2008; van der Meij & de Jong, 2011). Self-explanation prompts may be critical, because students typically struggle to make sense of connections (Ainsworth *et al.*, 2002), especially if they have low previous content knowledge (Stern *et al.*, 2003). For example, an experiment on fractions learning showed that students who were prompted to self-explain correspondences in how multiple visual representations of fractions (e.g. number lines, circle diagrams) depict core concepts related to the unit of the fraction or fraction equivalence showed higher learning outcomes on a domain knowledge test than students who were not prompted to do so (Rau *et al.*, 2015a).

Finally, research suggests that students need to actively establish these connections by themselves (as discussed earlier in the *Support for Visual Understanding* section). However, research also suggests that in complex domains, where students encounter a large number of novel concepts that are interrelated, they may need additional support in establishing connections. For example, providing students with linked representations in the form of simulations, where changes in one visual representation are automatically reflected in another, can be effective (Ainsworth & van Labeke, 2002; van der Meij & de Jong, 2006). However, it is still important that students actively process these connections themselves. For instance, they can be prompted to self-explain the connections that are presented to them (van der Meij & de Jong, 2011).

Figure 9.3 shows an example of instructional support for connectional understanding from Chem Tutor, a computer-based tutoring system for undergraduate chemistry learning (Rau *et al.*, 2015b). In this problem, students are asked to explicitly compare visual representations, and they are prompted to self-explain connections between the visual representations.

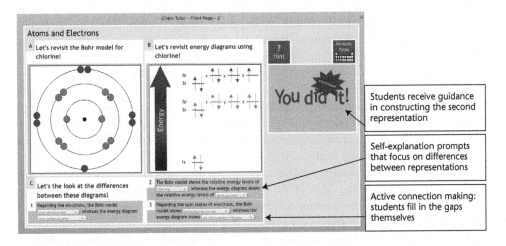

FIGURE 9.3 Example problem from Chem Tutor in which students first construct a different visual representation of the same atom, and then receive self-explanation prompts to reflect on the differences between the two visual representations.

Students are first given the visual representation of an atom (here the Bohr model of boron), and are then asked to use an interactive tool to construct a different representation of the same atom (the energy diagram). Students receive step-by-step guidance while they are constructing the visual representations. Next the students receive prompts to self-explain which concepts are depicted in both visual representations (e.g. both show the total number of electrons), or what information is shown in one representation but not in the other (e.g. the energy diagram shows the energy level of the electrons occupying each orbital, but the Bohr model does not).

For instructors, it is important to make sure that their students understand how each individual visual representation depicts conceptually relevant information before they ask the students to make connections between multiple visual representations. When they provide support for connectional understanding, they should ask the students to actively find corresponding concepts in different representations, and also ask them to explain what information about these concepts is depicted in one representation. The amount of guidance that students require in making these connections themselves may depend on the complexity of the domain. If the domain is novel, students may require more guidance in finding the correct connections. In this case, instructors should make sure that the students still become active in explaining the connections in their own words.

Support for Connectional Fluency

As with visual fluency (see *Support for Visual Fluency* section), students acquire connectional fluency by engaging perceptual, non-verbal inductive learning processes. Research on perceptual learning (Kellman & Massey, 2013; Kellman *et al.*, 2008; Wise *et al.*, 2000) provides principles that can guide the design of instructional support for perceptual fluency in connection making between multiple visual representations. First, to support non-verbal inductive processes, students should be exposed to numerous examples of multiple visual representations and asked to discriminate between them and to categorize them. Second, students should receive immediate feedback on these discrimination and classification tasks. Third, students should practice with varied instances that constitute contrasting cases (i.e. variations of irrelevant visual features while emphasizing relevant features). Typically, interventions that foster connectional fluency provide students with many short problems in which they are presented with one visual representation and are asked to select from a few options a different visual representation that shows the same phenomenon or concept (Kellman *et al.*, 2008, 2009; Wise *et al.*, 2000). For example, students may be presented with a Lewis structure that shows methane, and then be asked to select a ball-and-stick model that also shows methane. The options from which they can choose may vary visual features such as the color of the spheres in the ball-and-stick model, the number of total spheres shown, or the geometrical arrangement of the spheres.

Research suggests that connectional fluency builds on students' connectional understanding. Studies on fractions learning (Rau *et al.*, 2013c, 2013d, 2015a) and on chemistry learning (Rau & Wu, 2015) show that students only benefit from instructional support for connectional fluency if they also receive support for connectional understanding, or if they already have a high level of connectional understanding. These studies also indicate that providing students with instructional support for connectional fluency *before* they have acquired connectional understanding may be "harmful", in that students seem to benefit less from support for connectional understanding if they previously received support for connectional fluency

(Rau *et al.*, 2013d). Thus a fourth principle for supporting students in acquiring connectional fluency may be that they need to first conceptually understand connections between multiple visual representations.

Figure 9.4 shows another example from Chem Tutor, in which students are receiving instructional support for connectional fluency. In these problems, students are presented with one visual representation and have to select one out of four representations that shows the same atom. To foster non-verbal rather than verbal strategies, Chem Tutor prompts students to solve these problems fast, without overthinking them. Students receive immediate correctness feedback but no principle-based explanations. The four alternative representations build on the contrasting cases principle by emphasizing features that students should learn to pay attention to (e.g. an incorrect representation might show the same number of shells as the correct representation but a different number of valence electrons).

It is therefore important for instructors to consider students' level of connectional understanding before they provide them with support for connectional fluency. When they support students in engaging in perceptual learning processes involved in acquiring connectional fluency, instructors should expose students to a variety of examples of the visual representations and ask them to find matching representations without verbally explaining the connections, but by relying on visual features. In classrooms, interventions that foster connectional fluency include games in which students compete with one another as they try to find matching representations depicted on a screen or on cards (Eastwood, 2013; Moreira, 2013; Welsh, 2003). Other types of support for connectional fluency are technology based (Massey *et al.*, 2011; Rau *et al.*, 2015a, 2015b). Whichever platform an instructor uses to support connectional fluency, it is important that students are exposed to systematic variations of visual features and that they receive immediate feedback on whether their connections are correct or incorrect.

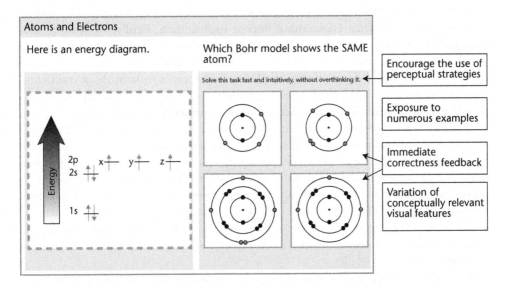

FIGURE 9.4 Example problem from Chem Tutor that supports connectional fluency. Students receive many rapid classification tasks, and are prompted to solve these tasks quickly, based on perceptual strategies. The choice options use contrasting cases to emphasize conceptually relevant visual features. Students receive immediate feedback.

Conclusions

This chapter has provided an overview of research-based principles that can help instructors provide appropriate support for representational competencies. Because representational competencies play a key role in students' success in STEM, fostering their representational competencies is likely to result in better learning of the targeted domain knowledge. Even though research has started to focus on interdependences between the different representational competencies described in this chapter, open questions remain as to how these representational competencies build on one another, and consequently how different types of instructional support should be sequenced. I have argued that visual understanding can be acquired by relating the novel visual representation to a well-mastered representation such as text-based explanations or symbols. However, it remains an open question what level of mastery of the familiar representation (e.g. text) is necessary for students to be able to understand the novel representation. This is an important question because it may suggest alternatives to relying on text-based representations to help students to acquire visual understanding—students may be able to use a well-understood visual representation to understand a novel visual representation. However, to date we know very little about how familiar students would need to be with the given representation (i.e. what level of visual understanding and visual fluency they need) in order to use it to understand a novel representation. Furthermore, although it seems reasonable to assume that students need to have at least a preliminary level of visual understanding in order to be able to acquire connectional understanding, it is not clear what level of visual understanding is necessary for connectional understanding interventions to be effective. Similarly, even though research shows that, if students are to benefit from instructional support that targets connectional fluency, this requires at least a preliminary level of connectional understanding, we know very little about what minimum level of connectional understanding is required for students to be able to benefit from connectional fluency interventions. Finally, an open question concerns the extent to which representational competencies are dependent on the specific visual representation used. For example, if a student understands connections between number lines and circle representations, will they find it easier to learn about connections between number lines and rectangle representations? In other words, does the representational competency of connectional understanding transfer across specific representations?

To address these questions, research needs to consider longer interventions as they happen in real classroom practice. Our understanding of students' acquisition of representational competencies and the interdependences among those competencies would greatly benefit from the collection of data about students' visual understanding and fluency, and about their connectional understanding and fluency over the course of an entire curriculum. Such observations would allow us to gain new insights into how students' representational competencies develop over time, how they build on one another, and whether the representational competencies transfer across representations that are used for a variety of curricular topics.

In conclusion, visual representations are powerful educational tools that can significantly promote students' learning of the domain knowledge. However, for students, visual representations are only helpful if they acquire representational competencies that allow them to make use of the visual representations to understand the domain knowledge. Too often we assume that our students understand visual representations. Only by conducting more research on how best to support students in acquiring crucial representational competencies can we provide effective instruction for STEM learning.

References

Ainsworth, S. (2006). DeFT: a conceptual framework for considering learning with multiple representations. *Learning and Instruction,* 16(3), 183–198.

Ainsworth, S. (2008). The educational value of multiple-representations when learning complex scientific concepts. In: J. K. Gilbert, M. Reiner, & M. Nakhleh (Eds), *Visualization: Theory and Practice in Science Education* (pp. 191–208). Dordrecht, The Netherlands: Springer.

Ainsworth, S. E. & van Labeke, N. (2002). *Using a Multi-Representational Design Framework to Develop and Evaluate a Dynamic Simulation Environment.* Paper presented at the International Workshop on Dynamic Visualizations and Learning, 18–19 July 2002, Knowledge Media Research Center, Tübingen, Germany.

Ainsworth, S. & Loizou, A. T. (2003). The effects of self-explaining when learning with text or diagrams. *Cognitive Science,* 27(4), 669–681.

Ainsworth, S., Bibby, P., & Wood, D. (2002). Examining the effects of different multiple representational systems in learning primary mathematics. *Journal of the Learning Sciences,* 11(1), 25–61.

Airey, J. & Linder, C. (2009). A disciplinary discourse perspective on university science learning: achieving fluency in a critical constellation of modes. *Journal of Research in Science Teaching,* 46(1), 27–49.

Arcavi, A. (2003). The role of visual representations in the learning of mathematics. *Educational Studies in Mathematics,* 52(3), 215–241.

Berthold, K. & Renkl, A. (2009). Instructional aids to support a conceptual understanding of multiple representations. *Journal of Educational Research,* 101(1), 70–87.

Berthold, K., Eysink, T. H. S., & Renkl, A. (2008). Assisting self-explanation prompts are more effective than open prompts when learning with multiple representations. *Instructional Science,* 27(4), 345–363.

Bodemer, D. & Faust, U. (2006). External and mental referencing of multiple representations. *Computers in Human Behavior,* 22(1), 27–42.

Bodemer, D., Ploetzner, R., Feuerlein, I., & Spada, H. (2004). The active integration of information during learning with dynamic and interactive visualisations. *Learning and Instruction,* 14(3), 325–341.

Bodemer, D., Ploetzner, R., Bruchmüller, K., & Häcker, S. (2005). Supporting learning with interactive multimedia through active integration of representations. *Instructional Science,* 33(1), 73–95.

Bodner, G. M. & Domin, D. S. (2000). Mental models: the role of representations in problem solving in chemistry. *University Chemistry Education,* 4(1), 24–30.

Butcher, K. R. (2006). Learning from text with diagrams: promoting mental model development and inference generation. *Journal of Educational Psychology,* 98(1), 182–197.

Butcher, K. & Aleven, V. (2007). *Integrating Visual and Verbal Knowledge During Classroom Learning with Computer Tutors.* Paper presented at the 29th Annual Conference of the Cognitive Science Society, 1–4 August 2007, Nashville, TN.

Charalambous, C. Y. & Pitta-Pantazi, D. (2007). Drawing on a theoretical model to study students' understandings of fractions. *Educational Studies in Mathematics,* 64(3), 293–316.

Chase, W. G. & Simon, H. A. (1973). Perception in chess. *Cognitive Psychology,* 4(1), 55–81.

Cheng, M. & Gilbert, J. K. (2009). Towards a better utilization of diagrams in research into the use of representative levels in chemical education. In: J. K. Gilbert & D. F. Treagust (Eds), *Multiple Representations in Chemical Education* (pp. 191–208). Berlin: Springer.

Chi, M. T., Bassok, M., Lewis, M. W., Reimann, P., & Glaser, R. (1989). Self-explanations: how students study and use examples in learning to solve problems. *Cognitive Science,* 13(2), 145–182.

Chi, M. T. H., Feltovitch, P. J., & Glaser, R. (1981). Categorization and representation of physics problems by experts and novices. *Cognitive Science*, 5, 121–152.

Cobb, P. (1995). Cultural tools and mathematical learning: a case study. *Journal for Research in Mathematics Education*, 26(4), 362–385.

Cokelez, A. & Dumon, A. (2005). Atom and molecule: upper secondary school French students' representations in long-term memory. *Chemistry Education Research and Practice*, 6(3), 119–135.

Coll, R. K. & Treagust, D. F. (2003a). Investigation of secondary school, undergraduate, and graduate learners' mental models of ionic bonding. *Journal of Research in Science Teaching*, 40(5), 464–486.

Coll, R. K. & Treagust, D. F. (2003b). Learners' mental models of metallic bonding: a cross-age study. *Science Education*, 87(5), 685–707.

Cook, M., Wiebe, E. N., & Carter, G. (2007). The influence of prior knowledge on viewing and interpreting graphics with macroscopic and molecular representations. *Science Education*, 92(5), 848–867.

Cramer, K. (2001). Using models to build an understanding of functions. *Mathematics Teaching in the Middle School*, 6(5), 310–318.

Davidowitz, B. & Chittleborough, G. (2009). Linking the macroscopic and sub-microscopic levels: diagrams. In: J. K. Gilbert & D. F. Treagust (Eds), *Multiple Representations in Chemical Education* (pp. 169–191). Dordrecht, The Netherlands: Springer.

de Croock, M. B. M., Van Merrienboër, J. J. G., & Paas, F. G. W. C. (1998). High versus low contextual interference in simulation-based training of troubleshooting skills: effects on transfer performance and invested mental effort. *Computers in Human Behavior*, 14(2), 249–267.

de Jong, T., Linn, M. C., & Zacharia, Z. C. (2013). Physical and virtual laboratories in science and engineering education. *Science*, 340(6130), 305–308.

Dori, Y. J. & Barak, M. (2001). Virtual and physical molecular modeling: fostering model perception and spatial understanding. *Educational Technology & Society*, 4(1), 61–74.

Eastwood, M. L. (2013). Fastest fingers: a molecule-building game for teaching organic chemistry. *Journal of Chemical Education*, 90(8), 1038–1041.

Gegenfurtner, A., Lehtinen, E., & Säljö, R. (2011). Expertise differences in the comprehension of visualizations: a meta-analysis of eye-tracking research in professional domains. *Educational Psychology Review*, 23(4), 523–552.

Gentner, D. (1983). Structure-mapping: a theoretical framework for analogy. *Cognitive Science*, 7, 155–170.

Gentner, D. & Markman, A. B. (1997). Structure mapping in analogy and similarity. *American Psychologist*, 52(1), 45–56.

Gibson, E. J. (1969). *Principles of Perceptual Learning and Development*. New York: Prentice Hall.

Gibson, E. J. (2000). Perceptual learning in development: some basic concepts. *Ecological Psychology*, 12(4), 295–302.

Gilbert, J. K. (2004). Models and modelling: routes to more authentic science education. *International Journal of Science and Mathematics Education*, 2(2), 115–130.

Gilbert, J. K. (2005). Visualization: a metacognitive skill in science and science education. In: J. K. Gilbert (Ed.), *Visualization in Science Education* (pp. 9–27). Dordrecht, The Netherlands: Springer.

Gilbert, J. K. (2008). Visualization: an emergent field of practice and enquiry in science education. In: J. K. Gilbert, M. Reiner, & M. Nakhleh (Eds), *Visualization: Theory and Practice in Science Education. Volume 3* (pp. 3–24). Dordrecht, The Netherlands: Springer.

Goldstone, R. (1997). *Perceptual Learning*. San Diego, CA: Academic Press.

Goldstone, R. L. & Barsalou, L. W. (1998). Reuniting perception and conception. *Cognition*, 65(2), 231–262.

Gutwill, J. P., Frederiksen, J. R., & White, B. Y. (1999). Making their own connections: students' understanding of multiple models in basic electricity. *Cognition and Instruction*, 17(3), 249–282.

Jong, O. D., Van Driel, J. H., & Verloop, N. (2005). Preservice teachers' pedagogical content knowledge of using particle models in teaching chemistry. *Journal of Research in Science Teaching*, 42(8), 947–964.

Justi, R. & Gilbert, J. K. (2002). Models and modelling in chemical education. In: *Chemical Education: Towards Research-Based Practice* (pp. 47–68). Dordrecht, The Netherlands. Kluwer Academic Publishers.

Kellman, P. J. & Garrigan, P. B. (2009). Perceptual learning and human expertise. *Physics of Life Reviews*, 6(2), 53–84.

Kellman, P. J. & Massey, C. M. (2013). Perceptual learning, cognition, and expertise. *Psychology of Learning and Motivation*, 58, 117–165.

Kellman, P. J., Massey, C. M., Roth, Z., Burke, T., Zucker, J., Saw, A., Aguero, K. E., & Wise, J. (2008). Perceptual learning and the technology of expertise: studies in fraction learning and algebra. *Pragmatics & Cognition*, 16(2), 356–405.

Kellman, P. J., Massey, C. M., & Son, J. Y. (2009). Perceptual learning modules in mathematics: enhancing students' pattern recognition, structure extraction, and fluency. *Topics in Cognitive Science*, 2(2), 285–305.

Koedinger, K. R., Corbett, A. T., & Perfetti, C. (2012). The knowledge-learning-instruction framework: bridging the science-practice chasm to enhance robust student learning. *Cognitive Science*, 36(5), 757–798.

Kordaki, M. (2010). A drawing and multi-representational computer environment for beginners' learning of programming using C: design and pilot formative evaluation. *Computers & Education*, 54(1), 69–87.

Kozma, R. & Russell, J. (2005a). Multimedia learning of chemistry. In: R. E. Mayer (Ed.), *The Cambridge Handbook of Multimedia Learning* (pp. 409–428). New York: Cambridge University Press.

Kozma, R. & Russell, J. (2005b). Students becoming chemists: developing representational competence. In: J. Gilbert (Ed.), *Visualization in Science Education* (pp. 121–145). Dordrecht, The Netherlands: Springer.

Kozma, R., Chin, E., Russell, J., & Marx, N. (2000). The roles of representations and tools in the chemistry laboratory and their implications for chemistry learning. *The Journal of the Learning Sciences*, 9(2), 105–143.

Lamon, S. J. (Ed.). (1999). *Teaching Fractions and Ratios for Understanding*. Mahwah, NJ: Lawrence Erlbaum Associates.

Lee, T. D. & Magill, R. A. (1983). The locus of contextual interference in motor-skill acquisition. *Journal of Experimental Psychology: Learning, Memory, and Cognition*, 9(4), 730–746.

Lee, T. D. & Magill, R. A. (1985). Can forgetting facilitate skill acquisition? In: D. Goodman, R. B. Wilberg, & I. M. Franks (Eds), *Differing Perspectives in Motor Learning, Memory, and Control* (pp. 3–22). Amsterdam, The Netherlands: Elsevier.

Lewalter, D. (2003). Cognitive strategies for learning from static and dynamic visuals. *Learning and Instruction*, 13(2), 177–189.

Massey, C. M., Kellman, P. J., Roth, Z., & Burke, T. (2011). Perceptual learning and adaptive learning technology: developing new approaches to mathematics learning in the classroom. In: N. L. Stein & S. W. Raudenbush (Eds), *Developmental Cognitive Science Goes to School* (pp. 235–249). New York: Routledge.

Moreira, R. F. (2013). A game for the early and rapid assimilation of organic nomenclature. *Journal of Chemical Education*, 90(8), 1035–1037.

Moss, J. (2005). Pipes, tubes, and beakers: new approaches to teaching the rational-number system. In: J. Brantsford & S. Donovan (Eds), *How People Learn: A Targeted Report for Teachers* (pp. 309–349). Washington, DC: National Academies Press.

Nathan, M. J., Walkington, C. A., Srisurichan, R., & Alibali, M. W. (2011). *Modal Engagements in Pre-College Engineering: Tracking Math and Science Concepts Across Symbols, Sketches, Software, Silicone, and Wood*. Washington, DC: American Society for Engineering Education.

Özgün-Koca, S. A. (2008). Ninth grade students studying the movement of fish to learn about linear relationships: the use of video-based analysis software in mathematics classrooms. *Mathematics Educator*, 18(1), 15–25.

Plötzner, R., Bodemer, D., & Neudert, S. (2008). Successful and less successful use of dynamic visualizations in instructional texts. In: R. K. Lowe & W. Schnotz (Eds), *Learning with Animation: Research Implications for Design* (pp. 71–91). New York: Cambridge University Press.

Post, T. R., Behr, M. J., & Lesh, R. (1982). Interpretations of rational number concepts. In: L. Silvey & J. R. Smart (Eds), *Mathematics for the Middle Grades (5–9)* (pp. 59–72). Reston, VA: National Council of Teachers of Mathematics.

Rau, M. A. (in press). Conditions for the effectiveness of multiple visual representations in enhancing STEM learning. *Educational Psychology Review*. DOI: 10.1007/s10648-016-9365-3

Rau, M. A. & Wu, S. P. (2015). ITS support for conceptual and perceptual connection making between multiple graphical representations. In: *Artificial Intelligence in Education* (pp. 398–407). Cham: Switzerland: Springer International Publishing.

Rau, M. A., Aleven, V., & Rummel, N. (2013a). How to use multiple graphical representations to support conceptual learning? Research-based principles in the Fractions Tutor. In: H. C. Lane, K. Yacef, J. Mostow, & P. Pavlik (Eds), *Artificial Intelligence in Education* (pp. 762–765). Berlin: Springer.

Rau, M. A., Aleven, V., & Rummel, N. (2013b). Interleaved practice in multi-dimensional learning tasks: which dimension should we interleave? *Learning and Instruction*, 23, 98–114.

Rau, M. A., Aleven, V., & Rummel, N. (2013c). Complementary effects of sense-making and fluency-building support for connection making: a matter of sequence? In: H. C. Lane, K. Yacef, J. Mostow, & P. Pavlik (Eds), *Artificial Intelligence in Education* (pp. 329–338). Berlin: Springer.

Rau, M. A., Scheines, R., Aleven, V., & Rummel, N. (2013d). Does representational understanding enhance fluency or vice versa? Searching for mediation models. In: S. K. D'Mello, R. A. Calvo, & A. Olney (Eds), *Proceedings of the 6th International Conference on Educational Data Mining (EDM 2013)* (pp. 161–169). Worcester, MA: International Educational Data Mining Society.

Rau, M. A., Aleven, V., Rummel, N., & Pardos, Z. (2014). How should intelligent tutoring systems sequence multiple graphical representations of fractions? A multi-methods study. *International Journal of Artificial Intelligence in Education*, 24(2), 125–161.

Rau, M. A., Aleven, V., & Rummel, N. (2015a). Successful learning with multiple graphical representations and self-explanation prompts. *Journal of Educational Psychology*, 107(1), 30–46.

Rau, M. A., Michaelis, J. E., & Fay, N. (2015b). Connection making between multiple graphical representations: a multi-methods approach for domain-specific grounding of an intelligent tutoring system for chemistry. *Computers and Education*, 82, 460–485.

Richman, H. B., Gobet, F., Staszewski, J. J., & Simon, H. A. (1996). Perceptual and memory processes in the acquisition of expert performance: the EPAM model. In: K. A. Ericsson (Ed.), *The Road to Excellence: The Acquisition of Expert Performance in the Arts and Sciences, Sports and Games* (pp. 167–187). Mahwah, NJ: Lawrence Erlbaum Associates.

Schnotz, W. (2005). An integrated model of text and picture comprehension. In: R. E. Mayer (Ed.), *The Cambridge Handbook of Multimedia Learning* (pp. 49–69). New York: Cambridge University Press.

Schnotz, W. & Bannert, M. (2003). Construction and interference in learning from multiple representation. *Learning and Instruction*, 13(2), 141–156.

Schönborn, K. J. & Anderson, T. R. (2006). The importance of visual literacy in the education of biochemists. *Biochemistry and Molecular Biology Education*, 34(2), 94–102.

Seufert, T. (2003). Supporting coherence formation in learning from multiple representations. *Learning and Instruction*, 13(2), 227–237.

Seufert, T. & Brünken, R. (2006). Cognitive load and the format of instructional aids for coherence formation. *Applied Cognitive Psychology*, 20, 321–331.

Shanks, D. (2005). Implicit learning. In: K. Lamberts & R. Goldstone (Eds), *Handbook of Cognition* (pp. 202–220). London: Sage.

Shea, C. H. & Morgan, R. L. (1979). Contextual interference effects on the acquisition, retention, and transfer of a motor skill. *Journal of Experimental Psychology: Human Learning and Memory*, 5(2), 179–187.

Siegler, R. S., Thompson, C. A., & Schneider, M. (2011). An integrated theory of whole number and fractions development. *Cognitive Psychology*, 62(4), 273–296.

Siegler, R. S., Duncan, G. J., Davis-Kean, P. E., Duckworth, K., Claessens, A., Engel, M., Susperreguy, M. I., & Chen, M. (2012). Early predictors of high school mathematics achievement. *Psychological Science*, 23(7), 691–697.

Stern, E., Aprea, C., & Ebner, H. G. (2003). Improving cross-content transfer in text processing by means of active graphical representation. *Learning and Instruction*, 13(2), 191–203.

Stieff, M. (2007). Mental rotation and diagrammatic reasoning in science. *Learning and Instruction*, 17(2), 219–234.

Sweller, J. (1990). Cognitive load as a factor in the structuring of technical material. *Journal of Experimental Psychology; General*, 119(2), 176–192.

Taber, S. B. (2001). *Making Connections among Different Representations: The Case of Multiplication of Fractions.* Paper presented at the Annual Meeting of the American Educational Research Association, Seattle, WA, 10–14 April 2001.

Talanquer, V. (2013). Chemistry education: ten facets to shape us. *Journal for Research in Mathematics Education*, 90, 832–838.

Uttal, D. H. & O'Doherty, K. (2008). Comprehending and learning from 'visualizations': a developmental perspective. In: J. K. Gilbert, M. Reiner, & M. Nakhleh (Eds), *Visualization: Theory and Practice in Science Education* (pp. 53–72). Dordrecht, The Netherlands: Springer.

van der Meij, J. & de Jong, T. (2006). Supporting students' learning with multiple representations in a dynamic simulation-based learning environment. *Learning and Instruction*, 16(3), 199–212.

van der Meij, J. & de Jong, T. (2011). The effects of directive self-explanation prompts to support active processing of multiple representations in a simulation-based learning environment. *Journal of Computer Assisted Learning*, 27(5), 411–423.

Van Labeke, N. & Ainsworth, S. E. (2002). Representational decisions when learning population dynamics with an instructional simulation. In: S. A. Cerri, G. Gouardères, & F. Paraguacu (Eds), *Proceedings of the 6th International Conference on Intelligent Tutoring Systems* (pp. 831–840). London, UK: Springer-Verlag.

Van Someren, M. W., Boshuizen, H. P. A., & de Jong, T. (1998). Multiple representations in human reasoning. In: M. W. Van Someren, H. P. A. Boshuizen, & T. de Jong (Eds), *Learning with Multiple Representations*. Oxford: Pergamon.

Vreman-de Olde, C. & De Jong, T. (2007). Scaffolding learners in designing investigation assignments for a computer simulation. *Journal of Computer Assisted Learning*, 22(1), 63–73.

Vygotsky, L. S. (1978). Internalization of higher psychological functions. In: M. W. Cole, V. John-Steiner, S. Scribner, & E. Souberman (Eds), *Mind in Society* (pp. 52–57). Cambridge, MA: Harvard University Press.

Welsh, M. J. (2003). Organic functional group playing card deck. *Journal of Chemical Education*, 80(4), 426–427.

Wertsch, J. V. & Kazak, S. (2011). Saying more than you know in instructional settings. In: T. Koschmann (Ed.), *Theories of Learning and Studies of Instructional Practice* (pp. 153–166). New York: Springer.

Wise, J. A., Kubose, T., Chang, N., Russell, A., & Kellman, P. J. (2000). Perceptual learning modules in mathematics and science instruction. In: P. Hoffman & D. Lemke (Eds), *Teaching and Learning in a Network World* (pp. 169–176): Amsterdam, The Netherlands: IOS Press.

Won, M., Yoon, H., & Treagust, D. F. (2014). Students' learning strategies with multiple representations: explanations of the human breathing mechanism. *Science Education*, 98(5), 840–866.

10

INVESTIGATING DYSCALCULIA

A Science of Learning Perspective

Brian Butterworth and Diana Laurillard

INSTITUTE OF COGNITIVE NEUROSCIENCE AND INSTITUTE OF EDUCATION, UNIVERSITY COLLEGE LONDON

Introduction

This chapter sets out to map the interdisciplinary journey from neuroscience findings that illuminate some form of conceptual understanding, to the analysis of how this might affect the learning process in formal education, and finally to a pedagogical design for practical application in a classroom. We contextualize this with reference to the phenomenon of dyscalculia, partly because it is a fascinating and difficult problem for education, and partly because its effects on behavior, cognition, and the brain can be quite precisely described. For education, psychology, and neuroscience to be able to collaborate effectively, we need to select the problems that provide a clear and rigorous account of what it takes to learn, and how the relevant processes and products of learning can be identified and measured for both neural and behavioral markers.

The section on the research program explains the nature of the neuroscience research program on dyscalculia, and the second section outlines some of the main findings. We then analyze what these findings mean for education, and use pedagogic theory and practice to specify the kind of intervention needed. Finally, we describe a particular application, which takes the form of an adaptive game-like teaching program, and the pedagogy that would be built around it in the classroom teaching context.

What Special Educational Needs (SEN) Teachers Know

People with typical numerical processing find it hard to imagine having no "number sense." They will often observe that some very poor learners of arithmetic can count, as they can recite the number sequence, and point to distinct objects as they do so. Around the same stage of development, children are also learning to recite another sequence, namely the alphabet, and as they do so they point to distinct objects. There are obvious similarities. The crucial difference is that whereas the alphabet is an entirely arbitrary sequence and could be in any order, the number sequence is ordered and has an internal structure. In the number sequence it is meaningful to ask "What number do you add to 5 to reach 9?" However, it makes no sense at all to ask "What letter do you add to K to reach P?"

If a child were to interpret the number sequence as being similar to the alphabet sequence, arithmetic would become a baffling series of arbitrary rules that has no logic to it. If the processing of numerosity, because of an abnormality in the intraparietal sulci (IPS), does not include seeing 5 as contained within 7, then what could "7 minus 5" possibly mean? It is rather like asking "What letter is equivalent to P minus K?"—we would start to recite the alphabet using our fingers as the only route to finding a possible answer.

Learners with *dyscalculia* can usually learn to count in the sense that they can recite the number sequence, and can often put it in one-to-one correspondence with objects, although they may not be completely systematic about this. The problem for them is that the number sequence is cognitively rather like the alphabet. With little intuitive sense of number magnitude, they try to solve all problems by their one reliable method, namely counting. For example:

- When asked to select a 9-dot card from a pile of cards, they select from cards at random and count the dots until they find nine.
- When asked to state which is the larger of two playing cards showing 5 and 8, they count all of the symbols on each card, and note that 8 comes after 5.
- When asked to count down from 10, they count from 1 to 10, then 1 to 9, then 1 to 8, etc.
- When asked to place a playing card of 8 in sequence between a 3 and a 9 they count up spaces between the two to identify where the 8 should be placed.

They do not rely on spatial representations of numbers to help them, except for finger counting. These procedures make it very hard work to do simple arithmetic. For example, to calculate 5 + 7 they have to count up to 5 on their fingers, then count a further 7 to see which finger they end up with, then go back to the start and count up to that finger again to find out what number it is. Remembering number facts can help, but these are essentially meaningless arbitrary facts, so it is like building on sand. They rely so heavily on counting because memory is not reliable whereas counting is. SEN teachers frequently find that ideas that appear to have been mastered in one lesson are forgotten by the next one, which may be several days later, with nothing in between to reinforce the learning they have achieved.

The Research Program on Dyscalculia

Dyscalculia: The Official Position

Poor numeracy is a serious disability. It leads to poor educational, employment, and health lifetime outcomes (Bynner & Parsons, 1997; Parsons & Bynner, 2005). One form of low numeracy is developmental dyscalculia. A major UK government report, *Mental Capital and Wellbeing*, summarized the current situation as follows: "Developmental dyscalculia is currently the poor relation of dyslexia, with a much lower public profile. But the consequences of dyscalculia are at least as severe as those for dyslexia" (Beddington *et al.*, 2008).

So what is dyscalculia? The term does not appear in the *Diagnostic and Statistical Manual of Mental Disorders, 5th edition (DSM-5)*, the researchers' and clinicians' official resource that is used to "diagnose and classify mental disorders" (American Psychiatric Association, 2013). Incidentally, the term "dyslexia" does not appear either. In this manual all "learning disabilities" are unhelpfully defined as "A persistent difficulty learning *academic skills* for at least 6 months despite intervention targeting the area(s) of difficulty." The definition comes with a "Specifier" to make it specific to mathematics (i.e. a difficulty "in number sense, fact and calculation, and in mathematical reasoning"), and in three degrees of "Severity" (i.e. mild, moderate, or severe). No norms are offered, and exclusions include intellectual disabilities, visual or hearing impairments, mental disorders (e.g. depression, anxiety, etc.), psycho-social difficulty, neurological disorders, and lack of access to adequate instruction.

To identify an individual as having this disability, the advice is as follows:

> The specific learning disorder is diagnosed through a clinical review of the individual's developmental, medical, educational, and family history, reports of test scores and teacher observations, and responses to academic interventions. The diagnosis requires persistent difficulties in reading, writing, arithmetic, or mathematical reasoning skills during formal years of schooling.
>
> *(American Psychiatric Association, 2013, DSM-5, 315.1)*

The exclusions mean that a child or adult cannot be diagnosed with dyscalculia if they are depressed, anxious, have a low IQ, or have a sensory impairment. These conditions can cause poor academic skills, but seem to take precedence over other possible causes. The exclusions also mean that different clinicians can operate with quite different criteria as to who should and who should not be classified, and therefore how an intervention strategy should be designed and implemented.

Moreover, the individual should have no "specific cognitive impairment." (It is unclear whether this would include a specific impairment in phonological processing for dyslexia.)

The General Approach

Our research-based approach is quite different from that of *DSM-5*. In the learning sciences, we want to understand *why* a learner is having difficulty in learning arithmetic, since this has to be the basis for an intervention strategy. We do not exclude learning disability (low IQ), or specific cognitive or neural differences, although we would of course take into account the learning context at home and at school (Butterworth *et al.*, 2011).

The general approach is as follows:

1. Start with the observed behavior of learners with low attainment in mathematics on a range of tests, on the basis of self-report, and on the basis of reports by their teachers and parents.
2. Develop a cognitive hypothesis based on the observations and reports, which may suggest a specific cognitive impairment.
3. Use cognitive theory about why some learners have difficulty or disability in learning arithmetic to develop a specific neural hypothesis based on the cognitive theory and other behavioral evidence.
4. Plan an intervention strategy based on the cognitive and neural theories, guided by the principles of pedagogic design and the best practice of reflective practitioners.
5. Implement the strategy in the form of guidance for teachers, parents, and learners, and for relevant professionals, including educational and clinical psychologists.

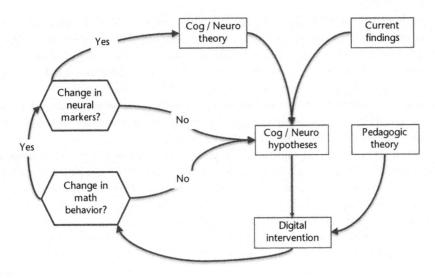

FIGURE 10.1 An iterative integration of neural and genetic factors with the development and testing of educational interventions.

6. Implement the strategy in the form of software that can help to identify sufferers, and to distinguish them from learners with low numeracy for reasons other than dyscalculia.
7. Implement the strategy in the form of digital games that can support learners in both formal and informal settings, including individual learning away from teachers and parents.
8. Evaluate the intervention against changes in behavior, following intervention, when modified and retested against further changes in behavior, and ultimately against predicted changes in neural activity and structure.

The general approach is illustrated in Figure 10.1, which shows how the two disciplines are interwoven in an iterative series of research activities.

Investigating Dyscalculia

In our first study of 9-year-olds, we asked teachers to identify the children who, behaviorally, performed very badly at arithmetic, but seemed to achieve normally in other subjects (Landerl *et al.*, 2004). Those identified were formally tested with item-timed arithmetic, since response times to answer a question such as "What is 3 plus 8?" can be diagnostic. For example, using a counting strategy to solve this problem is slow, especially if the child is "counting all" ("one, two, three; one, two, three, four, five, six, seven, eight; one, two, three, four, five, six, seven, eight, nine, ten, eleven"). We have found in a series of studies that the development of arithmetical skills in children is reliably predicted by the time it takes to do very simple numerical tasks such as timed enumeration of dot displays up to 9 dots, and selecting the larger of two digits (Butterworth, 2003; Landerl *et al.*, 2004; Reeve *et al.*, 2012; Reigosa-Crespo *et al.*, 2012).

Of these children, we selected those who were 3 standard deviations (SDs) worse than matched controls. There was no special reason for this criterion, except to ensure that these children performed very badly at arithmetic. These individuals we provisionally termed "dyscalculic." We constructed four groups who were matched on language ability, IQ, and short-term memory span (apart from the dyslexic groups who had a span of about one item fewer than the controls): (1) dyscalculic children, (2) dyslexic children, (3) a double deficit group who were both dyscalculic and dyslexic, and (4) a control group matched for age, gender, and classroom. We included learners who were dyslexic because many special needs teachers told us that dyslexics experienced difficulties with mathematics, although for this group we selected only those who were not bad at arithmetic.

It turned out to be easy to construct these groups, which in itself showed that differences in IQ, language, and short-term memory are not sufficient to cause dyscalculia. So what did make the difference? Our cognitive hypothesis was that the dyscalculic children differed in something very simple, which must be domain-specific, and that would prove to be foundational for learning arithmetic. We already knew that mathematical abilities had a heritable component, from twin studies (Alarcon et al., 1997) and from studies of genetic anomalies, such as Turner syndrome (Butterworth et al., 1999; Rovet et al., 1994; Temple & Marriott, 1998), and that infants even in the first weeks of life could make numerical discriminations (Antell & Keating, 1983; Starkey & Cooper, 1980). Therefore we tested these four groups on two tasks that seemed likely to capture differences in innate abilities, affected as little as possible by education. These tasks were timed enumeration of dot displays up to 9 dots, and magnitude comparison (selecting the larger of two digits). We found that the dyscalculic group and the double deficit group performed significantly less well than controls on these measures, but the dyslexic group did not.

These findings supported our cognitive hypothesis that the 9-year-old dyscalculic children had a "core deficit" in an inherited domain-specific mechanism that could be identified by simple tests of timed enumeration of sets of objects and by timed magnitude comparison (Butterworth, 2005). They also guided the development of a software product that a teacher or other professional could use to help to identify the dyscalculic children and differentiate them from other children who performed equally badly on a standardized test of timed simple arithmetic (Butterworth, 2003). Other studies used a somewhat different characterization of the domain-specific mechanism, but also used a very simple test that depended relatively little on education, namely "numerical acuity", a two-alternative forced-choice task to select the display with more dots. It turned out that children who performed badly on this test were also bad at learning arithmetic (Piazza et al., 2010). However, training (Dewind & Brannon, 2012) and education do seem to play a role even in this simple task (Piazza et al., 2013).

The early results encouraged us to conduct a longitudinal study based on the cognitive hypothesis of a core deficit in this mechanism (Reeve et al., 2012). Here we tested timed *dot enumeration* (DE) along with other numerical and cognitive tests on seven occasions between kindergarten and 11 years of age. DE is a very simple test, in which the learner states the number of dots in a visual array as quickly as possible. Using cluster analysis based on four parameters of the number of dots against reaction time (RT), namely slope of the subitizing range, slope of the counting range, the point of discontinuity where the slope changes, and the overall average RT (the term "subitizing" refers to the rapid, accurate, and confident judgments of number performed for small numbers of items), it is claimed that for up to about four items counting is not necessary for accuracy, whereas for larger numbers of items counting is needed for accuracy. We identified three clusters at each testing. Children tended to remain in the same cluster throughout the testing, which suggests that this is a stable measure of individual differences. The slowest cluster at kindergarten, about 7% of the total of 159 children, were also way behind their peers in the other two clusters at each testing in their accuracy of age-appropriate arithmetic, from single-digit addition at 6 years, to three-digit subtraction, multiplication, and division at 10 years.

At the same time, several other teams had identified very simple cognitive markers of dyscalculia using our method or similar ones. For example, Piazza *et al.* (2010) found that children and adults differed in how well they could tell which of two clouds of dots contained more dots (see Figure 10.2).

Accuracy on this task depends on the difference between the numerosities of the clouds—that is, the more different they are, the higher the accuracy, and also the faster the response. This is called the "distance effect." On this task, 10-year-old dyscalculic children performed at the level of typically developing 5-year-olds. That is, the distance effect was different for the dyscalculic children—they need a larger difference in order to be reliably accurate. More generally, individual differences on this task correlated with performance on arithmetic tasks (Halberda *et al.*, 2008; Mazzocco *et al.*, 2011). Several other studies have pointed to differences on very simple numerical tasks, such as deciding whether two squares match the digit 2, or placing the number 7 on a line with the ends marked 0 and 10 (e.g. Geary *et al.*, 2009). In fact a tool for screening for dyscalculia and differentiating from non-dyscalculic causes of poor arithmetic skills was based on measures of this kind (Butterworth, 2003), and a large-scale prevalence study used dot enumeration as the criterion for distinguishing dyscalculia from "calculation dysfluency" (Reigosa-Crespo *et al.*, 2012).

These studies suggested that it may be possible to find differences in brain activity when dyscalculic individuals carry out these simple tasks. Several studies have established that small regions in the parietal lobes, namely the left and right *intraparietal sulci* (IPS), are reliably activated when children or adults compare the numerosities of sets. In fact, activity in these regions shows the distance effect—that is, the more similar the numerosities of the sets to be compared, the greater the activation (Castelli *et al.*, 2006; Pinel *et al.*, 2001). A study of dyscalculic 12-year-olds revealed that these children did not show the distance effect in the right parietal lobe, whereas matched controls did (Price *et al.*, 2007). It is worth noting that although these tasks activate both the left and right parietal lobe in adults, the balance of

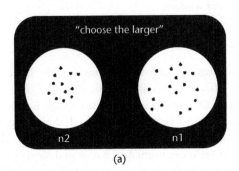
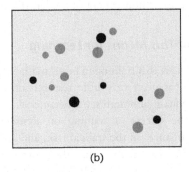

(a)   (b)

FIGURE 10.2 Two examples of the "clouds of dots" task. (a) The method used by Piazza *et al.* (2010). (b) The method used by Halberda *et al.* (2008), where the task is to say whether there are more blue or more yellow dots.

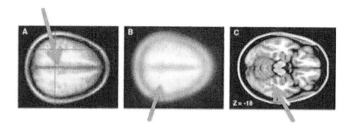

FIGURE 10.3 Structural abnormalities in young dyscalculic brains, suggesting a critical role for the IPS. A: There is a small region of reduced gray matter density in the left IPS in dyscalculic adolescents (Isaacs *et al.*, 2001). B: There is reduced gray matter density (indicated by grew arrows) in the right IPS in dyscalculic 9-year-olds (Rotzer *et al.*, 2008). C: There is a reduced likelihood of connections between the right fusiform gyrus and other parts of the brain, including the parietal lobes (Rykhlevskaia *et al.*, 2009).

Source: Reproduced from Butterworth *et al.* (2011).

activation changes with age, with children tending to show more activation in the right parietal lobe, whereas adults show more activation in the left one (Cantlon *et al.*, 2006).

The structure of the dyscalculic brain in these regions is also different from that of typically developing individuals. In adolescents, there is lower gray matter density in the left IPS of dyscalculic individuals compared with controls (Isaacs *et al.*, 2001), whereas in younger children there is lower gray matter density in the right IPS (Rotzer *et al.*, 2008). White matter—that is, the tracts that connect different gray matter regions—also differs in children with low numeracy (Rykhlevskaia *et al.*, 2009). From the ages of 8 to 14 years in typically developing children, white matter volume in several tracts increases with age, showing that the distant regions are becoming better connected. However, in dyscalculic children this does not appear to happen, although it may occur later (Ranpura *et al.*, 2013). There also seem to be differences in the white matter connections between the frontal lobes (the region that supports reasoning) and the hippocampus (the structure that supports long-term memory) (for a recent review, see Moeller *et al.*, 2015).

Figure 10.3 shows the regions where there are differences between the dyscalculic brain and that of typically developing controls. Both the left and right IPS are implicated, possibly with greater impairment of the left IPS in older learners.

What This Means for Learning

We know that training in novel math tasks changes the activity of brains in adults, but to date there has been very little research on the effects of training on the brains of dyscalculic individuals (although see Kucian *et al.*, 2011). One of the aims of our research is indeed to test the effects of training on dyscalculic brains. Training could and should improve performance on the trained task, and also on transfer tasks, but this in itself does not clarify whether the training makes the pattern of activity more normal, as it does in dyslexia training (Eden *et al.*, 2004), or whether alternative networks are created to perform the task. What is of primary importance for the teacher and the learner is whether performance improves, but for the science of learning it is important to determine whether improvement is caused by making the learner better at using typical strategies, or by recruiting compensatory strategies.

As we mentioned above, one important factor in dyscalculia is genetics. This is not to say that all dyscalculic individuals have inherited the condition. Neural abnormalities can have many other causes (e.g. prematurity, perinatal trauma, fetal alcohol syndrome). In fact, twin studies show that the effects of non-shared environment—the experiences of one of the twins but not the other—can be as important as genetics (for a review, see Butterworth & Kovas, 2013).

Figure 10.4 summarizes what is currently known about the causal basis of dyscalculia—the cognitive activities affected by the biology of regions of the brain, the arithmetic activities affected by cognition, and the educational contexts in which these are addressed.

If parietal areas, especially the IPS, fail to develop normally, there may be an impairment at the cognitive level in numerosity representation, and consequential impairments for other relevant cognitive systems revealed in behavioral abnormalities. The link between the occipitotemporal and parietal cortex is required for mapping number symbols (digits and number words) to numerosity representations. The prefrontal cortex supports the learning of new facts and procedures. The multiple levels of the theory suggest the instructional interventions on which educational scientists should focus.

To summarize, the basic science reveals a core deficit in numerosity processing specific to dyscalculia. That is, dyscalculic individuals have a deficit in their "number sense." In the next section we shall show how this can be a target for intervention.

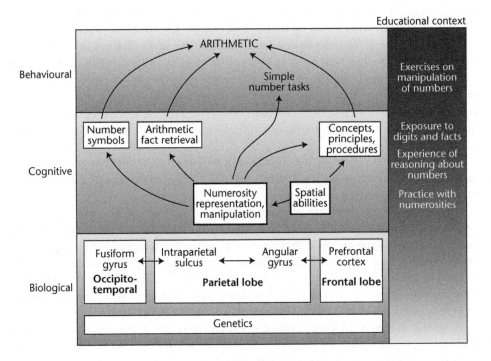

FIGURE 10.4 Causal model of possible interrelationships between educational context and biological, cognitive, and behavioral functions.

Source: Reproduced from Butterworth *et al.* (2011).

From Research to Education

To help SEN learners with mastery of basic number concepts, teachers use intensive practice with materials-based manipulation activities (Anning & Edwards, 1999), focused on the core concepts of number, as this can help to bring dyscalculic learners closer to the norm (Butterworth & Yeo, 2004). To help with retention, teachers ask their SEN learners to talk about what they are doing, and when they have done it successfully to describe what they did, and why it was right (Butterworth & Yeo, 2004). These methods take time, and have no place in the classroom for typically developing learners. SEN teachers are very aware that there is no point in forcing the age-stage link to the curriculum. These learners must be allowed to take their time, and build up the concepts that typically developing learners have been building throughout the preschool years (Yeo, 2003).

Diagnosis to Intervention

Neuroscience identifies the origin of dyscalculia, and explains it as a congenital neural difference that amounts to "a deficit in number sense." From this we can infer that an educational intervention must attempt to build the automatized connections between digit, numerosity, and length that a typically developing (TD) learner has. It does not yet tell us how those connections were built. We know from behavioral studies with infants that there is an innate basis to grasp of numerosity, and we know from studies of dyscalculic individuals that it is heritable (Butterworth, 2010). However, we do not yet know how the perception of numerosity builds up to the number sense (e.g. that 5 is contained within 7, or that 3 + 2 = 2 + 3). In order to develop an intervention that is likely to assist dyscalculic individuals we therefore turn to a combination of building on what SEN teachers know (and know to be successful) (Bird, 2007; Butterworth & Yeo, 2004), and making use of techniques that provide the vast number of transactions required to build the neural connections to form an efficient connection between the concepts of digit, numerosity, and length, enabling the representations and processing that are necessary for arithmetic (Butterworth *et al.*, 2011).

Our fundamental pedagogic aim, therefore, is to strengthen numerosity processing. We argue that the optimal approach is to create game-like digital environments that scaffold the learner's development of number sense.

The advantage of game-like digital environments is their highly engaging quality. Dyscalculic learners are able to focus and maintain attention on task for a long time, and hence practice far more examples than they could with a teacher, even working one to one (Butterworth & Laurillard, 2010). These digital environments offer the most effective means of enabling a learner to process a very large number of numerical transactions over sufficiently short periods of time for them to be likely to learn something about them, and to remember what they learn.

A second advantage of using a digital environment is that it can support independent learning by providing feedback and therefore supporting learning beyond the classroom. In the long gaps between one lesson and another at school it is very easy to forget the ideas that have been mastered, but the personal mobile device, with an enticing game that is satisfying to play, is an ever-present personal tutor—if it is well designed.

The Pedagogical Principles

The increasing popularity of tablets and personal mobile devices for children has led to the development of a huge number of game-like apps for basic mathematics. They are certainly engaging, because they have the motivational qualities of games, but they lack any game-play design based on pedagogic principles. The predominant form of feedback is the right/wrong response to multiple-choice questions, or their equivalent. This is the instructionist design that requires an external judge of what the learner has done.

The alternative pedagogy is "constructionist", which enables "learning without being taught" (Butterworth & Laurillard, 2010; diSessa, 2001; Healy & Kynigos, 2010; Noss *et al.*, 1997; Papert, 1980). Here the nature of the task, and therefore the learning process, are closer to learning in the real world, because the digital format creates a task environment in which the goal is shared (in the same sense in which a game goal is shared), the actions are within the learner's repertoire of possible actions, and the feedback is intrinsic (i.e. the environment changes according to the learner's action). There is no extrinsic judgmental feedback. The learner is situated within an environment that affords learning because they are able to self-correct, having seen the effect of their action in relation to the goal. For example, consider a child who is learning to use a spoon, aims for the yogurt pot, but using the wrong angle knocks it over. They are very aware of having to aim more carefully. They do not need to be told that they missed, so the processing of that action is more likely to integrate the form of the action with its result than if they had been blindfolded and simply told "Wrong, try again." In this case there would be no informational feedback to supply the link between action, goal, and improved action. The aim of a constructionist design is to emulate the nature of encounters with the world, which affords learning.

A second pedagogical principle is to adapt to the learner's current level, where the "zone of proximal development" (Vygotsky, 1978) is maintained not by a more competent individual, but by an algorithm that tracks current performance and decides whether or not to increase the difficulty level. In this way the tasks remain challenging, and the learner is motivated to move through different levels of the game, and so build the concept (Mariotti, 2009).

These two principles were used in the design of a game tested with typically developing learners aged 5–7 years.

Successful SEN teachers and the basic principles of good pedagogy therefore form the basis that allows us to specify the pedagogical features of the digital learning environment. It must:

- provide intensive learning
- set familiar materials-based tasks
- sequence tasks and stages to build a concept of numerosity
- adapt difficulty to the performance of the learner
- ask the learner to construct answers to achieve a goal
- give meaningful feedback that enables the learner to self-correct.

The contrast between instructionist and constructionist approaches is captured in the Conversational Framework account of learning in the context of formal education (Laurillard, 2012). It models learning in terms of two kinds of interaction—communication and practice. The teacher communicates ideas through language and representation, enabling the learner

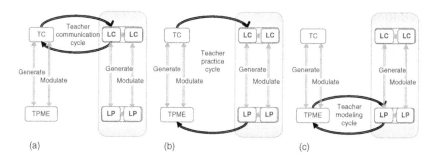

FIGURE 10.5 The learner learning concepts (LC) and learning practice (LP) through interaction in (a) the teacher communication cycle, (b) the teacher practice cycle, and (c) the teacher modeling cycle, from the teacher's conceptual organization (TC), and the practice modeling environment set up by the teacher (TPME).

Source: Reproduced from Laurillard (2012).

to learn through acquisition of concepts by listening or reading, and through discussion (Frith, 2007), as shown in Figure 10.5a. The teacher also sets up a learning practice modeling environment in which the learner puts their developing concepts into practice in order to achieve some defined goal, and through which those concepts are modified as a result of feedback on actions in relation to the goal. The feedback may be extrinsic in the practice cycle, from the teacher or from a computer program evaluating the learner's actions, as shown in Figure 10.5b, or it may be intrinsic in the modeling cycle, from the world or from a computer model giving informational feedback on the result of the learner's actions, as shown in Figure 10.5c.

The Conversational Framework represents the contrast between instructionist and constructionist pedagogies in terms of the contrast between extrinsic feedback in the practice cycle and intrinsic feedback in the modeling cycle.

Figure 10.6a shows the *instructionist* version of the goal → action → feedback → revised action sequence, where the teacher's evaluation or guidance can be put into practice without necessarily engaging the learner's conceptual processing, inevitably so if the feedback does not make explicit the connection between the goal, the action, and what is needed to improve the action, resulting in a trial-and-error response.

Figure 10.6b shows the *constructionist* version of the sequence, where the feedback on action comes from the world, or from the program representing the result of the action. In this case, there is an explicit relationship between the goal, the action, and what the action achieved in comparison with the goal. The learner may make a random trial-and-error attempt to revise their action, but they also have the information that they need to inform their own decision on how to revise it, without recourse to teacher guidance.

Engaging the learner in making a connection between their practice and their concepts is essential if they are to build a meaningful relationship between the two, and so develop a full conceptual understanding of the task set. This is what we aim for in designing a game-like digital environment for learning number concepts.

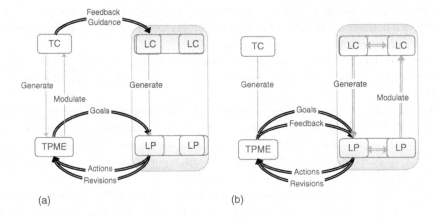

FIGURE 10.6 (a) The teacher reflects on the learner's actions to provide extrinsic feedback. (b) The practice/modeling environment provides intrinsic feedback, prompting learner reflection.

Source: Reproduced from Laurillard (2012).

Design for a Number Concepts Game

Several digital games, based on these pedagogic principles and aiming to develop aspects of number, have been tested with small numbers of learners (Butterworth & Laurillard, 2010; Butterworth *et al.*, 2011). The new Science of Learning Research Centre (based at the University of Queensland and the University of Melbourne, and funded by the Australian Research Council) provides an opportunity to test this approach with larger learner groups, comparing typically developing with dyscalculic learners. With its focus on the relationship between education, cognition, and neuroscience, it also enables the investigation of both behavioral and neural responses to this constructionist type of game design, in comparison with the typical educational app, which adopts an instructionist or simple testing approach.

To integrate number concepts with the basics of arithmetic manipulation, the aim of a new game is to enable dyscalculic learners to develop a sense of the meaning of numbers, not as an arbitrary sequence, but as a structure, which can be combined and split to make other numbers, and therefore represent a meaningfully ordered sequence. With this conceptual basis, the manipulations of addition and subtraction become meaningful.

The design of the "Sets Game" is as follows:

- The screen displays sets of discrete objects, clustered in sets of different numerosities.
- The objects are initially color-coded according to the set size.
- Two tools are always available, one for combining and one for splitting sets.
- The goal is to combine or split the sets to match the target set displayed at the top of the screen, until all of the sets are matched.
- Later levels of difficulty use larger sets, digits linked to the set to denote its cardinality, objects with digits but no colors, and finally just digits.
- When sets are combined or split, the resulting set changes color, or changes the digit to denote the new numerosity.

Figures 10.7, 10.8, and 10.9 show how the game play appears to the learner.

The total number of objects on the screen is programmed to be a multiple of the target number, to ensure that the task can be completed.

At the final level the learner is combining and splitting a screen full of just digits, and is then ready to move on to the formal representation of these manipulations of addition and subtraction.

The game has the concreteness of materials-based manipulations, but the significant advantage that it can represent the change of numerosity by the change in color, as well as other rewards, such as a small animated movement of the set, and sounds. There is nothing else visual, to avoid distraction. Other visual rewards come at the end of each game, along with the score and, with a sufficient score, a new level.

There is never any negative evaluation of the learner. They can tell for themselves when they have matched the target, and can repeat the manipulations as often as they wish, even playing with irrelevant manipulations without penalty. Games of this kind appear to be

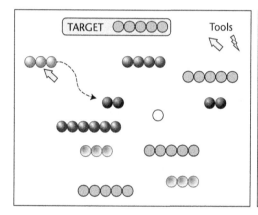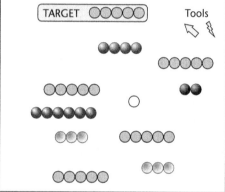

FIGURE 10.7 The learner moves the 3 group to combine with the 2 group, which makes a target 5 group, which changes color to match its size.

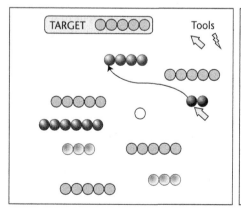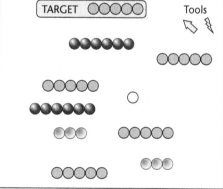

FIGURE 10.8 The learner moves the 2 group to combine with the 4 group, which makes a 6 group, which changes color to match its size.

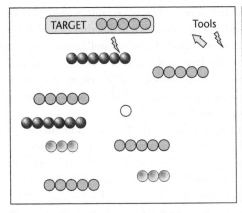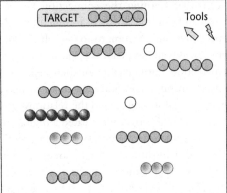

FIGURE 10.9 The learner now has to split the 6 group at the right place to make a target 5 group with an extra 1, both of which change color to match their size.

sufficiently rewarding for the learner to remain on task for long continuous periods, and this does help to establish the connections that they need to make between the nature of the goal and their action to achieve it.

Using Feedback

Further experimentation on games of this type should replicate the following established findings on feedback:

- Feedback is effective if it directs information to more effective self-regulation, so that students invest more effort or commitment in the task (Kluger & DeNisi, 1996).
- Teachers can help by creating a learning environment that emphasizes self-monitoring and self-regulation to enhance learning (Hattie *et al.*, 1996).
- Feedback about the task is powerful when the task information can be used for improving strategy processing (Hattie & Timperley, 2007).

However, as Hattie and Timperley (2007, p. 91) have pointed out, "too much feedback at the task level can lead to trial-and-error strategies and less cognitive effort to develop informal hypotheses about the relationship between the instructions, the feedback and the intended learning."

In an adaptive digital game the feedback is entirely focused on the task level, so it is important to investigate this aspect. However, as the nature of the task is conceptual, and the goal can only be achieved by using cognitive effort to clarify the relationship between goal and feedback, it should be the case that, under these conditions, task-level feedback could achieve the intended learning.

From the Laboratory to the Classroom

It has been found that dyscalculia occurs because of a specific and often severe deficit in the capacity to mentally represent the number of objects in a set—that is, its "numerosity." This means that learning the connection between the representation of numerosities and the words and symbols for them is difficult for dyscalculic learners. Remembering facts based on representations of numerosity—such as single digit additions and multiplication tables—as typically developing learners can, is also difficult for dyscalculic learners. Therefore effective remediation must strengthen their representations of numerosities, link them to counting words and numerals, and help them to make sense of the meaning of numbers in terms of their internal structures and the relationships between them.

As outlined above, we created a digital game that addresses all of these requirements.

This game can be used in the learner's own time, because the task adaptation and meaningful intrinsic feedback can support independent learning. However, this gives the learner no opportunity to discuss and articulate the mathematical concepts and relationships. Therefore it is important to integrate independent, technology-based learning with the classroom teaching, where learners manipulate concrete materials, work in pairs or groups, and have plenty of opportunity to articulate what they have done, as the expert SEN teachers do. A learning design for one such session is proposed here, based on the designs used by these teachers (Butterworth & Yeo, 2004).

The design has been implemented in the Learning Designer tool (http://learningdesigner. org)—an online design tool that is free and open to anyone who registers—and exported to a word document, as set out below. The design shows a plan for a 50-minute classroom session leading to individual learner use of the Sets Game described above, to be followed by a class discussion in the next session a few days later.

The design can be found on the Learning Designer website in the Browser screen, from where it can be loaded into the Designer screen for editing.

Appendix: A Learning Design for Developing Number Sense

Context

- Topic: set combinations.
- Total learning time: 180 minutes.
- Number of students: 10.

This is a design for a week's worth of teaching and learning for a student who attends class and has access to a personal mobile device for learning beyond the classroom. It assumes that the learner has learned to count using 1-1 correspondence (based on Butterworth & Yeo, 2004, pp. 55–59).

Aim

To develop a sense of the way that numbers can combine and split to make other numbers.

Outcome

Construct (application): able to construct a target number from combining or splitting different sets of numerosities.

Teaching–Learning Activities

Build Sets of 4 From Sets of 1, 2, and 3

Read Watch Listen—2 minutes, 10 students. Watch how I can make up a group of 4 counters. I have a group of 2 here, and another group of 2 here. Count each group. Now I bring them together. How many are in this group? From this one I am adding 3, 4, so I now have a group of 4. I added a group of 2 to a group of 2 to make a group of 4.

Practice—2 minutes, 1 student. Now take counters from the pile to make a group of 2 and another group of 2. Put them together and tell me what you have made. Use the counters to make groups of 2, then build a group of 4 from two groups of 2.

Read Watch Listen—2 minutes, 10 students. Watch how I can do this with lots of groups, and make them all into groups of 4. [Use several sets of 1, 2, and 3.] I can combine a 1 and a 1 to make a 2, and now I can add another 2 group to make a 4 group. Here's a group of 3. I add a 1 to that to make 4, and so on till I have just groups of 4.

Practice—3 minutes, 2 students. Work in pairs and take it in turns to combine these groups so that you make just groups of 4. Each time you make one, describe how you did it: "I added a group of 1 to a group of 3 to make a group of 4."

Produce—3 minutes, 2 students. Explain to your partner what you did. Is your partner's explanation correct?

Combine and Split Sets of 1 to 6 to Make Sets of 3

Read Watch Listen—3 minutes, 10 students. If I have a group of 6 and want to make a group of 3, what should I do? [Demonstrate splitting the group of 6 into two groups of 3.] How am I going to make this group of 5 into a group of 3? I can split it to make a group of 3 and now I have a group of 2 as well: "I took 2 away from 5 to make 3." How can I make that into a group of 3, if I add it to this 1. Here you have several groups of different numbers. Can you bring them together, or split them up until you have just groups of 3?

Practice—5 minutes, 2 students. Work in pairs and take it in turns to combine and split these groups so that you make just groups of 3. Each time you make one, describe how you did it: "I added a group of 2 to a group of 1 to make a group of 3", "I took 3 away from 6 to make 3", and so on.

Repeat the Same Design: Combine and Split Sets of 1 to 10 to Make Sets of 2 to 9

Produce—5 minutes, 1 student. Split the pile of counters into small groups of different size for their partner.

Practice—10 minutes, 1 student. Each learner rolls a dice to decide which number they are aiming to make, takes a pile of the counters and makes them into groups of the target number by combining and splitting them.

Do the Same Exercise with the Sets Game on a Tablet

Read Watch Listen—5 minutes, 10 students. In this game you have to make all the groups on the screen into the same as the one at the top. You can use the combine and split tools to combine and split the groups. When you have matched all of the groups on the screen you move on to the next level.

Practice—10 minutes, 1 student. Now work through Level 1 and see if you can get to Level 3 in 10 minutes.

Working Through Levels in the Sets Game

Practice—120 minutes, 1 student. Work individually to complete each successive level in the game. [They should use it for three sessions of 20 minutes each day before the next classroom session.]

Discuss—10 minutes, 10 students. In class, discuss which levels in the Sets Game were easy or difficult, and why. Each learner should describe what they did in the last game they used.

Conclusion

The interdisciplinary journey does not end here, but with the behavioral and neural testing now under way. The aim is to demonstrate that integrating neuroscience with personalized learning can be most effectively achieved by properly designed and evaluated digital learning environments.

References

Alarcon, M., Defries, J., Gillis Light, J., & Pennington, B. (1997). A twin study of mathematics disability. *Journal of Learning Disabilities*, 30, 617–623.

American Psychiatric Association (2013). *Diagnostic and Statistical Manual of Mental Disorders, 5th edition (DSM-5)*. Washington, DC: American Psychiatric Publishing.

Anning, A. & Edwards, A. (1999). *Promoting Children's Learning from Birth to Five: Developing the New Early Years Professional*. Maidenhead: Open University Press.

Antell, S. E. & Keating, D. P. (1983). Perception of numerical invariance in neonates. *Child Development*, 54, 695–701.

Beddington, J., Cooper, C. L., Field, J., Goswami, U., Huppert, F. A., Jenkins, R., Jones, H. S., Kirkwood, T. B. L., Sahakian, B. J., & Thomas, S. M. (2008). The mental wealth of nations. *Nature*, 455, 1057–1060.

Bird, R. (2007). *The Dyscalculia Toolkit*. London: Paul Chapman Publishing.

Butterworth, B. (2003). *Dyscalculia Screener*. London: nferNelson Publishing Company Ltd.

Butterworth, B. (2005). Developmental dyscalculia. In: J. I. D. Campbell (Ed.), *Handbook of Mathematical Cognition* (pp. 455–467). Hove: Psychology Press.

Butterworth, B. (2010). Foundational numerical capacities and the origins of dyscalculia. *Trends in Cognitive Sciences*, 14, 534–541.

Butterworth, B. & Yeo, D. (2004). *Dyscalculia Guidance*. London: nferNelson Publishing Company Ltd.

Butterworth, B. & Laurillard, D. (2010). Low numeracy and dyscalculia: identification and intervention. *ZDM Mathematics Education*, 42, 527–539.

Butterworth, B. & Kovas, Y. (2013). Understanding neurocognitive developmental disorders can improve education for all. *Science*, 340, 300–305.

Butterworth, B., Granà, A., Piazza, M., Girelli, L., Price, C., & Skuse, D. (1999). Language and the origins of number skills: karyotypic differences in Turner's syndrome. *Brain and Language*, 69, 486–488.

Butterworth, B., Varma, S., & Laurillard, D. (2011). Dyscalculia: from brain to education. *Science*, 332, 1049–1053.

Bynner, J. & Parsons, S. (1997). *Does Numeracy Matter?* London: The Basic Skills Agency.

Cantlon, J. F., Brannon, E. M., Carter, E. J., & Pelphrey, K. A. (2006). Functional imaging of numerical processing in adults and 4-y-old children. *PLoS Biology*, 4, e125.

Castelli, F., Glaser, D. E., & Butterworth, B. (2006). Discrete and analogue quantity processing in the parietal lobe: a functional MRI study. *Proceedings of the National Academy of Sciences of the United States of America*, 103, 4693–4698.

Dewind, N. K. & Brannon, E. M. (2012). Malleability of the approximate number system: effects of feedback and training. *Frontiers in Human Neuroscience*, 6, 68.

diSessa, A. (2001). *Changing Minds: Computers, Learning, and Literacy*. Cambridge, MA: MIT Press.

Eden, G., Jones, K., Cappell, K., Gareau, L., Wood, F., Zeffiro, T., Dietz, N., Agnew, J., & Flowers, D. (2004). Neural changes following remediation in adult developmental dyslexia. *Neuron*, 44, 411–422.

Frith, C. D. (2007). *Making up the Mind: How the Brain Creates our Mental World*. Oxford: Blackwell Publishing.

Geary, D. C., Bailey, D. H., Littlefield, A., Wood, P., Hoard, M. K., & Nugent, L. (2009). First-grade predictors of mathematical learning disability: a latent class trajectory analysis. *Cognitive Development*, 24, 411–429.

Halberda, J., Mazzocco, M. M. M., & Feigenson, L. (2008). Individual differences in non-verbal number acuity correlate with maths achievement. *Nature*, 455, 665–668.

Hattie, J. & Timperley, H. (2007). The power of feedback. *Review of Educational Research*, 77, 81–112.

Hattie, J., Biggs, J., & Purdie, N. (1996). Effects of learning skills intervention on student learning: a meta-analysis. *Review of Research in Education*, 66, 99–136.

Healy, L. & Kynigos, C. (2010). Charting the microworld territory over time: design and construction in mathematics education. *ZDM Mathematics Education*, 42, 63–76.

Isaacs, E. B., Edmonds, C. J., Lucas, A., & Gadian, D. G. (2001). Calculation difficulties in children of very low birthweight: a neural correlate. *Brain*, 124, 1701–1707.

Kluger, A. N. & DeNisi, A. (1996). The effects of feedback interventions on performance: a historical review, a meta-analysis, and a preliminary feedback intervention theory. *Psychological Bulletin*, 119, 254–284.

Kucian, K., Grond, U., Rotzer, S., Henzi, B., Schönmann, C., Plangger, F., Gälli, M., Martin, E., & von Aster, M. (2011). Mental number line training in children with developmental dyscalculia. *NeuroImage*, 57, 782–795.

Landerl, K., Bevan, A., & Butterworth, B. (2004). Developmental dyscalculia and basic numerical capacities: a study of 8–9-year-old students. *Cognition*, 93, 99–125.

Laurillard, D. (2012). *Teaching as a Design Science: Building Pedagogical Patterns for Learning and Technology*. New York: Routledge.

Mariotti, M. A. (2009). Artifacts and signs after a Vygotskian perspective: the role of the teacher. *ZDM Mathematics Education*, 41, 427–440.

Mazzocco, M. M., Feigenson, L., & Halberda, J. (2011). Impaired acuity of the approximate number system underlies mathematical learning disability (dyscalculia). *Child Development*, 82, 1224–1237.

Moeller, K., Willmes, K., & Klein, E. (2015). A review on functional and structural brain connectivity in numerical cognition. *Frontiers in Human Neuroscience*, 9, 227.

Noss, R., Healy, L., & Hoyles, C. (1997). The construction of mathematical meanings: connecting the visual with the symbolic. *Educational Studies in Mathematics*, 33, 203–233.

Papert, S. (1980). *Mindstorms: Children, Computers, and Powerful Ideas*. Brighton, UK: Harvester Press.

Parsons, S. & Bynner, J. (2005). *Does Numeracy Matter More?* London: National Research and Development Centre for Adult Literacy and Numeracy, Institute of Education.

Piazza, M., Facoetti, A., Trussardi, A. N., Berteletti, I., Conte, S., Lucangeli, D., Dehaene, S., & Zorzi, M. (2010). Developmental trajectory of number acuity reveals a severe impairment in developmental dyscalculia. *Cognition*, 116, 33–41.

Piazza, M., Pica, P., Izard, V., Spelke, E. S., & Dehaene, S. (2013). Education enhances the acuity of the nonverbal approximate number system. *Psychological Science*, 24, 1037–1043.

Pinel, P., Dehaene, S., Rivière, D., & Le Bihan, D. (2001). Modulation of parietal activation by semantic distance in a number comparison task. *NeuroImage*, 14, 1013–1026.

Price, G. R., Holloway, I., Räsänen, P., Vesterinen, M., & Ansari, D. (2007). Impaired parietal magnitude processing in developmental dyscalculia. *Current Biology*, 17, R1042–R1043.

Ranpura, A., Isaacs, E., Edmonds, C., Rogers, M., Lanigan, J., Singhal, A., Clayden, J., Clark, C., & Butterworth, B. (2013). Developmental trajectories of grey and white matter in dyscalculia. *Trends in Neuroscience and Education*, 2, 56–64.

Reeve, R., Reynolds, F., Humberstone, J., & Butterworth, B. (2012). Stability and change in markers of core numerical competencies. *Journal of Experimental Psychology: General*, 141, 649–666.

Reigosa-Crespo, V., Valdés-Sosa, M., Butterworth, B., Estévez, N., Rodriguez, M., Santos, E., Torres, P., Suarez, R., & Lage, A. (2012). Basic numerical capacities and prevalence of developmental dyscalculia: the Havana Survey. *Developmental Psychology*, 48, 123–135.

Rotzer, S., Kucian, K., Martin, E., von Aster, M., Klaver, P., & Loenneker, T. (2008). Optimized voxel-based morphometry in children with developmental dyscalculia. *NeuroImage*, 39, 417–422.

Rovet, J., Szekely, C., & Hockenberry, M.-N. (1994). Specific arithmetic calculation deficits in children with Turner syndrome. *Journal of Clinical and Experimental Neuropsychology*, 16, 820–839.

Rykhlevskaia, E., Uddin, L. Q., Kondos, L., & Menon, V. (2009). Neuroanatomical correlates of developmental dyscalculia: combined evidence from morphometry and tractography. *Frontiers in Human Neuroscience*, 3, 1–13.

Starkey, P. & Cooper, R. G. Jr. (1980). Perception of numbers by human infants. *Science*, 210, 1033–1035.

Temple, C. M. & Marriott, A. J. (1998). Arithmetical ability and disability in Turner's syndrome: a cognitive neuropsychological analysis. *Developmental Neuropsychology*, 14, 47–67.

Vygotsky, L. S. (1978). *Mind in Society: The Development of Higher Psychological Processes*. Cambridge, MA: Harvard University Press.

Yeo, D. (2003). A brief overview of some contemporary methodologies in primary maths. In: M. Johnson & L. Peer (Eds), *The Dyslexia Handbook*. Reading, UK: British Dyslexia Association.

11

LEARNING TO READ

The Science of Reading in the Classroom

Donna Coch

DEPARTMENT OF EDUCATION, DARTMOUTH COLLEGE

Introduction

The human brain is not designed for reading (LC1[1]). Humans have been reading and writing for only about 5,000 years; on an evolutionary scale, that is very little time for the development of a neural region specialized for the cultural invention of reading. Indeed, there is no single part of the brain that can be identified as "the part of the brain that does reading." And yet, if you have picked up this book, chosen this chapter, and are comprehending this text, you have a brain that can read. How did that come about?

You have developed a brain that can read, with assistance from your teachers (classroom, parent, sibling, and otherwise), by borrowing from, building on, and recycling many other neural systems that are specialized for different types of processing (e.g. Coch, 2010; Dehaene, 2009; Dehaene *et al.*, 2010). For example, you have borrowed from the auditory system to be able to parse spoken words, from the visual system to be able to expertly process the print on the page, and from the language system to be able to make meaning of the words on the page. With practice and over time, you have developed and connected those systems to work together in the service of reading.

The time course for this development is quite long. Despite educational beliefs about a shift from "learning to read" to "reading to learn" around the fourth grade (e.g. Chall, 1983), neuroscience studies have shown that learning to read is by no means over by the third grade, and that the development of networks involved in reading extends well into adolescence (e.g. Brem *et al.*, 2006; Coch, 2015; Eddy *et al.*, 2014). What this lengthy developmental time course implies in application is that not only primary grade teachers but all K-12 teachers are teachers of reading. That is, teachers and students are literally building brains that can read throughout elementary, middle, and high school, borrowing and specializing neural networks in the service of reading (LC2). In this chapter we shall take a closer look at some of the borrowed systems involved in beginning reading.

The Auditory System: Parsing Speech

In evolutionary terms, spoken language has been around for much longer than written language—long enough, in fact, for the human brain to have developed a specialized area within the auditory cortex, at the top of the temporal lobe, for speech processing (e.g. Binder *et al.*, 2000). Specialized processing for speech in this region has been demonstrated in functional magnetic resonance imaging (fMRI) studies not only in adults (e.g. Binder, 2000), but also in 5-year-old children (e.g. Ahmad *et al.*, 2003) and, remarkably, even in 2- to 3-month-old infants (Dehaene-Lambertz *et al.*, 2002). Reading builds on this auditory word-processing system (e.g. Moats, 2010). Indeed, this same auditory region at the top of the temporal lobe is active during *silent* reading, when there is no incoming sound information from the external environment (e.g. Joubert *et al.*, 2004; Simos *et al.*, 2000b). Thus this neural region appears to be involved in processing phonology, the sounds of a language, whether the language is spoken or written.

Phonological awareness is defined as a sensitivity to the sound structure of spoken language (e.g. Treiman, 2000). Not surprisingly, given the neural overlap in phonological processing for speech and print, phonological awareness is highly predictive of reading ability throughout the school years, from kindergarten through twelfth grade (e.g. Calfee *et al.*, 1973). Much of the reading literature has focused on phonological awareness, because children who begin school with poor phonological awareness tend to fall further and further behind their peers across the elementary school years—not only in reading, but in all academic tasks (most of which depend upon reading in some way; Stanovich, 1986). The term "Matthew effects" was coined by Stanovich (1986) to describe this pernicious pattern, to reflect the way that the rich (children with strong phonological awareness skills at school entry) get richer, while the poor (children with weak phonological awareness skills at school entry) get poorer.

In fact "phonological awareness" is an umbrella term (e.g. Lane *et al.*, 2002; Podhajski, 1995) that encompasses a set of skills for parsing speech at different levels of analysis, from the whole spoken word to the syllable to the rime to the smallest unit of sound that distinguishes one spoken word from another (the phoneme) (LC3). With increasing age, children become increasingly sensitive to smaller parts of spoken words, such as the rime and the phoneme (e.g. Anthony & Francis, 2005) (LC4).

Rhyme Awareness

Phonological awareness at the level of the rime allows children to play rhyming games, joyously linking the spoken words /bat/ and /cat/ and /rat/ and /hat/, and making up words such as /gat/ to fit, well before the age of school entry and before reading begins (e.g. Goswami, 1993). The linguistic unit of the rime consists of the vowel and the consonant sounds that follow within a syllable. For example, the spoken word /cat/ is composed of the onset /c/ and the rime /at/, and the spoken word /splat/ is composed of the onset /spl/ and the rime /at/. Phonological awareness at the level of onset and rime thus allows for separation and recognition of word-ending sound units (/at/ and /at/), which is the basis of rhyming (LC5). Illustrating the complex reciprocal relationship between spoken language and reading, rhyming ability is both a cause and a correlate of beginning reading ability (e.g. Bryant *et al.*, 1990a, 1990b; Goswami, 1999; Wood & Terrell, 1998). That is, increasing awareness of the spoken rime unit causes reading development, and increasing reading development is associated with increasing awareness of spoken word units.

In typically developing children, event-related potential (ERP, also known as brainwave recording) studies have shown that auditory rhyme processing is essentially adult-like in 6- to 8-year-old beginning readers, whether the stimuli are real words (e.g. *moose* and *juice* vs. *knee* and *fox*; Coch *et al.*, 2002), made-up words called pseudowords (e.g. *nin* and *rin* vs. *ked* and *voo*; Coch *et al.*, 2005), or single letters (e.g. *A* and *J* vs. *A* and *B*; Coch *et al.*, 2011). This neural evidence is consistent with the early development of the behavioral ability to rhyme. There is also a connection between these neural measures of rhyme processing and behavioral measures of phonological awareness. The point in time at which the brainwaves distinguish between a rhyming pair and a non-rhyming pair of pseudowords is correlated with a standardized behavioral measure of phonological awareness. Children with better phonological awareness differentiated the rhyming from the non-rhyming pairs 80 milliseconds earlier than children with poorer phonological awareness, even though all of the children scored within normal limits on the phonological awareness measure (Coch *et al.*, 2005). One millisecond is 1/1000 of 1 second, so 80 milliseconds would not make a noticeable difference in the classroom in terms of observable behaviors. However, in terms of neural processing time, an 80-millisecond difference is quite significant, particularly when the information being processed may need to be coordinated with other information, such as print. Indeed, one theory of dyslexia or poor reading focuses on just such desynchronized neural timing (e.g. Breznitz, 2006).

Phonemic Awareness

In English, children learn to produce phonemes, or speech sounds, from infancy (for sounds like /m/ and /p/) through middle childhood (extending to at least the age of 8 years for sounds like /zh/, as in "measure"; e.g. Sander, 1972). Moreover, there is marked variability across years with regard to when individual children master certain speech sounds (e.g. Sander, 1972). This means that it is within the range of normal for some third graders still to be working on articulation of some phonemes, which may seem a surprisingly long developmental time course to some teachers. This time course for production of phonemes contrasts sharply with the time course for reception or perception of phonemes. Infants during the first months of life are able to distinguish between the phonemes not only of their caretakers' language (phonemes in their native language), but also of other languages (non-native phonemes) (e.g. Werker & Tees, 2002). However, by about 12 months of age, infants can only distinguish between speech sounds in their native language(s), demonstrating rapid specialization and narrowing for native phoneme perception (e.g. Werker & Tees, 2002).

Phonological awareness at the level of the phoneme, or phonemic awareness, is particularly important for at least two reasons. First, there are many words in English that are "minimal pairs"—that is, words that differ by only a single phoneme. For example, consider the spoken words /bin/ and /pin/. Listeners and speakers must be able to differentiate between the /b/ and the /p/ sounds (in this case, both single phonemes and onsets) in order to hear and recognize these as two different words, as is the case for many other minimal pairs for these phonemes (e.g. /bear/ and /pear/ or /bale/ and /pail/). Second, phonemic awareness is particularly important for reading in alphabetic languages such as English because it is the phonemes that will be mapped onto printed letters during beginning reading. Thus learning to read requires explicit attention to the subunits of speech, at the level of the phoneme.

Breaking down spoken words into phonemes is not always an easy task, and it is more difficult than breaking down spoken words into onsets and rimes. For example, consider the spoken word /box/. Splitting it into onset and rime, we would have /b/ and /ox/. Splitting it into its constituent phonemes, we would count four: /b/ /o/ /k/ /s/.

It is a matter of concern that many students who are training to become elementary school teachers, as well as practicing elementary school teachers, are unable to accurately perform such phoneme counting tasks or phoneme manipulation tasks (e.g. "Say /string/ without the /r/") (e.g. Bos et al., 2001; Stainthorp, 2003). Indeed, Moats (2000, p. 7) claimed that most adults have never "analyzed language at the level required for explaining and teaching it." This is in part due to the fact that much of language processing is automatic; we are not consciously, effortfully aware of what we are doing when we are speaking (LC6). It may also in part be due to the fact that much of what we know about phonology comes from the field of linguistics, and most teachers have had little training in this field. In linguistics, consonant sounds are categorized along three dimensions: place of articulation (where in the mouth the speech sound is made); manner of articulation (how the speech sound is made in terms of airflow through the mouth); and voicing (whether or not the vocal cords vibrate when making the speech sound, which you can determine by gently resting your fingertips against your throat while making the sound) (e.g. Moats, 2000).

To continue with our example of the phonemes /b/ and /p/, both of these speech sounds are bilabials (i.e. the two lips come together in order to make these sounds), and they are both stops (i.e. the air flowing through your mouth is stopped, by your closed lips), but /p/ is voiceless (i.e. your vocal cords do not vibrate when you produce this sound), whereas /b/ is voiced (i.e. your vocal cords do vibrate when you produce this sound). Knowing how sonically similar these speech sounds are, teachers should not be surprised when, for example, a child spells "cab" as "cap" or "robe" as "rope"—whereas this might reflect a print confusion about where the "ball and the stick" go relative to one another to form a letter in print, it is more likely to reflect a sound confusion about the final phoneme. If this child also confuses /t/ and /d/, as well as /g/ and /k/, in speech or in spelling, this pattern would indicate that he/she would benefit from explicit instruction in distinguishing voiced from unvoiced speech sounds (each of these pairs is matched on all dimensions except voicing). Indeed, there are reading programs and curricula based on just this approach (e.g. Lindamood et al., 1997).

The concept of a phoneme comes from linguistics, and although we know that phonological processing in general occurs at the top of the temporal lobe in the human brain, few neuroscience studies have addressed phonemic processing specifically. Perhaps one of the most remarkable is a recent study using cortical recordings from adult patients undergoing neurosurgery for epilepsy (Mesgarani et al., 2014). In this study, electrodes were placed directly on the brains of the patients as they listened to speech. The recordings showed that specific populations of neurons at the top of the temporal lobe were activated for specific speech sounds—that is, specific groups of neurons processed specific phonemes. Moreover, specific phonemic features, such as place and manner of articulation and voicing, activated different subpopulations of neurons. This study was the first of its kind to discover how the human brain, at the top of the temporal lobe, encodes and processes spoken language at the level of the phoneme. The fact that the findings were consistent with behavioral evidence from linguistics is amazing.

Perhaps even more amazing is the existence of evidence that learning to read actually shapes the human brain in this way. Alexandre Castro-Caldas and his colleagues (e.g.

Castro-Caldas, 2004; Castro-Caldas *et al.*, 1998) have used positron emission tomography (PET) to study the brains of literate and illiterate women, by asking the women to repeat spoken words and spoken made-up words (pseudowords) while they were being scanned. A spoken pseudoword is essentially an unfamiliar string of phonemes—that is, phonemes put together in a way that you have never heard before. In the study, the literate women tended to repeat both the words and the pseudowords accurately, whereas the illiterate women repeated the words accurately but often changed the pseudowords into similar-sounding real words when they attempted to repeat them. Correspondingly, there were no differences in the neural activation patterns as measured in the PET scans when the two groups of women were repeating the words. However, the PET scans showed an extensive network of activation only in the literate women during the pseudoword repetition (as compared with the word repetition) task. The authors concluded that learning to read changes the neural phonological processing system: "learning the written form of a language … interacts with the function of oral language" (Castro-Caldas *et al.*, 1998, p. 1053). Thus it seems that the very act of learning to *read* affects *speech* processing, such that "whole word sounds are automatically broken up into sound constituents … by keeping track of phoneme constituents, novel word sounds are remembered more accurately" (Frith, 1998, p. 1011). Other authors have also reported evidence indicating that the acquisition of reading affects neural phonological networks (e.g. Brennan *et al.*, 2013; Nation & Hulme, 2010).

Is this pertinent to children who struggle to acquire reading skills? Although there are many theories regarding the core deficit in dyslexia, the one that is currently predominant is the phonological deficit theory. In this view, dyslexia is thought to be, fundamentally and independently of IQ, a sound (phonology) processing disorder (e.g. S. E. Shaywitz, 1996; Tanaka *et al.*, 2011; Vellutino *et al.*, 2004). Indeed, there is ample neuroimaging evidence from children and adults indicating that dyslexics not only struggle with reading but also process spoken language differently from good readers (e.g. Bonte & Blomert, 2004; Bonte *et al.*, 2007; Simos *et al.*, 2000a). There is even remarkable evidence from babies that supports the relationship between spoken sound processing and dyslexia. Brainwave (ERP) responses to spoken syllables recorded from newborn infants discriminated among these same individuals who subsequently, at age 8 years, were classified as dyslexic, poor, or normal readers (Molfese, 2000) (LC7).

Overall, we might interpret these findings as indicating that, in the course of typical development, learning to read builds on the specialties of the phonological processing system, and borrows and further specializes that processing in the service of reading.

The Visual System: Print on the Page

In typical reading, the only neural system that receives input from the environment is the visual system. Thus visual processing plays a key role in reading (e.g. Hattie, 2009, p. 131). In alphabetic languages, the print on the page—the orthography of a language—can be consistent and closely matched with the sounds of the language (i.e. there are many one-to-one mappings between letters and sounds), in which case it is known as a "shallow" orthography, or relatively inconsistent and poorly matched with phonology (i.e. there are numerous many-to-one mappings), in which case it is known as a "deep" orthography. A moment's reflection on English reveals that it is a language with a deep orthography. For example, we have the words *brake* and *break*, which are spelled quite differently but sound the same (they are homophones), and *lead* (to show the way) and *lead* (a heavy metal) that are spelled the same but sound quite different (they are homographs). It should not be surprising that the initial stages of learning to read are, for the most part, easier and faster in languages with shallow orthographies (Caravolas *et al.*, 2013). However, regardless of the depth of the orthography, at a basic level, it is the marks on the page that must be perceived and processed meaningfully by the reading brain. This is accomplished by borrowing and building on the processing capabilities of two branches of the neural visual system—the ventral visual pathway and the dorsal visual pathway (e.g. Ungerleider & Haxby, 1994).

The Ventral Visual Pathway

Most children have been exposed to print—for example, on the page, on signs, on cereal boxes—well before school entrance. Tagging this print as important and meaningful is key to children developing a familiarity with the printed symbols of a language (e.g. Burns & Snow, 1999). This familiarity forms a foundation for beginning to recognize and differentiate those symbols (in the case of English, the letters of the Roman alphabet) (LC8). This is not an easy task, because the letters in alphabetic languages such as English contain minimal perceptual information—they are abstract, arbitrary, and in some cases highly confusable (e.g. Adams, 1990; Dunn-Rankin *et al.*, 1968; Gervais *et al.*, 1984; Gibson, 1965). For example, there is no particular reason why a "stick and a ball" in one configuration are a "b," in another are a "d," and in a third are a "p," other than that we have culturally decided that this is so. It may not be surprising then that, by some accounts, being able to identify and name the letters of the alphabet is the best predictor in kindergarten of future reading scores (e.g. Chall, 1967; Scarborough, 2005).

In adults, individual letters are processed not just as visual objects, but with special abstract letter identities such that, for example, a "G" across many fonts (G, G, G, G, g, g, g, g) is mapped onto the abstract letter identity "g" (e.g. Flowers *et al.*, 2004; James *et al.*, 2005; Mitra & Coch, 2009; Petit *et al.*, 2006). This is an astonishing feat of perceptual generalization in order to form conceptual categories, particularly when you consider the variety of not only fonts but also handwriting. However, whereas individual letter identification may be necessary for reading, it is not sufficient—it is groups and patterns of letters that we must identify when we read fluently. This is accomplished as visual processing continues along the ventral visual pathway in the inferior (lower part of the) temporal lobe.

The ventral visual pathway is specialized for processing texture, color, pattern, form, and fine detail. Any incoming visual information characterized by these elements is further processed along this pathway (e.g. Livingstone & Hubel, 1988). The neural processing of letters and words borrows from the specialization of this visual system. For example, the overall form of each letter (e.g. recognizing the curved shape of the letter C), the details that distinguish one letter from another (e.g. the capital G and C in many fonts; Adams, 1990), and the patterns of letters that coalesce to form words (e.g. *cat*) or other meaningful sequences (e.g. *–ing*) capitalize on the specialties of this pathway (LC9). However, reading not only borrows from this perceptual system, but also builds on it in a quite amazing way. This is the story of the visual word form area.

In an early PET study, Petersen *et al.* (1988) presented adult fluent readers with four types of stimuli—real words (e.g. *ANT*), pseudowords (made-up words, e.g. *GEEL*), letter strings (e.g. *VSHFFT*), and strings of letter-like symbols. When comparing the blood flow patterns for each of these types of stimuli, they identified a region along the ventral visual pathway that was particularly active only for the strings of letters that formed words and pseudowords. Because these were the stimuli that were most word-like (i.e. the stimuli that looked like legitimate English words), they referred to this region as the "visual word form area." Remarkably, there appeared to be a region of the brain that was specialized for processing visual objects that took the form of words. Since the original PET report, numerous other studies using various neuroimaging techniques have confirmed the specialized nature of the visual word form area for processing words and word-like stimuli, and have associated activation in this region with the automatic, efficient processing of words that is characteristic of fluent reading (e.g. Cohen & Dehaene, 2004; Cohen et al., 2002; McCandliss et al., 2003).

Importantly, from an educational perspective, learning to read is thought to drive the development of the visual word form area such that this neural region becomes increasingly tuned to visual word processing over time and with experience with print (e.g. Cohen & Dehaene, 2004; McCandliss et al., 2003). This is a kind of expertise account of the visual word form area—as a reader becomes increasingly expert in reading words, specialization for word processing in the visual word form area develops (e.g. McCandliss et al., 2003; Wandell, 2011). Interestingly, however, it is not print exposure alone that appears to develop this specialization for orthography within the ventral visual processing stream.

At a behavioral level, there is evidence that the process of decoding—of "sounding out" printed words by mapping letters to speech sounds (i.e. phonemes)—is "critical to the acquisition of word-specific orthographic representations" (Share, 1999, p. 95). At a neural level, there is compatible evidence from fMRI studies showing that it is decoding ability, regardless of age, that is associated with activation levels in the visual word form area in 7- to 18-year-olds (e.g. Shaywitz et al., 2002). Furthermore, there is evidence from a brainwave recording (ERP) study showing that the amplitude of a specific brainwave component (called N1 and thought to originate in the visual word form area) was similar in kindergartners without decoding skills when they were looking at decodable real words and strings of meaningless symbols. However, after these same children were taught letter-to-speech sound correspondences in a training study totaling fewer than 4 hours, the amplitude of the N1 component did differentiate between the real words and the symbol strings (Brem et al., 2010) (LC10). Thus it is learning to map letters to sounds that appears to build a brain that can read along the ventral visual pathway. Remarkably, this differentiation of words and non-words in the visual word form area, as indexed by the N1 component, is not completely adult-like by late elementary school (Coch & Meade, 2016) or even by adolescence (Brem et al., 2006) (LC11). Educationalists suggest that older students may not develop more advanced orthographic knowledge "unless teachers introduce and guide the students' exploration" (Templeton & Gehsmann, 2014, p. 67) (LC12).

Along with evidence for a long developmental time course for the visual word form area, there is evidence for less activation in the visual word form area in readers with dyslexia. For example, in a PET study comparing single word reading in fluently reading adults and in adults with dyslexia across three languages with orthographies of various depths (French, Italian, and English), the consistent pattern was significantly less activation in the visual word form area for participants diagnosed with dyslexia than for controls (Paulesu et al., 2001). The same pattern of underactivation of the visual word form area has been reported in children diagnosed with dyslexia (e.g. Shaywitz et al., 2004). Thus less activation in the visual word form area along the ventral visual pathway has been associated with struggles in reading in both children and adults. This may be related to the fact that children and adults who struggle with reading tend to get relatively less practice in reading, and less experience with decoding printed words would be related to less development of expertise in word processing.

Overall, we might interpret these findings as indicating that, in the course of typical development, learning to read builds on the specialties of the ventral visual pathway, and borrows and further specializes that processing in the service of reading.

The Dorsal Visual Pathway

In contrast to the ventral visual pathway, the dorsal pathway is specialized for depth and motion processing (e.g. Livingstone & Hubel, 1988). Given that the letters on the page do not move, the contribution of this system to reading may not be so readily apparent. However, whereas the letters do not move, a reader's eyes do need to move across the letters on the page in a carefully coordinated fashion. For example, reading English from right to left across the page or skipping a line or two of text will certainly impede comprehension. Readers' eyes move across the page in a series of fixations (brief periods during which the eyes are relatively still) and saccades (periods when the eyes are jumping to the next fixation) (e.g. Rayner et al., 2001). Simply watching a beginning reader's eye movements will reveal that the skills involved in fluently moving the eyes across text develop over time. Beginning readers have longer fixations, shorter saccades, and more regressions (returns to look at text already read) than fluent readers (e.g. Blythe, 2014; Rayner et al., 2001).

Anecdotally, teachers report that students with dyslexia and other struggling readers sometimes claim that the words are moving on the page. It is possible that this subjective experience of moving print is actually related to unsteady binocular fixation (i.e. the two eyes not focusing steadily on the same point on the page), interpreted by the brain as movement. This unsteady visual fixation may be related to the findings from a study which showed that extra large letter spacing (i.e. moving the letters further apart from one another, allowing each letter to be perceived, uncrowded by others, in space) improved reading in Italian and French children with dyslexia (Zorzi et al., 2012). In fact, some authors have related dyslexia to deficits in dorsal stream processing (e.g. Boden & Giaschi, 2007; Stein, 2001a). In particular, Stein and colleagues have reported significant positive correlations between reading ability and motion processing ability, measured behaviorally (e.g. Stein, 2001b; Talcott et al., 2002). Consistent with this, neuroimaging studies of adults with dyslexia have shown reduced or no activation in a specific region along the dorsal pathway (an area called MT) that is strongly activated by motion in typically reading adults (e.g. Demb et al., 1997; Eden et al., 1996). This same pattern of a correlation between degree of activation in area MT and reading skill has also been observed in children (e.g. Olulade et al., 2013).

In a clever study designed to investigate the nature of the relationships between reading skill, motion processing, and activation in brain area MT, Olulade et al. (2013) determined that children who were poor readers showed much less activation in area MT in response to moving stimuli than age-matched controls, but as much activation in area MT as reading-age-matched controls. That is, there was an association between reading ability (but not age) and degree of activation in area MT in response to motion, as had been shown in previous studies. But which was causing which? Was dorsal stream processing affecting reading development, or was reading development affecting dorsal stream processing? The authors addressed this question by providing a reading intervention for poor readers, and comparing the degree of activation in area MT in response to motion before and after the intervention. After intervention, the fMRI results showed that activity in area MT in the right hemisphere had increased in these children, who were also better readers after the intervention. Thus learning to read actually changed dorsal stream motion processing.

Overall, we might interpret these findings as indicating that, in the course of typical development, learning to read builds on the specialties of the dorsal visual pathway, and borrows and further specializes that processing in the service of reading.

Connectivity

As hinted above, in learning to read it is not enough to develop and begin to specialize each of these neural auditory and visual processing systems. In addition, these systems must work in a coordinated and integrated fashion in order to develop a brain that can read. Beginning reading is fundamentally about connecting the visual and the auditory, print and sound, grapheme and phoneme—decoding based on the alphabetic principle (e.g. Adams, 1990; Moats, 2010; Strickland et al., 2002). Phonics methods of teaching reading focus on precisely these sorts of connections, and are included in many common reading programs, such as those based on Orton–Gillingham instruction (e.g. Gillingham & Stillman, 1983; Ritchey & Goeke, 2006). Indeed, phonics-based approaches are considered best practice in teaching beginning reading (e.g. Hattie, 2009, p. 133; National Institute of Child Health and Human Development, 2000; National Research Council, 1998).

This kind of phonological recoding or "sounding out" of printed words is not only an important means of lexical access in beginning reading, but also a useful tool for fluent and adult readers when they come across less familiar words in texts (e.g. Thompson et al., 2009; Wagner & Torgesen, 1987, p. 192). Overall, though, reliance on phonological recoding in reading for meaning decreases across the elementary school years, as the automatic visual encoding most associated with fluent reading progressively develops with increasing exposure to—and expertise in—printed words (e.g. Doctor & Coltheart, 1980). It follows that, although the decodable texts often used with phonics instruction provide useful opportunities for beginning readers to practice their grapheme-to-phoneme (i.e. orthography-to-phonology) mapping skills, the necessarily controlled and limited vocabulary in such texts calls for integration with more interesting and challenging selections that can facilitate wider exposure to words, as well as pique interest and motivation for reading (e.g. Templeton & Gehsmann, 2014, p. 252).

Whereas brief, explicit phonics instruction as part of a total reading program can be limited to the primary grades for typically developing readers (e.g. Anderson et al., 1985; Stahl, 1992), the development of integration of letters and speech sounds is not entirely adult-like even after 4 years of reading experience (e.g. Froyen et al., 2009; van Atteveldt et al., 2004). Findings from neuroimaging studies confirm the importance of integrating sight and sound in fluent reading. Dyslexics show reduced integration of letter and speech sound processing (e.g. Blau et al., 2009). Remarkably, intensive, phonics-based remedial instruction has been shown to "normalize" brain activation patterns during reading in children with dyslexia. For example, in one study, children who showed greater activation at the top of the temporal lobe in the *right* hemisphere when reading pseudowords before intervention showed greater activation at the top of the temporal lobe in the *left* hemisphere—the typical pattern of activation during phonological processing—after intervention. The children also scored within normal limits on a standardized reading test post-intervention (Simos *et al.*, 2002). Other researchers have reported similar neuroplasticity in struggling readers receiving intensive phonics-based interventions—both children (e.g. Meyler *et al.*, 2008; Shaywitz *et al.*, 2004) and adults (e.g. Eden *et al.*, 2004). First, such evidence supports the importance of connecting orthography and phonology in fluent reading. Second, it confirms that *teaching matters* (e.g. Hattie, 2012) in the development of the reading brain (LC13). Third, along with evidence from adults learning how to read for the first time (e.g. Dehaene *et al.*, 2010), such evidence suggests potentially lifelong plasticity for building a reading brain (LC14).

The Language System: Making Meaning

Although phoneme awareness, letter name knowledge, and letter-sound knowledge are causal influences on early reading development (e.g. Hulme *et al.*, 2012, p. 572), mapping speech sounds to print is not sufficient for reading. Rather, this mapping—the process of decoding—is simply a stepping-stone on the path to automatic word recognition and fluent reading with meaning. Decoding only serves its purpose in beginning reading if a child knows the meaning of the word that he/she has just decoded, and he/she would only know the meaning of the word, for the most part (e.g. with the exception of proper names and with a lack of pictures), if it were already in his/her spoken vocabulary. Thus learning to read builds on the spoken language system in terms of vocabulary knowledge. For example, decoding *cat* into /kuh/ /aah/ /tuh/ and blending those phonemes into /cat/ allows the child to recognize that that particular string of letters and phonemes maps on to a known lexical (i.e. vocabulary) item associated with the furry, purring, meowing animal that curls up in his/her lap. This is yet another example which illustrates that what students already know affects their learning (e.g. American Psychological Association & Coalition for Psychology in Schools and Education, 2015).

Given that early reading builds on spoken language vocabulary, it becomes that much more important that children enter school knowing a sufficient set of words. Studies of early vocabulary development have shown that up to 98% of the words that a 3-year-old child knows consist of words in the caregiver's vocabulary (e.g. Hart & Risley, 1995). The complexity of the language that preschool teachers use has also been associated with the language and reading development of their students (e.g. Dickinson, 2011; Huttenlocher *et al.*, 2002). Across studies, reading books with young children is consistently positively associated with vocabulary development, whereas watching television does not have an impact on vocabulary in toddlers (e.g. Alloway *et al.*, 2014; Burns & Snow, 1999). In particular, reading books in an interactive way that includes talking about the books, eliciting meaningful responses beyond "yes" or "no" or labels of objects in illustrations, and connecting to experiences in the child's life is associated with literacy development (e.g. Arnold *et al.*, 1994; Whitehurst *et al.*, 1998). Indeed, talking to and reading with young children in meaningful interactive contexts appear to be the best ways to develop their vocabulary (e.g. Burns & Snow, 1999) (LC15). Children who grow up in households in which they are not spoken to extensively (and are therefore not exposed to a variety of words) begin school with significantly fewer words in their vocabularies than their peers who grew up in households in which speaking with children was more frequent. Astoundingly, environments characterized by rich oral language experiences are associated with *millions* more words being heard by a child by the age of 3 years (e.g. Hart & Risley, 1995, 1999, 2003).

In the brain, spoken and written words are processed for meaning in similar ways—that is, there is one neural semantic system, regardless of whether the lexical input is sound- or sight-based (e.g. Barsalou, 2008; Booth *et al.*, 2002). That "semantic system" appears to be distributed throughout the brain (e.g. Binder *et al.*, 2009; Martin, 2007; Martin & Chao, 2001; Thompson-Schill, 2003). When we hear or read a word such as *telephone*, motor regions of the brain that are activated when we pick up and hold and dial our phone are reactivated, visual regions that are activated when we see our phones are reactivated, and so on (e.g. Goldberg *et al.*, 2006; Thompson-Schill, 2003). Indeed, reading words related to taste or smell, such as *cinnamon* or *salt*, elicits greater activation in neural regions associated with processing gustatory and olfactory information than reading similar control words that are not related to taste or smell (e.g. Barrós-Loscertales *et al.*, 2012; González *et al.*, 2006). This is true even idiomatically. When we read about *grasping the idea* or *kicking the habit*, the hand and foot areas of the motor cortex are activated (Boulenger *et al.*, 2009).

By about the fourth grade, most new vocabulary words are learned directly from print rather than from speech (e.g. Nippold, 1998), through encounters in text (e.g. Nagy & Anderson, 1984). This is one reason why all students should be reading widely (e.g. Kuhn *et al.*, 2010), beyond direct instruction in vocabulary (e.g. Hattie, 2009, p. 131). Not surprisingly, with this exposure to new vocabulary, time spent reading becomes one of the best predictors not only of reading achievement but also of general knowledge (e.g. Anderson *et al.*, 1988; Cunningham & Stanovich, 1998). Thus having the basic skills in place to tackle the new words embedded in a typical fourth-grade curriculum is important both for reading achievement specifically and for academic success more generally (Hernandez, 2011) (LC16).

Although most new words are learned from texts after the primary grades, there is only about a 10% chance that a child who encounters a new word in a grade-level text for the first time will be able to clearly express the meaning of that word (Adams, 1990, p. 150; Nagy & Anderson, 1984). Thus repeated exposures to a word, across a variety of contexts (e.g. literary and informational), is critical for developing a deep understanding of word meaning (e.g. Adams, 1990)—that is, acquiring long-term knowledge such as vocabulary is dependent on practice (e.g. American Psychological Association & Coalition for Psychology in Schools and Education, 2015). Given that different attributes of words are processed in different neural regions, thus resulting in a widely distributed semantic system, it seems evident that dictionary definitions are not nearly adequate for truly knowing the meaning of a word (e.g. Hattie, 2009, p. 132; Templeton *et al.*, 2015). Rather, explicitly analyzing the morphological structure of new words, considering the denotative and connotative meanings, generating antonyms and synonyms, and the like support deep processing and therefore the development of high-quality word representations (e.g. Beck *et al.*, 2013; Ford-Connors & Paratore, 2015; Moats, 2010) (LC17). Many graphic organizers, such as Frayer diagrams, word webs, or concept maps, can provide support for this kind of word work (e.g. Hyerle, 2000). At the middle-school level, school-wide programs for vocabulary development have been implemented around these ideas, particularly focused on critical "academic vocabulary" that occurs across content areas (e.g. Lawrence *et al.*, 2010; Nagy & Townsend, 2012). In turn, such high-quality, dense lexical representations have positive consequences for reading comprehension (e.g. Perfetti, 2007).

Overall, we might interpret these findings as indicating that, in the course of typical development, learning to read builds on the specialties of the semantic system, and borrows and further specializes that processing in the service of reading.

Conclusion

Even in our very selective overview of just a handful of the systems involved in learning to read, the breathtaking complexity of a brain that can read has become apparent—and so, too, I hope, has the power of bringing the science of reading into the classroom. Yet there is much more complexity to add. For example, we have not considered comprehension, genre, text complexity, syntax, context, memory, literature, attention, fluency, or motivation, to list just a few of the key ingredients that are missing from our recipe for a reading brain. Understanding this complexity at both the behavioral and neural levels is important in educational application because it "unpacks" reading. This unpacking allows for a deeper understanding of the component elements of "reading" (e.g. Coch & Benoit, 2015) (LC18).

In turn, this understanding allows for targeted assessment and modification of instructional practices to meet students where they are. This sort of knowledge is considered foundational for teachers of reading (e.g. International Reading Association, 2010). For evidence-based classroom reading instruction it is unlikely that "one size fits all", and differentiation requires mastery of foundational as well as instructional knowledge (e.g. Connor *et al.*, 2007). For example, given what we know about the science of learning to read, to describe a child as "a poor reader" is far too simplistic, as there are so many ways in which this complex system can break down. Rather, we can have a child with poor phonological awareness at the level of the rime but a strong oral vocabulary. This kind of approach, taking into account both strengths and weaknesses, allows both for differentiated instruction, and for leveraging of strengths in order to address weaknesses. This is one starting point of the process by which scientific findings become evidence-based practice in teaching reading (e.g. McCardle & Chhabra, 2004).

Evidence from neuroscience alone can rarely, if ever, provide directives for classroom practice (e.g. Ansari & Coch, 2006). However, in combination with psychological and educational evidence, the neuroscience evidence reviewed here may change the way that you think about reading, which in turn may change your instructional practices. For example, it may encourage you to try a new activity that includes a component of reading that you now realize may not be adequately addressed in your current approach. Or it may simply deepen your understanding of best practices, as instruction in phonemic awareness, phonics, and vocabulary represents three of the five "pillars" from the National Reading Panel report that outlines best practices in teaching reading (National Institute of Child Health and Human Development, 2000). Or, given that we know that many elementary teacher training programs fail to consider the science of reading, at least in the U.S.A. (e.g. Walsh *et al.*, 2006), perhaps some of this evidence will provide the missing *why* behind some of the *how to* that you learned or are learning as a student teacher. At the very least, it is hoped that the scientific evidence from multiple levels of analysis reviewed here will confirm what you have already experienced—or are going to experience—as a teacher of reading. To borrow from Moats (1999), teaching reading really *is* rocket science.

From the Laboratory to the Classroom

As noted at the beginning of this chapter, whereas findings from neuroscience studies generally cannot direct teachers with regard to what to do in the classroom, in combination with evidence from psychological and educational studies, the scientific evidence can speak to practical applications. Some of the main practical applications are extracted and summarized below.

LC1. The human brain is not designed for reading; therefore teaching approaches and philosophies that are based on the notion that reading is "natural" (e.g. Goodman & Goodman, 1979) are inconsistent with neuroscientific evidence. This does not mean that other aspects of such approaches, such as rich vocabulary development, reading for meaning, use of "authentic" texts, and developing students who believe in themselves as readers, must be abandoned, but simply that the foundational concept that reading is "natural"—that is, built into the human brain from day one—should be abandoned, as it is incorrect from a neurobiological perspective.

LC2. The complex process of learning to read is not limited to the primary grades. Therefore we need effective programs to teach reading through late elementary, middle, and high school, and even into college (e.g. Bean, 2011; Biancarosa & Snow, 2004; National Institute for Literacy, 2007; Slavin et al., 2008).

LC3. Because phonological awareness is such a strong predictor of reading achievement, early screening and intervention for phonological weaknesses are key. Because it is an umbrella concept, assessment of phonological awareness necessarily requires a wide range of phonological tasks, ranging from easier (e.g. oddity tasks such as identifying /man/ as the "odd one out" of /dog/, /day/, /man/) to more challenging (e.g. phoneme manipulation tasks such as saying /splat/ without the /p/). No single task can adequately reflect "phonological awareness." Such optimized assessments "will improve early identification of children at risk for reading problems, educational diagnosis, instructional planning, and resource allocation" (Anthony & Francis, 2005, p. 258).

LC4. "Literacy instruction may prove most successful if particular phonological awareness skills, spelling patterns, and word-reading strategies are linked and taught in a systematic, developmentally sensitive order" (Anthony & Francis, 2005, p. 258). Direct, explicit, systematic, sequential instruction is considered best practice in reading education (e.g. National Institute of Child Health and Human Development, 2000; National Research Council, 1998).

LC5. Any game or task that emphasizes the sound structure of language and requires children to break down spoken language into smaller parts will help to develop phonological awareness—for example, rhyming games, reciting poetry or nursery rhymes, or phoneme deletion tasks (e.g. say /cat/ without the /k/) (Adams, 1990; MacLean et al., 1987). Many such activities can be fun and engaging without appearing to be academic (e.g. Yopp & Yopp, 2000), which is important for children who have self-identified themselves as non-readers or poor readers.

LC6. Because speaking and reading are mostly automatic for many adults, teachers must "break" their own automaticity (i.e. become consciously aware of typically unconscious processing) in order to be able to teach phonemic awareness and many other aspects of speech-to-print connections to their young students.

LC7. The fact that differences in sound processing in infants can be predictive of reading difficulties 8 years later highlights the potential for early intervention. This means that children who are at risk of struggling with learning to read could receive remedial instruction even before they try to begin to read. Randomized intervention studies with pre-readers have shown that phonological awareness training, especially when coupled with letter name instruction, leads to improvements in reading and spelling (e.g. Anthony & Francis, 2005; Torgesen, 1998). Early intervention programs often have marked positive effects (Hattie, 2009, p. 58).

LC8. Children who have not been exposed to print and have not developed rudimentary print awareness at school entrance are at a critical disadvantage if early curricula assume, rather than develop, foundational print awareness (e.g. Justice *et al.*, 2006). The number of books in the home is a powerful predictor of academic success (e.g. Evans *et al.*, 2010).

LC9. There is a substantial amount of behavioral evidence that explicit teaching of the meaningful letter sequences called morphemes (i.e. instruction in morphological awareness) from elementary school through high school is related to improvements in literacy achievement (for reviews, see Bowers *et al.*, 2010; Carlisle, 2010; Goodwin & Ahn, 2010). A morpheme is the smallest unit of meaning in a language—for example, in English, the "-s" in *cats*, which carries the meaning "plural," or the "-chrono-" in *chronological*, which carries the meaning "time."

LC10. These results from neuroimaging studies using different techniques and populations are consistent in suggesting that learning to decode—the centerpiece of phonics instruction—is key to the development of specialized, efficient neural processing for words along the ventral visual pathway. Such automatic processing of words is the goal of fluent reading, and frees resources for comprehension (LaBerge & Samuels, 1974).

LC11. These neuroimaging studies indicate a long developmental time course, extending into adolescence, for fine-tuning and efficient processing of orthographic-to-phonological mappings. Therefore we should not assume adult-like neural processing even if observable behavior appears adult-like.

LC12. Much of orthographic instruction in later development is based on morphological analysis of words—for example, recognizing Latin roots such as *-agri-* or Greek combining forms such as *-chrono-* (e.g. Moats, 2010; Templeton *et al.*, 2015; Templeton & Gehsmann, 2014).

LC13. Teaching matters. Studies such as these show that the instructional practices used to teach reading (i.e. intensive phonics intervention) are able to change both the neural systems participating in the process of reading and reading behaviors and performance. Teachers and students, together, are literally building brains that can read.

LC14. Given evidence for lifelong plasticity of the human brain, teachers of reading should expect, within reason, that most students will be able to learn how to read. Teacher expectations have a powerful effect on the learning and development of their students (e.g. Hattie, 2012, p. 91), through many different pathways (e.g. American Psychological Association & Coalition for Psychology in Schools and Education, 2015).

LC15. Interactive read-alouds may serve similar purposes in the classroom, modeling the process of fluent reading, exposing older children to different types of texts, building vocabulary, and developing skills related to meaningfully thinking about and responding to texts (e.g. Templeton & Gehsmann, 2014).

LC16. Although this paragraph may appear innocent enough, it touches on the heart of one of the great debates in teaching reading. Should beginning instruction focus on lower-level, letter-sound skills (as in phonics approaches) or higher-level meaning building (as in whole language approaches)? Despite meta-analyses indicating that phonics approaches are best practice (e.g. National Institute of Child Health and Human Development, 2000; National Research Council, 1998), this debate continues (e.g. Hernández, 2014; Pondiscio, 2014). As the pendulum swings back and forth between these options over time, the answer, as with many false dichotomies in education, is that sound, print, and meaning are *all* important to beginning reading.

LC17. Isolated vocabulary lists and copying of dictionary definitions are not sufficient for word learning. Rather, deep learning leading to high-quality lexical representations involves encountering a new word in multiple meaningful contexts, considering a new word in relation to known words, analyzing the morphological structure of the word, and so on.

LC18. A deep understanding of the component elements of reading allows for both reflective practice in teaching reading and critical evaluation and use of reading approaches, curricula, and materials. Theoretically, considering reading from the multiple perspectives of mind, brain, and education, as has been done in this chapter, engenders this sort of deep understanding.

Note

1   A summary of some of the main practical applications is provided in the form of a numbered list in the *From the Laboratory to the Classroom* section at the end of this chapter. The numbers LC1, LC2, etc. in the main text refer to that numbered list.

References

Adams, M. J. (1990). *Beginning to Read: Thinking and Learning About Print*. Cambridge: MIT Press.

Ahmad, Z., Balsamo, L. M., Sachs, B. C., Xu, B., & Gaillard, W. D. (2003). Auditory comprehension of language in young children. *Neurology*, 60, 1598–1605.

Alloway, T. P., Williams, S., Jones, B., & Cochrane, F. (2014). Exploring the impact of television watching on vocabulary skills in toddlers. *Early Childhood Education Journal*, 42, 343–349.

American Psychological Association & Coalition for Psychology in Schools and Education (2015). *Top 20 Principles from Psychology for PreK–12 Teaching and Learning*. Washington, DC: American Psychological Association.

Anderson, R. C., Hiebert, E. H., Scott, J. A., Wilkinson, I. A. G., & members of the Commission on Reading (1985). *Becoming a Nation of Readers: the Report of the Commission on Reading*. Champaign, IL: University of Illinois.

Anderson, R. C., Wilson, P. T., & Fielding, L. G. (1988). Growth in reading and how children spend their time outside of school. *Reading Research Quarterly*, 23, 285–303.

Ansari, D. & Coch, D. (2006). Bridges over troubled waters: education and cognitive neuroscience. *Trends in Cognitive Sciences*, 10, 146–151.

Anthony, J. L. & Francis, D. J. (2005). Development of phonological awareness. *Current Directions in Psychological Science*, 14, 255–259.

Arnold, D. H., Lonigan, C. J., Whitehurst, G. J., & Epstein, J. N. (1994). Accelerating language development through picture book reading: replication and extension to a videotape training format. *Journal of Educational Psychology*, 86, 235–243.

Barrós-Loscertales, A., González, J., Pulvermüller, F., Ventura-Campos, N., Bustamante, J. C., Costumero, V., Parcet, M. A., & Ávila, C. (2012). Reading salt activates gustatory brain regions: fMRI evidence for semantic grounding in a novel sensory modality. *Cerebral Cortex*, 22, 2554–2563.

Barsalou, L. W. (2008). Cognitive and neural contributions to understanding the conceptual system. *Current Directions in Psychological Science*, 17, 91–95.

Bean, J. C. (2011). *Engaging Ideas: The Professor's Guide to Integrating Writing, Critical Thinking, and Active Learning into the Classroom*, 2nd edition. San Francisco, CA: Jossey-Bass.

Beck, I. L., McKeown, M. G., & Kucan, L. (2013). *Bringing Words to Life: Robust Vocabulary Instruction*, 2nd edition. New York: Guilford Press.

Biancarosa, G. & Snow, C. (2004). *Reading Next: A Vision for Action and Research in Middle and High School Literacy. A Report to the Carnegie Corporation of New York*. Washington, DC: Alliance for Excellent Education.

Binder, J. R. (2000). The new neuroanatomy of speech perception. *Brain*, 123, 2371–2372.

Binder, J. R., Frost, J. A., Hammeke, T. A., Bellgowan, P. S. F., Springer, J. A., Kaufman, J. N., & Possing, E. T. (2000). Human temporal lobe activation by speech and nonspeech sounds. *Cerebral Cortex*, 10, 512–528.

Binder, J. R., Desai, R. H., Graves, W. W., & Conant, L. L. (2009). Where is the semantic system? A critical review and meta-analysis of 120 functional neuroimaging studies. *Cerebral Cortex*, 19, 2767–2786.

Blau, V., van Atteveldt, N., Ekkebus, M., Goebel, R., & Blomert, L. (2009). Reduced neuronal integration of letters and speech sounds links phonological and reading deficits in adult dyslexia. *Current Biology*, 19, 503–508.

Blythe, H. I. (2014). Developmental changes in eye movements and visual information encoding associated with learning to read. *Current Directions in Psychological Science*, 23, 201–207.

Boden, C. & Giaschi, D. (2007). M-stream deficits and reading-related visual processes in developmental dyslexia. *Psychological Bulletin*, 133, 346–366.

Bonte, M. L. & Blomert, L. (2004). Developmental dyslexia: ERP correlates of anomalous phonological processing during spoken word recognition. *Cognitive Brain Research*, 21, 360–376.

Bonte, M. L., Poelmans, H., & Blomert, L. (2007). Deviant neurophysiological responses to phonological regularities in speech in dyslexic children. *Neuropsychologia*, 45, 1427–1437.

Booth, J. R., Burman, D. D., Meyer, J. R., Gitelman, D. R., Parrish, T. B., & Mesulam, M. M. (2002). Modality independence of word comprehension. *Human Brain Mapping*, 16, 251–261.

Bos, C., Mather, N., Dickson, S., Podhajski, B., & Chard, D. (2001). Perceptions and knowledge of preservice and inservice educators about early reading instruction. *Annals of Dyslexia*, 51, 97–120.

Boulenger, V., Hauk, O., & Pulvermüller, F. (2009). Grasping ideas with the motor system: semantic somatotopy in idiom comprehension. *Cerebral Cortex*, 19, 1905–1914.

Bowers, P. N., Kirby, J. R., & Deacon, S. H. (2010). The effects of morphological instruction on literacy skills: a systematic review of the literature. *Review of Educational Research*, 80, 144–179.

Brem, S., Bucher, K., Halder, P., Summers, P., Dietrich, T., Martin, E., & Brandeis, D. (2006). Evidence for developmental changes in the visual word processing network beyond adolescence. *NeuroImage*, 29, 822–837.

Brem, S., Bach, S., Kucian, K., Guttorm, T.K., Martin, E., Lyytinen, H., Brandeis, D., & Richardson, U. (2010). Brain sensitivity to print emerges when children learn letter-speech sound correspondences. *Proceedings of the National Academy of Sciences of the United States of America*, 107, 7939–7944.

Brennan, C., Cao, F., Pedroarena-Leal, N., McNorgan, C., & Booth, J. R. (2013). Reading acquisition reorganized the phonological awareness network only in alphabetic writing systems. *Human Brain Mapping*, 34, 3354–3368.

Breznitz, Z. (2006). *Fluency in Reading: Synchronization of Processes*. Mahwah, NJ: Lawrence Erlbaum Associates.

Bryant, P., MacLean, M., & Bradley, L. (1990a). Rhyme, language, and children's reading. *Applied Psycholinguistics*, 11, 237–252.

Bryant, P., MacLean, M., Bradley, L. L., & Crossland, J. (1990b). Rhyme and alliteration, phoneme detection, and learning to read. *Developmental Psychology*, 26, 429–438.

Burns, M. S. & Snow, C. E. (Eds) (1999). *Starting Out Right: A Guide to Promoting Children's Reading Success*. Washington, DC: National Academies Press.

Calfee, R. C., Lindamood, P., & Lindamood, C. (1973). Acoustic-phonetic skills and reading: Kindergarten through twelfth grade. *Journal of Educational Psychology*, 64, 293–298.

Caravolas, M., Lervåg, A., Defior, S., Málková, G. S., & Hulme, C. (2013). Different patterns, but equivalent predictors, of growth in reading in consistent and inconsistent orthographies. *Psychological Science*, 24, 1398–1407.

Carlisle, J. F. (2010). Effects of instruction in morphological awareness on literacy achievement: an integrative review. *Reading Research Quarterly*, 45, 464–487.

Castro-Caldas, A. (2004). Targeting regions of interest for the study of the illiterate brain. *International Journal of Psychology*, 39, 5–17.

Castro-Caldas, A., Petersson, K. M., Reis, A., Stone-Elander, S., & Ingvar, M. (1998). The illiterate brain: learning to read and write during childhood influences the functional organization of the adult brain. *Brain*, 121, 1053–1063.

Chall, J. S. (1967). *Learning to Read: The Great Debate*. New York: McGraw-Hill.

Chall, J. S. (1983). *Stages of Reading Development*. New York: McGraw-Hill.

Coch, D. (2010). Constructing a reading brain. In: D. A. Sousa (Ed.), *Mind, Brain, and Education: Neuroscience Implications for the Classroom* (pp. 139–162). Bloomington, IN: Solution Tree Press.

Coch, D. (2015). The N400 and the fourth grade shift. *Developmental Science*, 18, 254–269.

Coch, D. & Benoit, C. (2015). N400 ERP and standardized measures of reading in late elementary school children: correlated or independent? *Mind, Brain, and Education*, 9, 145–153.

Coch, D. & Meade, G. (2016). N1 and P2 to words and wordlike stimuli in late elementary school children and adults. *Psychophysiology*, 53, 115–128.

Coch, D., Grossi, G., Coffey-Corina, S., Holcomb, P. J., & Neville, H. J. (2002). A developmental investigation of ERP auditory rhyming effects. *Developmental Science*, 5, 467–489.

Coch, D., Grossi, G., Skendzel, W., & Neville, H. (2005). ERP nonword rhyming effects in children and adults. *Journal of Cognitive Neuroscience*, 17, 168–182.

Coch, D., Mitra, P., George, E., & Berger, N. (2011). Letters rhyme: electrophysiological evidence from children and adults. *Developmental Neuropsychology*, 36, 302–318.

Cohen, L. & Dehaene, S. (2004). Specialization within the ventral stream: the case for the visual word form area. *NeuroImage*, 22, 466–476.

Cohen, L., Lehéricy, S., Chochon, F., Lemer, C., Rivaud, S., & Dehaene, S. (2002). Language-specific tuning of visual cortex? Functional properties of the Visual Word Form Area. *Brain*, 125, 1054–1069.

Connor, C. M., Morrison, F. J., Fishman, B. J., Schatschneider, C., & Underwood, P. (2007). Algorithm-guided individualized reading instruction. *Science*, 315, 464–465.

Cunningham, A. E. & Stanovich, K. E. (1998). What reading does for the mind. *American Educator*, 22, 8–15.

Dehaene, S. (2009). *Reading in the Brain: The Science and Evolution of a Human Invention*. New York: Viking.

Dehaene, S., Pegado, F., Braga, L. W., Ventura, P., Nunes Filho, G., Jobert, A., Dehaene-Lambertz, G., Kolinsky, R., Morais, J., & Cohen, L. (2010). How learning to read changes the cortical networks for vision and language. *Science*, 330, 1359–1364.

Dehaene-Lambertz, G., Dehaene, S., & Hertz-Pannier, L. (2002). Functional neuroimaging of speech perception in infants. *Science*, 298, 2013–2015.

Demb, J. B., Boynton, G. M., & Heeger, D. J. (1997). Brain activity in visual cortex predicts individual differences in reading performance. *Proceedings of the National Academy of Sciences of the United States of America*, 94, 13363–13366.

Dickinson, D. K. (2011). Teachers' language practices and academic outcomes of preschool children. *Science*, 333, 964–967.

Doctor, E. A. & Coltheart, M. (1980). Children's use of phonological encoding when reading for meaning. *Memory and Cognition*, 8, 195–209.

Dunn-Rankin, P., Leton, D. A., & Shelton, V. F. (1968). Congruency factors related to visual confusion of English letters. *Perceptual and Motor Skills*, 26, 659–666.

Eddy, M. D., Grainger, J., Holcomb, P. J., Mitra, P., & Gabrieli, J. D. E. (2014). Masked priming and ERPs dissociate maturation of orthographic and semantic components of visual word recognition in children. *Psychophysiology*, 51, 136–141.

Eden, G. F., VanMeter, J. W., Rumsey, J. M., Maisog, J. M., Woods, R. P., & Zeffiro, T. A. (1996). Abnormal processing of visual motion in dyslexia revealed by functional brain imaging. *Nature*, 382, 66–69.

Eden, G. F., Jones, K. M., Cappell, K., Gareau, L., Wood, F. B., Zeffiro, T. A., Dietz, N. A., Agnew, J. A., & Flowers, D. L. (2004). Neural changes following remediation in adult developmental dyslexia. *Neuron*, 44, 411–422.

Evans, M. D. R., Kelley, J., Sikora, J., & Treiman, D. J. (2010). Family scholarly culture and educational success: books and schooling in 27 nations. *Research in Social Stratification and Mobility*, 28, 171–197.

Flowers, D. L., Jones, K., Noble, K., VanMeter, J., Zeffiro, T. A., Woord, F. B., & Eden, G. F. (2004). Attention to single letters activates left extrastriate cortex. *NeuroImage*, 21, 829–839.

Ford-Connors, E. & Paratore, J. R. (2015). Vocabulary instruction in fifth grade and beyond: sources of word learning and productive contexts for development. *Review of Educational Research*, 85, 50–91.

Frith, U. (1998). Literally changing the brain. *Brain*, 121, 1011–1012.

Froyen, D. J. W., Bonte, M. L., van Atteveldt, N., & Blomert, L. (2009). The long road to automation: neurocognitive development of letter-speech sound processing. *Journal of Cognitive Neuroscience*, 21, 567–580.

Gervais, M. J., Harvey, L. O., & Roberts, J. O. (1984). Identification confusions among letters of the alphabet. *Journal of Experimental Psychology: Human Perception and Performance*, 10, 655–666.

Gibson, E. J. (1965). Learning to read. *Science*, 148, 1066–1072.

Gillingham, A. & Stillman, B. (1983). *Remedial Training for Children with Specific Disability in Reading, Spelling, and Penmanship*. Cambridge, MA: Educator's Publishing Service, Inc.

Goldberg, R. F., Perfetti, C. A., & Schneider, W. (2006). Distinct and common cortical activations for multimodal semantic categories. *Cognitive, Affective, & Behavioral Neuroscience*, 6, 214–222.

González, J., Barrós-Loscertales, A., Pulvermüller, F., Meseguer, V., Sanjuán, A., Belloch, V., & Ávila, C. (2006). Reading *cinnamon* activates olfactory brain regions. *NeuroImage*, 32, 906–912.

Goodman, K. S. & Goodman, Y. M. (1979). Learning to read is natural. In: L. B. Resnick & P. A. Weaver (Eds), *Theory and Practice of Early Reading. Volume 1* (pp. 137–154). Hillsdale, NJ: Lawrence Erlbaum Associates.

Goodwin, A. P. & Ahn, S. (2010). A meta-analysis of morphological interventions: effects on literacy achievement of children with literacy difficulties. *Annals of Dyslexia*, 60, 183–208.

Goswami, U. (1993). Phonological skills and learning to read. *Annals of the New York Academy of Sciences*, 682, 296–311.

Goswami, U. (1999). Causal connections in beginning reading: the importance of rhyme. *Journal of Research in Reading*, 22, 217–240.

Hart, B. & Risley, T. R. (1995). *Meaningful Differences in the Everyday Experience of Young American Children*. Baltimore, MD: Paul H. Brookes Publishing Co.

Hart, B. & Risley, T. R. (1999). *The Social World of Children Learning to Talk*. Baltimore, MD: Paul H. Brookes Publishing Co.

Hart, B. & Risley, T. R. (2003). The early catastrophe: the 30 million word gap by age 3. *American Educator*, 27, 4–9.

Hattie, J. (2009). *Visible Learning: a Synthesis of Over 800 Meta-Analyses Relating to Achievement*. New York: Routledge.

Hattie, J. (2012). *Visible Learning for Teachers: Maximizing Impact on Learning*. New York: Routledge.

Hernandez, D. J. (2011). *Double Jeopardy: How Third-Grade Reading Skills and Poverty Influence High School Graduation*. Baltimore, MD: Annie E. Casey Foundation.

Hernández, J. C. (2014). New York schools chief advocates more 'balanced literacy.' *The New York Times*, 26 June. Available online at http://nyti.ms/TARA2O

Hulme, C., Bowyer-Crane, C., Carroll, J. M., Duff, F. J., & Snowling, M. J. (2012). The causal role of phoneme awareness and letter-sound knowledge in learning to read: combining intervention studies with mediation analyses. *Psychological Science*, 23, 572–577.

Huttenlocher, J., Vasilyeva, M., Cymerman, E., & Levine, S. (2002). Language input and child syntax. *Cognitive Psychology*, 45, 337–374.

Hyerle, D. (2000). *A Field Guide to Using Visual Tools*. Lyme, NH: Designs for Thinking.

International Reading Association (2010). *Standards for Reading Professionals: Revised 2010*. Newark, DE: International Reading Association, Inc.

James, K. H., James, T. W., Jobard, G., Wong, A. C.-N., & Gauthier, I. (2005). Letter processing in the visual system: different activation patterns for single letters and strings. *Cognitive, Affective, & Behavioral Neuroscience*, 5, 452–466.

Joubert, S., Beauregard, M., Walter, N., Bourgouin, P., Beaudoin, G., Leroux, J. M., Karama, S., & Lecours, A. R. (2004). Neural correlates of lexical and sublexical processes in reading. *Brain and Language*, 89, 9–20.

Justice, L. M., Bowles, R. P., & Skibbe, L. E. (2006). Measuring preschool attainment of print-concept knowledge: a study of typical and at-risk 3- to 5-year-old children using item response theory. *Language, Speech, and Hearing Services in Schools*, 37, 224–235.

Kuhn, M. R., Schwanenflugel, P. J., & Meisinger, E. B. (2010). Aligning theory and assessment of reading fluency: automaticity, prosody, and definitions of fluency. *Reading Research Quarterly*, 45, 230–251.

LaBerge, D. & Samuels, S. J. (1974). Toward a theory of automatic information processing in reading. *Cognitive Psychology*, 6, 293–323.

Lane, H. B., Pullen, P. C., Eisele, M. R., & Jordan, L. (2002). Preventing reading failure: phonological awareness assessment and instruction. *Preventing School Failure*, 46, 101–110.

Lawrence, J. F., White, C., & Snow, C. (2010). The words students need. *Educational Leadership*, 68, 23–26.

Lindamood, P., Bell, N., & Lindamood, P. (1997). Sensory-cognitive factors in the controversy over reading instruction. *Journal of Developmental and Learning Disorders*, 1, 143–182.

Livingstone, M. & Hubel, D. (1988). Segregation of form, color, movement, and depth: anatomy, physiology, and perception. *Science*, 240, 740–749.

McCandliss, B. D., Cohen, L., & Dehaene, S. (2003). The visual word form area: expertise for reading in the fusiform gyrus. *Trends in Cognitive Sciences*, 7, 293–299.

McCardle, P. & Chhabra, V. (Eds) (2004). *The Voice of Evidence in Reading Research*. Baltimore, MD: Paul H. Brookes Publishing Co.

MacLean, M., Bryant, P., & Bradley, L. (1987). Rhymes, nursery rhymes, and reading in early childhood. *Merrill-Palmer Quarterly*, 33, 255–281.

Martin, A. (2007). The representation of object concepts in the brain. *Annual Review of Psychology*, 58, 25–45.

Martin, A. & Chao, L. L. (2001). Semantic memory and the brain: structure and processes. *Current Opinion in Neurobiology*, 11, 194–201.

Mesgarani, N., Cheung, C., Johnson, K., & Chang, E. F. (2014). Phonetic feature encoding in human superior temporal gyrus. *Science*, 343, 1006–1010.

Meyler, A., Keller, T. A., Cherkassky, V. L., Gabrieli, J. D., & Just, M. A. (2008). Modifying the brain activation of poor readers during sentence comprehension with extended remedial instruction: a longitudinal study of neuroplasticity. *Neuropsychologia*, 46, 2580–2592.

Mitra, P. & Coch, D. (2009). A masked priming ERP study of letter processing using single letters and false fonts. *Cognitive, Affective, & Behavioral Neuroscience*, 9, 216–228.

Moats, L. C. (1999). *Teaching Reading Is Rocket Science: What Expert Teachers of Reading Should Know and Be Able To Do*. Washington, DC: American Federation of Teachers.

Moats, L. C. (2000). *Speech to Print: Language Essentials for Teachers*. Baltimore, MD: Paul H. Brookes Publishing Co.

Moats, L. C. (2010). *Speech to Print: Language Essentials for Teachers*, 2nd edition. Baltimore, MD: Paul H. Brookes Publishing Co.

Molfese, D. L. (2000). Predicting dyslexia at 8 years of age using neonatal brain responses. *Brain and Language*, 72, 238–245.

Nagy, W. & Anderson, R. C. (1984). How many words are there in printed school English? *Reading Research Quarterly*, 19, 304–330.

Nagy, W. & Townsend, D. (2012). Words as tools: learning academic vocabulary as language acquisition. *Reading Research Quarterly*, 47, 91–108.

Nation, K. & Hulme, C. (2010). Learning to read changes children's phonological skills: evidence from a latent variable longitudinal study of reading and nonword repetition. *Developmental Science*, 14, 649–659.

National Institute of Child Health and Human Development (2000). *Report of the National Reading Panel. Teaching Children to Read: An Evidence-Based Assessment of the Scientific Research Literature on Reading and its Implications for Reading Instruction*. NIH Publication No. 00-4769. Washington, DC: U.S. Government Printing Office.

National Institute for Literacy (2007). *What Content-Area Teachers Should Know About Adolescent Literacy*. Jessup, MD: National Institute for Literacy.

National Research Council (1998). *Preventing Reading Difficulties in Young Children*. Washington, DC: National Academies Press.

Nippold, M. A. (1998). *Later Language Development: The School-Age and Adolescent Years*, 2nd edition. Austin, TX: Pro-Ed.

Olulade, O. A., Napoliello, E. M., & Eden, G. F. (2013). Abnormal visual motion processing is not a cause of dyslexia. *Neuron*, 79, 180–190.

Paulesu, E., Démonet, J. F., Fazio, F., McCrory, E., Chanoine, V., Brunswick, N., Cappa, C. F., Cossu, G., Habib, M., Frith, C. D., & Frith, U. (2001). Dyslexia: cultural diversity and biological unity. *Science*, 291, 2165–2167.

Perfetti, C. A. (2007). Reading ability: lexical quality to comprehension. *Scientific Studies of Reading*, 11, 357–383.

Petersen, S. E., Fox, P. T., Posner, M. I., Mintun, M., & Raichle, M. E. (1988). Positron emission tomographic studies of the cortical anatomy of single-word processing. *Nature*, 331, 585–589.

Petit, J.-P., Midgley, K. J., Holcomb, P. J., & Grainger, J. (2006). On the time course of letter perception: a masked priming ERP investigation. *Psychonomic Bulletin & Review*, 13, 674–681.

Podhajski, B. (1995). *TIME for Teachers*. Williston, VT: Stern Center for Language and Learning.

Pondiscio, R. (2014). Why Johnny won't learn to read: balanced literacy is baaaack. *New York Daily News*, 3 July. Available online at http://nydn.us/1jL2SZp

Rayner, K., Foorman, B. R., Perfetti, C. A., Pesetsky, D., & Seidenberg, M. S. (2001). How psychological science informs the teaching of reading. *Psychological Science in the Public Interest*, 2, 31–74.

Ritchey, K. D. & Goeke, J. L. (2006). Orton-Gillinghman and Orton-Gillingham-based reading instruction: a review of the literature. *Journal of Special Education*, 40, 171–183.

Sander, E. K. (1972). When are speech sounds learned? *Journal of Speech and Hearing Disorders*, 37, 55–63.

Scarborough, H. S. (2005). Developmental relationships between language and reading: reconciling a beautiful hypothesis with some ugly facts. In: H. W. Catts & A. G. Kamhi (Eds), *The Connections Between Language and Reading Disabilities* (pp. 3–24). Mahwah, NJ: Lawrence Erlbaum Associates.

Share, D. L. (1999). Phonological recoding and orthographic learning: a direct test of the self-teaching hypothesis. *Journal of Experimental Child Psychology*, 72, 95–129.

Shaywitz, B. A., Shaywitz, S. E., Pugh, K. R., Mencl, E., Fulbright, R. K., Skudlarski, P., Constable, R. T., Marchione, K. E., Fletcher, J. M., Lyon, G. R., & Gore, J. C. (2002). Disruption of posterior brain systems for reading in children with developmental dyslexia. *Biological Psychiatry*, 52, 101–110.

Shaywitz, B. A., Shaywitz, S. E., Blachman, B. A., Pugh, K. R., Fulbright, R. K., Skudlarski, P., Mencl, W. E., Constable, R. T., Holahan, J. M., Marichione, K. E., Fletcher, J. M., & Gore, J. C. (2004). Development of left occipitotemporal systems for skilled reading in children after a phonologically-based intervention. *Biological Psychiatry*, 55, 926–933.

Shaywitz, S. E. (1996). Dyslexia. *Scientific American*, 275, 98–104.

Simos, P. G., Breier, J. I., Fletcher, J. M., Bergman, E., & Papanicolaou, A. C. (2000a). Cerebral mechanisms involved in word reading in dyslexic children: a magnetic source imaging approach. *Cerebral Cortex*, 10, 809–816.

Simos, P. G., Breier, J. I., Wheless, J. W., Maggio, W. W., Fletcher, J. M., Castillo, E. M., & Papanicolaou, A. C. (2000b). Brain mechanisms for reading: the role of the superior temporal gyrus in word and pseudoword naming. *NeuroReport*, 11, 2443–2447.

Simos, P. G., Fletcher, J. M., Bergman, E., Breier, J. I., Foorman, B. R., Castillo, E. M., Davis, R. N., Fitzgerald, M., & Papanicolaou, A. C. (2002). Dyslexia-specific brain activation profile becomes normal following successful remedial training. *Neurology*, 58, 1203–1213.

Slavin, R. E., Cheung, A., Groff, C., & Lake, C. (2008). Effective reading programs for middle and high schools: a best-evidence synthesis. *Reading Research Quarterly*, 43, 290–322.

Stahl, S. A. (1992). Saying the "p" word: nine guidelines for exemplary phonics instruction. *The Reading Teacher*, 45, 618–625.

Stainthorp, R. (2003). Use it or lose it. *Literacy Today*, 34, 16–17.

Stanovich, K. E. (1986). Matthew effects in reading: some consequences of individual differences in the acquisition of literacy. *Reading Research Quarterly*, 21, 360–407.

Stein, J. (2001a). The magnocellular theory of developmental dyslexia. *Dyslexia*, 7, 12–36.

Stein, J. (2001b). The neurobiology of reading difficulties. In: M. Wolf (Ed.), *Dyslexia, Fluency, and the Brain* (pp. 3–21). Timonium, MD: York Press.

Strickland, D., Snow, C., Griffin, P., Burns, S. M., & McNamara, P. (2002). *Preparing Our Teachers: Opportunities for Better Reading Instruction*. Washington, DC: Joseph Henry Press.

Talcott, J., Witton, C., Hebb, G. S., Stoodley, C. J., Westwood, E. A., France, S. J., Hansen, P.C., & Stein, J. F. (2002). On the relationship between dynamic visual and auditory processing and literacy skills: results from a large primary-school study. *Dyslexia*, 8, 204–225.

Tanaka, H., Black, J. M., Hulme, C., Stanley, L. M., Kesler, S. R., Whitfield-Gabrieli, S., Reiss, A. L., Gabrieli, J. D., & Hoeft, F. (2011). The brain basis of the phonological deficit in dyslexia is independent of IQ. *Psychological Science*, 22, 1442–1451.

Templeton, S. & Gehsmann, K. M. (2014). *Teaching Reading and Writing: The Developmental Approach*. Boston, MA: Pearson.

Templeton, S., Bear, D. R., Invernizzi, M., Johnston, F., Flanigan, K., Townsend, D. R., Helman, L., & Hayes, L. (2015). *Vocabulary Their Way: Word Study With Middle and Secondary Students*, 2nd edition. Boston, MA: Pearson.

Thompson, G. B., Connelly, V., Fletcher-Flinn, C. M., & Hodson, S. J. (2009). The nature of skilled adult reading varies with type of instruction in childhood. *Memory and Cognition*, 37, 223–234.

Thompson-Schill, S. L. (2003). Neuroimaging studies of semantic memory: inferring "how" from "where." *Neuropsychologia*, 41, 280–292.

Torgesen, J. K. (1998). Catch them before they fall: identification and assessment to prevent reading failure in young children. *American Educator*, 22, 32–39.

Treiman, R. (2000). The foundations of literacy. *Current Directions in Psychological Science*, 9, 89–92.

Ungerleider, L. G. & Haxby, J. V. (1994). 'What' and 'where' in the human brain. *Current Opinion in Neurobiology*, 4, 157–165.

van Atteveldt, N., Formisano, E., Goebel, R., & Blomert, L. (2004). Integration of letters and speech sounds in the human brain. *Neuron*, 43, 271–282.

Vellutino, F. R., Fletcher, J. M., Snowling, M., & Scanlon, D. M. (2004). Specific reading disability (dyslexia): what have we learned in the past four decades? *Journal of Child Psychology and Psychiatry*, 45, 2–40.

Wagner, R. K. & Torgesen, J. K. (1987). The nature of phonological processing and its causal role in the acquisition of reading skills. *Psychological Bulletin*, 101, 192–212.

Walsh, K., Glaser, D., & Wilcox, D. D. (2006). *What Education Schools Aren't Teaching About Reading And What Elementary Teachers Aren't Learning*. Washington, DC: National Council on Teacher Quality.

Wandell, B. A. (2011). The neurobiological basis of seeing words. *Annals of the New York Academy of Sciences*, 1224, 63–80.

Werker, J. F. & Tees, R. C. (2002). Cross-language speech perception: evidence for perceptual reorganization during the first year of life. *Infant Behavior & Development*, 25, 121–133.

Whitehurst, G. J., Falco, F. L., Lonigan, C. J., Fischel, J. E., DeBaryshe, B. D., Valdez-Menchaca, M. C., & Coulfield, M. (1998). Accelerating language development through picture book reading. *Developmental Psychology*, 24, 552–559.

Wood, C. & Terrell, C. (1998). Pre-school phonological awareness and subsequent literacy development. *Educational Psychology*, 18, 253–274.

Yopp, H. K. & Yopp, R. H. (2000). Supporting phonemic awareness development in the classroom. *The Reading Teacher*, 54, 130–143.

Zorzi, M., Barbiero, C., Facoetti, A., Lonciari, I., Carrozzi, M., Montico, M., Bravar, L., George, F., Pech-Georgel, C., & Ziegler, J. C. (2012). Extra-large letter spacing improves reading in dyslexia. *Proceedings of the National Academy of Sciences of the United States of America*, 109, 11455–11459.

SECTION 4
Special Student Groups

12

DEVELOPMENTAL CHARACTERISTICS OF GIFTED CHILDREN

Educational Approaches

Evie Malaia, Vicki K. Hinesley, and Elena Egorova

NETHERLANDS INSTITUTE FOR ADVANCED STUDY, WASSENAAR, THE NETHERLANDS; GRAPEVINE-COLLEYVILLE ISD, TEXAS, USA; AND LYCEUM #44, CHEBOKSARY, RUSSIA

Goals of Gifted Education

Throughout modern history, students have attended school to acquire the knowledge and skills that they need in order to become productive citizens. School programs and lesson plans are typically structured to allow most children within a specific society to develop the required skills and acquire knowledge appropriate to the cultural norms. The approach that involves a system-wide focus on specific skills in the transition from education to the workforce has historically paid off. Now, with increasing flexibility of the requirements for the modern workforce, there are increasing opportunities for high achievers to have an impact. In fact, the quality of human capital can determine a country's role in the world marketplace (Hausmann & Hidalgo, 2011), and drive competitiveness at the global level.

Subotnik *et al.* (2011) offer the framework of *eminence* as an approach to the education of gifted children. Every year, teachers encounter students who are capable of more than is expected of them in the typical classroom, and typically these children will be considered gifted, or high-ability. The eminence framework offers a long-term view with regard to the education of these children. It suggests that their education, both within and outside formal schooling, should center on identifying and nurturing those abilities that can be beneficial to society at large. The overarching idea is that providing children with challenges and opportunities that match their abilities will allow society to benefit from the innovation and creativity of these individuals at a later stage, once they have developed eminence within their fields of expertise. This way of framing gifted education allows a compelling case to be made for the development of gifted programs at the national level, with a long-term outlook. More locally and immediately, however, from the viewpoint of individual teachers who are working with a new group of students every year, gifted students present a special case that requires additional resources. In the short term, gifted children could be more appropriately viewed as students in need of *special education* (Borland, 1989).

School teachers are in a somewhat conflicted yet quite powerful position at the intersection of societal interests and individuals in their classrooms. On the one hand, as part of the established school system, teachers are charged with the primary tasks of delivering curricula and socializing young people. The introduction of outliers—whether gifted or learning-challenged—into the classroom appears to interfere with these tasks. On the other hand, it is teachers who have the most information and experience with regard to early identification of ability or talent. Crucially, teachers who are knowledgeable about the structure of and information flow in their country's educational system are uniquely equipped to direct gifted students to appropriate challenges and specialized programs.

In this chapter, we shall discuss the characteristics of high-ability students that can aid their early identification, and the strategies available to enable teachers to contribute to ability development within their classroom. First, let us consider high-ability children in context, starting with real-life observations from the teacher's viewpoint.

Gifted Children in Context

The following observations were made by a teacher from an elementary school in the U.S.A. However, as any experienced teacher will tell you, similar stories play out daily with gifted kids in any classroom or country.

> Sam, a ten-year-old 4th grader, sits at the back of the classroom tearing a sheet of notebook paper into tiny pieces. He rolls each piece tightly between his fingers and places one at a time between his lips and spits it toward any one of several nearby targets. Within seconds I realize the class has turned their attention to Sam and his attempts to launch spit wads of paper toward the cage where the class pet hamster is exercising on the wheel. Sam is busy demonstrating to the other students how he has perfected the art of placing his mouth between the bars of the cage so the spit wads can actually land on his moving target. Naturally, the other students find Sam's experiment quite entertaining, which brings classroom instruction to an abrupt halt. The next ten minutes are spent reprimanding Sam for unwise choices. As Sam is the instigator of many high jinks that lead to classroom interruptions, he often does not complete his school work. I am at my wits' end trying to coerce him into passing his assignments and, most importantly, his state-mandated exams.
>
> On the other side of the classroom, a new student named Susanna works alone and finishes her work quickly. During recess, Susanna walks alone around the perimeter of the playground reading a book. No one invites her to join the group, as the children chase each other through the maze of playground equipment. When I ask some of the girls in her class if they have considered asking Susanna to join the group, they reply that they invited her to play with them once, but she didn't know how to play the games the girls enjoy at recess. As it turns out, Susanna's passion is creating robots, and her book is teaching her how to write a code to make the robot follow commands. For the local community, this is something quite outside the norm.

The teacher is concerned about Susanna, as well as about Sam. She suspects that Susanna is a gifted student, but she may be surprised to find that Sam is also gifted. She realizes that these two students have different needs—socially, emotionally, and cognitively—from other children in the class. She begins a search for a recipe to create the right environment for individuals with diverse backgrounds, interests, and abilities similar to those of Susanna and Sam, but she soon realizes that there is no readily available curriculum that fits the needs of everyone.

For several months now, the teacher has been working with Sam to figure out how to get him to complete his work. When the class began a study of decimals and statistics, the teacher noticed that Sam demonstrated an unexpected grasp of complex math skills. During a class discussion of favorite sports teams, Sam mentions his love of baseball, and demonstrates his ability to quote team and player statistics with ease. The teacher makes the connection between learning to calculate decimals and the use of percentages in baseball statistics, and realizes what fuels Sam's extraordinary memory for player and team standings. She begins to suspect that Sam's dislike of her mathematics assignments may stem from the lack of complexity and application that is embedded in the authentic problem solving that Sam prefers. Sam is not interested in merely changing fractions into decimals, when he can apply that skill to comparing teams and their players and understanding why they win or lose their games. Sam needs to see the benefit of practicing isolated skills; he tires quickly in the face of monotony and lack of relevance to other contexts that he values.

Susanna is quite the opposite of Sam. She is quiet and prefers to work alone. She is unfailingly polite to the other students and the teacher, but is reluctant to share much about herself. The teachers realize that she excels in all class assignments, but rarely adds her opinion to class discussions. On the rare occasions when she does so, her insights are often quite abstract. Other students dismiss her comments—not because they dislike Susanna, but because they do not understand her or do not know how to respond. Susanna's thinking processes are more complex than those of her peers. The teacher smiles and says something like "That's an interesting idea", but rarely asks her to elaborate, and the teacher herself is not sure how to direct Susanna's thinking. She often regrets not giving Susanna much of an opportunity to contribute to class, and wishes that she had the skill to engage others in conversation with Susanna.

As the school year comes to an end, Sam is still using most of his time to find ways to entertain his classmates. He struggles to finish his assignments, but manages to pass his end-of-term exams and state-mandated tests. Susanna still prefers to work and play alone. She performs exceptionally well in the math and science areas, but dislikes reading novels and writing stories. The teacher watches Susanna trying to write codes similar to the ones she studies in her coding book.

Neural and Behavioral Characteristics of High-Ability Students

There are two dominant neurocognitive characteristics of gifted children—the high rate at which they acquire new cognitive structures, and the depths at which they interact with information (Brant et al., 2013; Malaia & Newman, 2013). To date, several specific patterns of cognitive neurodynamics have been shown to contribute to both measurable intelligence and ability to learn (Sternberg & Kaufman, 2011).

High Capacity of Working Memory (Processing Buffer), and its Efficient Interaction with Both Sensory and Long-Term Memory Networks

The behavioral literature (Montgomery et al., 2008) reports a positive correlation between children's ability to understand complex sentences, and the speed of attention reallocation among items in working memory. Neural studies have shown that highly skilled readers use rapid, online strategies of information consolidation, quickly recoding incoming information to references to semantic (long-term) memory (Malaia et al., 2009; Newman et al., 2013).

Quality of Within- and Between-Network Connectivity in the Brain

Individuals with high ability in a specific cognitive processing task are able to filter the incoming sensory information, and process it using task-specific neural networks. The student's effectiveness in controlling attention and gating sensory information is a critical determinant of individual differences in a wide range of complex cognitive abilities (Brumback *et al.*, 2004; Malaia *et al.*, 2012, 2014b). Furthermore, this modality- and task-specific ability is developed by way of continuous exposure to the specific stimulus (reading), or by engagement in the specific activity (e.g. sports, or playing a musical instrument). Interestingly, parents often report that gifted children have problems with everyday sensory integration (e.g. sensitivity to sound or touch, extreme concentration ability/filtering of sensory input) (see Gilman *et al.*, 2013).

Flexibility of Switching among Multiple Neural Networks Involved in a (Learning) Task

The brain networks responsible for specific task (e.g. numerical processing, lexical retrieval, deductive reasoning) interact to allow for specific cognitive tasks. The switching along networks is carried out through central hubs (cognitive control centers) in the frontal and cingulate cortices. The process of learning a novel task consists of separating the task-specific networks (e.g. sensorimotor; see Bassett *et al.*, 2015), and release of the cognitive control hubs. This process is faster and more efficient in high-performing learners (e.g. Mantzaris *et al.*, 2013; Malaia *et al.*, 2014a).

It is important to note that high ability manifested in neural efficiency is shaped by both genetic and environmental factors (Tucker-Drob & Briley, 2014; Gray & Thompson, 2004). The human brain has the potential for learning and processing highly complex information. However, if that potential is not actualized by exposure to appropriately complex stimuli within the developmentally appropriate period, neural processing, although taking place, will not be productive (see Malaia *et al.*, 2012). In practical terms, this means that children need to be exposed to complex applications of basic ideas covered in the classroom in order to use the experiences for further, individualized, and possibly implicit learning.

Behaviorally, the high level of interconnectedness and flexibility of neural networks yields a recognizable set of behaviors in children. Although some of these behaviors (listed below) can be considered disruptive in a standard classroom, they are consistent in indicating a deeper need for cognitive load in high-ability students:

- abstract, logical thinking—the child can be argumentative if not responded to at the appropriate level
- a keen sense of justice and fairness aimed outside immediate experience (other epochs and countries)
- intense concentration (possibly only on specific or internal tasks, so daydreaming may occur)
- interest in experimenting, and exploring the possibilities beyond common practice
- enjoyment of contradictions and paradoxes, an acute sense of humor, and language play (e.g. puns, intentional playful use of foreign languages)
- interest in organizing or planning complex systems (either social, mechanical, verbal, or visual).

If one tries to imagine all of these behaviors taking place in the everyday classroom, it becomes very clear that the identification and development of high-ability students is a high-level skill, which crucially depends on a confident and resourceful teacher.

Classroom Considerations for High-Ability Students

Many adults assume that gifted students should be high achievers in all academic subjects and areas, and willing to do whatever work is assigned to them. School administrators and parents expect gifted students not only to complete all assignments on time, but also to demonstrate products of the highest quality in terms of depth of understanding, creativity, and appearance. In reality, a student may, for example, demonstrate exceptional skill in mathematics, but struggle in writing or history. It is also possible for a student who is exceptionally skilled in experimental science to have a learning disability in another essential area, such as reading. The developmental profile of an 8-year-old gifted student might match that of a 15-year-old in abstract analysis, and that of a 5-year-old in self-control (Peterson, 2015). Many adults find these seemingly conflicting trajectories of ability development difficult to contend with, even after continuous observation of the child. Standard expectations for success in mathematics, for example, clearly do not apply to a child who has already learned multiplication and powers at 6 years of age. Thus it is crucially important that teachers and parents, as well as school administrators, continuously assess their expectations for the students. What will it mean for this particular high-ability student to demonstrate learning? This is where a special-education approach to education of the gifted, where school education is viewed from the standpoint of added value to individual development, is more appropriate.

Establishing Appropriate Individual Learning Criteria

Standard grading schemes are poorly applicable to high-ability students, as it takes one minimal effort to demonstrate equivalent levels of achievement. Although the teacher, as a public employee, might have to provide official grade assessments, the more practicable approach with high-ability students is to convey that, in the real world, actual skills and knowledge are meaningful assets—for example, in searching for employment. Assembling a portfolio of projects that can demonstrate mastery of specific domains can also be intensely meaningful for high-ability students, and the form of the portfolio can differ depending on the domain of ability. It is crucially important not to limit the preferred areas of development early on—for example, a child can demonstrate high ability in mathematics and cello performance. Without deliberate, focused coordination of efforts between the parents, teachers, and coaches of gifted students, some (well-meaning) adults might be tempted to suggest that the child should direct their efforts towards a single, more socially promising area of learning. However, from the developmental perspective, retaining maximum variety with regard to exposure to different activities is beneficial both to long-term brain health and to mental stability in young adulthood. Thus, whether a child demonstrates one or more areas of high ability, continued exposure to novel domains and exploration within existing ones is highly encouraged.

Individualized Depth of Curriculum

By the time a gifted child is enrolled in an educational institution, they will have had years of this type of intense interaction with the world around them, resulting in deep asynchrony between their development and that of their typically developing peers. The difficulty encountered by educators and parents is typically that of appropriate grouping, given the high variability in levels of giftedness among gifted children. *Ability grouping* has been established as the most appropriate approach to gifted education (Neihart, 2007; Richardson & Benbow, 1990). One problem that teachers encounter when trying to establish an appropriate level of engagement for the gifted children in the class is that the standard curriculum material is insufficient to maintain a taxing cognitive load for this group. Therefore ability-related acceleration needs to be supported by more in-depth material (enrichment). Another problem is ensuring that the child is able to communicate with others in the classroom. One strategy is to engage the gifted student as "teacher's helper", and allow them to demonstrate creativity and engagement with material while teaching it to their same-age peers. This technique can be helpful as a temporary solution, while the family and school identify which of the more permanent solutions—acceleration, specialized/gifted program, or change of school system or homeschooling—is most appropriate in the long term.

An important step in individualization of the curriculum is to involve the child as an active agent and, if practicable within the specific school system, to secure agreement for the grading scale based on individual growth, rather than grade standards, which are likely to be too low. For example, the teacher can explain that since the grade-level material is too easy, the child will be given more complex or difficult projects to complete, such that their time at school is spent on improving their skills, rather than simply showing them off. This approach establishes the so-called "growth mindset" (Dweck, 2006), where the progress, rather than specific achievement level, is considered valuable in the social contract between the teacher and the student.

Psychosocial Development

The growth mindset can be helpful within another problem area for gifted children, namely psychosocial development. Due to asynchrony in ability manifestation, gifted children often receive highly conflicting cues from their environment from the early years. An elementary school child is likely to feel confused or ambivalent about demonstrating their ability, precisely because of the mixed messages that they might have received early on, whether because of reading before the age of 4 years, or being able to do mental mathematics beyond typical expectations. Teachers who continuously observe the progress of gifted students are at the forefront of forming psychosocial skills that can ensure sustained effort in learning in gifted children. Gifted students might need some social skills earlier than their peers (e.g. self-presentation, constructive response to criticism). A child who is compelled to excel in one or multiple domains for the purpose of self-actualization needs to learn to take risks, and be able to deal with criticism and competitiveness in their environment. Thus it is important to identify individual ways of transforming internal motivation into external efforts. In this domain, parents' experience of observing emotional patterns in their child's behavior should be engaged. Since psychosocial skills are a crucial component in the development of eminence in high-ability children, parents and teachers need to provide a consistent environment in which to deal with problem areas, such as perfectionism or insufficient risk taking.

Opportunity Opening

The opportunities for gifted children to engage with individuals and assignments that are instrumental for their development are often limited by lack of information on the part both of children and of parents, and by lack of mobility (e.g. the parents cannot take the child to all of the opportunities that they know about, such as area chess tournaments). Austin (1978) identified two types of chance factors in the development of talent that are malleable to influence, especially by professional educators. The first is opportunity opening as a function of exploratory behavior (e.g. a child learning about chess while browsing a board games store). The second is domain-specific (e.g. the child being able to play with a chess Grandmaster at a local tournament, and learning a novel endgame).

Teachers can encourage the development of high-ability young people by promoting exploratory behavior, and informing students of opportunities that already exist within the school. For example, a focused kindergartener can be encouraged to join a chess club, even if to date she has never heard of chess. Although parents and other family members are expected to provide the majority of such exploratory opportunities prior to adolescence, not all communities and levels of income can provide adequate access to the experiential involvement necessary for a high-ability child. Another level of opportunity opening involves connecting students who already excel in a particular domain with regional and national networks, groups, and opportunities to perform or compete. Because of the noted asynchrony in cognitive development of gifted children, interaction with older and younger children should be consistently encouraged, both within and outside academic environments. In schools, these interactions can be organized, for example, by pairing up first- and third-grade "reading buddies", or forming mathematics-contest teams from all grades in a high school. Gifted children need a peer support network, but it is difficult to recognize the opportunities for forming this. Some organizations for the gifted (e.g. Davidson's Gifted Network in the U.S.A.) organize and run interest-specific camps for high-ability children. Where such networks are not available, an equivalent result can be achieved by encouraging mixed-age interactions in the classroom and within the fields of interest. This can involve additional (extracurricular) work for the teacher, and this work should be recognized at the school level.

Outcomes

At this point, you may be wondering what happened to the two real-life students with whom we began our discussion—Sam and Susanna. Here are the letters that their fourth-grade teachers wrote to them at their graduation from high school 8 years later.[1]

Dear Susanna,

When you walked into my classroom, I must admit I didn't expect you to excel at the level and in the areas you chose. As a young Hispanic female who still struggled with the English language, I expected that you had little formal education and would be satisfied to graduate from high school. Unfortunately I didn't question the prevailing stereotype of minority females, and I failed to see you as the student you were. As a society, we expected our gifted students to be Caucasian males, but over time, we have realized gifted individuals come from all groups of people; some are identified more easily and more often. Some of these prejudices come from the belief that genetics determine potential for intelligence; others believe it is a combination of genetics and experience; while others see intelligence as a function of economic status. It was obvious you had experienced life in ways most students had not as your family struggled financially and socially to begin a new life in this country. As I learned more about you, I realized not all experiences can be measured on a test of achievement or intelligence. Your insight into the value of freedom and the ways it impacted your perceptions of right and wrong, what was a necessity for life, and what blessings meant to those less fortunate was formed from personal experience. Now I understand the context from which you viewed the world and the opportunity you had to change the course of your future and that of your family.

At first, you preferred to learn alone and keep to yourself during free time. I thought it was because you were self-conscious about speaking to other members of the class because you might make a mistake, and I knew that making mistakes was unacceptable in your eyes. Many times I wanted to tell you that I admired your desire to succeed, but sometimes I worried that you suffered from perfectionism, the belief that everything you did had to be perfect or there was a flaw in you as a person. I know now I should have told you that all accomplishments are the result of much trial and error, and that the errors we make are the stepping stones to our learning. Learning doesn't come from knowing the answers; it comes from finding out what we don't know and how we can improve. Sadly, our culture emphasizes the end result of most discoveries and achievements as if they were easy to attain. We don't usually hear about the thousands of attempts that failed before achieving some measure of success, and the perseverance demonstrated by those who worked months and years to finally find the answers that lay buried below the obvious. You were one of those who wanted to succeed, and now I wish I had supported you more with something as small as "I see that you are fascinated by robots." Just to validate your interests and efforts to learn on your own could have fueled your willingness to self-direct your desire to learn, if I had only known the power of hearing someone say "I notice you, I accept you for who you are, and I respect you as a student and an individual."

As the year continued to pass, I realized you were becoming a fluent English-speaker, but more than that, I could tell you thought about our class discussions in a deeper, more complex way. I remember having concerns before allowing you to ask questions because I knew I didn't always have answers that I felt were good enough to satisfy your passion for knowing and understanding the "why and how" about the topics of our discussion. The connections you made between ideas from one topic to another made me realize how different you were to most other students in the class. Years later I recognize how difficult it must have been to find other students who would listen to your concerns and questions with a real desire to understand and respond with thoughts of their own. I'm sure it was disappointing to have those "aha" moments when you found symbolic meanings or insight into something you read, but I often passed you by when you raised your hand. I thought I was giving others the chance to share answers so they'd stay engaged in the dialogue. I didn't consider what it might do to you emotionally to have no one to share your excitement, no one to celebrate your thinking or think along with you as you pieced your ideas together. I can't imagine how it must be for individuals like you who sit and think alone day after day, year after year without someone who listens and responds on a similar level or even acknowledges your ideas as worth consideration. I'm sure my classroom was a lonely place for you to spend a school year. Now that I look back I understand the reasons you withdrew from classroom interaction. I'm sure it became easier to look inward to find validation that you understood many things and felt deeply about situations we never imagined. I regret that I didn't see the importance of giving you opportunities to develop relationships with other students with similar interests or academic abilities that could spur your thinking to deeper levels both emotionally, socially, and intellectually. Now I understand how important it is to cluster gifted individuals into classrooms so they have peers with whom they can think and communicate even in the early years, before boredom and detachment become an issue.

Throughout my years as a teacher I succumbed to other stereotypical ideas about gifted students. I remember thinking that students who learned quickly should be capable and willing to tutor other students who were slower to understand. I assigned two other girls who I thought might benefit from your explanations for you to mentor. I thought they would be cooperative and eager to learn from someone their own age, but now I look back at those tutoring sessions and understand why you asked to be relieved from that responsibility. Just because you were quick to catch on to the concepts I taught did not mean you had the ability to think as the girls and figure out where they were making mistakes. Your mind worked differently, and I was naïve to think you could accomplish what was challenging for me as their teacher. The girls were less than gracious to you because they too were victims of cultural biases. You were a quick learner and intrinsically motivated, which may have threatened their self-esteem. As a result, you were excluded from the cliques that formed during free time and after school. Your eyes expressed your intense sensitivity to their criticism and rejection of you as a classmate. I wish I had been more proactive in guiding the students into getting to know you so they could have seen their assumptions that you were a "know-it-all" were inaccurate. I might have been able to prevent many misconceptions and prejudice that continued during that school year and possibly years later.

You are probably unaware that I kept up with your progress throughout high school. I was impressed by your willingness to take risks and accept challenges. You may not recall this conversation we had toward the end of the school the year you came to my class. You mentioned wanting to take a test to advance a year in math. I supported your desire to take the test to grade skip in math. Later in the week I asked if you had turned in the form to the principal, and you admitted that you changed your mind. At first I hesitated to ask why, but now I am so glad I did. You were reluctant to take the test because you were afraid to fail. Usually you didn't let a challenge stop you, but this time you acknowledged this meant so much to you and your parents. I took the opportunity to share a topic I had recently researched, the "growth mindset" by Dr. Carol Dweck at Stanford University. I explained that Dr. Dweck had identified two basic mindsets: the fixed mindset and the growth mindset. The fixed mindset dictates that our abilities are fixed. We are born with a specific intelligence that will not change no matter what we do to improve. On the other hand, the growth mindset promotes the idea that we have the power to change our intelligence through deliberate study and practice. People with growth mindsets believe they can control their destiny in life, whereas those with a fixed mindset believe they cannot change themselves or the situations they face. We talked on several occasions about how to adopt the growth mindset, and I watched as a different person developed inside of you. You changed your perception of success and failure as you took that test and failed the first time. I was worried that you might give up, but relieved you tried again and passed the second time. You reminded me of the lessons I taught about those who failed but decided it was just one way something didn't work. The failure didn't define you—it meant you tried again using a different strategy until you succeeded. It was a time I can recall saying, "Susanna, you were able to take a risk and prepare yourself to pass that exam, and it worked." I watched you smile and nod in agreement. This time we both had learned a great deal.

Now as I watch you walk across the stage to receive your high-school diploma, I realize how narrow-minded I had been years before when you first entered my classroom. Without conscious thought, I expected you would struggle to learn English, lag behind the class in reading, and my most egregious mistake was to expect you would never excel in academics. Fortunately I was wrong. I discovered you learned faster than I could teach. I have changed my attitude about gifted students and the responsibility I have to provide the appropriate education to all students. Some people assume gifted students will succeed regardless of the quality of instruction provided. This is not true. Gifted students deserve the best instruction possible to help them navigate social and emotional issues that prevent them from developing to their potential just as any other group of individuals. I have grown as an educator in experiencing what it is like to have a gifted student very different from the stereotype I expected. Now as you graduate with honors and have received more than one scholarship to college, I'm not sure who has learned the most … you or me.

Best wishes for your continued success,

Your 4th Grade Teacher

Dear Sam,

I wanted to take this opportunity to share with you a few important memories I have as your 4th grade teacher. Early in our year together I wondered who would survive. Our class enjoyed the spit wad contests you held at the back of the room with anyone who accepted your challenge: to launch the most spit wads into a trash can near my desk. Unfortunately, not all of the spit wads found the intended target; some must have been random launches because they landed on various individuals sitting close by. Not a day went by without an interruption stemming from your direction of the room. I will admit it was entertaining to watch from a distance the skill you had developed in rolling the pieces of paper so tightly before placing them on your tongue, then blowing them out with great force. I was amazed at your ability to gather the attention of so many students without capturing my eye. I often wondered what would have happened if you had put as much effort into finishing your assignments as you put into improving your aim in wad spitting.

You and I had many conversations about finishing your work. I tried everything I knew to convince you that goofing off was a poor choice. I made you sit alone at lunch in the cafeteria, and tried taking away your free time during recess. Nothing changed. Day after day I struggled with finding the way to make you complete your work on time. One day as I sat in the classroom exhausted from teaching, planning, and scouring my brain for new strategies that might prevent more interruptions, I realized I couldn't make you do anything. The only person who could make any real, lasting change was you, and that was unlikely unless you perceived a compelling reason to do so.

The day began like most. I began teaching fractions and decimals, and explaining how they were different ways of talking about parts of something. I tried to make the connection to percentages and how they were based on decimals. Most of the class looked lost, and I realized I had made a mistake in jumping too quickly from one concept to the other. I assumed you weren't listening, so I put the lesson away when I overheard you mention voting for the best hitter to ever play baseball. Being a baseball fan myself, I asked you who you thought would win, and then you began to quote baseball statistics unlike anyone I had ever heard. My interest continued to build while you expounded on a number of ways the list could be compiled. I could hardly contain my excitement to hear you compare the old players I grew up watching to young players that capture the attention of current fans. For the next several days, I tried to connect the daily lesson on decimals to the application in baseball. For the first time I could remember, you finished the math assignment and gladly invited others to sit around you as you worked the problems and explained the application to baseball and the strategy used to bring up new players and choose where to place a hitter in the team's line-up. It was an overnight change in your interest and participation in class. I felt like you had transformed into a gifted mathematical guru who had taken over Sam's body. For two weeks you focused on the daily math assignments, asking if you might share a digital presentation you had made to explain the game of baseball and how statistics were necessary for decision-making. At first, I thought the transformation was the result of introducing the topic of fractions and decimals to you, but fortunately I soon realized it wasn't me who was doing the teaching.

You didn't need my lesson on fractions or decimals. You understood those concepts long before I wrote my lesson plans. You not only understood decimals, you applied them to problems that sports teams face every day. Learning to identify a decimal or change a common fraction into a decimal wasn't your goal. Your goal was to determine how baseball owners, scouts, and managers make the decisions necessary to run a baseball team. Your understanding of how math is a tool to be applied to decision-making is the ultimate goal we all strive to attain. Yes, Sam, you are a gifted individual—I didn't see it because I wasn't giving you an opportunity to demonstrate your interests and abilities. I kept looking at the minute skills I thought you needed before I gave you a real problem to solve. After all, solving problems takes a lot of time, and I thought you needed a short leash, so to speak, so you could finish something I could grade. Isn't it ironic that you needed and craved a complex problem that provided a number of choices and processes to consider before coming to a conclusion? I never would have dreamed that you, Sam, could change from a spit wad champion to a data analyst during the course of a math class.

Again and again, I am reminded that I do not have all the knowledge needed to teach my students as I once thought. I am not an expert on every topic I teach, but I do need to allow students who show an interest to delve deeper by giving them tools and resources to explore. Most importantly, I need to allow them to experiment with their ideas and give them opportunities to fail and try again.

Sam, 8 years have passed and I watch as students gravitate to you as they did years ago. I wonder if you hid your abilities as a 4th grader because you believed your peers were more likely to admire your ability to be funny rather than being quick to learn. You enjoyed being a non-conformist in the eyes of most teachers, but I now see that conforming to the norm has never been your goal. When you were in my class I thought you didn't work to your potential. I see that my definition of your potential simply was not the same as yours. I also know it was never my job to make you "successful"—it is ultimately up to you to decide what success means for your life.

With best wishes for your future,

Your 4th Grade Teacher

From the Laboratory to the Classroom

- Demand that you, as a teacher, are given adequate resources to work with high-ability students. These students need special programming that is as labor-intensive as that for other special education learners. Work with high-ability students needs to be recognized and rewarded as part of the teaching workload.
- Allow your class to differentiate among levels of engagement with material. Give more challenging tasks to students who need them, after ensuring the child's agreement about viewing the challenge in terms of growth mindset. Challenge will provide high-ability children with crucial experiences in the use of intuition, cognitive flexibility, and understanding the limits of their knowledge.
- Create room for growth and failure for all of the students in your class. The opportunity for failure will be different for your high-ability students (e.g. not winning in a regional math contest), but it has to be there. Growth opportunities are necessary to encourage knowledge-seeking behavior. They can be larger assignments that engage the high-ability child outside the classroom, or group projects.
- Offer multiple varied experiential opportunities to your class (e.g. contests, practical engagements, industry observations, etc.). Ensure a variety of learning experiences to help individuals to find, and you to identify, their specific domains of high ability.
- High-ability students need social interaction with individuals who can provide them with emotional validation of their (different) ways of thinking, goals, and ideas. Allow students to interact with others regardless of age or curriculum standing (cross-grade "peer learning", mixed-age classrooms, etc., are excellent starters).

NOTE

1   These letters have been adapted from those written by Vicky K. Hinesley. Some of the names and details have been changed to protect the identities of all involved.

References

Austin, J. H. (1978). *Chase, Chance, and Creativity: The Lucky Art of Novelty.* New York: Columbia University Press.

Bassett, D., Yang, M., Wymbs, N.F., & Grafton, S.T. (2015). Learning-induced autonomy of sensorimotor systems. *Nature Neuroscience*, 18(5), 744–751.

Borland, J. H. (1989). *Planning and Implementing Programs for the Gifted.* New York: Teachers College Press.

Brant, A. M., Munakata, Y., Boomsma, D. I., DeFries, J. C., Haworth, C. M., Keller, M. C., Martin, N. G., McGue, M., Petrill, S. A., Plomin, R., Wadsworth, S. J., Wright, M. J., & Hewitt, J. K. (2013). The nature and nurture of high IQ: an extended sensitive period for intellectual development. *Psychological Science*, 24(8), 1487–1495.

Brumback, C. R., Low, K. A., Gratton, G., & Fabiani, M. (2004). Sensory ERPs predict differences in working memory span and fluid intelligence. *NeuroReport*, 15(2), 373–376.

Dweck, C. (2006). *Mindset: The New Psychology of Success.* New York: Random House, Inc.

Gilman, B. J., Lovecky, D. V., Kearney, K., Peters, D. B., Wasserman, J. D., Silverman, L. K. *et al.* (2013). Critical issues in the identification of gifted students with co-existing disabilities: the twice-exceptional. *Sage Open*, 3(3), 1–16.

Gray, J. R. & Thompson, P. M. (2004). Neurobiology of intelligence: science and ethics. *Nature Reviews: Neuroscience*, 5, 471–482.

Hausmann, R. & Hidalgo, C. A. (2011). The network structure of economic output. *Journal of Economic Growth*, 16(4), 309–342.

Malaia, E. & Newman, S. (2013) Neural bases of giftedness. In: J. A. Plucker & C. M. Callahan (Eds), *Critical Issues and Practices in Gifted Education: What the Research Says.* Waco, TX: Prufrock Press Inc.

Malaia, E., Wilbur, R. B., & Weber-Fox, C. (2009). ERP evidence for telicity effects on syntactic processing in garden-path sentences. *Brain and Language*, 108(3), 145–158.

Malaia, E., Ranaweera, R., Wilbur, R. B., & Talavage, T. M. (2012). Event segmentation in a visual language: neural bases of processing American Sign Language predicates. *NeuroImage*, 59(4), 4094–4101.

Malaia, E., Talavage, T., & Wilbur, R. B. (2014a) Functional connectivity in task-negative network of the Deaf: effects of sign language experience. *PeerJ*, 2, e446.

Malaia, E., Tommerdahl, J., & Mckee, F. W. (2014b) Deductive and heuristic reasoning processing markers in EEG. *Journal of Psycholinguistic Research*, 1–12.

Mantzaris, A. V., Bassett, D. S., Wymbs, N. F., Estrada, E., Porter, M. A., Mucha, P. J., Grafton, S. T., & Higham, D. J. (2013). Dynamic network centrality summarizes learning in the human brain. *Journal of Complex Networks*, 1(1), 83–92.

Montgomery, J. W., Magimairaj, B. M., & O'Malley, M. H. (2008). Role of working memory in typically developing children's complex sentence comprehension. *Journal of Psycholinguistic Research*, 37(5), 331–354.

Neihart, M. (2007). The socioaffective impact of acceleration and ability grouping recommendations for best practice. *Gifted Child Quarterly*, 51(4), 330–341.

Newman, S. D., Malaia, E., Seo, R., & Cheng, H. (2013). The effect of individual differences in working memory capacity on sentence comprehension: an fMRI study. *Brain Topography*, 26(3), 458–467.

Peterson, J. S. (2015). School counselors and gifted kids: respecting both cognitive and affective. *Journal of Counseling & Development*, 93(2), 153–162.

Richardson, T. M. & Benbow, C. P. (1990). Long-term effects of acceleration on the social-emotional adjustment of mathematically precocious youths. *Journal of Educational Psychology*, 82(3), 464–470.

Sternberg, R. J. & Kaufman, S. B. (Eds) (2011). *The Cambridge Handbook of Intelligence.* New York: Cambridge University Press.

Subotnik, R. F., Olszewski-Kubilius, P., & Worrell, F. C. (2011). Rethinking giftedness and gifted education: a proposed direction forward based on psychological science. *Psychological Science in the Public Interest*, 12(1), 3–54.

Tucker-Drob, E. M. & Briley, D. A. (2014). Continuity of genetic and environmental influences on cognition across the life span: a meta-analysis of longitudinal twin and adoption studies. *Psychological Bulletin,* 140(4), 949–979.

13

EDUCATIONAL APPROACHES FOR STUDENTS EXPERIENCING LEARNING DIFFICULTIES

Anne Bellert and Lorraine Graham

SCHOOL OF EDUCATION, SOUTHERN CROSS UNIVERSITY, AND
MELBOURNE GRADUATE SCHOOL OF EDUCATION, UNIVERSITY OF MELBOURNE

Introduction

This chapter focuses on the strategies and approaches of effective teaching and learning for students who experience learning difficulties. This "special student group" is both diverse and variable, and the implementation of effective classroom teaching and learning strategies to meet the needs of these students has the potential both to prevent them from falling further behind and to reduce the impact of learning difficulties during their school years and over their lifespan. A considerable body of work from intervention research in education and psychology informs this discussion, especially with regard to effective teaching strategies and approaches suitable for these students (e.g. Baker *et al.*, 2002; Geary, 2004; Kroesbergen & van Luit, 2003; Swanson & O'Connor, 2009; Swanson & Hoskyn, 1998; Torgesen, 2002; Vaughn *et al.*, 2000, 2010; Wolf & Katzir-Cohen, 2001). However, this chapter's focus will be primarily on regular classroom teaching practices that effective teachers employ in supporting students with learning difficulties to engage with grade-level curriculum.

In Australia, as the forthcoming discussion will explain, intervention programs are not consistently available in schools for students experiencing learning difficulties, especially after the first few years of schooling. Subsequently, "first" teaching and learning in regular classrooms is where the research from education and psychology, and new sources of information from other fields related to the science of learning, can potentially have the most impact and make the greatest difference in improving educational outcomes for students who are experiencing learning difficulties.

The following discussion sits broadly within the perspective of sustainable education that advocates holistic and relational views of education and learning (Sterling, 2001, 2008). Sustainable learning (Graham *et al.*, 2015) is a conceptualization of effective teaching and learning for students with additional learning needs that incorporates the overarching frameworks of equity (learning for all), relevance (teaching that matters), and sustainability (learning that lasts). Within this construct, individual difference and diversity in students' learning (e.g. developmental readiness, learning capabilities, and need for learning support) are accepted as part of the normal ecology of classrooms, schools, and communities. Hence, difference and diversity are to be expected in classrooms, and teaching and learning should be designed from the outset to accommodate variability, rather than viewing students with learning difficulties as requiring "add-on" considerations in a one size fits all curriculum. This is an important perspective to incorporate into the science of learning—that students who experience learning difficulties are not viewed as deficient, but rather as representing part of the diversity that exists in schools and in society more broadly. Sustainable learning provides a powerful framework for orchestrating effective teaching practices that respond to individual learning needs, and for using resources effectively.

This chapter examines learning difficulties from educational and cognitive psychology perspectives, and proposes three broad approaches that are known to be effective in supporting classroom learning and participation for students who are experiencing learning difficulties. These approaches are differentiation, direct instruction and strategy instruction, and teaching for self-regulation and metacognition. The chapter concludes with a discussion of the promises, threats, and implications, for students with learning difficulties and their teachers, of effective translation of cognitive neuroscience from the laboratory to the classroom.

Learning Difficulties

The field of learning difficulties is beset by definitional issues, not only because of the varying terminology used internationally and in the overarching disciplines of psychology and education, but also due to the profusion of terms with overlapping meanings—for example, learning disability, learning difficulty, specific learning difficulty, learning delays, and dyslexia or dyscalculia. In this chapter the term "learning difficulties" is used—as it is most commonly adopted in Australia—to refer broadly to those students who experience problems learning at the same rate as their age peers.

Key areas of difficulty experienced by students with learning difficulties include reading, writing, language comprehension and expression, understanding arithmetic concepts and skills, and problem solving. At least 20% of school students are considered to have such problems at some time during their schooling (Ashman & Elkins, 2009). Of these students, approximately 5% are considered to have notable learning disabilities in a specific area, most commonly reading (Westwood & Graham, 2000).

There is no assumption that students who are experiencing learning difficulties have a disability, although some certainly may. In fact, students who do not have a disability or other condition and yet experience difficulties in learning academic skills comprise the largest and most rapidly increasing group of students with additional learning needs (Bentley & Cazaly, 2015; Kavale & Forness, 2000; Westwood, 2015). Many students with a disability also experience learning difficulties, and, in some contexts, so do students with English as an additional language or dialect, indigenous students, students from diverse cultural backgrounds, and, notably, students who have not been well served by their past educational provision.

Although the scale of difficulty in learning is not precisely defined by the use of the term "learning difficulties" in Australia, the notion of educationally significant differences (Westwood, 2013, p. 11) is relevant. Differences in literacy and numeracy capability may be small at first—for example, students who on school entry cannot identify rhyming words or order numbers as proficiently as their peers. As time passes and differences persist, however, the gap between students with learning difficulties and their peers grows. Subsequently, the composition of any given school grade may represent a 5- to 6-year achievement gap between the highest and lowest achieving students (Masters, 2013).

As the term "learning difficulties" tends to be used as a catch-all category, students with learning difficulties are a diverse group. Their low achievement in academic subjects may result from any combination of factors that can affect an individual's ability to learn and participate. Although factors within learners and within their environments may contribute to learning difficulties, it must also be acknowledged that ineffective or inadequate teaching, poor curricula, and poor teacher–student relationships contribute to, and can exacerbate, educational risk (Westwood, 2004). When teachers have high expectations of all their learners, and expect that achievement can always be enhanced, students perform and achieve better (Kaplan & Owens, 2013). For all students, high-quality teaching is a singularly powerful influence on their achievement (Hattie, 2003).

In terms of additional support for students who are experiencing learning difficulties, definitional issues have an impact on service provision. Broadly speaking, in Australia, targeted resources are allocated to schools for the learning and support needs of students with a confirmed disability (i.e. intellectual disability, physical disability, vision impairment, hearing impairment, mental health conditions, or autism). Provisions for students with other additional learning needs, including learning difficulties, executive function disorders (e.g. attention deficit hyperactivity disorder, or ADHD), language disorders, or dyslexia are usually derived from school-based resources, based on models that offer combined consultation and professional learning opportunities for teachers, and limited, intermittent direct support to students. Even when resources are available to provide intensive intervention support, such measures may not be implemented with efficacy, as school-developed programs may be piecemeal, poorly sequenced, or inappropriately targeted, and furthermore they may not draw on critical research findings. This is despite the fact that sound, evidence-based programs are available (see, for example, Buckingham *et al.*, 2012; Graham & Pegg, 2011), although the costs associated with implementing such programs with fidelity can be a barrier to their use. Consequently, many students progress through their school years under the "soft" tag of learning difficulties and do not receive enough appropriate, evidence-informed intervention to enable them to overcome and/or learn to work around, their difficulties.

Australia's "long tail" of underachievement in literacy and numeracy (Commonwealth of Australia, 2007) and declining rates of adult literacy (Australian Bureau of Statistics, 2008) attest to the pressing need for better targeting of available resources, so that evidence-based practices can be sustainably implemented to achieve equity, with real and lasting impact. Whereas competent learners can be successful when given instruction of variable quality, students with learning difficulties are particularly vulnerable to poor pedagogy, and are disproportionately disadvantaged by ineffective teachers (Petty, 2009; Sanders & Horn, 1998; Sanders & Rivers, 1996; Strain & Hoyson, 2000). Clearly, the quality of the daily work of teachers matters for students with learning difficulties. It influences not only learning outcomes, but also long-term vocational outcomes and standards of living. Higher levels of literacy and school completion enhance opportunities for personal fulfilment, meaningful work, and increased earnings, all of which are key factors associated with workforce participation, productivity, and lifelong well-being (Coulombe *et al.*, 2004; Masters, 2007).

Given the challenges faced by students with learning difficulties, the translation of the learning sciences from the laboratory to the classroom is of great promise for teachers, particularly if it is aimed at securing the best possible initial classroom teaching for all students.

Otherwise, the profession may remain vulnerable to fads because teachers' work takes place in classroom contexts where "everything works" (to a degree) and pseudoscience enhances "the allure of everything neuro" (Anderson & Della Sala, 2012, p. 6) at the cost of implementing effective, evidence-based instructional approaches.

Cognitive Characteristics of Students with Learning Difficulties

Students experience learning difficulties for a wide range of reasons. Despite these differences, there are some common cognitive "characteristics" that students with learning difficulties share. Generally, students with learning difficulties are inefficient in the ways that they go about the process of learning—they use immature or inefficient strategies and do not change or adapt these readily enough when required, resulting in repeated errors that undermine their confidence and motivation. Gersten *et al.* (2001) describe such patterns of behavior as difficulties of strategic processing and metacognition, and emphasize that these are issues of "inefficiency rather than deficiency" (p. 280). Students who are experiencing learning difficulties also have memory problems, resulting in difficulty accessing and coordinating knowledge encountered previously, and the flexible use of that knowledge (Ashbaker & Swanson, 1996), with short-term memory, working memory, and long-term memory all potentially implicated. Unsurprisingly, after repeatedly experiencing difficulty with learning tasks and low achievement, these students also display patterns of behavior and thinking that are detrimental to learning, including task avoidance, inadequate inhibitory control, lack of persistence, and poor self-efficacy (Chan & Dally, 2001; Greulich *et al.*, 2014; Harris *et al.*, 2004).

A key cognitive attribute of students who are experiencing learning difficulties, highlighted primarily by the work of Swanson and colleagues (see Swanson, 2008; Swanson & Sachse-Lee, 2001; Swanson & Siegel, 2001; Ashbaker & Swanson, 1996; Keeler & Swanson, 2001), is the apparent relationship between inefficient working memory function and learning disabilities. Poor working memory capacity, with constraints on processing and functioning, is a common underlying factor for students who are experiencing delays because of learning difficulties (Gathercole & Alloway, 2007; Keeler & Swanson, 2001). These limitations in working memory, linked to deficiencies in executive processes such as memory, attention, and cognitive flexibility, present significant obstacles to successful learning and participation in academic work.

Cognitive load theory (Sweller, 1988, 1994, 2010) also suggests that one reason why some students have difficulty learning new or challenging material is linked to the demands of the task and the learning processes on working memory. When learning new information is a complex task with a challenging number of elements (bearing in mind that even simple tasks can be complex for young or inexperienced learners), it draws on working memory processes and functions that can be too demanding for some learners. As educational psychologists, Sweller and his colleagues are concerned with identifying how instruction can be designed to reduce the "cognitive load" of tasks in order to facilitate the working memory processes required for learning academic work. Examples of instructional design strategies that support students who experience the kind of cognitive attributes that impede learning are listed in Table 13.1.

Teachers' use of strategies for adapting methods, resources, and instructional approaches offers students with learning difficulties more of a "level playing field" by ensuring that they

TABLE 13.1 Teaching strategies to minimize cognitive load for students who are experiencing learning difficulties.

Student cognitive characteristics	Responsive instructional design strategies
Inappropriate or inefficient use of strategies	• Model efficient strategies in a supportive environment • Use teacher and peer "think-alouds" • Teach by showing, demonstrating, and questioning • Discuss if, when, or why strategies *do not* work • Encourage reflection and talk about learning processes
Difficulty recalling previously encountered knowledge	• Begin every lesson with a review of previous content • Make strong connections with the students' previous knowledge, interests, and experiences • Provide explicit, repeated review and practice • Use mnemonics, page traces, and other memory aids • Provide visual cues and other sensory cues to support recall
Working memory constraints	• Teach and review cognitive strategies and procedures • Use advanced organizers (preview and pre-teach) • Start with an overview, and then chunk (break up) the content or task into achievable steps; conclude with a holistic review • Use graphic organisers (concept maps, timelines, etc.) • Provide scaffolds or pro formas, especially for writing tasks
Limitations in attention and task persistence	• Ensure that the task set is within the students' capabilities • Reward effort, strategy use, and achievement • Break tasks up into steps, acknowledge progress, and provide feedback after each step • Provide short lesson segments with breaks in between • Provide feedback that focuses on effort and strategies • Use individual goal-setting and reward schedules

are given increased opportunities from which to learn the same curriculum as their peers. Such approaches also offer teachers guidance on designing initial instructional experiences that are more inclusive and learning focused, rather than looking to cater for learning difficulties by simplifying the complexity of the content or offering an alternative curriculum. Students who are experiencing learning difficulties are disadvantaged if teachers offer them alternative "busy-work" tasks while the other students are engaged in challenging, novel, or innovative learning opportunities. Indeed, in many instances it is preferable for teachers not to modify what they teach, but how they teach it. An understanding of the cognitive demands of instructional tasks can help teachers to make more appropriate adjustments—for example, by presenting new information in small increments, or explaining new content using a concept map to link it to what the students already know. Modification of the curriculum to suit the learning needs of individual students is, of course, necessary at times. However, because of the impact of perceived low expectations on self-efficacy, care must be taken to avoid increasing the achievement gap and unnecessarily restricting opportunities for students with learning difficulties to engage in complex and higher-order thinking (Westwood, 2013).

Supporting Students with Learning Difficulties in the Regular Classroom: Applications

When every learner is considered in terms of capabilities rather than deficits, and when curricula are constructed from the outset to offer multiple ways of engaging with content and demonstrating understanding, "abelist" assumptions (Cologon, 2013) become less influential and authentic inclusion may prevail. The role of school systems and teachers, and perhaps more broadly the science of learning, is to remove as many barriers as possible so that all students routinely encounter the best opportunities to learn. From this perspective, the focus is on enabling students to learn through effective teaching, and supporting them to overcome, or "work around", the cognitive characteristics that impede progress. Three important applications of research progress towards these overarching goals: using differentiation of and adjustments to instruction; direct instruction and strategy instruction; and teaching for self-regulation and metacognition.

Using Differentiation of and Adjustments to Instruction

Acknowledging that students are different from each other and that their differences matter in terms of how they engage with content and learning activities is an important starting point for planning and delivering effective pedagogy. The kind of classroom teaching that *really* matters for students with learning difficulties is effectively differentiated instruction—a genuine response to diversity that can be simply defined as "teaching things differently according to observed differences in learners" (Westwood, 2001, p. 5). Differentiation addresses the needs of all students, from those who struggle to those who excel, by tailoring teaching and learning according to educationally important student needs. It follows, then, that differentiation is an essential foundational approach to effective pedagogy for students who are experiencing learning difficulties. The facets of instructional practice that can be adjusted through differentiation include approaches to teaching content, assessment methods and response modes, classroom organization procedures, grouping practices, and the duration and intensity level of teacher interactions.

Tomlinson (2001, p. 1), a leading U.S. author on the topic of differentiation, states that differentiated instruction "means 'shaking up' what goes on in the classroom so that students have multiple options for taking in information, making sense of ideas, and expressing what they learn." According to Tomlinson, differentiated instruction is a careful combination of individual, group, and whole-class instruction that is proactive, student centered, and grounded in assessment. It provides multiple instructional pathways related to content, process, and product so that students encounter different approaches to what they learn, how they learn, it and how they demonstrate their learning.

Differentiation recognizes that important differences exist among learners, and that these differences must be responded to so that students can maximize their learning opportunities. It should be acknowledged, though, that teaching increasingly diverse classes is challenging! As Rose (2001, p. 147) has noted, "The teaching methods and practices required for the provision of effective inclusion are easier to identify than they are to implement." Taking this further, Westwood (2005, p. 69) has observed that "in countries where differentiation has been implemented there is accumulating evidence that teachers have great difficulty in applying differentiation strategies in practice, and particularly in sustaining their use over time."

Research that has examined what happens in classrooms, through either self-report questionnaires or observational studies, confirms that the most commonly used differentiation strategies tend to be those that do not require prior planning, but instead are instigated as on-the-spot differentiation within the flow of a general whole-class lesson. On-the-spot differentiation is the appropriate adjustment of instructional factors at the point of need—for example, repeating or simplifying instructions, providing extra support, or giving specific guidance to some students (Chan *et al.*, 2002; Yuen *et al.*, 2005).

A paradox exists between the variety of differentiation strategies available and the desirability of a simple approach for making decisions about when and how to differentiate to meet students' needs. More than two or three strategies actively in play at the same time in a lesson have the potential to confuse learners, unless adjustments are made skilfully. As a general teaching heuristic, applying the simplicity principle means that differentiated instruction is provided only when necessary, and should be faded as soon as possible to ensure that all of the students have as much access as possible to the curriculum.

Although there is no one "right" way to plan for and deliver differentiated instruction, there certainly is a singular "wrong" way to approach differentiation, and that is not to plan for it at all. The starting point for planning effective differentiation is to consider the nominated learning outcomes, the diversity, strengths, and needs of the learners, what they already know, and what they need to learn next. Some broad approaches for planning for differentiation are presented in Table 13.2.

TABLE 13.2 Planning for differentiation to support effective teaching for students with learning difficulties.

Differentiation approaches for planning	*Implementation prompts*
Planning inclusively	• Use a structured and sequenced learning curriculum to identify specific learning outcomes • Pre-test to establish prior knowledge. What do students need to learn next? • Identify evidence-based practice that represents the best ways to present this content and these concepts to this group of learners within this learning environment • Consider task difficulty. Ensure that all students can demonstrate progress in this learning sequence
Identifying clear learning intentions and success criteria	• Ensure that the students know and can articulate what it is the teacher wants them to learn, and why this learning matters • Make clear to the students what the success criteria are. Show what success looks like (e.g. provide annotated work samples) • Use learning taxonomies (e.g. SOLO) to explain and identify student progress in thinking and learning • Use personalized success criteria, as progress or achievement is not the same for every student
Using routine procedures for interactions and organization	• Give clear instructions • Manage transitions • Provide appropriate feedback on learning process, progress, and product • Implement classroom management that focuses on behavior for learning

Implementing effective differentiation in the classroom is now the expected "work" of all teachers, even beginning teachers. Differentiation is an approach to instruction that permeates all key aspects of classroom learning—teaching, assessment, and feedback—rather than an identifiable set of strategies or activities. Approaches that can be used to support the delivery of differentiated instruction in the classroom are described in Table 13.3.

TABLE 13.3 Approaches for "doing" differentiation as part of effective classroom teaching for students with learning difficulties.

Differentiation approaches for teaching★	Implementation prompts
Implementing learning activities with flexibility	• Provide content variations (e.g. more or less, different levels of complexity, different modalities) • Use a variety of approaches (e.g. explicit teaching, peer learning, frequent and innovative practice opportunities, and problem solving) when the "usual" way is not working • Ensure relatedness to previous learning, prior experiences, and background knowledge • Maintain high expectations for all students in terms of progress and achievement levels
Probing understanding	• Observe • Listen • Question • Notice help seeking
Re-teaching and extending	• Use formative assessment information to identify students who "don't get it." Consider how to best change instruction, and then re-teach specific content to small groups • Use pre-test or formative assessment information to identify students whose work shows mastery
Using "different" ways: take a fresh look at the same content using another approach, different examples, or a specific intervention	• Implement reciprocal teaching routines ("take turns teaching") • Reorganize learning groups (change group sizes, configurations, and roles within the groups) • Consider innovative and creative uses of the available resources • Vary the mode of response required to allow for different ways to demonstrate learning outcomes • Provide a variety of options for students to show what they have learned, including an alternative format for assessment tasks • Vary the strategies and thinking aids to enhance and enliven explanations (e.g. use stories or metaphors, non-examples and binary opposites, worked examples, images, and multimedia)
Adjusting on the spot	• Adjust task demands (e.g. allow more or less time) • Nominate peers to provide explanations and examples • Provide direct teacher help during the lesson • Change the level or type of ICT use within the task

★ "Teaching" encompasses teaching, assessment, and feedback.

Importantly, for effective teaching and learning for all students, evaluation is a vital final phase that needs to be included in the instructional cycle. Both teachers and students need to incorporate evaluation into effective, differentiated teaching and learning. For teachers, this approach is perhaps best expressed by the first of Hattie's eight teacher mind frames (ways of thinking for teachers and school leaders) (Hattie, 2012), stated in the phrase "Know thy impact." This mind frame shifts the focus of student progress and achievement away from student factors (ability, motivation, effort, etc.) and teaching strategies to focus directly on the teacher—the effectiveness of the teaching and feedback provided to the students, and the resulting growth in student learning outcomes. Questions that teachers may ask in order to evaluate their instructional impact can target the magnitude of the impact, the differential impact for individuals or groups of students, the impact of various differentiated approaches, whether another approach would have had more impact, and the range of evidence—including feedback from students about teaching—that is available to support the evaluation.

Students' evaluation of their own learning progress, including making predictions about their future achievement levels, inherently involves students setting goals for their learning and progress. Once students achieve or exceed their expectations, they gain confidence in their ability to learn. The instructional approach of facilitating students' prediction of their own achievement was found to be the most powerful influence on student achievement in Hattie's meta-analysis (Hattie, 2009). Students' self-evaluation of their learning may focus on progress compared with previous performance, progress compared with nominated success criteria, strategies tried and the effectiveness of those strategies, and ratings for self-regulation factors such as time on task, persistence, and self-efficacy. An overview of approaches for evaluating the impact of teaching is provided in Table 13.4.

Commonly, classroom teachers may group students to facilitate differentiation, and although this approach can enable teachers to better target their instruction, the idea has been somewhat confounded by linking differentiation with the neuromyth of "learning styles", with proponents advocating differentiated teaching and learning activities based on identified learning preferences (see, for example, Gregory & Chapman, 2013; Sprenger, 2008). However, as there is insufficient evidence to support learning styles as a useful

TABLE 13.4 Evaluating instruction and differentiation.

Approaches for evaluation	Implementation prompts
Following through with data	• Teachers can compare pre-test and post-test scores and review anecdotal records, observations, other test scores, work samples, and verbal or written feedback from the students in order to gauge student learning and evaluate the impact of their teaching • Students can graph performance on basic academic skills, collect work examples to illustrate their progress, and participate in self-assessment and peer assessment procedures
Reflecting and refining	• Ask yourself "Was this differentiated instruction effective? Did it have an appropriate impact on student learning?" • Undertake reflection "in action" (thinking on your feet) and "on action" (retrospective reflection, or thinking after the event)

instructional concept for planning and delivering differentiated instruction (Landrum & McDuffie, 2010), this approach should be assiduously avoided. Similarly, grouping for differentiated instruction based on ability should also be carefully considered, as there is evidence to indicate that ability grouping is an ineffective practice (Baines, 2013; Hattie, 2009), and the risk of presenting students with learning difficulties with an impoverished curriculum, beset by low expectations (as described earlier), is amplified. Appropriate considerations to underpin flexible student grouping for differentiated instruction include students' readiness, interests, preferences, strengths, and needs (Rock *et al.*, 2008).

Direct Instruction and Strategy Instruction

Experiencing ongoing difficulties in acquiring basic academic skills undoubtedly evokes frustration for some affected students and has a negative impact on their academic self-efficacy. They may well observe their peers using well-developed academic skills, seemingly effortlessly, to successfully participate in and contribute to teaching and learning activities. Yet even when a topic or subject is of particular interest to students with learning difficulties, or their effort and motivation to succeed exceeds that of their peers, they may be unable to achieve to the same level because of underlying, often unidentified, processing difficulties. Classroom teachers may also be disheartened when they encounter students who struggle to read or fully understand a carefully chosen text, or who have difficulty recalling and applying recently taught information, strategies, or procedures. Both for students with learning difficulties and for their teachers, "opting out" of authentic teaching and learning by presenting a limited curriculum and succumbing to low expectations for progress and success may offer a tempting alternative. However, as the discussion above identified, such options have potentially dire consequences for students throughout their lifespan, and also undermine the reputation of the teaching profession.

Accordingly, it is incumbent on teachers, when working with students who are experiencing learning difficulties, to consistently implement approaches to instruction that are most likely to be effective, based on evidence from educational and psychological research. There is now sound evidence to support the notion that student-centered or discovery-learning instructional approaches are not effective in improving learning outcomes for students with learning difficulties (Baker *et al.*, 2002; Ellis, 2005; Kirschner *et al.*, 2006; Pincott, 2004; Rowe, 2006), and consequently such approaches either should not be implemented (Clark *et al.*, 2012), or implementation should be preceded and scaffolded by direct instruction (Martin, 2015; Rowe, 2006). In contrast, direct instructional approaches have a sound evidence base to support their efficacy in improving learning outcomes (Arief *et al.*, 2013; Kirschner *et al.*, 2006; Purdie & Ellis 2005; Rowe, 2006), and are noted to be particularly effective for students with learning difficulties (Adams & Carnine, 2003; Ellis, 2005). All teachers, across all grade levels and in all curriculum areas, need to be proficient in delivering direct instructional approaches, and should implement them frequently, especially when working with students with learning difficulties.

Direct instruction "is a systematic method for presenting learning material in small steps, pausing to check for understanding and eliciting active and successful participation from all students" (Rosenshine, 1986, p. 60). Direct instruction is especially applicable when teaching new or difficult information, and when content is critical to subsequent learning (Mercer *et al.*, 1996). Other terms, including teacher-directed instruction, explicit instruction, guided instruction, and instructivism, are used to describe variants of direct instruction. Direct and explicit instruction can take many forms, including highly scripted lessons focusing on mastery of content, lessons with demonstration and practice routines, and lessons that use supports such as graphic organizers or specific scaffolding strategies to help students to perform a task or procedure. Direct and explicit instructional approaches commonly feature fast-paced lessons, and require iterative interactions between students and the teacher. Although direct instruction is not a singular procedure, lessons commonly contain key sequential components, as described below.

- *Scaffolding learning.* Before teaching, plan how to support student learning:
    - What do the students know now, and what do they need to learn next? Use a pre-test or activity to gauge the students' current performance.
    - Aim for clarity. What do the students need to do before, during, and after the task?
    - Anticipate common errors and develop a procedure for error correction.
    - Develop a routine to acknowledge progress and effort.
    - Consider how to make connections with the students' prior learning and experiences.
    - Establish how high expectations of success for all students will be communicated.
- *Targeting learning intentions.* Clearly communicate to the students what they are going to learn, and how they will know when they have learned it:
    - Discuss and display the learning outcome, in accessible language.
    - Use acronyms such as WALT (we are learning to), WALHT (we are learning how to), and WILF (what I'm looking for).
    - Show the students what the task looks like when it is satisfactorily completed. For example, provided an annotated work sample indicating the target new knowledge, skill, or concept.
- *Delivering information.* Explaining and teaching critical content most commonly relies on teacher talk, modeling, and demonstration (at times augmented by peer contributions):
    - Consider "scripting" this instructional input part of the lesson prior to teaching, so that what needs to be said has already been "thought through" to specifically target student learning needs.
    - Focus exclusively on aspects of content directly related to the outcome.
    - Break down tasks into steps, and then provide step-by-step demonstrations and explanations.
    - Sequence conceptual knowledge from easy (known) to hard (new).
    - Provide and elicit examples and non-examples.
    - Include metacognitive strategies—that is, not just what to do but how to think about and approach the task, and what to do if students get "stuck."
    - Ensure that the duration of instructional input is considered and the pacing is brisk, to avoid too much teacher talk.
- *Questioning to check understanding.* Use questioning to promote student interaction and to gauge student learning:
    - Require the students to respond frequently, using a variety of response modes.
    - Ask questions that the students will be able to answer. Avoid the use of trick questions or trying to "catch out" students.
    - Use strategies that randomly select students (with some discretion) to answer questions, rather than having them raise their hand to be selected.

- Use response cards or devices, such as mini whiteboards, true–false or yes–no cards, and appropriate technology, so that the whole group can respond simultaneously, providing the teacher with instant feedback.
- *Providing the opportunity for practice.* During and after the information delivery stage of the lesson, provide opportunities for guided and independent practice of the target knowledge or skill:
  - Practice both previously encountered (known) and new knowledge and skills, as appropriate.
  - Use a variety of modes—individual, small group, and whole class.
  - Use a variety of approaches—oral, written, and demonstrations.
  - Consider how technology can be incorporated into practice routines.
  - Monitor progress resulting from practice, and ensure that this information is available to the students.
- *Seeking proof of learning.* After instruction and practice, ensure that the students can generalize the new knowledge or skill:
  - Situate the new knowledge or skill in a different context—for example, in a different topic.
  - Make links between the new knowledge and everyday living situations.
  - "Turn it around" by having the students set problems, or providing the students with "the answer" and asking them to create a relevant problem.
  - Have the students complete a formative or summative assessment task.
- *Evaluating the impact of instruction.* Both students and teachers reflect on the effectiveness of teaching and learning (see Table 13.4).

In a series of influential meta-analyses, Swanson and colleagues (e.g. Swanson, 1999, Swanson *et al.*, 1996, Swanson & Hoskyn, 1998) established that two models of instruction, namely direct instruction and strategy instruction, had the greatest potential to improve learning outcomes, and that when combined these approaches are particularly powerful and effective. Although most of the meta-analyses were linked to reading, Swanson *et al.* (1996) found no significant differences across domains of reading, spelling, and mathematics. This indicated that direct instruction and strategy instruction are generally effective for students who are experiencing learning difficulties, regardless of the domain. Effective teaching for students with learning difficulties requires emphasis on content (direct instruction) and on teaching "how to" (strategy instruction). Students with learning difficulties require consistent, repeated instruction about how to appropriately select and implement learning strategies. Importantly, such strategy instruction also needs to include a focus on identifying when a strategy is not working, ceasing to use inefficient strategies, and providing motivation and direction to try a more appropriate strategy. Information about how to effectively teach learning strategies is summarized below.

- *Preparation.* Develop the students' metacognitive awareness and self-knowledge:
  - Discuss the strategies that the students already use to complete specific tasks.
  - Interview small groups of students about how they complete tasks successfully.
  - Administer simple learning strategy questionnaires to see how often the students use particular strategies for particular tasks.
  - Use a thinking-aloud format to observe how the students approach general and specific tasks.

- *Explicit instruction.* Teach the strategy explicitly:
  - Model strategy application by thinking aloud through a task.
  - Name the strategy and refer to it consistently by that name.
  - Explain how the strategy will help.
  - Describe when, how, and on what kinds of tasks the strategy is useful.
  - Ask the students for examples of when the strategy might not be useful.
- *Practice.* Provide many opportunities for strategy practice during complex activities:
  - Solving mathematical problems.
  - Predicting, recalling, questioning, and summarizing to develop comprehension.
  - Analyzing the results of science experiments.
  - Writing different texts for different purposes.
- *Self-assessment.* Develop the students' metacognitive awareness of what strategies work for them and why, by using self-assessment activities:
  - Debrief after strategy use (for example, use the questions "Why?" and "Why not?"), and compare the students' use of strategies within peer groups.
  - Write reflections in learning logs about effective strategy use.
  - Compare the students' performance on similar tasks with and without the use of particular strategies.
  - Have students rate their confidence levels with regard to their strategy use.
- *Support.* Provide support for the transfer and generalization of strategies to new tasks or settings:
  - Scaffold independent strategy use by gradually reducing reminders.
  - Give descriptively encouraging feedback when students independently use an appropriate strategy.
  - Analyze and discuss strategies that individual students find effective for certain tasks.
  - Analyze and discuss strategies that individual students find ineffective for certain tasks.
  - Hold "thought-storm" sessions in which the students brainstorm all of the possible uses for the strategies that they are learning (adapted from Centre for Advanced Research on Language Acquisition [CARLA], 2014; Wong & Butler, 2012; Wong et al., 2008).

Direct instruction and strategy instruction are generally effective instructional approaches for teachers to implement for students with learning difficulties, regardless of the content area.

Teaching for Self-Regulation and Metacognition

The development of self-regulated learners is a major goal of schooling, and is particularly relevant for students with learning difficulties. Self-regulated learners are those who are engaged in an active constructive process in which they set goals for their learning and then attempt to monitor, regulate, and control their cognition, motivation, and behavior, guided and constrained by their goals and the contextual features in the environment (Pintrich, 2000). Autonomous learners who are sensitive to their own thinking and to the learning environment, and who are able to regulate their own behavior in relation to appropriate goals, make very effective learners. In fact, it was the recognition that although all learners may have particular self-management skills, their use of them is inconsistent and inefficient at times that led to the formulation of the concept of metacognition (Brown, 1980; Flavell, 1976). Flavell's conception of metacognition consists of two interrelated factors—self-awareness and self-regulation—which support an individual's effective learning.

The emphasis in recent models of effective learning has shifted to self-regulation as the overarching concept within which metacognition operates alongside motivational dimensions such as attributions and a sense of self-efficacy. Graham and Berman (2012) proposed an adapted version of Pintrich's model of self-regulated learning, in which learners are influenced by both affect and motivation as they demonstrate behaviors and strategic functioning within a particular learning context, as depicted in Table 13.5. Teachers can use this framework to guide their support of students with learning difficulties through the phases of planning, monitoring, encouraging students' independence, and reflecting on evidence of self-regulation, and also as a way of making the behaviors of independent learners explicit for older students.

Generally, students with learning difficulties have constrained awareness of their cognitive processes as learners. For these students, metacognition is slow to develop, tends to be less sophisticated, and needs to be fostered through explicit instruction (Wong & Wong, 1986; Wong et al., 1996). Indeed, many learners may have difficulty assessing whether learning has

TABLE 13.5 Adapted version of Pintrich's model of self-regulated learning (Pintrich, 2000).

| Phases | Possible areas for regulation | | | |
	Cognition	Motivation/affect	Behavior	Context
1. Forethought, planning, and activation	Target goal setting Prior content and knowledge activation Metacognitive knowledge activation	Adoption of goal orientation Efficacy judgments Ease of learning judgments Perceptions of task difficulty Task value activation Interest activation	Time and effort planning Planning for self-observations of behavior	Perceptions of task Perceptions of context
2. Monitoring	Metacognitive awareness and monitoring of cognition	Awareness and monitoring of motivation and affect	Awareness and monitoring of effort, time use, and need for help Self-observation of behavior	Monitoring and changing task and context conditions
3. Control	Selection and adaptation of cognitive strategies for learning and thinking	Selection and adaptation of strategies for managing motivation and affect	Increase or decrease in effort Persist or give up Help-seeking behavior	Change or renegotiate task Change or leave context
4. Reaction and reflection	Cognitive judgments Attributions	Affective reactions Attributions	Choice behavior	Evaluation of task Evaluation of context

been achieved because "conditions that enhance performance during learning can fail to support long-term retention and transfer, whereas other conditions that appear to create difficulties and slow the acquisition process can enhance long-term retention and transfer" (Bjork *et al.*, 2013, p. 438). This is especially so for students with learning difficulties.

Overall, it is important to acknowledge the research-based finding that students with learning difficulties have significant difficulties with "strategic processing and metacognition" (Gersten *et al.*, 2001, p. 280). This perspective supports the usefulness of instruction that focuses on teaching cognitive and metacognitive strategies. Like cognition, metacognition is developmental—both thinking itself, and thinking about thinking, improve with maturity and experience, and can be facilitated by the explicit teaching of appropriate strategies.

From the Laboratory to the Classroom

Education is a discipline set to benefit from, and experience considerable change as a result of, emerging findings from research into cognitive neuroscience (Blakemore & Frith, 2000; Organisation for Economic Co-operation and Development [OECD], 2007; Prime Minister's Science, Engineering and Innovation Council [PMSEIC], 2009). The future translation of neuroscientific findings from the laboratory to the classroom will bring with it considerable potential benefit for schools, teachers, and students. In particular, students who are experiencing learning difficulties, their teachers, and their families have much to gain from both an increased scrutiny of everyday educational practices, and the incorporation of carefully evaluated contributions from the learning sciences.

Currently, however, many teachers are susceptible to accepting "neuromyths" (misapplications, over-extensions and over-simplifications of findings from cognitive neuroscience) and pseudoscience as fact (Anderson & Della Sala, 2012; Beauchamp and Beauchamp, 2012; Bellert & Graham, 2013; Dekker *et al.*, 2012; Geake, 2008). The influence of neuromyths, pseudoscience, and "brain-based" educational programs that are not substantiated by evidence of efficacy is of concern, because they divert resources that could otherwise be used to implement proven practices for more sustainable effect. Students with learning difficulties and their teachers and families are often the target market for spurious "brain-based" programs, which can mean that while they are offered false hope, they must eventually confront another failure when promised results are not achieved or sustained. This can have a negative impact on students' academic self-concept and motivation to participate in learning and continue their education.

A further complication associated with "brain-based" educational approaches that claim to be founded on neuroscience is the apparent confusion between cognitive psychology and neuroscience. In many cases, what is promoted as "neuroscience" in brain-based learning programs is more accurately considered to be cognitive psychology. For example, Anderson and Della Sala (2012, p. 1) claim that cognitive psychology does the "heavy lifting" for neuroscience in education, and that the study of cognition offers education more relevant classroom-related information than neuroscience.

The important premise that neuroscience research must be behaviorally translated (through cognitive psychology) before being applied to education (see Chapter 1) provides clarity in this context, and supports teachers and other educators in more readily identifying the over-extension of findings that become neuromyths, and the kind of misinformation that results from misapplication. The fact that teachers can learn much more about effective teaching from cognitive and behavioral studies than they can from neuroscience affirms the important link between cognitive psychology and education, and also has implications for teacher education and in-service teacher professional learning programs.

With the generation of increasing information from all levels of inquiry within the learning sciences, it is vital for teachers to develop robust conceptualizations of what happens for students as they learn, so that instruction can support optimal levels of engagement and the acquisition of knowledge. This is especially so for those students whose learning trajectories may be delayed or inconsistent. Accordingly, at least some teachers, particularly learning support teachers, special education teachers, and teacher educators, need to be "literate" in cognitive psychology and associated explanations relating to how students learn and how to teach effectively (Byrnes, 2007). For example, an understanding of the limited capacity of working memory and the constraints imposed on efficient processing by complex tasks provides informed educators with a sound rationale for "chunking" instructions and tasks into step-by-step components for students who are experiencing difficulties. Similarly, an understanding of how schemata are developed and refined enriches teachers' understanding of how to teach new concepts effectively by making clear links to students' prior knowledge, and employing strategies such as advance organizers that represent and scaffold students' organization of new knowledge (Hattie & Yates, 2014).

A more prominent place for the study of cognitive psychology in initial teacher education programs (and in-service teacher professional learning programs) in Australia is warranted, in order to support teachers in developing informed and responsive practice and more readily detecting spurious claims. This will require those closest to the interface between cognitive psychology and pedagogy—educational and cognitive psychologists, education academics, and specialist teachers—to work together with their teacher and psychologist colleagues to contribute to research and knowledge development.

Although direct prescriptive translation of neuroscience findings from the laboratory to the classroom is only possible if it is facilitated by cognitive psychology, this should not exclude educators from having "a seat at the table" during interdisciplinary collaborations. Experienced teachers can provide researchers with rich insights, and can steer the research agenda towards exploring educationally relevant issues and real-world educational processes, practices, and constraints (Ansari & Coch, 2006; Geake, 2009). As Kaufmann has commented, "Educational experts must share their expertise in pedagogy, and neuroscience researchers must develop ecological paradigms that are capable of investigating cognitive processes and learning mechanisms instead of circumscribed skills" (Kaufmann, 2008, p. 168). Looking ahead to the future, the educational community can perhaps look forward to a time when educators are in partnership with cognitive psychologists and neuroscientists in directing joint scientific investigations into essential questions that matter, leading to more effective teaching and improved educational experiences for all students.

References

Adams, G. & Carnine, D. (2003). Direct instruction. In: H. L. Swanson, K. R. Harris, & S. Graham (Eds), *Handbook of Learning Disabilities* (pp. 403–416). New York: Guilford Press.

Anderson, M. & Della Sala, S. (2012). Neuroscience in education: an (opinionated) introduction. In: S. Della Sala & M. Anderson (Eds), *Neuroscience in Education: The Good, the Bad and the Ugly* (pp. 3–12). Oxford: Oxford University Press.

Ansari, D. & Coch, D. (2006). Bridges over troubled waters: education and cognitive neuroscience. *Trends in Cognitive Sciences*, 10(4), 146–151.

Arief, G., Liem, D., & Martin, A. J. (2013). Direct instruction. In: J. Hattie & E. Anderman (Eds), *International Guide to Student Achievement* (pp. 366–368). New York: Routledge.

Ashbaker, M. H. & Swanson, H. L. (1996). Short-term memory and working memory operations and their contribution to reading in adolescents with and without learning disabilities. *Learning Disabilities Research and Practice*, 11(4), 206–213.

Ashman, A. & Elkins, J. (2009). *Education for Inclusion and Diversity*. Frenchs Forest, New South Wales: Pearson Education Australia.

Australian Bureau of Statistics (2008). *Australian Social Trends: Adult Literacy*. Available online at www.abs.gov.au/AUSSTATS/abs@.nsf/Lookup/4102.0Chapter6102008

Baines, E. (2013). Ability grouping. In: J. A. C. Hattie & E. M. Anderman (Eds), *International Guide to Student Achievement* (pp. 116–118). New York: Routledge.

Baker, S., Gersten, R., & Lee, D. S. (2002). A synthesis of empirical research on teaching mathematics to low-achieving students. *The Elementary School Journal*, 103(1), 51–73.

Beauchamp, M. H. & Beauchamp, C. (2012). Understanding the neuroscience and education connection: themes emerging from a review of the literature. In: S. Della Sala & M. Anderson (Eds), *Neuroscience in Education: The Good, the Bad and the Ugly* (pp. 13–30). Oxford: Oxford University Press.

Bellert, A. & Graham, L. (2013). Neuromyths and neurofacts: information from cognitive neuroscience for classroom and learning support teachers. *Special Education Perspectives*, 22(2), 7–20.

Bentley, T. & Cazaly, C. (2015). *The Shared Work of Learning: Lifting Educational Achievement Through Collaboration. Research Report*. Melbourne: Mitchell Institute for Health and Education Policy and the Centre for Strategic Education.

Bjork, R. A., Dunlosky, J., & Kornell, N. (2013). Self-regulated learning: beliefs, techniques, and illusions. *Annual Review of Psychology*, 64, 417–444.

Blakemore, S.-J., & Frith, U. (2000). *The Implications of Recent Developments in Neuroscience for Research on Teaching and Learning*. A consultation paper commissioned by the Teaching and Learning Research Program, ESRC. Available online at www.tlrp.org/acadpub/Blakemore2000.pdf

Brown, A. (1980). Metacognitive development and reading. In: R. J. Spiro, B. Bruce, & W. F. Brewer (Eds). *Theoretical Issues in Reading Comprehension* (pp. 453–481). Hillsdale, NJ: Lawrence Erlbaum.

Buckingham, J., Beaman, R., & Wheldall, K. (2012). A randomized control trial of a MultiLit small group intervention for older low-progress readers. *Effective Education*, 4(1), 1–26.

Byrnes, J. P. (2007). Some ways in which neuroscience research can be relevant to education. In: D. Coch, K. W. Fischer, & G. Dawson (Eds), *Human Behavior and the Developing Brain*, 2nd edition (pp. 30–49). New York: Guilford Publishers.

Centre for Advanced Research on Language Acquisition (CARLA) (2014). *Content-Based Language Teaching with Technology*. Available online at http://carla.umn.edu/cobaltt/lessonplans/frames.php?lessonID=ULP94

Chan, C., Chang, M. L., Westwood, P., & Yuen. M. T. (2002). Teaching adaptively: how easy is "differentiation" in practice? A perspective from Hong Kong. *The Asia-Pacific Education Researcher*, 11(1), 27–58.

Chan, L. & Dally, K. (2001). Learning disabilities and literacy and numeracy development. *Australian Journal of Learning Disabilities*, 6(1), 12–19.

Clark, R. E., Kirschner, P. A., & Sweller, J. (2012). Putting students on the path to learning: the case for fully guided instruction. *American Educator*, 36(1), 6–11.

Cologon, K. (2013). *Inclusion in Education: Towards Equality for Students with Disability*. Sydney, New South Wales: Children with Disability Australia.

Commonwealth of Australia (2007). *Quality of School Education*. Senate Standing Committee on Education, Employment and Workplace Relations. Available online at http://apo.org.au/node/3739

Coulombe, S., Tremblay, J.-F., & Marchand, S. (2004). *Literacy Scores, Human Capital and Growth across Fourteen OECD Countries*. Ottawa: Statistics Canada.

Dekker, S., Lee, N., Howard-Jones, P. & Jolles, J. (2012). Neuromyths in education: prevalence and predictors of misconceptions among teachers. *Frontiers in Psychology*, 3, 429.

Ellis, L. A. (2005). *Balancing Approaches: Revisiting the Educational Psychology Research on Teaching Students with Learning Difficulties*. Australian Education Review. Camberwell, Victoria: ACER Press.

Flavell, J. H. (1976). Metacognitive aspects of problem solving. In: L. B. Resnick (Ed.), *The Nature of Intelligence* (pp. 231–235). Hillsdale, NJ: Lawrence Erlbaum.

Gathercole, S. E. & Alloway, T. P. (2007). *Understanding Working Memory: A Classroom Guide*. London: Harcourt Assessment. Available online at www.york.ac.uk/res/wml/Classroom%20guide.pdf

Geake, J. (2008). Neuromythologies in education. *Educational Research*, 50(2), 123–133.

Geake, J. (2009). *The Brain at School: Educational Neuroscience in the Classroom*. Maidenhead: Open University Press.

Geary, D. C. (2004). Mathematics and learning disabilities. *Journal of Learning Disabilities*, 37(1), 4–15.

Gersten, R., Fuchs, L., Williams, J., & Baker, S. (2001). Teaching reading comprehension strategies to students with learning disabilities: a review of research. *Review of Educational Research*, 71(2), 279–320.

Graham, L. & Pegg, J. (2011). Evaluating the QuickSmart numeracy program: an effective Australian intervention that improves student achievement, responds to special education needs, and fosters teacher collaboration. *Journal of Educational Administration and History*, 29(2), 87–102.

Graham, L. & Berman, J. (2012). Self-regulation and learning disabilities. *Special Education Perspectives*, 21(2), 41–52.

Graham, L. Berman, J., & Bellert, A. (2015). *Sustainable Learning: Inclusive Practices for 21st Century Classrooms*. Melbourne: Cambridge University Press.

Gregory, G. & Chapman, C. (2013). *Differentiated Instructional Strategies: One Size Doesn't Fit All*, 3rd edition. Thousand Oaks, CA: Corwin Press.

Greulich, L., Al Otaiba, S., Schatschneider, C., Wanzek, J., Ortiz, M., & Wagner, R. K. (2014). Understanding inadequate response to first-grade multi-tier intervention: nomothetic and ideographic perspectives. *Learning Disability Quarterly*, 37(4), 204–217.

Harris, K., Reidy, R., & Graham, S. (2004). Self-regulation among students with LD and ADHD. In: B. Y. L. Wong (Ed.), *Learning about Learning Disabilities*, 3rd edition (pp. 167–189). New York: Academic Press.

Hattie, J. A. C. (2003). *Teachers Make a Difference: What is the Research Evidence?* Background paper to invited address presented at the 2003 ACER Research Conference, Carlton Crest Hotel, Melbourne, Australia, 19–21 October 2003. Available online at https://cdn.auckland.ac.nz/assets/education/hattie/docs/teachers-make-a-difference-ACER-(2003).pdf

Hattie, J. A. C. (2009). *Visible Learning: A Synthesis of Over 800 Meta-Analyses Relating to Achievement*. Abingdon: Routledge.

Hattie, J. A. C. (2012). *Visible Learning for Teachers: Maximizing Impact on Learning*. Abingdon: Routledge.

Hattie, J. A. C. & Yates, G. (2014). *Visible Learning and the Science of How We Learn*. Abingdon: Routledge.

Kaplan, L. & Owens, W. (2013). *Culture Re-Boot: Reinvigorating School Culture to Improve Student Outcomes*. Thousand Oaks, CA: Corwin.

Kaufmann, L. (2008). Dyscalculia: neuroscience and education. *Educational Research*, 50(2), 163–175.

Kavale, K. A. & Forness, S. R. (2000). What definitions of learning disability say and don't say: a critical analysis. *Journal of Learning Disabilities*, 33, 239–256.

Keeler, M. L. & Swanson, H. L. (2001). Does strategy knowledge influence working memory in children with mathematical disabilities? *Journal of Learning Disabilities*, 34(5), 418–434.

Kirschner, P. A., Sweller, J., & Clark, R. E. (2006). Why minimal guidance during instruction does not work: an analysis of the failure of constructivist, discovery, problem-based experiential and inquiry-based teaching. *Educational Psychologist*, 41(2), 75–86.

Kroesbergen, E. H. & van Luit, J. (2003). Mathematics interventions for children with special educational needs. *Remedial and Special Education*, 24(2), 97–114.

Landrum, T. J. & McDuffie, K. A. (2010). Learning styles in the age of differentiated instruction. *Exceptionality*, 18(1), 6–17.

Martin, A. J. (2015). Teaching at-risk students in middle school. In: S. Groundwater-Smith & N. Mockler (Eds), *Big Fish, Little Fish: Teaching and Learning in the Middle Years* (pp. 29–39). Port Melbourne: Cambridge University Press.

Masters, G. (2007). *Restoring our Edge in Education*. Available online at http://research.acer.edu.au/resdev/vol18/iss18/3

Masters, G. (2013). *Towards a Growth Mindset in Assessment*. Available online at http://research.acer.edu.au/ar_misc/17

Mercer, C. D., Jordan, L. A., & Miller, S. P. (1996). Constructivistic math instruction for diverse learners. *Learning Disabilities Research & Practice*, 11(3), 290–306.

Organisation for Economic Co-operation and Development (OECD) (2007). *Understanding the Brain: The Birth of a Learning Science*. Available online at www.oecd.org/edu/ceri/38811529.pdf

Petty, G. (2009). *Evidence-Based Teaching: A Practical Approach*. Oxford: Oxford University Press.

Pincott, R. (2004). Are we responsible for our children's maths difficulties? In: B. Knight & W. Scott (Eds), *Learning Difficulties: Multiple Perspectives*. French's Forest, New South Wales: Pearson SprintPrint.

Pintrich, P. R. (2000). An achievement goal theory perspective on issues in motivation terminology, theory and research. *Contemporary Educational Psychology*, 25, 92–104.

Prime Minister's Science, Engineering and Innovation Council (PMSEIC) (2009). *Transforming Learning and the Transmission of Knowledge*. Canberra: Commonwealth of Australia. Available online at www.chiefscientist.gov.au/wp-content/uploads/Transforming-Learning-EWG-report-FINAL.pdf

Purdie, N. & Ellis, L. (2005). *A Review of the Empirical Evidence Identifying Effective Interventions and Teaching Practices for Students With Learning Difficulties in Years 4, 5 and 6*. A report prepared for the Australian Government Department of Education, Science and Training. Camberwell, Victoria: Australian Council for Educational Research.

Rock, M. L., Gregg, M., Ellis, E., & Gable, R.A. (2008). REACH: a framework for differentiating classroom instruction. *Preventing School Failure*, 52(2), 31–47.

Rose, D. (2001). Universal design for learning. *Journal of Special Education Technology*, 16(2), 66–67.

Rosenshine, B. V. (1986). Synthesis of research on explicit teaching. *Educational Leadership*, 43(7), 60–69.

Rowe, K. (2006). Effective teaching practices for students with and without learning difficulties: issues and implications surrounding key findings and recommendations from the National Inquiry into the Teaching of Literacy. *Australian Journal of Learning Disabilities*, 11(3), 99–115.

Sanders, W. L. & Rivers, J. C. (1996). *Cumulative and Residual Effects of Teachers on Future Student Academic Achievement*. Knoxville, TN: University of Tennessee Value-Added Research and Assessment Center.

Sanders, W. & Horn, S. (1998). Research findings from the Tennessee Value-Added Assessment System (TVAAS) database: implications for educational evaluation and research. *Journal of Personnel Evaluation in Education*, 12(3), 247–256.

Sprenger, M. (2008). *Differentiation Through Learning Styles and Memory*, 2nd edition. Thousand Oaks, CA: Corwin Press.

Sterling, S. (2001). *Sustainable Education: Re-Visioning Learning and Change*. Cambridge, UK: Green Books.

Sterling, S. (2008). Sustainable education – towards a deep learning response to unsustainability. *Policy & Practice: A Development Education Review*, 6, 63–68.

Strain, P. S. & Hoyson, M. (2000). The need for longitudinal intervention: follow-up outcomes for children. *Topics in Early Childhood Special Education*, 20(2), 116–122.

Swanson, H. L. (1999). Reading research for students with LD: a meta-analysis of intervention outcomes. *Journal of Learning Disabilities*, 32(6), 503–534.

Swanson, H. L. (2008). Working memory and intelligence in children: what develops? *Journal of Educational Psychology*, 100(3), 581–602.

Swanson, H. L. & Hoskyn, M. (1998). Experimental intervention research on students with learning disabilities: a meta-analysis of treatment outcomes. *Review of Educational Research*, 68(3), 277–321.

Swanson, H. L. & Sachse-Lee, C. (2001). A subgroup analysis of working memory in children with reading disabilities: domain-general or domain-specific deficiency? *Journal of Learning Disabilities*, 34(3), 249–263.

Swanson, H. L. & Siegel, L. (2001). Learning disabilities as a working memory deficit. *Issues in Education*, 7(1), 1–48.

Swanson, H. L. & O'Connor, R. E. (2009). The role of working memory and fluency practice on the reading comprehension of students who are dysfluent readers. *Journal of Learning Disabilities*, 42(6), 548–575.

Swanson, H. L., Carson, C., & Sachse-Lee, C. (1996). A selective synthesis of intervention research for students with learning disabilities. *School Psychology Review*, 25(3), 370–391.

Sweller, J. (1988). Cognitive load during problem solving: effects on learning. *Cognitive Science*, 12(2), 257–285.

Sweller, J. (1994). Cognitive load theory, learning difficulty, and instructional design. *Learning and Instruction*, 4(4), 295–312.

Sweller, J. (2010). Element interactivity and intrinsic, extraneous, and germane cognitive load. *Educational Psychology Review*, 22(2), 123–138.

Tomlinson, C. A. (2001). *How to Differentiate Instruction in Mixed-Ability Classrooms*. Alexandria, VA: Association for Supervision and Curriculum Development.

Torgesen, J. K. (2002). Lessons learned from intervention research in reading: a way to go before we rest. In: R. Stanhope (Ed.), *Learning and Teaching Reading. Volume 1* (pp. 89–103). London: British Psychological Society.

Vaughn, S., Gersten, R., & Chard, D. J. (2000). The underlying message in LD intervention research: findings from research syntheses. *Exceptional Children*, 67(1), 99–114.

Vaughn, S., Cirino, P. T., Wanzek, J., Wexler, J., Fletcher, J. M., Denton, C. A., Barth, A., Romain, M., & Francis, D. J. (2010). Response to intervention for middle school students with reading difficulties: effects of a primary and secondary intervention. *School Psychology Review*, 39(1), 3–21.

Westwood, P. (2001). Differentiation as a strategy for inclusive classroom practice: some difficulties identified. *Australian Journal of Learning Difficulties*, 6(1), 5–11.

Westwood, P. (2004). *Learning and Learning Difficulties: A Handbook for Teachers*. Camberwell, Victoria: ACER Press.

Westwood, P. (2005). *Reading and Learning Difficulties: Approaches to Teaching and Assessment*. Abingdon, UK: David Fulton Publishers.

Westwood, P. (2013). *Inclusive and Adaptive Teaching: Meeting the Challenge of Diversity in the Classroom*. Abingdon, UK: Routledge.

Westwood, P. (2015). *Commonsense Methods for Children with Special Educational Needs*, 7th edition. Abingdon, UK: Routledge.

Westwood, P. & Graham, L. (2000). How many children with special needs in regular classes? Official predictions vs teachers' perceptions in South Australia and New South Wales. *Australian Journal of Learning Disabilities*, 5(3), 24–35.

Wolf, M. & Katzir-Cohen, T. (2001). Reading fluency and its intervention. *Scientific Studies of Reading*, 5(3), 211–239.

Wong, B. Y. L. & Wong, R. (1986). Study behavior as a function of metacognitive knowledge about critical task variables: an investigation of above average, average, and learning disabled readers. *Learning Disabilities Research*, 1(2), 101–111.

Wong, B. Y. L. & Butler, D. (2012). *Learning about Learning Disabilities*, 4th edition. San Diego, CA: Elsevier.

Wong, B. Y. L., Butler, D., Ficzere, S. A., & Kuperis, S. (1996). Teaching low achievers and students with learning disabilities to plan, write, and revise opinion essays. *Journal of Learning Disabilities*, 29(2), 197–212.

Wong, B. Y. L., Graham, L., Hoskyn, M., & Berman, J. (2008). *The ABCs of Learning Disabilities*, 2nd edition. San Diego, CA: Elsevier Academic Press.

Yuen, M., Westwood, P., & Wong, G. (2005). Meeting the needs of students with specific learning difficulties in the mainstream education system: data from primary school teachers in Hong Kong. *International Journal of Special Education*, 20(1), 67–76.

SECTION 5

Looking Ahead—The Future of Educational Research

14

NEUROSCIENCE RESEARCH AND CLASSROOM PRACTICE

Paul Howard-Jones and Wayne Holmes

GRADUATE SCHOOL OF EDUCATION, UNIVERSITY OF BRISTOL, AND
UCL INSTITUTE OF EDUCATION, UNIVERSITY COLLEGE LONDON

Introduction

We all know that learning involves the brain, so the idea of improving classroom practice by understanding the brain has a common-sense appeal. The idea has gained considerable traction in the last 15 years, with a step change in the number of academic papers, reports, and books published recently that connect the brain with education (Howard-Jones, 2014a).

The demand for neuroscience-informed education comes from both directions, with neuroscientists emphasizing the potential of their work to improve education, and many educators being keen to learn what neuroscience has to offer. This enthusiasm does, however, mean that the topic needs to be approached with care, to ensure that neuroscience research is not adopted too early, before it has been properly translated for classroom use. This enthusiasm also means that interventions simply *associated* with neuroscience (Fernandez-Duque *et al.*, 2015), whether or not they are genuinely grounded in neuroscience research or indeed have any evidence of educational impact, are sometimes welcomed uncritically—highlighting the importance of both dispelling myths (Dekker *et al.*, 2012; Howard-Jones, 2014b; Pasquinelli, 2012) and accurately disseminating evidence.

This chapter sets out to address these concerns. Building upon a detailed review (Howard-Jones, 2014a), it critically considers the readiness of a broad range of insights from neuroscience research, supported by psychology research, for application in classroom practice.

First, we discuss the areas of neuroscience that are most developed in terms of educational application and that also have the most promising evidence about their impact on educational outcomes. Then we consider approaches that have a good scientific basis, but require further work to ensure that they are appropriately applied within the classroom, and would benefit from further evidence about their educational effectiveness. Next, we provide two examples of topics that are gaining interest, such that it is important to be aware of their potential, but which face significant challenges in their application. The chapter concludes by describing a teaching application, the development of which was grounded in neuroscience research, specifically around the putative impact of uncertain rewards on dopaminergic activity and learning.

Areas of Neuroscience That Have the Most Promising Evidence about Their Impact on Educational Outcomes

We have identified five areas with a theoretical basis that can be clearly constructed from findings in the scientific literature, from laboratory studies showing improvements in tasks related to academic achievement and classroom-based trials. Both the strength of evidence and the number of classroom-based trials do vary, however, with some examples requiring further testing to determine best practice in applying the knowledge within the classroom. Two of the five areas are domain-specific (mathematics anxiety and reading), and the other three are more general (spaced learning, testing, and exercise).

Mathematics Anxiety

Mathematics anxiety has been shown to have detrimental effects on achievement (Ashcraft et al., 2007), which may be due to the effects of anxiety on working memory (Vukovic et al., 2013). When performing calculations, children who are anxious when doing mathematics have greater activity in the amygdala (which is associated with the processing of negative emotions) and reduced activity in the brain regions that support working memory and the processing of numbers, compared with children who are not anxious (Young et al., 2012). However, such neural differences should not be seen as evidence of a biologically determined condition. Indeed, it appears that mathematics anxiety can be culturally transmitted from teacher to student (Beilock et al., 2010). Nevertheless, a recent neuroimaging study found that the difficulties experienced by young adult students who were anxious about mathematics were predicted by how much they recruited neural circuits for cognitive control (Lyons & Beilock, 2012).

There is, then, some neural evidence that helps us to understand how mathematics anxiety affects learning. The question that needs to be addressed is how we can use this understanding of its impact to address mathematics anxiety and so help to improve achievement. A classroom study focused on controlling negative emotional response has reported improved achievement. In this intervention amongst math-anxious students aged 14–15 years (N=106), those who write about their anxieties before a test significantly outperformed those who did not (Ramirez and Beilock, 2011).

Reading

A vast amount of research has been undertaken into the neurocognitive and psychological processes that underlie reading. In addition, a number of laboratory-based and classroom trials of reading approaches and software informed by this understanding have been conducted.

To be a proficient reader, one must decode accurately and read fluently with understanding (Snowling & Hulme, 2011). Mapping letters (known as graphemes) and letter strings onto the sounds of language (known as phonemes) is a vital first step in this process, and difficulties learning to read are frequently attributed in the neuroscience literature to problems with this "phonological decoding" process (e.g. Temple et al., 2003). Several interventions have had some success in ameliorating these difficulties (e.g. Shaywitz et al., 2004). Such studies have helped to raise awareness of the general importance of phonological decoding for reading acquisition, and contributed to the widespread adoption of "phonics" approaches to reading.

However, although phonological decoding remains the prime candidate for early problems with reading, reading proficiency also requires comprehension, which is another key difficulty for many children. An imaging study of adults revealed that reading-related brain regions respond differently when reading fluency is manipulated by varying the speed with which text is presented (Benjamin & Gaab, 2012). Although the study focused on adults, this suggests that fluent reading should be understood as the product of multiple contributing reading sub-skills. It also suggests that varying reading speeds may be an effective means by which to subtype differing forms of dysfluency through behavioral and neural measures, and so support the personalization of remediation programs.

Spaced Learning

Spaced learning—that is, learning content multiple times with breaks in between—is an approach that can be applied immediately in the classroom. Although in the recent past it has been strongly associated with neuroscience (e.g. a brain imaging study suggested that spaced learning operates via enhanced maintenance rehearsal; Callan & Schweighofer, 2008), the vast majority of what we now know about the underlying processes is derived from the psychological literature. The effect has been documented for adults (e.g. Cepeda et al., 2006), preschoolers and infants (Toppino, 1991), and primary (Sobel et al., 2011) and secondary school children (Carpenter et al., 2009). As was examined further in Chapters 4 and 6 of this volume, these and other studies provide clear guidance for the optimal application of spaced practice, including the ideal length of learning periods and the gaps in between.

Testing

There is a strong neuroscientific and educational evidence base for the effectiveness of testing in improving learning, although further research might usefully focus on how it is best used and the factors that influence its effectiveness. Many laboratory studies have established that being tested on studied material improves the ability to remember it on a final test—more so than simply rereading the material for reviews (e.g. McDaniel et al., 2007). There is also evidence that testing slows the rate of forgetting in the longer term (Roediger & Karpicke, 2006). The effect has been confirmed as robust for a wide range of material and contexts (Rohrer & Pashler, 2010), including computer-mediated scientific explanations with adults (Johnson & Mayer, 2009), multiple-choice questions during undergraduate lectures (Campbell & Mayer, 2009), and science quizzes with 13- to 14-year-olds (McDaniel et al., 2011), and has been shown to be superior to concept mapping for undergraduate scientists (Karpicke & Blunt, 2011).

Rather than the testing effect simply being due to heightened attention, behavioral studies have suggested that it may arise from rehearsing retrieval (Kang et al., 2007), although, perhaps counter-intuitively, testing can also improve memory for associated material that is not tested (Chan, 2010). Testing can improve performance on applying the learned information to make inferences (Butler, 2010), and can promote meaningful conceptual links (Karpicke, 2012), although there is some evidence which suggests that this may not apply to the retention of problem-solving skills (van Gog & Kester, 2012).

Ongoing neuroimaging studies are now identifying candidate processes that may underpin the testing effect, and these insights may contribute to its optimal application. Suggested explanations include the notion that testing increases attention during restudy, which may lead to enhanced encoding and subsequently better performance (Vestergren & Nyberg, 2014), the possible role of reward in testing (Shohamy & Adcock, 2010), different processes of semantic processing being involved during retrieval and restudying (van den Broek *et al.*, 2013), and a decreased need for executive processing along with a strengthening of semantic representations (Wiklund-Hörnqvist *et al.*, 2013).

Finally, recent research links the potential benefits of using so-called "clickers" (systems originally designed for audience response) with the "testing effect" (Anderson *et al.*, 2013). In studies of undergraduates, use of clickers has been shown to reduce teaching time (Anderson *et al.*, 2011) and improve learning outcomes (e.g. Campbell & Mayer, 2009). This is one example where a more scientific understanding may help to develop improved practice and outcomes in the school classroom, by combining behavioral evidence for its effectiveness (Roediger III *et al.*, 2011) with neural evidence of how the brain's response to reward influences learning, and the influence of contextual factors such as peer presence on this response (Chein *et al.*, 2011).

Exercise

There is a strong basis in the neuroscience literature for justifying an exercise intervention to increase the efficiency of neural networks, with many studies exploring the effects of exercise on academic achievement (e.g. Lakes & Hoyt, 2004). However, the mixed results of these academic studies suggest that some of the factors that influence outcomes have yet to be identified, and there is a need to design future interventions carefully with this in mind. Indeed, for one particular approach, the so-called *educational kinesiology exercises* (sometimes sold under the brand name of Brain Gym®, which remains popular in some classrooms), there is little evidence of any real practical value (e.g. Spaulding *et al.*, 2010).

Nevertheless, it has been shown that there are some beneficial effects of *aerobic* exercise on selective aspects of brain function (Hillman *et al.*, 2008). In adults, regular exercise has been shown to improve the efficiency of the frontal, posterior, and temporal networks that are important for learning (Voss *et al.*, 2010), including the fronto-parietal networks that help to guide our attention (Colcombe *et al.*, 2004). Physical exercise also increases blood flow and connectivity in the hippocampus, a key region for memory formation and consolidation, and hippocampal volume is related to physical fitness in children (Chaddock *et al.*, 2010) and adults (Erickson *et al.*, 2009).

In adult studies, exercise has been shown to increase a range of white and gray matter regions, and such increases in the size of the hippocampus have been related to improved spatial memory and more *brain-derived neurotropic factor* (BDNF), a protein associated with the survival of existing neurons and the growth and differentiation of new neurons and synapses. These data support evidence that exercise increases BDNF gene expression in the hippocampus (Neeper *et al.*, 1995), which contributes to the effects of physical exercise on cognition (e.g. Gomez-Pinilla *et al.*, 2008). A study of healthy adults revealed increased levels of BDNF in the blood after two 3-minute sprints (Winter *et al.*, 2007). When compared with sedentary or moderate exercise conditions, participants showed a 20% increase in the speed of recall for words that they learned immediately following their intense exercise.

Several studies of school-age children have also revealed positive effects of exercise on cognitive functions crucial for learning, and some have linked these to improvements in brain function. For example, Kubesch *et al.* (2009) showed that on-task attention in the face of distraction was improved among 13- to 14-year-olds after a single 30-minute physical education program, in contrast to a 5-minute movement break. Meanwhile, kindergarten children show improved attention and improved efficiency in associated neural function after two 35-minute sessions per week for 8 weeks (Chang *et al.*, 2013). On a longer timescale, a 9-month randomised controlled physical activity intervention involving 7- to 9-year-olds (Kamijo *et al.*, 2011) produced improvements in working memory function (Dehaene, 2001) and its associated event-related brain potential measurements (Dehaene *et al.*, 1999). Brain-related improvements in function were also found in a study of 8- to 9- year-old children participating in 60 minutes of physical activity for 5 days a week over a 9-month period (Chaddock-Heyman *et al.*, 2013). This intervention improved efficiency in the prefrontal networks (De Smedt *et al.*, 2009) and performance on measures of cognitive control. Finally, it has been reported that a 3-month program of Tae Kwon Do with primary school children preceded improvements in cognitive self-regulation, affective self-regulation, prosocial behavior, classroom conduct, and performance on a mental math test, all relative to a control group (Lakes & Hoyt, 2004).

However, although these findings are all very encouraging, these many studies have not provided especially strong evidence for the impact of exercise on classroom learning. Yet some recent interventions have been mindful of the emphasis on aerobic content, with results showing impact on academic indicators (e.g. Mullender-Wijnsma *et al.*, 2015), and a systematic analysis of studies examining the effect of exercise on academic achievement revealed that the findings were almost equally split between no effect and positive effects, with a distinct lack of negative effects (Rasberry *et al.*, 2011). The authors suggest that, as noted previously, further interventions would benefit from better theoretical foundations which include reference to neurobiology.

Approaches That Have a Good Scientific Basis But Require Further Work to Ensure They are Appropriately Applied within the Classroom

This second group of approaches to classroom practice benefits from a theoretical basis that can be clearly constructed from findings in the scientific literature, from laboratory studies showing improvements in academic learning, and/or from some exploratory research in classrooms. However, these approaches still require translational work and piloting to test their feasibility within the classroom—and sometimes their impact has been shown to be negligible or negative.

We have identified a diverse mix of such approaches—non-symbolic and symbolic number representations in mathematics, embodied cognition, finger gnosis for mathematics (including counting on fingers), interleaving, learning games, creativity, "brain training", sleep, and neurofeedback.

Non-Symbolic and Symbolic Number Representations

Cognitive neuroscience and psychological research have made a substantial contribution to understanding how numerical abilities develop in young children, and the foundational role of a non-symbolic number system and symbolic representation in acquiring formal mathematical skills. The non-symbolic number system, or "numerosity", is the ability to quickly understand and approximate numerical quantities (Dehaene, 2001), which is evident in animals and present very early in human development. The symbolic number system involves representations such as "3" or "three", and its development is strongly linked to that of early language, beginning at around 2 to 3 years of age. Quantitative skills also involve the ability to map between these non-symbolic and symbolic systems, which appears to be linked to the use of fingers and develops through early childhood.

A brain imaging study suggests that as adults we still use our approximate non-symbolic number system (which involves a region in the parietal lobe) when estimating quantity, but we switch to a more language-dependent symbolic system when calculating with precision (Dehaene et al., 1999). Studies in typically developing children also attribute a crucial role to numerical magnitude representations in predicting individual differences in mathematics achievement (e.g. Holloway & Ansari, 2009). However, these studies involved several subdomains of mathematics. A study that focused on arithmetic, where deficits in fact retrieval are often regarded as the hallmark of mathematical difficulty (Geary, 2010), suggests that access to numerical meaning from Arabic symbols ("1", "2", "3", etc.) is key for children's arithmetic strategy development (Vanbinst et al., 2012). This study along with other evidence shows a critical role for this access, and makes a clear case for also exploring interventions based on connecting Arabic symbols to the quantities that they represent (Kolkman et al., 2013).

Some children who experience difficulties in learning functional mathematics—sometimes identified as "dyscalculics"—suffer from a severely impaired ability to identify number representations, with 10-year-old dyscalculics scoring at the level of 5-year-old normally achieving children (Piazza et al., 2010). Neuroimaging findings corroborate deficits of number representation observed in the behavior of children identified as having developmental dyscalculia, implicating functional impairments and structural alterations in parietal brain regions associated with representing the number line (e.g. Mussolin et al., 2010).

Reflecting the emergent state of understanding in this area, mixed results have been obtained from the small number of studies that have attempted to train children's non-symbolic representations, with some studies also reporting an impact of training on symbolic representation and transfer to other numeracy skills. However, these results have not provided a clear indication of the most important types of representation to target, and further research is needed to understand their role within the classroom. Nevertheless, a recent educational intervention with 6- to 7-year-olds compared the effects of training with exact and approximate number systems, and found that each approach led to the same level of improvements in arithmetic ability, lending further support to the notion that two distinct systems are involved in representing approximate and exact information about quantity (Obersteiner et al., 2013).

The combination of technology and a scientific understanding of learning potentially has much to offer education, with the promise of learning software that has a sound theoretical basis and that adapts to learners' needs. Research on how to combine technology and neuroscience in the development of new educational approaches to support children's learning has been identified as an important area for future investment (Frith et al., 2011), and we shall focus specifically on the challenges of combining neuroscience and learning game technologies later in this chapter. "The Number Race" was one of the first examples to attempt such a combination, with a design that drew on the concepts discussed above to remediate low attainment in mathematics (Wilson et al., 2006a). It focused on three areas thought to be involved in learning arithmetic: number sense, including numerical comparison (deciding which is the larger of two numbers) and the link between number and space; links between non-symbolic and symbolic number representations; and understanding of, and access to, basic addition and subtraction facts. In an initial study (Wilson *et al.*, 2006b), The Number Race software was shown to improve performance on non-symbolic as well as symbolic tasks for nine 7- to 9-year-olds identified as having mathematical difficulties. A study of 30 low-numeracy kindergarten children who played the game for 10–15 minutes daily for 3 weeks revealed improvements in comparison of Arabic numbers but not in other areas of number skills (Räsänen *et al.*, 2009). An evaluation with 53 young children (aged 4–6 years) revealed improvements in tasks that involved comparing digits and words, but no improvement on non-symbolic measures of number sense (Wilson *et al.*, 2009). This suggests that the underlying improvement produced by using the software was better number sense and/or better linking of non-symbolic representations of number to symbols.

Another mathematics learning game, "Rescue Calcularis", was developed by Karin Kucian and colleagues. This game requires young children to land a spaceship on a number line, with the aim of helping them to develop their own internal number line representation. In a 5-week intervention, 16 children (aged 8–10 years) diagnosed with dyscalculia and 16 matched controls played the game for 15 minutes a day at home (Kucian *et al.*, 2011). The outcomes of the training were evaluated using behavioral tests and neuroimaging of brain function when the children were performing a number line task. Both groups, with and without developmental dyscalculia, showed an improvement in various aspects of spatial number representation and mathematical reasoning 5 weeks after training. The intensive training led initially to a general activation decrease in the relevant brain regions, probably due to reorganization and fine-tuning processes (which were greater for the dyscalculic children), and then to an increase in the task-relevant regions after a period of consolidation. A further evaluation of this software was performed with 40 children who had difficulties in learning mathematics, as indicated simply by their below-average performance in arithmetic (Käser *et al.*, 2013). Playing the game for 20 minutes a day, 5 days a week for 6 weeks improved their arithmetic performance, especially subtractions (where performance is considered to represent a main indicator for development of spatial number representations and numerical understanding).

Other researchers have used non-technological means to encourage children to connect symbols to meaning. Gabriel *et al.* (2012) asked around 300 children aged 9–11 years to use wooden disks to help them to represent and manipulate fractions while playing card games for 30 minutes twice a week over 10 weeks. Compared with usual instruction, this was shown to have improved the children's conceptual understanding of fractions and their ability to associate fractional notations with numerical magnitude through a learning-by-doing approach. In another recent study, Brankaer *et al.* (2015) reported improvements in children's symbolic number comparison after using a domino game designed to foster connections between magnitude and symbol, compared with using a control domino game.

Embodied Cognition

Although a unified theory of embodiment is still work in progress (Barsalou, 2010), embodied cognition refers to the idea that mental processes are mediated by a range of bodily systems that include, but are not restricted to, the neural systems engaged in action planning and execution (Alibali & Nathan, 2012). Theories of embodied (or "grounded" or "situated") cognition suggest that we cannot consider those neurocognitive systems that are involved in learning as separate from those involved with action (Osgood-Campbell, 2015).

Embodied cognition also provides a theoretical basis for the well-established "enactment effect." This effect is illustrated by better memory of action verbs after they are performed than after they are simply read (Engelkamp et al., 2004). The enactment effect has been successfully applied in studies of foreign language learning (e.g. Kelly et al., 2009). For example, a within-subjects experimental study of 20 adult German speakers learning abstract Italian words showed better memory for words encoded with gestures, and improved frequency of use in transfer tasks, suggesting enhanced accessibility in memory (Macedonia & Knösche, 2011).

Increased memory after observing a teacher using gesture cannot be explained by the enactment effect, but such effects have been shown for adults and children (So et al., 2012), and could be predicted by an embodied cognition perspective. Embodied concepts may have further applications. For example, one study found that when a teacher imitated students' behavior during interactions, the students later reported significantly higher perceptions of rapport, more confidence about and satisfaction with learning outcomes, and scored significantly higher in a subsequent quiz (Zhou, 2012).

A range of different ways in which gestures can embody mathematical concepts has been postulated (Alibali & Nathan, 2012), although experimental work exploring testable hypotheses remains sparse in this area. The interrelationship between fingers and mathematics is well known (see the section on "finger gnosis" below), and this is one example of embodied cognition that has given rise to interventions. An extension of this approach has led to the use of dance mats to enable children to explore number lines with their whole body. In a small study, around 20 kindergarten children were asked to compare magnitudes using a full-body spatial movement on a digital dance mat (Fischer et al., 2011). Spatial training was demonstrated to be more effective than non-spatial training in enhancing the children's performance on a number line estimation task and on a subtest of a standardized mathematical assessment.

Brain imaging is also beginning to provide unexpected insights into vicarious learning as another example of embodied cognition. When we observe others carrying out actions, some of the same cortical areas are activated as if we were carrying out the actions ourselves (Rizzolatti & Craighero, 2004). This so-called mirror neuron system is thought to mediate imitation-based learning, and this capacity of the brain may have evolved as a type of "mind reading." Our mirror neuron system may not be innate but instead derive from the sensorimotor learning that we acquire when observing ourselves and others (Catmur et al., 2008). Nevertheless, the functioning of the mirror neuron system provides some evidence that our neural representation of others' actions is influenced by our own embodied experience of those actions (e.g. Gazzola et al., 2007).

Finger Gnosis

As already mentioned, another insight with potential application in the classroom comes from neuroscience research into the role of fingers in early mathematical development (Penner-Wilger & Anderson, 2013). Finger gnosis—that is, being able to distinguish between different fingers in response to touch—has been identified as a predictor of mathematical ability (Noël, 2005). Using functional magnetic resonance imaging (fMRI), a study has shown variation with age of the brain regions that are activated when fingers are used to approximate (Kaufmann *et al.*, 2008). In 8-year-old children there is an increase in activity in the parietal regions associated with number sense when fingers are involved, but there is no such increase in adults. The authors of this study suggest that fingers represent concrete embodied tokens involved in the estimation of number magnitude (i.e. they have an intimate involvement with our number sense), although it is not yet clear whether the link is logarithmic or discrete. There is also some evidence that the disproportionate number of split-five errors made in later years might be due to intermediate results using hands being forgotten. In addition, an fMRI study of 6- to 12-year-olds suggests that finger counting also mediates the step from non-symbolic to symbolic and exact number processing (Krinzinger *et al.*, 2011). On this basis, the suggestion is that children should not be discouraged from using their fingers, and teachers may be able to exploit the natural role of fingers more fully (Kaufmann, 2008).

Nevertheless, some mathematics educators still recommend the fostering of mentally based numerical representations, so as to induce children to abandon finger counting. In part this may be due to results for the impact of finger gnosis on mathematical learning being represented by only a single classroom-based study, in which the long-term impact of the approach was not tracked. In this study, Gracia-Bafalluy and Noel (2008) assessed new arrivals at three Belgian primary schools for finger gnosis, and formed three groups: children with poor finger gnosis who followed the finger-differentiation training program (G1); a control-intervention group who were trained in story comprehension (G2); and a group with high finger gnosis scores who just continued with normal school lessons (G3). Initially, children in G3 performed better in finger gnosis and enumeration than those in G1 and G2. Children in G1 then trained for two 30-minute sessions per week over 8 weeks. Training consisted of games played with colored stickers on each fingernail. For example, in one game the children followed each colored pathway in a labyrinth with the correspondingly colored finger. After the training period, the children in G1 were significantly better than those in G2 at finger gnosis when using their fingers to represent a numerosity (i.e. the number of objects in a set), in quantification tasks, and in the processing of Arabic digits. Nonetheless, these positive results have not resolved the debate between neuroscientists and mathematics educators regarding the role of fingers (Moeller *et al.*, 2011).

Interleaving

As mentioned earlier, research has consistently shown that learning performance improves if multiple study sessions are spaced rather than massed together, which raises the question of how different activities undertaken in the spacing period might influence outcomes. In fact, other research has shown that interleaving topics can increase the efficiency with which learned material is remembered (e.g. Carson & Wiegand, 1979). A typical interleaving strategy might involve each lesson being followed by practice problems drawn from previous lessons, such that no two problems of the same kind appear consecutively. For example, at the end of a lesson about electricity, a teacher might alternate questions about electricity with questions about heat, light, and motion (if these were taught in previous lessons).

However, the processes underlying the interleaving effect remain poorly understood. Neuroimaging studies suggest that the processes involved are not under conscious control, and that interleaving reduces the suppression of neural activity in memory regions that occurs when similar stimuli are repeatedly presented (Xue *et al.*, 2011). There are fewer studies of interleaving in education, compared with spaced learning, and they have been conducted relatively recently. One example is a study of 10- to 12-year-olds learning fractions (Rau *et al.*, 2013). Here the results showed an advantage of learning effectiveness and efficiency for interleaving task types (with representations blocked together). In another study, involving 10- to 11-year-old children learning to solve mathematical problems (Taylor & Rohrer, 2010), interleaving impaired performance during the practice session but boosted performance in a delayed test. The science of interleaving is discussed in more detail in Chapter 5 of this volume.

Learning Games

For several decades, a lack of established understanding about how games engage their players, and how these processes relate to learning, has hampered attempts to combine learning and games. These difficulties have led some commentators to state that the "only consensus in this whirlwind of activity seems to be that educational games are something of a failure" (Zimmerman & Fortugno, 2005). However, this activity may be aided by findings from cognitive neuroscience which provide insight into the motivating and learning roles of *uncertain rewards* in games, including educational games. Uptake of dopamine from the midbrain regions is closely related to many of our motivations, and the chance-mediated uncertainty of an outcome is thought to result in midbrain dopamine neurons "ramping up" their output until the outcome is known. This helps to explain why uncertain rewards are more enticing than either wholly predictable or wholly unexpected rewards, and perhaps why we find games of chance so attractive. Reward response peaks at 50% certainty in games, and research in cognitive neuroscience has established that declarative memory formation is strongly related to this response of the brain to reward (Shohamy & Adcock, 2010). This implies that the neural response to reward should be of educational interest, since it may inform interventions to improve motivation, engagement, and learning, based on a scientifically informed approach to scheduling rewards.

An array of neuroimaging studies provides insight into this neural response and how team-based competitive learning games can support our learning. Briefly, our reward response is egocentric, so that we respond to our competitor's loss as our gain (Howard-Jones *et al.*, 2010). It can become heightened in the presence of peers (Chein *et al.*, 2011), and it increases with reward size, but it is also dependent on context, such that it is scaled with regard to the maximum reward available in a particular context (Nieuwenhuis *et al.*, 2005). (This suggests, for example, that the absolute value of the winner's prize may not be an issue in terms of engagement.) However, these neural processes are still the subject of scientific research. For example, the exact mechanism by which reward response enhances declarative memory formation has yet to be determined. In addition, although it is known that response is mediated by the many factors described above, and more besides, their relative significance for education and their interaction remain the subject of neuroscientific, psychological, and educational research. (In the final section of this chapter we shall discuss in more detail one such project.)

An understanding of neural concepts such as reward uncertainty can provide a scientific basis for designing learning games (Howard-Jones *et al.*, 2011). In short, such findings suggest a games-based approach to learning that increases the emotional and/or motivational response by disrupting the learning-reward relationship with chance, in order to encourage greater reward activity without endangering self- and social esteem. A recent laboratory study of computing undergraduates learning about database concepts has confirmed that reward uncertainty can improve motivation and learning. Importantly, the study demonstrated the potential of the approach with what the authors call "deep learning" (in terms of meaningful understanding), rather than just factual recall (Ozcelik *et al.*, 2013).

Creativity

Neuroscience is providing some insights into strategies that have been found to foster creativity in the classroom, but there is a lack of studies showing the impact on tasks closely related to children's academic achievement. Further scientific progress in demonstrating the potential academic efficacy of concepts will be required before school-based interventions can be implemented and appropriately evaluated.

Creativity is an important quality of thought that is highly prized by many types of enterprise, from science to business and the arts. Advances in the expanding field of creative neurocognition confirm that creativity involves a daunting range of complex processes (Abraham, 2013). These advances support a model of creativity based on moving between a *generative process* that facilitates the production of novel ideas and an *evaluative process* that enables the assessment of their appropriateness (Ellamil *et al.*, 2012). Whereas evaluation is considered to require narrowly focused critical attention, the generation of ideas appears to benefit from a broader focus of attention. A study using electroencephalography (EEG) has shown how individual differences can be explained in terms of an individual's resting state of attention (i.e. whether they are more broadly or narrowly focused) (Kounios *et al.*, 2008). In addition, fMRI techniques have been used to validate and explore strategies that are considered to foster creativity. One of these suggests that sharing ideas with others can boost our creative output by reducing our need to suppress our own automatic associations (Fink *et al.*, 2010). A study that investigated the effect of incorporating an unrelated stimulus into a product suggests that this strategy boosts creativity by automatically increasing neural function in regions related to creative effort and the making of meaningful connections (Howard-Jones *et al.*, 2005).

At least one attempt has been made to develop strategies for drama teaching that are informed by the neuroscience of creativity (Howard-Jones *et al.*, 2008). However, there have been few attempts to subject neuroscientifically informed strategies to classroom-based trials. For example, some classroom studies report positive results in terms of impact on creativity for strategies that broaden the attention of young children (Howard-Jones & Murray, 2003), and a similar type of strategy for broadening attention has been investigated in adults, using fMRI (Howard-Jones *et al.*, 2005). However, there have been no field trials of strategies with a design and/or implementation influenced by current neuroscientific understanding.

"Brain Training"

"Brain training"—that is, the use of programs to enhance executive functions, such as reasoning, working memory, and inhibition control—has recently become very popular. However, there is conflicting evidence for the effects of such training on executive function, and little evidence for the effects of such training on academic achievement. Nevertheless, the number of studies reporting positive effects on executive function, the clear links between executive function and academic achievement, and the popularity of some of the programs warrant brief discussion here.

Brain training has its roots in neuropsychological attention training of individuals who have suffered brain damage. Some success in rehabilitating the cognitive functions of this population resulted in efforts to apply similar techniques to children with impaired control of their impulses. For example, there is evidence that attention training can improve attentional capacity in autistic children (Whalen & Schreibman, 2003) and the attentive abilities and academic efficiency of children with ADHD (Kerns *et al.*, 1999). This has led to research efforts focused on the supplementation of normally developing cognitive function with training, often accompanied by neuroimaging studies of associated changes in brain function.

A well-known commercial product, Dr Kawashima's Brain Training Game®, has been reported to improve executive functions, working memory, and processing speed in young adults (Nouchi *et al.*, 2013). In addition, in a classroom-based study (Miller & Robertson, 2010), positive effects on mathematics were reported after 10- to 11-year-olds played this game for 20 minutes a day for 10 weeks. However, this classroom study was heavily criticized for its flaws in design, statistical analysis, and reporting (Logie & Sala, 2010), while the game itself rehearses the player's numerical skills directly.

Computer-based cognitive training that transfers to academic achievement remains a possibility, but evidence has been difficult to find and many claims are highly contested. Few commercial brain-training games have been convincingly evaluated, but some studies suggest that reasoning skills and working memory are amenable to computer-based training. For example, studies of the commercial product Cogmed® have shown transfer of improved working memory to untrained tasks in students with ADHD (e.g. Klingberg *et al.*, 2005), and this improvement is retained for up to 6 months (Holmes *et al.*, 2010). Transfer is critical, as the ultimate goal is to generate improvements not only on the task used to train the cognitive function, but also on untrained tasks. However, the evidence so far is that transfer remains restricted to types of task that are similar to the training task (i.e. near-transfer effects). For example, training in reasoning improves performance on untrained reasoning tasks, but does not improve processing speed (Mackey *et al.*, 2011). In addition, a recent meta-analysis (Melby-Lervåg & Hulme, 2013) joins the voices of others (e.g. Shipstead *et al.*, 2012) in pointing out methodological flaws in some of these studies, proposing that there is a lack of convincing evidence for anything other than short-term, specific training effects that cannot be generalized. Debate about the effectiveness of cognitive training has continued as the design of training algorithms and interventions has improved, with some of the first evidence of transfer to academic achievement being published only recently (Goldin *et al.*, 2014).

Studies of executive function training using more physical activities that do not require technology, such as games involving resources that are found in typical preschool settings, have also reported some promising results (Röthlisberger *et al.*, 2012). Furthermore, two school curricula have been reported to have positive effects on executive functions in the early years, namely Montessori (Lillard & Else-Quest, 2006) and Tools of the Mind (Diamond *et al.*, 2007). These curricula share a number of features in common, including an emphasis on rehearsing executive functions and reducing stress (Diamond & Lee, 2011). However, a meticulously executed randomized controlled trial of Tools of the Mind has reported disappointing results (Farran & Wilson, 2014).

Sleep

The need to ensure proper cognitive function and the consolidation of the day's learning through proper sleep boasts a sound theoretical basis and a strong common-sense rationale for interventions.

Sleep does not merely provide rest that enables us to begin the next day in a more wakeful, attentive, and alert state. It also helps us to "lay down" and consolidate the day's experiences in long-term memory, so that our recollection of them becomes more robust and accessible to us in the future. Whereas the waking brain appears to be optimized for first encoding memories in a biological form, neuroscientists characterize sleep as the brain state that best consolidates them (Rasch & Born, 2013). This consolidation process starts by reactivating neuronal memory representations during slow-wave sleep, before these are transformed for integration into long-term memory. This is most strikingly illustrated by neuroimaging studies. One of these reveals how the sleeping brain reproduces the neural activities characterizing whatever we experienced in our preceding hours of wakefulness (Maquet *et al.*, 2000). The ensuing rapid-eye-movement (REM) sleep may be important for stabilizing these transformed memories. Sleep, by providing rest and better access to long-term memory, also helps us to access remotely associated ideas more efficiently, improving our ability to generate insights the next day (Wagner *et al.*, 2004). Regular and sufficient sleep is thus essential in order for the brain to learn and create efficiently.

An important component in the processes that help us to maintain regular sleep patterns (or so-called *circadian rhythms*) is the melatonin secreted by the brain's pineal gland. Teenagers often suffer a shortened sleep period, mainly because of falling asleep late. This is partly due to biological reasons, with puberty disrupting melatonin secretion, as well as psychosocial reasons (such as increased freedom), further exacerbated by forced awakenings on school days (Kirby *et al.*, 2011). The result is widespread daytime teenage sleepiness and associated reductions in cognitive function. Late-night use of electronic media is also commonly perceived as a cause of poor sleep (e.g. Suganuma *et al.*, 2007), with a study in the U.S.A. of teenagers' technology use after 9 pm indicating an average dose of 55 minutes of online computer use plus 24 minutes of video games (Calamaro *et al.*, 2009, p. 24).

In some countries, there is evidence that a double-shift school schedule seems to benefit the fulfilment of teenage sleep needs. There is a lack of reported interventions of the effects of school starting late in the U.K., although two notable studies report improvements in the U.SA. In one study, shifting the start of school from 7.15 am to 8.40 am improved attendance and reduced the number of students falling asleep in a cohort of primary and secondary school students (Wahistrom, 2002). In a more recent study, moving start times from 8.00 am to 8.30 am for 14- to 18-year-olds improved self-reported motivation and attendance (Owens *et al.*, 2010). However, it should be noted that the new start times trialled in these studies are frequently earlier than the times at which many schools in the U.K. and elsewhere currently begin their day.

Rather than change the school day, an alternative type of intervention involves educating adolescent students about the chronobiology of their sleep, in the hope that this will empower and encourage them to make wiser decisions about night-time sleep habits. Such interventions can successfully impart knowledge about sleep, with good retention of the knowledge, but appear to be unsuccessful in changing sleep habits (e.g. Cain *et al.*, 2011). This has led to calls for improved research efforts that focus upon, among other potential factors, how to create a cultural change in the importance assigned to sleep by adolescents (Blunden *et al.*, 2012). A more intense intervention involving a range of resources (a wall poster, fridge magnets, and a progress chart) supported by fortnightly telephone calls has, with some caution, reported more positive results (Tan *et al.*, 2012).

It has also been suggested that interventions concerned with sleep might benefit from considering the interrelationship of circadian rhythms of sleep with those more closely associated with nutritional issues. Specifically, receiving breakfast at school might delay the timing of nutritional intake to a later circadian phase, when both appetite and the intestinal systems are activated, making it possible to ingest larger and perhaps more nutritional meals. This may contribute to the improved school functioning that is sometimes observed when students are enrolled on school breakfast programs (Kleinman *et al.*, 2002).

Sleep and Technology

Excessive use of video games, partly identified by the disruption it causes in important areas of life such as sleeping, can be detrimental to a broad range of health measures, and also influences educational achievement (e.g. Bener *et al.*, 2010). A 2-year longitudinal study of children aged 8–14 years (Gentile *et al.*, 2011) linked pathological gaming to increased aggression, likelihood of being a victim of aggression, and poorer academic grades. Such evidence, together with the data on attentional problems discussed earlier, tends to support current guidelines from the American Academy of Pediatrics (AAP), which recommend a maximum of 2 hours of total screen time per day for children (American Academy of Pediatrics, 2009).

However, even when use is not excessive, the arousing effect of video-game play on a school evening may also influence sleep. In a small experimental study (Dworak *et al.*, 2007), 10 school children (average age 13.5 years) played a computer game for 60 minutes on one night of the week, watched television for the same amount of time on another evening, and also experienced one evening with no technology (as a control). Game playing resulted in significantly disrupted sleep patterns (including an approximately 20-minute further delay in sleep onset). Significantly, there was also reduced memory for material that students were exposed to after the game-playing session. Whereas playing video games results in a higher arousal state of the central nervous system (Wang & Perry, 2006), television viewing expends the same amount of energy as sitting quietly, and does not produce such large negative effects on sleep and memory. However, small screens may also be particularly problematic, due to their bright display terminals suppressing nocturnal melatonin secretion (Higuchi *et al.*, 2003). In a Belgian study of 13- to 16-year-olds, Van den Bulck (2007) found that mobile phone use after "lights out" was very common (most of the participants used their phones several times a month in this way), and was significantly related to increased tiredness.

Anxieties about children's use of technology have been the focus of media attention. However, at present little advice is offered to students, teachers, and parents in the U.K. about using technology healthily, beyond the critical issues of online safety. It has recently been suggested that digital hygiene might usefully be included in sleep intervention programs aimed at schoolchildren and their parents (Garmy *et al.*, 2012).

Sleep and Caffeine

Like technology, caffeine also disrupts sleep, with one study estimating that children who drink caffeinated beverages sleep 15 minutes less every night (Calamaro *et al.*, 2009). Caffeine is the only psychoactive drug legally available to children, and their consumption of it is very widespread. A small 500-mL bottle of cola contains the same amount of caffeine as a cup of coffee. In addition to the effects of reduced sleep, caffeine can contribute to poor cognitive functioning in other ways. Rather than making us more alert, habitual use of caffeine tends to suppress cognitive function, which only returns to baseline levels after ingestion of caffeine, and then, of course, only temporarily (James & Rogers, 2005). Many children commonly experience caffeine withdrawal (James, 1997). A study of children aged 9–10 years who habitually drank more than two cans a day showed decreased alertness compared with low users (Heatherley et al., 2006). As in studies of caffeine in adults, the alertness of these children only rose to baseline levels after they had received more caffeine. It would appear that, rather than making children fizzy for their lessons, the cola "caffeine fix" provides only a momentary return to the state of alertness offered by a caffeine-free lifestyle. A clinical review of the evidence confirmed clear links between caffeine and daytime sleepiness for both adults and children, and concluded that these effects are greatly underestimated both by the general population and by physicians (Roehrs & Roth, 2008). Caffeine may influence student achievement directly via its suppression of cognitive function, but the disruption of night-time sleep by caffeine can also induce tiredness and, as discussed earlier, potentially disrupt memory consolidation.

Neurofeedback

Neurofeedback—that is, the monitoring of one's own brain activity with a view to influencing it—is becoming cheaper, and studies with undergraduates and children, especially with children who have ADHD (Holtmann et al., 2014), point to its potential effectiveness. However, the fact that the theoretical basis of neurofeedback is still emerging, as well as questions about the optimal approaches to its application, highlight that at present neurofeedback research is still mostly exploratory.

Recent research has involved participants increasing the ratio of theta to alpha waves using auditory feedback with their eyes closed (a protocol originally designed to induce hypnogogia, a state historically associated with creativity) (Gruzelier, 2009). Another study investigating EEG neurofeedback concluded that it produced improvements in the performance ability of music students that were not observed with alternative interventions. In that study, conservatoire students received training using neurofeedback, and improvements in their musical performance were highly correlated with their ability to progressively influence neural signals associated with attention and relaxation (e.g. Gruzelier & Egner, 2004). Similar results have been found for dancers (Raymond et al., 2005).

The underlying neural mechanisms are the subject of active research, with evidence that self-induced changes in neural rhythms can produce detectable changes in neural function that last for 20 minutes or more (Ros et al., 2010). This supports the potential effectiveness of neurofeedback as a tool for mediating the plasticity of the brain, but many questions remain about the processes involved and how these can be best exploited for educational benefit. However, recently an initial study with 11-year-olds showed improved musical performance, creative improvisation, and measures of attention after ten 30-minute sessions of neurofeedback (Gruzelier et al., 2014). One study with adults has also shown improvements in mental rotation skills (Doppelmayr & Weber, 2011), which are thought to contribute to mathematical and scientific ability.

Neurofeedback may also be shared with the teacher. Alongside an understanding of technology use by children, Battro's review of the teaching brain identifies the use of wearable brain-image technologies in classrooms as having significant potential (Battro, 2010). Whereas studies such as those described above used high-quality multiple-electrode EEG apparatus, simple EEG devices retail for around $70. The manufacturers of one such device claim that it "safely measures brainwave signals and monitors the attention levels of students as they interact with math, memory and pattern recognition applications" (NeuroSky, 2015). Although these devices are primitive compared with those more often used in research environments, there are a number of ways in which even a noisy indicator of attention level might have a positive impact on learning. Further research is still required, but such an impact might arise from the learner's self-monitoring of their cognitive state, or by passing information to the teacher about individual or global levels of attention in a classroom. A recent study used such a device to inform an adaptive artificial agent designed to recapture diminished attention using verbal and non-verbal cues, and found that it significantly improved student recall of the learning content (Szafir & Mutlu, 2012).

Approaches for Which There is Least Evidence about Their Educational Impact and That Also Require the Most Translational Work

There are various other approaches that draw on neuroscience research, but that face significant challenges in terms of either their theoretical basis or their limited evidence for an impact on learning. This means that additional scientific questions need to be answered, or that substantially more developmental research needs to be done to allow the approach to be applied within the classroom. Nevertheless, it is important to be aware of these areas of research, their potential, and their limitations, not only because they are fast becoming the focus of media attention, but also because it is important to guard against a new generation of neuromyths. Accordingly, we shall briefly discuss one such approach—personalization—here.

Personalization

Although neuroscience is contributing an increasing number of insights about individual differences, and despite intuitive understandings of such differences, we know little about how to attend to these differences when designing learning technology, or about the magnitude and nature of any potential advantages.

Insights about individual differences may aid the selection of teaching approaches for different students. Examples of neuroimaging studies that might contribute in this way include the examination of gender difference in response to games (Hoeft *et al.*, 2008), and of age-related difference in response to different types of feedback (van Duijvenvoorde *et al.*, 2008). At a European Association for Research on Learning and Instruction Special Interest Group conference (2012) on neuroscience and education, Lee *et al.* (2012) reported on adult neural activities related to choice, suggesting that choice induces high levels of cognitive engagement, and that the impact of choice becomes stronger as the level of interest in topics increases.

However, although it is known that providing choice can improve motivation, the identification of learner preference does not always guarantee a learning advantage. There is, for example, a distinct lack of evidence for teaching to so-called learning styles (Krätzig & Arbuthnott, 2006). However, it is established that offering the freedom to make some choices can in itself provide motivation (Patall *et al.*, 2008). Although the benefits of personalization might seem intuitive or obvious, there has been a dearth of evaluated attempts to apply authentic neurocognitive understanding of individual differences (in terms of gender, age group, and measured ability) to the personalization of teaching and learning approaches or resources.

From the Laboratory to the Classroom

This chapter will conclude by briefly describing a games-based teaching application that is grounded in neuroscience research, that has been researched with children and students in authentic settings (Holmes *et al.*, 2013; Howard-Jones *et al.*, 2014), and the principles of which have been investigated as part of an fMRI study (Howard-Jones *et al.*, 2015a). Key ideas from this application might be implemented in any classroom.

The teaching application (an app known as zTP) draws on the role of uncertain rewards in games. As summarized earlier in this chapter, our motivation to win points in a game generates signals in the brain's reward system that involve the neurotransmitter dopamine in the midbrain regions. Primate studies show that a brief dopamine spike will be generated simply by the awareness that a reward will certainly be provided, or when a totally unexpected reward is received. However, when uncertainty exists about whether a reward will be received or not, there is a brief spike plus an additional ramping up of dopamine until the outcome is known (Fiorillo *et al.*, 2003). This results in more dopamine being released for uncertain rewards, peaking when the likelihood of receiving a reward is 50%. Importantly for education, a positive relationship between dopaminergic reward activity in the brain and memory formation has also been demonstrated, such that whether or not a reward is uncertain will predict the success of memory recall more effectively than the size of the reward itself (Howard-Jones & Demetriou, 2009).

Other related insights derived from the neuroscientific research are that the brain's response to rewards can be very brief (Bogacz *et al.*, 2007), which suggests that a close intermingling of learning and game-play elements is needed for the game-play to support the learning, whereas anticipation of an uncertain reward is likely to generate a more extended "window of enhanced attention" or "teachable moment" (Howard-Jones & Demetriou, 2009).

In a design-based research process that required five cycles of iterative design, intervention, analysis, and reflection, the authors and their colleagues simultaneously developed and researched what eventually became the design principles underlying zTP (Howard-Jones *et al.*, 2015b). The research was both prompted by and drew on the neuroscientific research outlined above. In early cycles, the app consisted of a standard PowerPoint presentation, some colored cards for students to use to indicate their answers, and a cardboard "wheel of fortune"—all of which might be implemented in any classroom. The latest version involved an Internet-based app that reduced some of the game's administrative burden, but in functionality was identical to the original version.

In all versions of the game, the teacher teaches a topic, perhaps using PowerPoint slides to structure and illustrate it, and then reveals a related question with color-coded multiple-choice answers. The students, sometimes working in teams, choose their answer and respond either by showing an appropriate-colored card or by clicking the appropriate-colored button in the Internet-based app. This approach to using multiple-choice questions in whole-class teaching is so far conventional. However, chance-based uncertainty is used to mediate the receipt of rewards. Having responded with their answer to the question, teams choose whether, if their answer turns out to be correct, they wish to receive one point, or to take a chance and receive either two or zero points based on a spin of a "wheel of fortune" that has a 50/50 chance of landing on "win" or "lose."

In each cycle of the research, the students were observed to be engaged by this novel approach to teaching and learning. They were animated and clearly excited by the challenges, absorbed in the activity, enjoying the immediate feedback, and attending closely to the teacher's talk. Observations also revealed that notable moments of heightened attention occurred when the correct answer was about to be announced and the wheel of fortune was turning—in other words, as the students were about to find out whether they would gain some points. Accordingly, if the enhanced levels of dopaminergic activity are to be usefully exploited and students are to achieve the potential learning gains, it is necessary for the teacher to exploit the teachable moments, discussing misconceptions or prompting extended answers while the correct answers are being revealed. Without this expert input from the teacher, the app has been shown to be less effective.

As noted earlier, for most learning games there is limited evidence of any impact in terms of improved engagement or enhanced academic achievement. Early cycles of this research also highlighted how, in any case, engagement does not necessarily translate into learning. Although they were obviously engaged, the students showed few if any learning gains. However, in the classroom-based study of a later cycle, for which the teacher had been shown how best to take advantage of teachable moments, statistically significant and encouraging learning gains were achieved. A subsequent fMRI study with adults used an adapted form of the software to identify the neural correlates of this positive impact on learning. Results showed gamification with uncertain reward increased learning as measured behaviorally. Gamification did not result in changes in task-positive (e.g. working memory) brain regions, but instead it reduced participants' activation during learning sessions in the default mode network (DMN—a network associated with mind wandering). Individual differences in learning performance were predicted by differences in DMN deactivation (Howard-Jones et al., 2016), providing insight into the neural processes underlying individual differences in response to the gamification of learning. In summary, these research outcomes suggest the importance of collaborative work between neuroscientists and educators in generating neuroscience-informed games-based teaching approaches and technologies.

References

Abraham, A. (2013). The promises and perils of the neuroscience of creativity. *Frontiers in Human Neuroscience*, 7, 246.

Alibali, M. W. & Nathan, M. J. (2012). Embodiment in mathematics teaching and learning: evidence from learners' and teachers' gestures. *Journal of the Learning Sciences*, 21, 247–286.

American Academy of Pediatrics (2009). Media violence. *Pediatrics*, 124, 1495–1503.

Anderson, L. S., Healy, A. F., Kole, J. A., & Bourne, L. E. (2011). Conserving time in the classroom: the clicker technique. *Quarterly Journal of Experimental Psychology*, 64, 1457–1462.

Anderson, L. S., Healy, A. F., Kole, J. A., & Bourne, L. E. (2013). The clicker technique: cultivating efficient teaching and successful learning. *Applied Cognitive Psychology*, 27, 222–234.

Ashcraft, M. H., Krause, J. A., & Hopko, D. R. (2007). Is math anxiety a mathematical learning difficulty? In: D. B. Berch & M. M. M. Mazzocco (Eds), *Why Is Math So Hard for Some Children? The Nature and Origins of Mathematical Learning Difficulties and Disabilities* (pp. 329–348). Baltimore, MD: Paul H. Brookes Publishing Co.

Barsalou, L.W. (2010). Grounded cognition: past, present, and future. *Topics in Cognitive Science*, 2, 716–724.

Battro, A. M. (2010). The teaching brain. *Mind, Brain, and Education*, 4, 28–33.

Beilock, S. L., Gunderson, E. A., Ramirez, G., & Levine, S. C. (2010). Female teachers' math anxiety affects girls' math achievement. *Proceedings of the National Academy of Sciences of the United States of America*, 107, 1860–1863.

Bener, A., Al-Mahdi, H. S., Vachhani, P. J., Al-Nufal, M., & Ali, A. I. (2010). Do excessive internet use, television viewing and poor lifestyle habits affect low vision in school children? *Journal of Child Health Care*, 14, 375–385.

Benjamin, C. F. A. & Gaab, N. (2012). What's the story? The tale of reading fluency told at speed. *Human Brain Mapping*, 33, 2572–2585.

Blunden, S. L., Chapman, J., & Rigney, G. A. (2012). Are sleep education programs successful? The case for improved and consistent research efforts. *Sleep Medicine Reviews*, 16, 355–370.

Bogacz, R., Usher, M., Zhang, J., & McClelland, J. L. (2007). Extending a biologically inspired model of choice: multi-alternatives, nonlinearity and value-based multidimensional choice. *Philosophical Transactions of the Royal Society of London B: Biological Sciences*, 362, 1655–1670.

Brankaer, C., Ghesquière, P., & De Smedt, B. (2015). The effect of a numerical domino game on numerical magnitude processing in children with mild intellectual disabilities. *Mind, Brain, and Education*, 9, 29–39.

Butler, A. C. (2010). Repeated testing produces superior transfer of learning relative to repeated studying. *Journal of Experimental Psychology: Learning, Memory, and Cognition*, 36, 1118–1133.

Cain, N., Gradisar, M., & Moseley, L. (2011). A motivational school-based intervention for adolescent sleep problems. *Sleep Medicine*, 12, 246–251.

Calamaro, C. J., Mason, T. B. A., & Ratcliffe, S. J. (2009). Adolescents living the 24/7 lifestyle: effects of caffeine and technology on sleep duration and daytime functioning. *Pediatrics*, 123, e1005–e1010.

Callan, D. E. & Schweighofer, N. (2008). Positive and negative modulation of word learning by reward anticipation. *Human Brain Mapping*, 29, 237–249.

Campbell, J. & Mayer, R. E. (2009). Questioning as an instructional method: does it affect learning from lectures? *Applied Cognitive Psychology*, 23, 747–759.

Carpenter, S. K., Pashler, H., & Cepeda, N. J. (2009). Using tests to enhance 8th grade students' retention of U.S. history facts. *Applied Cognitive Psychology*, 23, 760–771.

Carson, L. M. & Wiegand, R.L. (1979). Motor schema formation and retention in young children: a test of Schmidt's schema theory. *Journal of Motor Behavior*, 11, 247–251.

Catmur, C., Gillmeister, H., Bird, G., Liepelt, R., Brass, M., & Heyes, C. (2008). Through the looking glass: counter-mirror activation following incompatible sensorimotor learning. *European Journal of Neuroscience*. 28, 1208–1215.

Cepeda, N. J., Pashler, H., Vul, E., Wixted, J. T., & Rohrer, D. (2006). Distributed practice in verbal recall tasks: a review and quantitative synthesis. *Psychological Bulletin*, 132, 354–380.

Chaddock, L., Erickson, K. I., Prakash, R. S., Kim, J. S., Voss, M. W., VanPatter, M., Pontifex, M. B., Raine, L. B., Konkel, A., Hillman, C. H., Cohen, N. J., & Kramer, A. F. (2010). A neuroimaging investigation of the association between aerobic fitness, hippocampal volume, and memory performance in preadolescent children. *Brain Research*, 1358, 172–183.

Chaddock-Heyman, L., Erickson, K. I., Voss, M. W., Knecht, A. M., Pontifex, M. B., Castelli, D. M., Hillman, C. H., & Kramer, A. F. (2013). The effects of physical activity on functional MRI activation associated with cognitive control in children: a randomized controlled intervention. *Frontiers in Human Neuroscience*, 7, 72.

Chan, J. C. K. (2010). Long-term effects of testing on the recall of nontested materials. *Memory*, 18, 49–57.

Chang, Y.-K., Tsai, Y.-J., Chen, T.-T., & Hung, T.-M. (2013). The impacts of coordinative exercise on executive function in kindergarten children: an ERP study. *Experimental Brain Research*, 225, 187–196.

Chein, J., Albert, D., O'Brien, L., Uckert, K., & Steinberg, L. (2011). Peers increase adolescent risk taking by enhancing activity in the brain's reward circuitry. *Developmental Science*, 14, F1–F10.

Colcombe, S. J., Kramer, A. F., Erickson, K. I., Scalf, P., McAuley, E., Cohen, N. J., Webb, A., Jerome, G. J., Marquez, D. X., & Elavsky, S. (2004). Cardiovascular fitness, cortical plasticity, and aging. *Proceedings of the National Academy of Sciences of the United States of America*, 101, 3316–3321.

Dehaene, S. (2001). Précis of the number sense. *Mind & Language*, 16, 16–36.

Dehaene, S., Spelke, E., Pinel, P., Stanescu, R., & Tsivkin, S. (1999). Sources of mathematical thinking: behavioral and brain-imaging evidence. *Science*, 284, 970–974.

Dekker, S., Lee, N. C., Howard-Jones, P., & Jolles, J. (2012). Neuromyths in education: prevalence and predictors of misconceptions among teachers. *Frontiers in Psychology*, 3, 429.

De Smedt, B., Verschaffel, L., & Ghesquière, P. (2009). The predictive value of numerical magnitude comparison for individual differences in mathematics achievement. *Journal of Experimental Child Psychology*, 103, 469–479.

Diamond, A. & Lee, K. (2011). Interventions shown to aid executive function development in children 4 to 12 years old. *Science,* 333, 959–964.

Diamond, A., Barnett, W. S., Thomas, J., & Munro, S. (2007). Preschool program improves cognitive control. *Science*, 318, 1387–1388.

Doppelmayr, M. & Weber, E. (2011). Effects of SMR and theta/beta neurofeedback on reaction times, spatial abilities, and creativity. *Journal of Neurotherapy*, 15, 115–129.

Dworak, M., Schierl, T., Bruns, T., & Struder, H. K. (2007). Impact of singular excessive computer game and television exposure on sleep patterns and memory performance of school-aged children. *Pediatrics*, 120, 978–985.

Ellamil, M., Dobson, C., Beeman, M., & Christoff, K. (2012). Evaluative and generative modes of thought during the creative process. *NeuroImage*, 59, 1783–1794.

Engelkamp, J., Seiler, K. H., & Zimmer, H. D. (2004). Memory for actions: item and relational information in categorized lists. *Psychological Research*, 69, 1–10.

Erickson, K. I., Prakash, R. S., Voss, M. W., Chaddock, L., Hu, L., Morris, K. S., White, S. M., Wójcicki, T. R., McAuley, E., & Kramer, A. F. (2009). Aerobic fitness is associated with hippocampal volume in elderly humans. *Hippocampus*, 19, 1030–1039.

Farran, D. C. & Wilson, S. J. (2014). *Achievement and Self-Regulation in Pre-Kindergarten Classrooms: Effects of the Tools of the Mind Curriculum*. Nashville, TN: Peabody Research Institute. Available online at https://my.vanderbilt.edu/toolsofthemindevaluation/files/2011/12/Tools-Submission-Child-Development-7-27-14.pdf

Fernandez-Duque, D., Evans, J., Christian, C., & Hodges, S. D. (2015). Superfluous neuroscience information makes explanations of psychological phenomena more appealing. *Journal of Cognitive Neuroscience*, 27, 926–944.

Fink, A., Grabner, R. H., Gebauer, D., Reishofer, G., Koschutnig, K., & Ebner, F. (2010). Enhancing creativity by means of cognitive stimulation: evidence from an fMRI study. *NeuroImage*, 52, 1687–1695.

Fiorillo, C. D., Tobler, P. N., & Schultz, W. (2003). Discrete coding of reward probability and uncertainty by dopamine neurons. *Science*, 299, 1898–1902.

Fischer, U., Moeller, K., Bientzle, M., Cress, U., & Nuerk, H.-C. (2011). Sensori-motor spatial training of number magnitude representation. *Psychonomic Bulletin & Review*, 18, 177–183.

Frith, U., Bishop, D., Blakemore, C., Blakemore, S.-J., Butterworth, B., Goswami, U., Howard-Jones, P., Laurillard, D., Maguire, E., Sahakian, B. J., Smith, A. *et al.* (2011). *Brain Waves Module 2: Neuroscience: Implications for Education and Lifelong Learning*. London, UK: The Royal Society.

Gabriel, F., Coché, F., Szucs, D., Carette, V., & Rey, B. (2012). Developing children's understanding of fractions: an intervention study. *Mind, Brain, and Education*, 6, 137–146.

Garmy, P., Nyberg, P., & Jakobsson, U. (2012). Sleep and television and computer habits of Swedish school-age children. *Journal of School Nursing*, 28, 469–476.

Gazzola, V., Rizzolatti, G., Wicker, B., & Keysers, C. (2007). The anthropomorphic brain: the mirror neuron system responds to human and robotic actions. *NeuroImage*, 35, 1674–1684.

Geary, D. C. (2010). Mathematical disabilities: reflections on cognitive, neuropsychological, and genetic components. *Learning and Individual Differences*, 20, 130–130.

Gentile, D. A., Choo, H., Liau, A., Sim, T., Li, D., Fung, D., & Khoo, A. (2011). Pathological video game use among youths: a two-year longitudinal study. *Pediatrics*, 127, e319–e329.

Goldin, A. P., Hermidac, M. J., Shaloma, D. E., Costaa, M. E., Lopez-Rosenfelda, M., Segretinc, M. S., Fernández-Slezakd, D., Lipinac, S. J., & Sigmana, M. (2014). Far transfer to language and math of a short software-based gaming intervention. *Proceedings of the National Academy of Sciences of the United States of America*, 111, 6443–6448.

Gomez-Pinilla, F., Vaynman, S., & Ying, Z. (2008). Brain-derived neurotrophic factor functions as a metabotrophin to mediate the effects of exercise on cognition. *European Journal of Neuroscience*, 28, 2278–2287.

Gracia-Bafalluy, M. & Noel, M. (2008). Does finger training increase young children's numerical performance? *Cortex,* 44, 368–375.

Gruzelier, J. (2009). A theory of alpha/theta neurofeedback, creative performance enhancement, long distance functional connectivity and psychological integration. *Cognitive Processing*, 10 (Suppl. 1), S101–S109.

Gruzelier, J. H., Foks, M., Steffert, T., Chen, M.-L., & Ros, T. (2014). Beneficial outcome from EEG-neurofeedback on creative music performance, attention and well-being in school children. *Biological Psychology*, 95, 86–95.

Heatherley, S. V., Hancock, K. M. F., & Rogers, P. J. (2006). Psychostimulant and other effects of caffeine in 9- to 11-year-old children. *Journal of Child Psychology and Psychiatry*, 47, 135–142.

Higuchi, S., Motohashi, Y., Liu, Y., Ahara, M., & Kaneko, Y. (2003). Effects of VDT tasks with a bright display at night on melatonin, core temperature, heart rate, and sleepiness. *Journal of Applied Physiology*, 94, 1773–1776.

Hillman, C. H., Erickson, K. I., & Kramer, A. F. (2008). Be smart, exercise your heart: exercise effects on brain and cognition. *Nature Reviews: Neuroscience*, 9, 58–65.

Hoeft, F., Watson, C., Kesler, S., Bettinger, K., & Reiss, A. (2008). Gender differences in the mesocorticolimbic system during computer game-play. *Journal of Psychiatric Research*, 42, 253–258.

Holloway, I. D. & Ansari, D. (2009). Mapping numerical magnitudes onto symbols: the numerical distance effect and individual differences in children's mathematics achievement. *Journal of Experimental Child Psychology*, 103, 17–29.

Holmes, J., Gathercole, S. E., Place, M., Dunning, D. L., Hilton, K. A., & Elliott, J. G. (2010). Working memory deficits can be overcome: impacts of training and medication on working memory in children with ADHD. *Applied Cognitive Psychology*, 24, 827–836.

Holmes, W., Howard-Jones, P., Tanimoto, E., Jones, C., Demetriou, S., Morgan, O., Perkins, P., & Davies, N. (2013). Neuroeducational research in the design and use of games-based teaching. In: P. Escudeiro & C. Vaz de Carvalho (Eds), *Presented at the 7th European Conference on Games Based Learning, Porto, Portugal* (pp. 235–243). Reading: Academic Conferences and Publishing International Limited.

Holtmann, M., Sonuga-Barke, E., Cortese, S., & Brandeis, D. (2014). Neurofeedback for ADHD: a review of current evidence. *Child and Adolescent Psychiatric Clinics of North America*, 23, 789–806.

Howard-Jones, P. (2014a). *Neuroscience and Education: A Review of Educational Interventions and Approaches Informed by Neuroscience*. London: Education Endowment Foundation.

Howard-Jones, P. (2014b). Neuroscience and education: myths and messages. *Nature Reviews: Neuroscience*, 15, 817–824.

Howard-Jones, P. A. & Murray, S. (2003). Ideational productivity, focus of attention, and context. *Creativity Research Journal*, 15, 153–166.

Howard-Jones, P. A. & Demetriou, S. (2009). Uncertainty and engagement with learning games. *Instructional Science*, 37, 519–536.

Howard-Jones, P. & Jay, T. (in press). Reward, learning and games. *Current Opinion in Behavioral Sciences*. DOI: 10.1016/j.cobeha.2016.04.015

Howard-Jones, P. A., Blakemore, S.-J., Samuel, E. A., Summers, I. R., & Claxton, G. (2005). Semantic divergence and creative story generation: an fMRI investigation. *Cognitive Brain Research*, 25, 240–250.

Howard-Jones, P. A., Winfield, M., & Crimmins, G. (2008). Co-constructing an understanding of creativity in drama education that draws on neuropsychological concepts. *Educational Research*, 50, 187–201.

Howard-Jones, P. A., Bogacz, R., Yoo, J. H., Leonards, U., & Demetriou, S. (2010). The neural mechanisms of learning from competitors. *NeuroImage*, 53, 790–799.

Howard-Jones, P., Demetriou, S., Bogacz, R., Yoo, J. H., & Leonards, U. (2011). Toward a science of learning games. *Mind, Brain, and Education*, 5, 33–41.

Howard-Jones, P., Holmes, W., Demetriou, S., Jones, C., Tanimoto, E., Morgan, O., Perkins, E., & Davies, N. (2015a). Neuroeducational research in the design and use of a learning technology. *Learning, Media and Technology*, 40, 227–246.

Howard-Jones, P., Ott, M., van Leeuwen, T., & De Smedt, B. (2015b). The potential relevance of cognitive neuroscience for the development and use of technology-enhanced learning. *Learning, Media and Technology*, 40, 131–151.

Howard-Jones, P. A., Jay, T., Mason, A., & Jones, H. (2016). Gamification of learning deactivates the default mode network. *Frontiers in Psychology*, 6, 16. DOI: 10.3389/fpsyg.2015.01891

James, J. E. (1997). *Understanding Caffeine: A Biobehavioral Analysis*. Thousand Oaks, CA: Sage Publications, Inc.

James, J. E. & Rogers, P. J. (2005). Effects of caffeine on performance and mood: withdrawal reversal is the most plausible explanation. *Psychopharmacology*, 182, 1–8.

Johnson, C. I. & Mayer, R. E. (2009). A testing effect with multimedia learning. *Journal of Educational Psychology*, 101, 621–629.

Kamijo, K., Pontifex, M. B., O'Leary, K. C., Scudder, M. R., Wu, C.-T., Castelli, D. M., & Hillman, C. H. (2011). The effects of an afterschool physical activity program on working memory in preadolescent children. *Developmental Science*, 14, 1046–1058.

Kang, S. H. K., McDermott, K. B., & Roediger, H. L. (2007). Test format and corrective feedback modify the effect of testing on long-term retention. *European Journal of Cognitive Psychology*, 19, 528–558.

Karpicke, J. D. (2012). Retrieval-based learning: active retrieval promotes meaningful learning. *Current Directions in Psychological Science*, 21, 157–163.

Karpicke, J. D. & Blunt, J. R. (2011). Retrieval practice produces more learning than elaborative studying with concept mapping. *Science*, 331, 772–775.

Käser, T., Busetto, A. G., Solenthaler, B., Baschera, G.-M., Kohn, J., Kucian, K., von Aster, M., & Gross, M. (2013). Modelling and optimizing mathematics learning in children. *International Journal of Artificial Intelligence in Education*, 23, 115–135.

Kaufmann, L. (2008). Dyscalculia: neuroscience and education. *Educational Research*, 50, 163–175.

Kaufmann, L., Vogel, S., Wood, G., Kremser, C., Schocke, M., Zimmerhackl, L., & Koten, J. (2008). A developmental fMRI study of nonsymbolic numerical and spatial processing. *Cortex*, 44, 376–385.

Kelly, S. D., McDevitt, T., & Esch, M. (2009). Brief training with co-speech gesture lends a hand to word learning in a foreign language. *Language and Cognitive Processes*, 24, 313–334.

Kerns, K. A., Eso, K., & Thomson, J. (1999). Investigation of a direct intervention for improving attention in young children with ADHD. *Developmental Neuropsychology*, 16, 273–295.

Kirby, M., Maggi, S., & D'Angiulli, A. (2011). School start times and the sleep–wake cycle of adolescents: a review and critical evaluation of available evidence. *Educational Researcher*, 40, 56–61.

Kleinman, R. E., Hall, S., Green, H., Korzec-Ramirez, D., Patton, K., Pagano, M. E., & Murphy, J. M. (2002). Diet, breakfast, and academic performance in children. *Annals of Nutrition & Metabolism*, 46 (Suppl.1), 24–30.

Klingberg, T., Fernell, E., Olesen, P. J., Johnson, M., Gustafsson, P., Dahlström, K., Gillberg, C. G., Forssberg, H., & Westerberg, H. (2005). Computerized training of working memory in children with ADHD—a randomized, controlled trial. *Journal of the American Academy of Child & Adolescent Psychiatry*, 44, 177–186.

Kolkman, M. E., Kroesbergen, E. H., & Leseman, P. P. M. (2013). Early numerical development and the role of non-symbolic and symbolic skills. *Learning and Instruction*, 25, 95–103.

Kounios, J., Fleck, J. I., Green, D. L., Payne, L., Stevenson, J. L., Bowden, E. M., & Jung-Beeman, M. (2008). The origins of insight in resting-state brain activity. *Neuropsychologia*, 46, 281–291.

Krätzig, G. P. & Arbuthnott, K. D. (2006). Perceptual learning style and learning proficiency: a test of the hypothesis. *Journal of Educational Psychology*, 98, 238–246.

Krinzinger, H., Koten, J. W., Horoufchin, H., Kohn, N., Arndt, D., Sahr, K., Konrad, K., & Willmes, K., (2011). The role of finger representations and saccades for number processing: an fMRI study in children. *Frontiers in Psychology*, 2, 373.

Kubesch, S., Walk, L., Spitzer, M., Kammer, T., Lainburg, A., Heim, R., & Hille, K. (2009). A 30-minute physical education program improves students' executive attention. *Mind, Brain, and Education*, 3, 235–242.

Kucian, K., Grond, U., Rotzer, S., Henzi, B., Schönmann, C., Plangger, F., Gälli, M., Martin, E., & von Aster, M. (2011). Mental number line training in children with developmental dyscalculia. *NeuroImage*, 57, 782–795.

Lakes, K. D. & Hoyt, W. T. (2004). Promoting self-regulation through school-based martial arts training. *Journal of Applied Developmental Psychology*, 25, 283–302.

Lee, K., Bong, M., & Kim, S. (2012). *Does Choice Increase Cognitive Engagement? Neural Basis of Choice Effect*. Poster presented at the Neuroscience and Education Special Interest Group of the European Association for Research on Learning and Instruction (EARLI), London, UK, 24–26 May 2012.

Lillard, A. & Else-Quest, N. (2006). The early years: evaluating Montessori education. *Science*, 313, 1893–1894.

Logie, R. H. & Sala, S. D. (2010). Brain training in schools: where is the evidence? Colloquium. *British Journal of Educational Technology*, 41, E127–E128.

Lyons, I. M. & Beilock, S. L. (2012). Mathematics anxiety: separating the math from the anxiety. *Cerebral Cortex*, 22, 2102–2110.

McDaniel, M. A., Roediger, H. L., & McDermott, K. B. (2007). Generalizing test-enhanced learning from the laboratory to the classroom. *Psychonomic Bulletin & Review*, 14, 200–206.

McDaniel, M. A., Agarwal, P. K., Huelser, B. J., McDermott, K. B., & Roediger, H. L. (2011). Test-enhanced learning in a middle school science classroom: the effects of quiz frequency and placement. *Journal of Educational Psychology*, 103, 399–414.

Macedonia, M. & Knösche, T. R. (2011). Body in mind: how gestures empower foreign language learning. *Mind, Brain, and Education*, 5, 196–211.

Mackey, A. P., Hill, S. S., Stone, S. I., & Bunge, S. A. (2011). Differential effects of reasoning and speed training in children: effects of reasoning and speed training in children. *Developmental Science*, 14, 582–590.

Maquet, P., Laureys, S., Peigneux, P., Fuchs, S., Petiau, C., Phillips, C., Aerts, J., Del Fiore, G., Degueldre, C., Meulemans, T., Luxen, A., Franck, G., Van Der Linden, M., Smith, C., & Cleeremans, A. (2000). Experience-dependent changes in cerebral activation during human REM sleep. *Nature Neuroscience*, 3, 831–836.

Melby-Lervåg, M. & Hulme, C. (2013). Is working memory training effective? A meta-analytic review. *Developmental Psychology*, 49, 270–291.

Miller, D. J. & Robertson, D. P. (2010). Using a games console in the primary classroom: effects of 'Brain Training' programme on computation and self-esteem. *British Journal of Educational Technology*, 41, 242–255.

Moeller, K., Martignon, L., Wessolowski, S., Engel, J., & Nuerk, H.-C. (2011). Effects of finger counting on numerical development – the opposing views of neurocognition and mathematics education. *Frontiers in Psychology*, 2, 328.

Mullender-Wijnsma, M. J., Hartman, E., de Greeff, J. W., Bosker, R. J., Doolaard, S., & Visscher, C. (2015). Improving academic performance of school-age children by physical activity in the classroom: 1-year program evaluation. *Journal of School Health*, 85, 365–371.

Mussolin, C., De Volder, A., Grandin, C., Schlögel, X., Nassogne, M.-C., & Noël, M.-P. (2010). Neural correlates of symbolic number comparison in developmental dyscalculia. *Journal of Cognitive Neuroscience*, 22, 860–874.

Neeper, S. A., Gomezpinilla, F., Choi, J., & Cotman, C. (1995). Exercise and brain neurotrophins. *Nature*, 373, 109.

NeuroSky (2015). MindWave. Available online at http://store.neurosky.com/products/mindwave-1 (accessed 17 June 2015).

Nieuwenhuis, S., Heslenfeld, D. J., Alting von Geusau, N. J., Mars, R. B., Holroyd, C. B., & Yeung, N. (2005). Activity in human reward-sensitive brain areas is strongly context dependent. *NeuroImage*, 25, 1302–1309.

Noël, M.-P. (2005). Finger gnosia: a predictor of numerical abilities in children? *Child Neuropsychology*, 11, 413–430.

Nouchi, R., Taki, Y., Takeuchi, H., Hashizume, H., Nozawa, T., Kambara, T., Sekiguchi, A., Miyauchi, C. M., Kotozaki, Y., Nouchi, H., & Kawashima, R. (2013). Brain training game boosts executive functions, working memory and processing speed in the young adults: a randomized controlled trial. *PLoS One*, 8, e55518.

Obersteiner, A., Reiss, K., & Ufer, S. (2013). How training on exact or approximate mental representations of number can enhance first-grade students' basic number processing and arithmetic skills. *Learning and Instruction*, 23, 125–135.

Osgood-Campbell, E. (2015). Investigating the educational implications of embodied cognition: a model interdisciplinary inquiry in mind, brain, and education curricula. *Mind, Brain, and Education*, 9, 3–9.

Owens, J. A., Belon, K., & Moss, P. (2010). Impact of delaying school start time on adolescent sleep, mood, and behavior. *Archives of Pediatrics and Adolescent Medicine*, 164, 608–614.

Ozcelik, E., Cagiltay, N. E., & Ozcelik, N. S. (2013). The effect of uncertainty on learning in game-like environments. *Computers & Education*, 67, 12–20.

Pasquinelli, E. (2012). Neuromyths: why do they exist and persist? *Mind, Brain, and Education*, 6, 89–96.

Patall, E. A., Cooper, H., & Robinson, J. C. (2008). The effects of choice on intrinsic motivation and related outcomes: a meta-analysis of research findings. *Psychological Bulletin*, 134, 270–300.

Penner-Wilger, M. & Anderson, M. L. (2013). The relation between finger gnosis and mathematical ability: why redeployment of neural circuits best explains the finding. *Frontiers in Psychology*, 4, 877.

Piazza, M., Facoetti, A., Trussardi, A. N., Berteletti, I., Conte, S., Lucangeli, D., Dehaene, S., & Zorzi, M. (2010). Developmental trajectory of number acuity reveals a severe impairment in developmental dyscalculia. *Cognition*, 116, 33–41.

Ramirez, G. & Beilock, S. L. (2011). Writing about testing worries boosts exam performance in the classroom. *Science*, 331, 211–213. DOI: 10.1126/science.1199427

Räsänen, P., Salminen, J., Wilson, A. J., Aunio, P., & Dehaene, S. (2009). Computer-assisted intervention for children with low numeracy skills. *Cognitive Development*, 24, 450–472.

Rasberry, C. N., Lee, S. M., Robin, L., Laris, B. A., Russell, L. A., Coyle, K. K., & Nihiser, A. J. (2011). The association between school-based physical activity, including physical education, and academic performance: a systematic review of the literature. *Preventive Medicine*, 52, S10–S20.

Rasch, B. & Born, J. (2013). About sleep's role in memory. *Physiological Reviews*, 93, 681–766.

Rau, M. A., Aleven, V., & Rummel, N. (2013). Interleaved practice in multi-dimensional learning tasks: which dimension should we interleave? *Learning and Instruction*, 23, 98–114.

Raymond, J., Sajid, I., Parkinson, L., & Gruzelier, J. H. (2005). The beneficial effects of alpha/theta and heart rate variability training on dance performance. *Applied Psychophysiology and Biofeedback*, 30, 65–73.

Rizzolatti, G. & Craighero, L. (2004). The mirror-neuron system. *Annual Review of Neuroscience*, 27, 169–192.

Roediger, H. L. & Karpicke, J. D. (2006). Test-enhanced learning: taking memory tests improves long-term retention. *Psychological Science*, 17, 249–255.

Roediger III, H. L., Putnam, A. L., & Smith, M. A. (2011). Ten benefits of testing and their applications to educational practice. In: J. P. Mestre & B. H. Ross (Eds), *Cognition in Education* (pp. 1–36). San Diego, CA: Academic Press.

Roehrs, T. & Roth, T. (2008). Caffeine: sleep and daytime sleepiness. *Sleep Medicine Reviews*, 12, 153–162.

Rohrer, D. & Pashler, H. (2010). Recent research on human learning challenges conventional instructional strategies. *Educational Researcher*, 39, 406–412.

Ros, T., Munneke, M. A., Ruge, D., Gruzelier, J. H., & Rothwell, J. C. (2010). Endogenous control of waking brain rhythms induces neuroplasticity in humans. *European Journal of Neuroscience*, 31, 770–778.

Röthlisberger, M., Neuenschwander, R., Cimeli, P., Michel, E., & Roebers, C. M. (2012). Improving executive functions in 5- and 6-year-olds: evaluation of a small group intervention in prekindergarten and kindergarten children. *Infant and Child Development*, 21, 411–429.

Shaywitz, B. A., Shaywitz, S. E., Blachman, B. A., Pugh, K. R., Fulbright, R. K., Skudlarski, P., Mencl, W. E., Constable, R. T., Holahan, J. M., Marchione, K. E., Fletcher, J. M., Lyon, G. R., & Gore, J. C. (2004). Development of left occipitotemporal systems for skilled reading in children after a phonologically-based intervention. *Biological Psychiatry*, 55, 926–933.

Shipstead, Z., Redick, T. S., & Engle, R. W. (2012). Is working memory training effective? *Psychological Bulletin*, 138, 628–654.

Shohamy, D. & Adcock, R. A. (2010). Dopamine and adaptive memory. *Trends in Cognitive Sciences*, 14, 464–472.

Snowling, M. J. & Hulme, C. (2011). Evidence-based interventions for reading and language difficulties: creating a virtuous circle. *British Journal of Educational Psychology*, 81, 1–23.

So, W. C., Sim Chen-Hui, C., & Low Wei-Shan, J. (2012). Mnemonic effect of iconic gesture and beat gesture in adults and children: is meaning in gesture important for memory recall? *Language and Cognitive Processes*, 27, 665–681.

Sobel, H. S., Cepeda, N. J., & Kapler, I. V. (2011). Spacing effects in real-world classroom vocabulary learning. *Applied Cognitive Psychology*, 25, 763–767.

Spaulding, L. S., Mostert, M. P., & Beam, A. P. (2010). Is Brain Gym® an effective educational intervention? *Exceptionality*, 18, 18–30.

Suganuma, N., Kikuchi, T., Yanagi, K., Yamamura, S., Morishima, H., Adachi, H., Kumano-Go, T., Mikami, A., Sugita, Y., & Takeda, M. (2007). Using electronic media before sleep can curtail sleep time and result in self-perceived insufficient sleep. *Sleep and Biological Rhythms*, 5, 204–214.

Szafir, D. & Mutlu, B. (2012). Pay attention! Designing adaptive agents that monitor and improve user engagement. In: *Proceedings of the SIGCHI Conference on Human Factors in Computing Systems* (pp. 11–20). New York: Association for Computing Machinery.

Tan, E., Healey, D., Gray, A. R., & Galland, B. C. (2012). Sleep hygiene intervention for youth aged 10 to 18 years with problematic sleep: a before-after pilot study. *BMC Pediatrics*, 12, 189.

Taylor, K. & Rohrer, D. (2010). The effects of interleaved practice. *Applied Cognitive Psychology*, 24, 837–848.

Temple, E., Deutsch, G. K., Poldrack, R. A., Miller, S. L., Tallal, P., Merzenich, M. M., & Gabrieli, J. D. (2003). Neural deficits in children with dyslexia ameliorated by behavioral remediation: evidence from functional MRI. *Proceedings of the National Academy of Sciences of the United States of America*, 100, 2860–2865.

Toppino, T. C. (1991). The spacing effect in young children's free recall: support for automatic-process explanations. *Memory & Cognition*, 19, 159–167.

Vanbinst, K., Ghesquiere, P., & De Smedt, B. (2012). Numerical magnitude representations and individual differences in children's arithmetic strategy use. *Mind, Brain, and Education*, 6, 129–136.

van den Broek, G. S. E., Takashima, A., Segers, E., Fernández, G., & Verhoeven, L. (2013). Neural correlates of testing effects in vocabulary learning. *NeuroImage*, 78, 94–102.

Van den Bulck, J. (2007). Adolescent use of mobile phones for calling and for sending text messages after lights out: results from a prospective cohort study with a one-year follow-up. *Sleep*, 30, 1220–1223.

van Duijvenvoorde, A. C., Zanolie, K., Rombouts, S. A., Raijmakers, M. E., & Crone, E. A. (2008). Evaluating the negative or valuing the positive? Neural mechanisms supporting feedback-based learning across development. *Journal of Neuroscience*, 28, 9495–9503.

van Gog, T. & Kester, L. (2012). A test of the testing effect: acquiring problem-solving skills from worked examples. *Cognitive Science*. 36, 1532–1541.

Vestergren, P. & Nyberg, L. (2014). Testing alters brain activity during subsequent restudy: evidence for test-potentiated encoding. *Trends in Neuroscience and Education*, 3, 69–80.

Voss, M. W., Prakash, R. S., Erickson, K. I., Basak, C., Chaddock, L., Kim, J. S., Alves, H., Heo, S., Szabo, A. N., White, S. M., Wójcicki, T. R., Mailey, E. L., Gothe, N., Olson, E. A., McAuley, E., & Kramer, A. F. (2010). Plasticity of brain networks in a randomized intervention trial of exercise training in older adults. *Frontiers in Aging Neuroscience*, 2, 32.

Vukovic, R. K., Kieffer, M. J., Bailey, S. P., & Harari, R. R. (2013). Mathematics anxiety in young children: concurrent and longitudinal associations with mathematical performance. *Contemporary Educational Psychology*, 38, 1–10.

Wagner, U., Gais, S., Haider, H., Verleger, R., & Born, J. (2004). Sleep inspires insight. *Nature*, 427, 352–355.

Wahistrom, K. (2002). Changing times: findings from the first longitudinal study of later high school start times. *NASSP Bulletin*, 86, 3–21.

Wang, X. & Perry, A. C. (2006). Metabolic and physiologic responses to video game play in 7- to 10-year-old boys. *Archives of Pediatrics and Adolescent Medicine*, 160, 411–415.

Whalen, C. & Schreibman, L. (2003). Joint attention training for children with autism using behavior modification procedures. *Journal of Child Psychology and Psychiatry*, 44, 456–468.

Wiklund-Hörnqvist, C., Karlsson, L., Eriksson, J., Andersson, M., Jonsson, B., & Nyberg, L. (2013). Activity in left temporal-parietal regions characterizes long-term retention after repeated testing. *Journal of Cognitive Neuroscience*, S114.

Wilson, A. J., Dehaene, S., Pinel, P., Revkin, S. K., Cohen, L., & Cohen, D. (2006a). Principles underlying the design of "The Number Race", an adaptive computer game for remediation of dyscalculia. *Behavioral and Brain Functions*, 2, 19.

Wilson, A. J., Revkin, S. K., Cohen, D., Cohen, L., & Dehaene, S. (2006b). An open trial assessment of "The Number Race", an adaptive computer game for remediation of dyscalculia. *Behavioral and Brain Functions*. 2, 20.

Wilson, A. J., Dehaene, S., Dubois, O., & Fayol, M. (2009). Effects of an adaptive game intervention on accessing number sense in low-socioeconomic-status kindergarten children. *Mind, Brain, and Education*. 3, 224–234.

Winter, B., Breitenstein, C., Mooren, F. C., Voelker, K., Fobker, M., Lechtermann, A., Krueger, K., Fromme, A., Korsukewitz, C., Floel, A., & Knecht, S. (2007). High impact running improves learning. *Neurobiology of Learning and Memory*, 87, 597–609.

Xue, G., Mei, L., Chen, C., Lu, Z.-L., Poldrack, R., & Dong, Q. (2011). Spaced learning enhances subsequent recognition memory by reducing neural repetition suppression. *Journal of Cognitive Neuroscience*, 23, 1624–1633.

Young, C. B., Wu, S. S., & Menon, V. (2012). The neurodevelopmental basis of math anxiety. *Psychological Science*, 23, 492–501.

Zhou, J. (2012). The effects of reciprocal imitation on teacher–student relationships and student learning outcomes. *Mind, Brain, and Education*, 6, 66–73.

Zimmerman, E. & Fortugno, N. (2005). *Soapbox: Learning to Play to Learn – Lessons in Educational Game Design*. Gamasutra: The Art and Business of Making Games. Available online at www.gamasutra.com/view/feature/2273/soapbox_learning_to_play_to_learn_.php (accessed 16 June 2015).

15

LABORATORY SCHOOLS

Bridging Theory, Research, and Practice to Improve Education

Sharon M. Carver, Wendell McConnaha, Richard Messina, Elizabeth Morley, and Yingmin Wang

CARNEGIE MELLON UNIVERSITY, UNIVERSITY OF PITTSBURGH AND TSINGHUA UNIVERSITY, UNIVERSITY OF TORONTO, UNIVERSITY OF TORONTO, AND TSINGHUA UNIVERSITY

Introduction

The interdisciplinary field of learning sciences aims to advance theory, research, and practice related to human learning, learning environments, and learning support systems (e.g. curricula, instructional methods, educational policy, etc.) in ways that are directly relevant to improving real-world learning in a variety of educational contexts, including classrooms. Researchers in this new field experience a balance of challenges and rewards from their interdisciplinary collaborations, but they do not often experience the same level of reciprocity in their researcher–practitioner partnerships, which means that the challenges of collaboration with educators often outweigh the benefits. Practitioners may be similarly wary of research involvement, particularly when the school is simply viewed as the research site and not as a full partner in the investigation.

From the perspective of the first author of this chapter, as a developmental psychologist serving as a laboratory school director on the campus of a research university, it seems that the difficulty in forming beneficial researcher–practitioner relationships arises from a linguistic and cultural divide—one that she has attempted to bridge for the past three decades (Carver & Klahr, 2001). In that time, she has determined that laboratory schools on college and university campuses are uniquely poised to lead the bridge building, because laboratory school leaders already share the culture of the academy with researchers and can more easily become "bilingual", such that they can help to decrease the barriers to constructive collaboration by translating for both researchers and educators interested in improving education. Furthermore, laboratory school educators who intentionally focus on interpretation from research to practice and vice versa can purposefully encourage practitioners from the broader community beyond the academy to engage in collaborative research, while encouraging researchers to view their collaborations in a more reciprocal manner. In this way, partnerships become more positive and productive, especially for the learners, who benefit from the principles discovered and the educational innovations designed.

Tackling the complex educational problems of interest to the researchers whose work is included in this volume and the educators who endeavor to apply it requires focused programs of research to investigate the nuances of the learning principles, particularly as they relate to individual learners mastering distinct domains in diverse learning venues. Laboratory school research sites benefit from institutional support for innovation, yet freedom from excessive constraints, as well as a balance between access to new ideas and time to develop relationships and long-term projects. What we hope to demonstrate in this chapter is the value of researcher–practitioner collaboration in laboratory school contexts, so that both researchers and educators may seek opportunities for similar collaborations to advance the learning sciences.

What is a Laboratory School?

The earliest laboratory schools served primarily as demonstration sites within teacher-training programs (National Association of Laboratory Schools, 1991). In 1896, John Dewey shifted the focus of campus schools to research when he founded the laboratory school at the University of Chicago. According to Dewey,

> Conducted under the management and supervision of the university's Department of Philosophy, Psychology, and Education, [the laboratory school] bore the same relation to the work of the department that a laboratory bears to biology, physics, or chemistry. Like any such laboratory, it had two main purposes: (a) to exhibit, test, verify and criticize theoretical statements and principles, and (b) to add to the sum of facts and principles in its special line.
>
> *(Mayhew & Edwards, 1965, p. 3)*

Although several hundred laboratory schools had emerged by the mid-twentieth century, it was not until 1958 that the Laboratory School Administrators Association (LSAA) was formed to develop resources for and synergies among laboratory schools. The laboratory schools varied in terms of the age levels served (from early childhood only to full pre-K to twelfth-grade programs), but the academy provided a common context for laboratory school administrators. By 1974, the association had broadened to include laboratory school faculty, and had changed its name to the National Association of Laboratory Schools (NALS). By 2006, the Association decided to recognize its international members and those with diverse governance structures by adding a tag line—NALS: International Association of Laboratory and University Affiliated Schools. In 2012, the Association signaled its full commitment to serving an international cadre of colleagues by becoming the International Association of Laboratory Schools (IALS) and adopting a mission statement broad enough to include a wide range of laboratory schools:

> The IALS is an international association of pre-kindergarten through graduate laboratory and university affiliated schools engaged in practices of *teacher training, curriculum development, research, professional development,* and *educational experimentation* for the purpose of supporting members' schools, and as a voice speaking for the improvement of learning for all children.

Laboratory schools that take Dewey's mission seriously cultivate the dispositions necessary for effective research collaborations among all of the learners in the school and are proactive in seeking partnership opportunities that deepen research investigations and broaden the impact of findings by facilitating wide dissemination and encouraging dialogue and application to inform the learning sciences and improve education.

The bulk of this chapter focuses on introducing three individual laboratory schools as exemplars of reciprocal bridge building that has advanced educational theory, research, and practice. From these models, we then highlight the important role that laboratory school educators can play in advancing the translation between research and practice, such that all learning sciences researchers can develop more fruitful partnerships with educators in the learning contexts most relevant to their investigations.

Laboratory School Exemplars

The unique context of each laboratory school and strategic niche within the campus and community affords different opportunities for proactively facilitating the translation of psychological, educational, and neuroscientific research to inform teaching practice. By introducing the Carnegie Mellon University Children's School (U.S.A.) (www.psy.cmu.edu/cs/), the Fanny Edel Falk Laboratory School (U.S.A.) (www.falkschool.pitt.edu), and the Jackman Institute of Child Study Laboratory School (Canada) (www.oise.utoronto.ca/ics), all in the voices of their own leaders, we seek to demonstrate the varied possibilities for laboratory school roles and highlight the significant impact that laboratory school educators can have on the effectiveness of researcher–educator collaboration that enhances the effectiveness of both.

Carnegie Mellon University Children's School

Origins of the School

The Children's School began as the Child Development Laboratory, a small nursery program serving as an observation site for the Margaret Morrison Carnegie School for Women that opened in 1906 as one of the four colleges of the Carnegie Technical Schools, which then became the Carnegie Institute of Technology in 1912. In 1968, just after the Carnegie Institute of Technology became Carnegie Mellon University, a grant from the ESSO Foundation supported faculty design of a larger laboratory program inspired by John Dewey's progressive philosophy and the open classrooms of the English infant schools, where "children are expected and encouraged to explore and use the total environment" (Regan, 1973). At that point, the program was renamed the "Children's School" and moved into the Margaret Morrison Carnegie (MMC) building to accommodate a capacity of 48 half-day preschoolers. Within the next few years, the programs and students of the School for Women became integrated into the CMU departments, and the Children's School became part of the Psychology Department within the College of Humanities and Social Sciences. Gradual acquisition of additional space in the MMC building afforded program growth to its current capacity of 72 half-day preschoolers and 24 full-day kindergartners. The Children's School achieved accreditation by the National Association for the Education of Young Children in 2003 and has been re-accredited every 5 years, as well as becoming licensed as a private academic school in the State of Pennsylvania in 2014.

The Children's School's approach to preschool and kindergarten education is based on theories and research in developmental psychology. It uses a set of developmental goals as a systematic framework for focusing its program and assessment design. It has specified detailed learning goals for 3-, 4-, and 5-year-olds in each of the following categories: self-esteem and independence, interaction and cooperation, communication, discovery and exploration, physical capabilities/health and safety, and artistic expression and appreciation. Its teachers are familiar with a wide variety of educational approaches, and they choose teaching strategies, daily routines, classroom arrangements, and curriculum structure that will encourage each child's development. Teacher observations and documentation of individual development are used to adjust the program to better challenge each child, as well as to conference with parents about ways in which teachers and parents can work as a team to provide support.

The teachers prepare an engaging learning environment for exploring a theme, such as birds, music, or building. They use a group meeting time each day to set the stage for the investigation and introduce relevant concepts. Then the children pursue a variety of activities that reinforce the learning goals in an open classroom environment. The educators monitor the children's activities, so that they may facilitate the children's learning and challenge them at an appropriate level. Children's explorations enrich their development of concepts related to the theme and strengthen their skills in all areas. They extend and apply their concepts by experimenting with various materials in the school, and they express their understanding by creating their own representations in a variety of media.

The Children's School's program is strengthened by the school's relationship with Carnegie Mellon University. As part of the Psychology Department, the school serves as a laboratory for research in child development. Its children eagerly participate in "special games" with researchers, and the teachers and parents receive summary results of current studies. As part of the university community, the school has access to facilities such as the gym and track, can schedule walking field trips to interesting places such as the post office, food services, and the robotics lab, and has visits from university musicians, security officers, construction workers, etc. Undergraduate interns and student employees enhance the children's experiences, and at the same time their involvement at the school strengthens their understanding of child development theory, research, and practice.

Mission and Purpose of the School

As a university laboratory school, we aim to lead through excellence and innovation as we:

1. facilitate interdisciplinary research in developmental psychology and related fields,
2. support undergraduate and graduate students studying child development theory, research, and applications,
3. create and implement developmentally appropriate, inclusive half-day preschool, full-day kindergarten, extended day, and camp programs for children ages 3–6,
4. collaborate with families in nurturing and educating their children, particularly as family challenges arise and developmental difficulties emerge,
5. organize professional development experiences and provide resources for practicing educators locally, nationally, and internationally, and
6. mentor students exploring careers in early childhood, elementary education, and related fields.

To model best practices that promote positive and productive learning for all members of its learning community, we foster a professional climate of hospitality, communication, trust, teamwork, and flexible problem solving. We strive to recruit a diverse staff and student population to provide a diverse subject pool for research, broad experiences for university students, and an enriched learning environment for our children and their families. By continually striving for quality improvement in all aspects of our mission, including the foundational finances and facilities, our laboratory school exemplifies progressive design in education and the learning sciences that can be utilized by professionals in various disciplines to meet the changing needs of society.

The phrasing and priority of this mission statement highlight the unique context of a laboratory school within a Psychology Department on the campus of a major research university that does not have a Department or School of Education. Carnegie Mellon does have a rich tradition of interdisciplinary inquiry within and between the seven colleges, and there is a significant emphasis on the learning sciences and brain sciences on its campus, both of which are enhanced by sophisticated technological methods (see www.cmu.edu/simon/ and www.cmu.edu/research/brain/). This context challenges Children's School educators to bridge from their own training in education to the culture of psychology and other disciplines, while also striving to serve as translators between researchers and practitioners.

The key to the Children's School's effectiveness in this translation process is having a director who not only has training and experience in both psychology and education, which means that she is bilingual and understands both disciplinary cultures, but also has a long tenure on campus during which to build relational bridges. The school's strategy has been multifaceted, with proactive bridge building for all of the laboratory school's constituent groups. Within the school, the director models bilingualism for the educators by sharing relevant lessons from her own reading and talks she has attended, by arranging reading groups and research presentations, by helping with translation during dialogue and subsequent efforts to apply research in the laboratory school classrooms, and by facilitating collaborations that involve educators directly in research. She then coaches these educators as they share what they have learned with practicing and pre-service educators via workshops offered on campus, consulting done in the community, and conference presentations through the local Pittsburgh Association for the Education of Young Children (PAEYC), the National Coalition for Campus Children's Centers (NCCCC), and the International Association of Laboratory Schools (IALS).

Undergraduate and graduate students have opportunities to explore the interdisciplinary links within the learning sciences through their course and project work. Undergraduates from all colleges begin by conducting comparative observations in the preschool and kindergarten classrooms as part of their Principles of Child Development course, and can choose to deepen their learning by taking a Developmental Research Methods course and a Practicum in Child Development to complete the "theory–research–practice" triangle. As their interests develop, students can join a faculty research team and also conduct their senior thesis project at the laboratory school. These theses may involve experimental psychology work, interdisciplinary design projects, or even literary compositions to communicate broadly about some aspect of child development. Similarly, graduate students tour the school and conduct observations as part of learning sciences courses and have access to the laboratory school for advanced projects and dissertation research. In all of these cases, learning experiences at the Children's School prepare students for interdisciplinary work bridging theory, research, and practice related to child development, regardless of their particular majors or career trajectories.

Finally, Carnegie Mellon faculty members involved in the learning sciences community on campus benefit from having the Children's School director and educators in the audience, asking questions and making connections from an educator's point of view. These educator perspectives may shape researchers' topics, research questions, methods, analysis techniques, and so on, and they certainly help them prepare to approach potential collaborators within the community of practitioners. Those actually conducting research at the Children's School benefit even more from these interactions at multiple stages of the research, from the initial request for collaboration, through the task design, and even into the analysis phase because they share written drafts and engage in dialogue throughout the process, particularly when they conduct an extended series of projects over a period of years.

From the Laboratory to the Classroom

In a collaboration spanning more than two decades, Children's School educators have supported Dr. Robert Siegler's research on the development of mathematical thinking in young children (www.psy.cmu.edu/~siegler/). Both the director and classroom educators have engaged in design discussions with research team members about creating children's games that highlight numerical magnitude to help children to develop a more linear representation of numbers. In one case, Children's School educators also suggested that researchers include an interview about home game play in the research protocol, which led to the finding that types of game play in the home vary significantly by income level, which then has an impact on children's understanding of numerical magnitude. In the case of one graduate student, they also arranged a longitudinal classroom experiment in which one group of 4-year-olds learned a Chinese finger-counting system that enables children to represent numbers up to 99 on their two hands, while another group continued with standard classroom practice. In all cases, research on children's initial levels of mathematical thinking and change after playing a new game or learning a new counting system then serves as a foundation for more extensive studies with broader populations beyond the school.

Working with Children's School educators during the early stages of a research program helps the team to refine their tasks and study protocols to resonate with educators and to align with early childhood program culture, and conducting pilot work at the Children's School is particularly helpful in enabling novice researchers to learn effective ways of interacting with professionals in school contexts in the community. Dissemination of this research is broader than the typical journal papers produced by the research team (Laski & Siegler, 2014; Siegler, 2009), because Children's School educators present findings to other educators at the conferences and workshops mentioned earlier, particularly when the studies involve classroom interventions (Carver et al., 2009). In addition, as a result of this collaboration, Dr. Carver had the opportunity to serve on the national panel charged by the Institute of Education Sciences (IES) with making research-based recommendations on Teaching Math to Young Children (available for free download at http://ies.ed.gov/ncee/wwc/PracticeGuide.aspx?sid=18). Panel membership has then afforded numerous opportunities to present workshops linking research with classroom practice for educators, curriculum coaches, administrators, and faculty in schools of education around the country. Drawing on a wide range of Siegler's research, the practice guide recommends that educators "Use games to teach math concepts and skills and to give children practice in applying them" (p. 2). One specific study demonstrated that as little as 1 hour of scaffolded game play on a 1 to 10 board over the course of 2 weeks made a significant difference in HeadStart children's ability to count, recognize numerals, locate numbers on a number line, and choose the larger of two numbers, compared with children who played an equivalent color game (Siegler, 2009).

In an even deeper collaboration, Dr. Anna Fisher, graduate student Karrie Godwin, and their research team have conducted a series of studies on children's attention that have gone well beyond the typical laboratory studies of cognitive development (for an introduction to the full range of Dr. Fisher's research, see www.psy.cmu.edu/~cognitivedevelopmentlab/). The collaboration to study the impact of classroom displays on children's attention and subsequent learning began with classroom observations and progressed to a multi-year series of microgenetic studies in a simulated classroom environment situated adjacent to the Children's School kindergarten. In the simulated classroom, researchers could control the type of displays to vary potential distractions, and they negotiated with the kindergarten educators to arrange for half of the class to come at the same time for a lesson and assessment of their comprehension. During the lesson, the researchers used multiple video cameras to capture the children's behavior so that independent raters could score their attention and the sources of their distraction. Ratings of attention were then correlated with the children's performance on assessments of comprehension, tracked over time to test the impact of increasing familiarity with the simulated classroom, and finally compared across sessions with high vs. low visual distraction.

Insights gained from these studies informed both subsequent laboratory studies designed to investigate the relationship between attention and learning and subsequent *in-vivo* classroom research in a broad range of schools within the region. Again, publications included standard disciplinary venues (Fisher *et al.*, 2013, 2014), as well as broader platforms for the general public (Kantrowitz, 2014). To summarize the findings briefly, "children were more distracted by the visual environment, spent more time off task, and demonstrated smaller learning gains when the walls were highly decorated than when the decorations were removed" (Fisher *et al.*, 2014). This finding challenges early childhood educators to be intentional about the quantity and relevance of the displays that they add to their classroom environments.

Many of the Children's School's other research collaborations involve the design of technology tools for use by children. In one extensive collaboration, the educators partnered with the Community Robotics, Education, and Technology Empowerment (CREATE) Lab at Carnegie Mellon and the Pittsburgh Association for the Education of Young Children (PAEYC) with grant support from several local foundations to design "Message from Me." According to the CREATE Lab website,

Kiosks at childcare centers enable young children to record their daily experiences through pictures and speech and send them to their parents' cell phones or email. This age appropriate adaptation of existing technologies allows young children to practice their communication skills and build their self-confidence by talking about their day, their accomplishments, and their discoveries. Message from Me enhances parent–child conversations and involves families in the educational experience of their children.

(*www.cmucreatelab.org/projects/Message_from_Me*)

Children's School educators worked directly with the kiosk designers to develop a hardware system that was easy for the children to use, as well as a software system that was user-friendly for the educator entering all of the children's names and all the family members entering contact information. Initial trials of the original bulky kiosk led to its refinement into a tabletop kiosk that was moveable for the educators' ease and transparent for the children's exploration. In preparation for the distribution of these kiosks to 30 sites around the city, Children's School educators wrote curriculum and implemented training sessions. PAEYC then provided the long-term technical support for community educators, while Children's School educators worked with the designers to transition to an iPad version of Message from Me (further information on Message from Me is available at www.messagefromme.org). The research section of the Children's School website (www.psy.cmu.edu/cs/research/index.html) provides more examples of research that has been conducted in recent years.

Across all of these collaboration examples, and many more, the Children's School director and educators utilize their professional networks within the education community to help researchers to forge collaborations that reach well beyond the laboratory school so that they can incorporate the perspectives of more diverse educators and include a broader range of children in their studies. This approach increases the ecological and external validity of the research, which then leads to the development of more robust theories with clearer applications for practice.

The Fanny Edel Falk Laboratory School

Origins of the School

The Fanny Edel Falk Laboratory School was born of two wishes. The first was that of Leon Falk and Marjory Falk-Levy, who wished to honor their late mother by establishing a school that promoted progressive methods of teaching children that could be observed and studied by those who wished to pursue teaching as a vocation. The second was that of the University of Pittsburgh, which wanted to establish and maintain a laboratory that was progressive, experimental, and would become an integral part of the School of Education's educational mission. The Falk family purchased land next to the University campus and paid for the construction of the original building. Upon completion of the facility, the family created a charter agreement that gave the school and property to the University, and in 1931 the school opened.

The school has grown from its initial group of six students into a Kindergarten through Grade Eight, tuition-based facility with approximately 400 students. The students attending Falk are diverse in every sense of the word, which strengthens the external validity of the research conducted there. Of those enrolled, 43% are classified as "Children of Color." There is economic diversity, with 21% of the students receiving need-based tuition support. Falk also serves students with a wide variety of educational issues, with 9% of those attending having identified learning needs. Falk is known for providing a learning environment that is grounded in community, diversity, progressive and experiential education, and a low adult:student ratio. The fact that it is grounded in progressive education means that there is a child-centered approach to learning that focuses on the social, emotional, and academic needs of each individual. It also means that there is an emphasis on collaboration, intrinsic motivation, and active learning. Instruction revolves around an inquiry base that requires children to reflect on and take ownership of their own learning.

As students move from Kindergarten through Grade Eight, they experience a variety of classroom structures. Kindergarten is self-contained, and first and second grade are self-contained with looping. Third-, fourth-, and fifth-grade classes are semi-departmentalized with looping, and the middle grades are fully departmentalized. The core curriculum is enhanced by weekly classes in art, music, Spanish, physical education, yoga, library, and technology. There are currently 67 faculty and staff members who work each year with interns or student teachers in each of the grade-level classrooms and with practicum students, interns, or student teachers in each of the non-core classes as well.

Mission and Purpose of the School

From the outset, the Falk Laboratory School has maintained a four-part mission within the University of Pittsburgh's School of Education. Educators assist in the preparation of teachers, educators participate in the development of new curriculum materials, the school serves as a demonstration site for observing progressive and experimental education practices, and educators assist in conducting research. Although the Laboratory School serves as a research partner for divisions from throughout the campus, many of the projects have been undertaken in collaboration with the Learning Research and Development Center (LRDC) (www.lrdc.pitt.edu).

The LRDC is part of the University of Pittsburgh, and its mission is to advance the learning sciences by bringing together leading researchers in the cognitive, social, and educational sciences. This mission has guided the LRDC in its programs of basic and applied research, its demonstration projects, and its direct support of school improvement and reform. In the LRDC's multidisciplinary setting, scientists study the cognitive, neural, social, and organizational aspects of learning, making research and development links to formal education practice, policy, and out-of-school settings. The LRDC research portfolio includes large programs of extended duration as well as single-investigator projects of smaller scope and shorter duration.

Families who select the Falk School for their children are aware that it is a laboratory school engaged in experimental practice and research. At the time of registration, parents sign forms acknowledging their understanding of the research components of the school. If whole-class research is conducted, with the classroom teacher present, no further permission is needed for the researcher to work with the students. If the study is to involve working with individuals within the school, or students working away from the school site, parents need to provide individual permission.

From the Laboratory to the Classroom

In 2010, investigators Suzanne Adlof, Gwen Frishkoff, and Charles Perfetti from LRDC began a long-term study related to children's word learning from context (Adlof *et al.*, 2011; Frishkoff *et al.*, 2009). The initial phase looked at the effects of word familiarity on learning from context. Children frequently encounter words in text that they have seen or heard before, but whose meanings they do not know. The researchers wanted to determine whether children found it easier to learn the meanings of such familiar words compared with completely novel words.

To address this question, they began with very rare words that they were fairly certain children had never seen or heard before. Some words were "pre-familiarized" and others were not. The children were then given opportunities to learn words from context. The study began with a general whole-class assessment. The researchers then worked at the school with individuals and pairs of students. Finally, identified students accompanied the researchers to the LRDC lab. At this site, the students were fitted with what they termed the "spaghetti hat", which holds the sensors for near-infrared spectroscopy (NIRS). This non-invasive optical imaging technique related changes in cerebral blood oxygenation measured by sensors placed on the head to the temporal dynamics of cognitive behavior in order to localize the student's brain response to familiar versus unfamiliar words.

The results showed that there was a small benefit for words that had been pre-familiarized in four sentences prior to the learning opportunities, and that children with higher levels of reading comprehension skill tended to learn more new words overall. Portions of this work were then presented at the annual meetings of the Institute of Education Sciences in Washington, DC and the American Speech-Language-Hearing Association in Philadelphia, PA.

Follow-up studies continued from this initial phase, and various LRDC investigators worked with the students and teachers at Falk over the next few years. Each of the subsequent studies looked at various aspects of the same general question: *How do students learn vocabulary from context?* The researchers returned for the 2014–2015 school year with a follow-up of more practice-related value. They are now testing an online vocabulary tutor that is indirectly the result of the previous projects and studies at Falk. Once this project is complete, educators will have an online tool that will be an aid to improving students' vocabulary skills (additional examples of research projects conducted at the Falk Laboratory School can be found at www. falkschool.pitt.edu/about-falk/recent-research-projects).

A second way in which laboratory school leaders support the translation of research into practice and promote research in broader contexts is by collaborating with laboratory schools across the U.S.A. and worldwide. While at the Falk School, director Wendell McConnaha demonstrated the integration of theory, research, and practice by mentoring educators as they developed laboratory schools in Nigeria, Romania, Chile, Hong Kong, the United Arab Emirates, and Indonesia. Applying research to educational practice across cultures challenges the underlying learning principles, and conducting research in a variety of cultural contexts helps researchers to determine which educational programs can be directly transported to an international school without adaptation, which can be "made to fit" with slight modifications, and which simply will not work in the new environment and must be discarded in favor of a different approach.

Before learning sciences research can be conducted at the new sites, there are lessons to be learned from the design process itself. For example, while working in Abu Dhabi, Dr. McConnaha discovered that the design of every public school building throughout the entire country was identical. Schools were all three-story structures built around a central courtyard, with a specified configuration of classrooms and offices. Although this commonality of design is cost-effective from a construction standpoint, it ignores the impact of school design on learning as highlighted in *The Third Teacher: 79 Ways You can Use Design to Transform Teaching and Learning* (Cannon Design, Inc., VS Furniture, & Bruce Mau Design, 2014). The authors suggest that much of Howard Gardner's multiple intelligences theory implicitly suggests the need for a variety of learning spaces. If one starts with the school's vision, then creates a physical design for the building and a selection process for the personnel as expressed through that vision, it is remarkable how agile the space becomes and how richly the educators can engage students in different modes of learning.

Upon retirement from the University of Pittsburgh, Dr. McConnaha was recruited by Tsinghua University in Beijing to design, construct, and launch a new campus school, the Tsinghua International School (see www.this.edu.cn). Tsinghua University was established in the north-western section of Beijing, China (PRC) in 1911. Today, the university consists of 12 colleges, 48 departments, 41 research institutes, 35 research centers, and 167 laboratories. The major focus of the university is scientific research, and national and international rankings consistently position Tsinghua as one of China's leading universities.

Tsinghua's initial campus school was founded in 1915 as "the school affiliated with Tsinghua University", or THHS. THHS gives top priority to nurturing individual talents, respecting the student's individuality, facilitating the student's overall development, focusing on hands-on experiences and a global vision, advancing scientific research, innovating approaches to moral education, and emphasizing sports and arts education. The school consists of a Junior Secondary (Grades 7–9) and a Senior Secondary (Grades 10–12). The two programs include 85 classes, with approximately 3,500 students and 300 faculty/staff.

In 2009, Tsinghua University established a second campus school. Tsinghua International School (THIS) is affiliated with both the university and THHS. Whereas THHS serves only Chinese national students, THIS was established to provide international students and foreign-born Chinese students returning from overseas with courses featuring a Western educational philosophy and practice. The school emphasizes the integration of Chinese and Western cultures and is designed to prepare students to succeed in American, Canadian, and European universities. THIS teachers seek to educate their students holistically, to equip them with global vision, and to prepare them for a global future. They focus on laying a solid educational foundation, and they attach great importance to the development of personal integrity and leadership skills. The school includes Grades One to Twelve, has approximately 360 students, and has faculty and staff members from over a dozen different countries.

Within the past 3 years, the Ministry of Education passed a regulation which states that international schools may not enroll students holding only Chinese passports. Because this requirement means that Chinese national students may no longer attend THIS, Tsinghua University is in the process of designing a third campus school. This school will attempt to integrate the most current research regarding campus school design and school–university partnerships. It will also create a framework for curriculum design, facility planning, teacher preparation, and classroom pedagogy that can be a model for other schools to emulate. This framework will blend Western educational design with the examination schedule required of all Chinese students, so that Chinese students can benefit from the same preparation that is now being offered only to international students.

The vision for the school was to develop a facility and program that would prepare Chinese national students to apply to, be selected by, and succeed academically and socially in American and Canadian universities. The university purchased a set of buildings that had originally been constructed for the 2008 Olympic Games in Beijing. The concept of school planning described above highlights the importance of designing a facility to suit the needs of the school rather than the other way round, so in collaboration with Yingmin Wang, Director of the International Education Office, Dr. McConnaha established the aims and objectives and, on the basis of these, the correct subject matter to include and the most appropriate teaching and learning strategies were adopted. A clear understanding of these learning and teaching strategies then guided the design of the classrooms and other facilities. The project leaders are optimistic about both the impact of this school and the research conducted there, because there are strong connections between the university and the laboratory school researchers. There is also a commitment from the Central Ministry of Education to work toward the development of a completely different model of education for China. Tsinghua University has established a planning team that includes representation from the University, THHS, THIS, and external resources. With careful notes being taken to record the process of development, and a constant eye toward the research as it currently exists, discoveries related to the development of classroom and program design will be shared with the broader education community so that this school design for university-bound students can be replicated throughout China.

The Dr. Eric Jackman Institute of Child Study Laboratory School
Origins of the School

The Dr. Eric Jackman Institute of Child Study (ICS) Laboratory School was founded in 1925–1926 with seed funding from the Laura Spelman Rockefeller Memorial Foundation, as one of six laboratory schools in North America created to advance the Child Study Movement's multidisciplinary approach to understanding childhood and, importantly, the betterment of learning potential and life possibilities for children. This movement applies social science disciplines to the study of the health, education, and welfare of children. The mission of the Dr. Eric Jackman Institute of Child Study Laboratory School today remains unchanged in its essential focus from that of its founding days—excellence in childhood education, teacher education, and research in an intentionally diverse environment. This mission guides the school's work in creating meaningful links between research and practice. This connection occurs in the Jackman ICS classrooms, with their 2-year MA program in Child Study and Education that emphasizes the relationship between theory and application in educational research, and in the context of their Dr. R.G.N. Laidlaw Centre for multidisciplinary research in child development (see www.oise.utoronto.ca/ics/Laidlaw_ Research_Centre/index.html).

The philosophy of the school is inspired by the thinking of American educational philosopher John Dewey. There is a strong commitment to an inquiry-based approach to learning and intentional emphasis on the application of child development knowledge to teaching. At Jackman ICS, the school strives to create a secure learning environment that inspires exploration, creativity, curiosity, and confidence to flourish.

Since its inception in 1925, the Dr. Eric Jackman Institute of Child Study Laboratory School has been a place where the exploration of ideas is central to all stakeholders—the children, parents, teachers, and researchers. Within the classrooms, children are challenged to use their natural curiosity to critically investigate the social and natural world, to gain the skills to communicate with others, to think independently, and to become engaged citizens.

As a unique Nursery to Grade Six laboratory school in downtown Toronto, Jackman ICS makes a noted contribution to the understanding of strong educational practices and research application in elementary schools. The school is part of the Ontario Institute for

Studies in Education (OISE) at the University of Toronto and meets a threefold mandate—teacher education, research, and exemplary education for the 200 children who attend the school.

Mission and Purpose of the School

As a laboratory school, the Dr. Eric Jackman Institute of Child Study shares characteristics that are common to many good schools across North America. These include a focus on children and learning, involved parents, competent and reflective teachers, responsive leadership, a caring environment, and curricular, teaching, and assessment strategies that are appropriate and effective. In addition, it enjoys several unique characteristics, including a university setting, strong research capability, involvement in initiating and disseminating new ideas related to improving education, daily contributions to teacher training, and a measure of autonomy that allows a critical thinking lens to be used when evaluating and selecting curriculum and assessment strategies of and for learning.

Research-based initiatives that are part of this laboratory school include the following:

- The teachers in each classroom are teacher-researchers, with capacities to provide exemplary teaching as well as research facilitation in each grade and specialty subject.
- Educators regularly attend conferences, including the American Educational Research Association, the Canadian Society for the Study of Education, and Computer Supported Collaborative Learning.
- Teachers conduct research in, for example, knowledge building, early mathematics, and lesson study.
- Teachers and research partners publish research work in journals and books, including *The National Council of Teachers of Mathematics Yearbook*, the *Journal of the Learning Sciences*, and *Young Children*.
- The ICS hosts over 700–1,000 visits to the laboratory school each year from international, national, and local educators and researchers.
- The Jackman ICS provides over 8,000 hours of supervised practicum annually to teacher candidates in a research-based Master of Arts in Child Study and Education program.

The laboratory school's connection to the University of Toronto influences everything from academic standards to the spirit of inquiry that pervades its classrooms. The university provides the school's faculty with a research-related mandate—to explore what is possible in education—as well as professional development opportunities, resources, library facilities, and research support that make the lively community of professional learners a uniquely positioned school in terms of linking theory and practice. The school contributes on many levels to the academic work of the University, so its students are also learning in an environment where research is everywhere. There are four main ways in which research is part of the school experience at Jackman ICS: first, conducting research within the Jackman ICS Laboratory School; second, partnering with researchers to demonstrate research-based practice; third, mentoring practicing and pre-service teachers in applying research to their practice; and fourth, disseminating research findings for the use of a wide community of educators that includes policy makers, national and international researchers, and professors who teach in teacher education degree programs at the University of Toronto and in other faculties of education.

From the Laboratory to the Classroom

Conducting original research is an important goal at Jackman ICS. For example, for more than 10 years, the school has refined and researched Japanese Lesson Study (JLS), a process of teacher professional development. This work began with an interest on the part of teachers in considering alternatives to the common professional development model in which knowledge is delivered by an expert in a brief presentation that might be inspiring but is short term in impact. The school was drawn to JLS as a unique way for teachers to reflect on their own practice with a fresh perspective (Stigler & Hiebert, 1999), and because its classroom context, ongoing collaborative process, focus on students, and attention to teachers' concerns and questions (Bruce & Ladky, 2010) fitted the existing educational culture at Jackman ICS.

In partnership with Kobe Shinwa Women's University in Japan, the Jackman ICS research took the form of an initial investigation into the JLS process, which involves a four-stage cycle of clear and concise focus on teachers' goal setting, planning, teaching, and reflections about a carefully chosen "research lesson" (Lewis et al., 2006). To adapt this form of professional development for the North American educator and educational context, where early childhood educators are often inadequately prepared to teach mathematics, the school integrated four additional stages—an initial phase of educators engaging in content-related explorations (which in the school's focus were geometry and spatial reasoning), designing and conducting clinical interviews, using the data to plan and implement exploratory activities with children, and finally creating resources for other educators.

In the Jackman ICS context, Lesson Study was made a staff-wide part of the school's annual professional learning (Moss et al., 2012), thereby involving teachers in considering disciplines and age groups beyond their own classroom focus. The sessions were expanded to include the student teachers, who would eventually carry this technique with them into their schools. The teachers and the research team piloted the adapted eight-stage lesson study process with 15 "Professional Learning Teams" in seven public districts in urban and rural communities throughout Ontario, and the process was documented by Moss et al. (2015), together with one extended case study of the impact on teachers serving an urban immigrant population. That impact included effectively "supporting teachers' content knowledge of and comfort level with geometry and spatial reasoning, increasing teachers' perceptions of young children's mathematical competencies, increasing teachers' awareness and commitment for the inclusion of high quality geometry and spatial reasoning as a critical component of early years mathematics, and the creation of innovative resources for other educators."

This original lesson study investigation dovetailed with Jackman ICS teachers' collaborative work with a team of researchers exploring professional growth in teaching mathematics to young children (Math for Young Children, M4YC). The first role of the team of teachers and administrators was to plan and implement, with their partners, full-day sessions in the school that would demonstrate evidence-based inquiry techniques for teaching math in the early years, such as the kindergarten teacher's focus on spatial reasoning in her rigorous block play program (see Tepylo et al., 2015). There was research funding to bring representatives from many school districts to visit the school for these sessions and to participate in a year-long hands-on practical intervention with the school's teachers assisting in supporting an inquiry-based approach in participants' own classrooms.

M4YC was salient and successful on many levels, including a strong proliferation of sites using inquiry-based practices when teaching math to young children. Related research continues today through the school and the Institute's Robertson Program for Inquiry-Based Teaching of Math and Science. The focus of the current math-related research is now also in First Nations Communities that invited the school's teachers and researchers to join their teachers, who are working for change in long-term student outcomes in mathematics. An even broader impact resulted from Jackman ICS Professors Dr. Joan Moss and Dr. Beverly Caswell, and Research Associate Zack Hawes, being invited by the Ministry of Education of the Province of Ontario to produce a monograph available to all K–12 teachers about the strand of Mathematics that was the focus of this research (Ontario Ministry of Education, 2014). This resource is a part of the province of Ontario's *Paying Attention to Mathematics Education* series, and it highlights the evidence that focusing on spatial thinking strengthens a broad range of student skills and allows mathematics to become more accessible, engaging, and relevant (see www.edu.gov.on.ca/eng/literacynumeracy/LNSPayingAttention.pdf).

Jackman ICS also partners with researchers to apply research-based practices. For more than 15 years, the ICS has been a hub school for knowledge-building research for the Institute for Knowledge Innovation and Technology (IKIT) (www.ikit.org), under the leadership of Dr. Carl Bereiter and Dr. Marlene Scardamalia. The school's teachers have worked closely in a design research mode with researchers who are exploring knowledge building through collaboration and use of an online program, Knowledge Forum.® The IKIT principles of knowledge building all relate to "giving students collective responsibility for idea improvement" such that they "initiate students into the knowledge creating culture." This approach involves engaging students in deeply constructivist learning "in which learners come together to pose questions, posit theories, and to revisit, negotiate, and refine ideas." This research collaboration has now fully influenced the way that the teaching staff teach everyone, every day. They also encourage all teachers to explore their own pedagogical questions and share their curriculum breakthroughs within professional learning circles using Knowledge Forum.® They have shared the principles and benefits of knowledge building on the Ontario Ministry of Education's *Learn Teach Lead* website (http://learnteachlead.ca/projects/knowledge-building/). In addition, they always engage in at least one specific research project, funded through the Principal Investigators' grants, to enhance and advance understanding of knowledge construction (see, for example, Zhang *et al.*, 2011). Having a specific research focus enables every teacher to work in a research environment and to contribute through bi-weekly research design meetings.

Recently, the school's emphasis has been on using the knowledge-building approach in the context of environmental inquiry. The resulting pedagogical framework has four branches: inquiry-based learning to nurture children's sense of wonder; experiential learning about, for, and in the environment; integrated learning to help students to see the big picture; and stewardship to foster civic responsibility. To make the principles and the knowledge-building approach to the practice of environmental inquiry more accessible to a broad range of educators, the ICS teachers collaborated to write a book for early years and elementary teachers, entitled *Natural Curiosity: A Resource for Teachers* (The Laboratory School at The Dr. Eric Jackman Institute of Child Study, 2011). This book includes an emphasis on the theoretical underpinnings of each branch of the framework and practical advice on implementing the idea while still meeting the Ministry of Education's standards, and it also includes stories of inquiry experiences both in the ICS laboratory school classrooms and in diverse public schools. The guide is already in wide use throughout the province of Ontario, Canada, and there are 25,000 copies in the hands of teachers (it is available for free download at www.naturalcuriosity.ca).

As the above examples illustrate, the ICS laboratory school makes robust, collaborative contributions to the advancement of theory, research, and practice. The educators conduct and contribute to research that strengthens education for all. In general, laboratory school educators can be an uncommonly rich resource, providing several populations of educators with tools for change. As research findings are translated into living laboratory classrooms in schools that are open for all to see and reflect upon, one finds theory made visible. Universities with laboratory schools know the value that this demonstration adds to the utility and reach of research. Although translation may be helpful and needed between the world of the academic and that of the classroom teacher, it is uptake of good ideas by both communities that will eventually mean the research that we do truly reaches those whom it is designed to support—the children.

Laboratory School Roles and Opportunities for Partnership

The laboratory school examples described in this chapter demonstrate a variety of strategies for bridging the linguistic and cultural divide between educators and researchers. In each case, laboratory school leaders capitalized on potential synergies between the laboratory school mission and that of learning sciences researchers, dedicated the time to developing a common language and shared vision, provided a welcoming experimental context for advancing the researchers' agendas, took the risk of becoming true partners in the investigation, and went beyond the original studies to explore applications of the findings, develop effective dissemination mechanisms, and reflectively iterate on the process, which then opened the door to continued investigation and offers of new collaborations on different topics. Furthermore, inquiry learning approaches and cultures of respect were characteristic of each laboratory school environment, so learners of all ages adopted a growth mindset and the contributions of both educators and researchers were valued.

These factors align well with research on critical elements for teacher–researcher collaboration. Reflecting on a partnership using a design experiment approach, Herrenkohl *et al.* (2010, p. 74) highlight features for "building a culture of research-based practice in schools." These elements include:

> (1) shared understanding and vision with both complementary and overlapping roles and perspectives, (2) place, status, power, position, and control, (3) social and emotional support and acceptance, (4) intellectual rigor and debate among ourselves and with the larger field for the sake of students.
>
> *(Herrenkohl et al., 2010, p. 86)*

Furthermore, we suggest that laboratory school educators who intentionally focus on interpretation from research to practice, and vice versa, can purposefully encourage practitioners from the broader community beyond the academy to engage in collaborative research, while encouraging diverse researchers to view their collaborations in a more reciprocal manner, such that the resulting partnerships are more positive and productive for everyone, but most importantly for the learners who benefit from the principles they discover and the educational innovations they design (Carver, 2001).

Regarding the direct improvement of education, laboratory schools provide opportunities for:

1. exposing researchers and undergraduates to educational settings in order to better understand the challenges faced by educators, so that they are more likely to focus research on solving educationally relevant topics
2. training researchers and undergraduates to communicate their findings to parents and educators in ways that are directly and immediately applicable
3. coaching practicing educators and pre-service teachers in the applications of research—both basic research and research on educational interventions
4. connecting researchers and educators across professional cultures in order to explore ways to bridge theory, research, and practice.

These opportunities and related benefits can extend to educators within the broader communities surrounding universities and, via technology, in every corner of the world. Today's learning sciences researchers are increasingly attuned to practitioners' interest in collaborating on research that involves testing straightforward predictions based on relevant learning principles with a practical level of assessment and analysis that can be undertaken in near real time so that it is useful for influencing the current learning endeavors (McCandlis *et al.*, 2003). Finding partners to develop designs for entire units or courses with multiple refinements over a period of years, such as the thermodynamics case reported by Clark and Linn (2003), benefits both researchers and educators as they gradually learn to speak each other's language and contribute meaningfully to both the research and the educational innovation agendas. We encourage everyone interested in improving education to proactively identify an area of interest, boldly approach potential collaborators, seek administrative support for the necessary time and resources, and then share the lessons learned with both the educator and researcher communities so that together we can create bridges to strengthen learning for all.

References

Adlof, S. M., Perfetti, C. A., & Catts, H. W. (2011). Developmental changes in reading comprehension: implications for assessment and instruction. In: S. J. Samuels & A. E. Farstrup (Eds), *What Research Has to Say About Reading Instruction* (pp. 186–214). Newark, DE: International Reading Association.

Bruce, C. & Ladky, M. (2010). *Using Design Research to Test and Refine a Lesson Study Model: A Close Examination of the Complexities of the Lesson Study Cycles.* Paper presented at the Annual Meeting of the American Educational Research Association, Denver, CO.

Cannon Design, Inc., VS Furniture, & Bruce Mau Design (2014). *The Third Teacher: 79 Ways You Can Use Design to Transform Teaching and Learning.* New York: Abrams.

Carver, S. M. (2001). Cognition and instruction: enriching the laboratory school experience of children, teachers, parents, and undergraduates. In: S. M. Carver & D. Klahr (Eds), *Cognition and Instruction: Twenty-Five Years of Progress* (pp. 385–426). Mahwah, NJ: Lawrence Erlbaum Associates, Inc.

Carver, S. M. & Klahr, D. (Eds) (2001). *Cognition and Instruction: Twenty-Five Years of Progress.* Mahwah, NJ: Lawrence Erlbaum Associates, Inc.

Carver, S. M., Bird, J., & Hancock, L. (2009). *Teaching Chinese Hand Gestures to Build Understanding of Numerical Magnitude in Preschoolers and Kindergartners.* Paper presented at the Annual Conference of the National Association of Laboratory Schools, Nashville, TN.

Clark, D. & Linn, M. C. (2003). Designing for knowledge integration: the impact of instructional time. *Journal of the Learning Sciences*, 12, 451–492.

Fisher, A. V., Thiessen, E. D., Godwin, K., Kloos, H., & Dickerson, J. P. (2013). Assessing selective sustained attention in 3- to 5-year-old children: evidence from a new paradigm. *Journal of Experimental Child Psychology*, 114, 275–294.

Fisher, A. V., Godwin, K. E., & Seltman, H. (2014). Visual environment, attention allocation, and learning in young children: when too much of a good thing may be bad. *Psychological Science*, 25, 1362–1370.

Frishkoff, G. A., White, G., & Perfetti, C. A. (2009). In vivo testing of learning and instructional principles: the design and implementation of school-based experimentation. In: L. M. Dinella (Ed.), *Conducting Science-Based Psychology Research in Schools* (pp. 153–173). Washington, DC: American Psychological Association.

Herrenkohl, L. R., Kawasaki, K., & Dewater, L. S. (2010). Inside and outside: teacher-researcher collaboration. *The New Educator*, 6, 74–92.

Kantrowitz, B. (2014). The science of learning. *Scientific American*, 311, 69–73.

Laski, E. V. & Siegler, R. S. (2014). Learning from number board games: you learn what you encode. *Developmental Psychology*, 50, 853–864.

Lewis, C., Perry, R., & Murata, A. (2006). How should research contribute to instructional improvement? The case of lesson study. *Educational Researcher*, 35, 3–14.

McCandlis, B. D., Kalchman, M., & Bryant, P. (2003). Design experiments and laboratory approaches to learning: steps toward collaborative exchange. *Educational Researcher*, 32, 14–16.

Mayhew, K. C. & Edwards, A. C. (1965). *The Dewey School: The Laboratory School of the University of Chicago, 1896–1903.* New York: Atherton Press.

Moss, J., Messina, R., Morley, E., & Tepylo, D. (2012) Sustaining professional collaborations over 6 years: using Japanese Lesson Study to improve the teaching and learning of mathematics. In: J. Bay-Williams (Ed.), *Professional Collaborations in Mathematics Teaching and Learning: Seeking Success for All: The National Council of Teachers of Mathematics 70th Yearbook.* Reston, VA: National Council of Teachers of Mathematics.

Moss, J., Hawes, Z., Naqvi, S., & Caswell, B. (2015). Adapting Japanese Lesson Study to enhance the teaching and learning of geometry and spatial reasoning in early years classrooms: a case study. *ZDM Mathematics Education*, 47, 377–390.

National Association of Laboratory Schools (1991). *Laboratory Schools: An Educational Resource.* Honolulu: University of Hawaii Curriculum Research and Development Group.

Ontario Ministry of Education (2014). *Paying Attention to Spatial Reasoning.* Available online at www.edu.gov.on.ca/eng/literacynumeracy/LNSPayingAttention.pdf

Regan, E. M. (1973). Review of Lillian Weber's 1971 book "The English Infant School and Informal Education." *Interchange*, 4, 88–95.

Siegler, R. S. (2009). Improving the numerical understanding of children from low-income families. *Child Development Perspectives*, 3, 118–124.

Stigler, J. W. & Hiebert, J. (1999). *The Teaching Gap: Best Ideas from the World's Teachers for Improving Education in the Classroom.* New York: Free Press.

Tepylo, D. H., Moss, J., & Stephenson, C. (2015). A developmental look at a rigorous block play program. *Young Children*, 70, 18–25.

The Laboratory School at The Dr. Eric Jackman Institute of Child Study (2011). *Natural Curiosity: a resource for teachers.* Toronto, ON: Miracle Press Ltd.

Zhang, J., Hong, H.-Y., Scardamalia, M., Teo, C., & Morley, E. (2011). Sustaining knowledge building as a principle-based innovation at an elementary school. *Journal of the Learning Sciences*, 20, 262–307.

INDEX

References to figures are shown in *italics*. References to tables are shown in **bold**. References to endnotes consist of the page number followed by the letter "n" followed by the number of the note, e.g. 38n3 refers to note no. 3 on page 38